FUNDAMENTALS OF PERVASIVE INFORMATION MANAGEMENT SYSTEMS

FUNDAMENTALS OF PERVASIVE INFORMATION MANAGEMENT SYSTEMS

VIJAY KUMAR
Computer Science Electrical Engineering
University of Missouri-Kansas City

Dedicated to the One who taught me the wisdom of selfless action

CONTENTS

PREFACE

The trajectory of wireless discoveries and innovations is a long and interesting one. We believe that a concise description of this trajectory and the events that occurred surrounding it are worth telling to the readers of this book.

The discovery of electromagnetism by Hans Christian Oersted and Andre-Marie Ampere, early in the 1820s, seems to provide a glimpse of the evolution of the wireless era. A number of other significant discoveries followed that provided necessary flesh and bones to the idea of wireless communication. In 1831, the physicist Michael Faraday, a book-binder by profession, became interested in electricity and discovered the principle of electromagnetic induction. The Scottish mathematician James Maxwell investigated this principle in 1864 and formulated it using a set of equations known as *Maxwell's* equations. They were published in *A Treatise on Electricity and Magnetism* in 1873, and they showed the propagation of electromagnetic waves through free space at the speed of light and also set the foundation of wireless communication. Heinrich Hertz verified and demonstrated this propagation first in 1880, and then he followed it by another demonstration in 1887. In Italy, Guglielmo Marconi started an investigation into electromagnetic waves, but he did not get much support from his government for it, so in February 1896 he moved to England to continue his work. In 1897, Marconi and Popov experimented with a radio-telegraph in which they used electromagnetic waves to transmit and receive signals. In the same year, Marconi patented a complete wireless system that sent and received Morse Code. These successes motivated Marconi to experiment with practical mobile radio communication. He successfully established radio transmission from a ship in New York Harbor (the Twin Lights in Highland, New Jersey), and he used this transmission technique to cover the arrival of Admiral Dewey from Manila followed by the coverage of the Americas Cup races. He used high-energy wideband pulses of radio noise that were created by using a spark generator connected to an antenna. On December 12, 1901, Marconi successfully transmitted the first transatlantic wireless signal from Poldhu, Cornwall to St. John's, Newfoundland, covering a distance of 2100 miles. He used this technique to report the movement of many sea vessels, including the sinking of the Titanic in 1912. These uses of radio transmissions ignited a global interest in wireless communication that led to a series of innovations. His system used long radio waves (wavelengths much longer than 1 km), and through this work he initiated transmitter technology.

The discovery of the diode by J. A. Fleming in 1904 and of a triode amplifier by Lee DeForest in 1906 added a third dimension to wireless transmission. In 1906, the Canadian-born Reginald Aubrey Fessenden, working in the United States, success-fully transmitted speech on a wireless channel using a triode amplifier. The credit for inventing wireless telegraphy, therefore, goes to Marconi and Fessenden. In 1907, commercial Trans-Atlantic Wireless Service, using huge ground stations with an an-tenna the size of 30-m × 100-m masts began. Initially, most of these facilities were driven primarily by military needs; but in 1919 an experimental inter-ship radio tele-phone service was launched, and commercial radiotelephony for passengers on ships in the Atlantic started in 1929. This marked the beginning of the end for cable-based telegraphy. For many years, Americans called the receiver *wireless* because there were no wires linking to the transmitting station, and the British called it *radio* because the station used electromagnetic waves.

Along with these experimentations, some real-world deployment of radio telephony was taking shape. In 1921, the Detroit police department began experimenting with a frequency band of 2 MHz for vehicular mobile service. The success of this experiment led to the deployment of regular one-way radio communication called "land mobile" in police cars for managing traffic. It was adopted throughout the country. Unfortunately, as expected, the channels in this low-frequency band became too crowded to be used effectively. In 1933, the Bayonne, New Jersey police department implemented a regu-lar two-way communication system and deployed it in their patrol cars. This was a ma-jor advance over the previous one-way systems. They used a very high frequency sys-tem in patrol cars that enabled patrolmen to communicate with headquarters and other cars and to receive calls. This police radio became standard throughout the country.

In 1940, the Connecticut State Police took this facility a step further and initiated a two-way, frequency-modulated (FM) system in Hartford with the help of Daniel E. Noble of the University of Connecticut and engineers from the Fred M. Line Company. This improvement greatly reduced interference due to static; as a result, FM mobile radio became standard throughout the country. The success prompted the FCC (Fed-eral Communication Commission) to allocate 40 MHz of spectrum ranging between 30 and 500 MHz for private and public organizations. With the availability of a wider spectrum, the Bell system initiated a project to connect a variety of users wirelessly. The FCC identified these systems as *Domestic Public Land Mobile Radio Service (DPLMRS)*. In 1946, the first Bell DPLMRS was inaugurated in St. Louis. In 1947, a 35- to 44-MHz *highway* system between New York and Boston was inaugurated.

The success of these devices motivated the FCC to release more channels for public wireless communication. This prompted many companies to develop more powerful communication systems. In 1964, the first automatic full duplex 150-MHz service, called *MJ*, was introduced. Then in 1969 this automatic service was enhanced by using 450 MHz for communication and was called *MK*. The combination of these two services was called *Improved Mobile Telephone Service (ITMS)*. This remained a standard until AMPS was developed and introduced. To make further development of mobile systems, the FCC allocated 666 duplex channels in the 800- to 900-MHz frequency range and authorization was granted to Illinois Bell in 1978.

There were two serious limitations with early mobile telephone systems: (a) They acted as broadcast systems, so powerful transmitters were used to cover a distance of 20–30 miles from a high tower or rooftop and (b) to avoid interference (co-channel and adjacent channel) in frequency reuse, they required a separation of more than 50 miles. Thus, the New York channels were reused in Philadelphia and beyond and supported only 40 simultaneous calls in each city and its suburbs. Furthermore, calls in both directions were placed through a mobile operator. It was not until the 1960s that advanced automatic systems were introduced where an *idle tone* was put on an idle channel for a scanning receiver to hold on to that channel. This allowed a mobile telephone to decode its own dialed number on the channel and to send dialed digits for outgoing calls.

With the evolution of wireless communication, the notion of personal communication began to emerge. The competing manufacturers from Denmark, Finland, Iceland, Norway, and Sweden collaborated and developed an automatic radio telephony system called the Nordic Mobile Telephone (NMT) cellular system. In the United States, Bell Laboratories played a leading role in the development of novel cellular technology in the early 1970s called *Advanced Mobile Phone Systems (AMPS)*. AMPS quickly captured two-thirds of the mobile market worldwide. By 1995, AMPS had an estimated 13 million subscribers in the United States.

Note that the cellular system actually began in automobiles where large radios were stored in the trunk and connected to control units mounted on the dashboard. Hand-held devices were quite large and heavy. For example, Motorola introduced the "DynaTAC," a hand-held unit that was about the size of a brick, weighed a couple of pounds, and was carried around in an attaché case.

AMPS was an analog device based on FM modulation. It used RF bandwidth of 30 kHz (824–849 MHz for downlink and 869–894 MHz for uplink traffic) that accommodated 832 duplex channels, among which 21 were reserved for call setup while the rest were reserved for voice communication. In 1978, field trials of AMPS using 850 MHz began in Chicago and ARTS (American Radio Telephone Service) in Washington, DC.

The FCC opted for an all-digital operation that was fully compatible with the existing analog AMPS system. This move was mainly to reduce the cost of communication with more efficient use of the available spectrum. The digital system provided better speech coding, improved security, better user privacy, and better protection against unauthorized use. By 1988, a 1900-MHz version of AMPS was developed that was capable of using dual-band/dual-mode with 800-/1900-MHz frequencies. This marked the advent of *PCS (Personal Communication System)* that provided identical services in both bands, and a subscriber on D-AMPS 1900 could seamlessly migrate (handoff) to/from a D-AMPS and analog AMPS channels.

The cellular systems of the first decade used digital signals for control, but analog signals carried the voice because the technology was not ready for a fully digital cell phone to avail its benefits. The situation, however, changed by late 1980. In the early 1980s, analog cellular telephone systems spread rapidly in a few European countries (Scandinavia, United Kingdom, France, and Germany.) However, each country developed its own system that was largely incompatible with the other countries. This created an uneasy situation, and thus in 1982 the *Conference of European Posts and Telegraphs (CEPT)* formed a study group called the *Groupe Spécial Mobile (GSM)* to study and develop a system that (a) had good speech quality, (b) incurred low costs, (c) provided support for international roaming, (d) had the ability to support hand-held terminals, (e) provided support for a range of new services and facilities, (f) possessed spectral efficiency, and (g) was ISDN compatible. This digital system became popularly known as the *Global System for Mobile communications (GSM)*. Phase I of the GSM specifications was published in 1990, and commercial service started from mid-1991. Its use and subscription spread rapidly; by 1993 there were 36 GSM networks in 22 countries, and this increased to about 58 million in 1997. The GSM was not deployed in North America; rather, it appeared as its derivative called *PCS1900*. It was originally intended to be used in vehicles but rapidly became a favorite hand-held gadget. By 1994, about 102 operators in 60 countries opted for GSM. By early 1997, GSM captured about 25% of the world market where 198 networks were operational in 75 countries and the number of subscribers exceeded 30 million. It allowed global roaming using 900-, 1800-, and 1900-MHz frequency bands. By the end of 1997, GSM had 60 million subscribers in 110 countries, giving GSM a 35% share of the world market in mobile telephony; whereas the US GSM system PCS 1900 had 670,000 subscribers. In Europe, two digital systems began to operate, GSM and *DECT (Digital Enhanced Cordless Telecommunication)*; in the United States, *IS54 (Interim Standard-54)* and *IS95 (Interim Standard-95)* and *Iridium*.

The history of wireless and mobile disciplines will lose a lot of its flavor if we do not include a discussion on remote controls. The fascination with these disciplines began to affect many other day-to-day household activities—for example, opening garage doors from inside the cars, switching TV channels, controlling stereo units, and setting microwaves, to name a few. The discovery began for military use and the German navy deployed remote controls extensively to control their motorboats, bombs, and so on. United States scientists experimented to find nonmilitary uses for the remote control. In the United States, scientists and engineers began to develop remote control units for everyday activities. In the late 1940s, automatic garage door openers were invented, and in the 1950s, the first TV remote controls were introduced.

In 1950, the Zenith Electronics Corporation (initially known as Zenith Radio Corporation) began investigating the idea of a TV remote control, and in 1952 they developed a wired remote control called "Lazy Bones" that was attached to the TV through a long cable. The controller had a number of buttons to change the channel. Although the controller lost popularity quickly, it did set a track for others to follow. The first wireless control called "Flashmatic" was invented by Zenith's engineer

Eugene Polley. It used four photo cells, each located at one of the four corners of the TV screen. It had a number of limitations, but it did pioneer the concept of wireless TV remote controls. In 1956, Dr. Robert Adler of the Zenith corporation proposed to use ultrasonic, and in 1957 the company introduced a wireless remote control called "Space Command." It used ultrasonic waves to change TV channels. It had problems such as interference from clinking metal that interfered with channel changing, and its high frequencies sometimes made dogs bark. In spite of these problems, this kind of remote was used for two decades. The next improvement replaced ultrasound with infrared frequencies. The remote control had a number of buttons, and each button had its own unique digital code that was captured by the sensor in the TV set and changed the channel. Remote control started with one controller to one TV set but in 1987, Steve Wozniak of Apple developed a universal remote control called *CORE (Controller of Remote Equipment)*. Unfortunately, it did not become popular because it was far too complicated for the average user. By 2000, there were a large number of universal remote controls manufactured by nearly all consumer electronics companies. Table 0.1 lists important events in mobile communication.

These discoveries and developments in wireless and mobile disciplines have created a platform for us where we can fulfill our vision of pervasive computing—in particular, mobile database systems. This book presents useful information about the management of data on a system where processors and the entire database (or portions of it) are moving around in geographical space. The entire mobile database processing paradigm is relatively new, born out of the needs of highly mobile workers. In the beginning, the workforce satisfied their data processing needs by filling their laptops with relevant parts of the database before they set out on a trip. At the end of the trip, or sometime in the middle, they also then refreshed the main database with up-to-date data values. However, this intermittent connectivity approach quickly became inadequate in satisfying global consistency requirements. In addition, the persistent background nagging of cell phone users for ubiquitous access to desired data added additional urgency for the development of a system that came to be known as *Mobile Database Systems (MDS)*. This stimulated database and wireless communities to join forces to look into this new discipline. Members of these communities, from academia as well as from industries, accepted the challenge and created a new research direction with several names such as *pervasive computing, ubiquitous computing, nomad computing*, and *anywhere anytime computing*. Since then, mobile data processing became a discipline and significant progress has been made in research and development areas. Along with this, a few more new names have been used to identify this discipline, and many more will continue to appear as the area gets more and more mature. One consoling factor, however, is that everybody has a clear notion of this new discipline, and these names address the same concept.

The excitement to write this book morphed into a lot of difficulties. A central problem is the immaturity of research findings. Most of these, such as mobile database transaction models, concurrency control mechanisms, recovery protocols, location-dependent data, and so on, have not been fully deployed and validated in the real world. However, there are clear indications that in the near future, they will become available on most mobile devices. As mobile database technology is deployed, a plethora of

Table 0.1   Important Events in Mobile Communication

Date	Event
1867	Maxwell speculated the existence of electromagnetic waves.
1887	Hertz showed the existence of electromagnetic waves.
1890	Branly developed technique for detecting radio waves.
1896	Marconi demonstrated wireless telegraph.
1897	Marconi patented wireless telegraph.
1898	Marconi awarded patent for tuned communication.
1898	Wireless telegraphic connection between England and France established.
1901	Marconi successfully transmited radio signal from Cornwall to Newfoundland.
1909	Marconi received Nobel prize in physics for Voice over Radio system.
1928	Detroit police installed mobile receivers in police patrol cars.
1930	Mobile transmitters were deployed in most cars.
1935	Armstrong demonstrated frequency modulation (FM) scheme.
1940	Majority of police systems converted to FM.
1946	Mobile systems were connected to public switched telephone network (PSTN).
1949	FCC recognizes mobile radio as a new class of service.
1950	Number of mobile users increased more than 500,000.
1960	Number of mobile users grew more than 1.4 million.
1960	Improved Mobile Telephone Service (IMTS) introduced.
1976	Bell Mobile used 12 channels to support 543 customers in New York.
1979	NTT/Japan deploys first cellular communication system.
1983	Advanced Mobile Phone System (AMPS) deployed in the United States.
1989	GSM appeared as European digital cellular standard.
1991	US Digital Cellular phone system introduced.
1993	IS-95 code-division multiple-access (CDMA) digital cellular system deployed in the United States.
1994	GSM Global System for Mobile Communications deployed in the United States.
1995	FCC auctioned band 1.8-GHz frequencies for Personal Communications System (PCS).
1997	Number of cellular telephone users in the United States increased to 50 million.
2000	Third-generation cellular system standards? Bluetooth standards?

useful applications will be developed and deployed, making MDS an essential gadget for most of us.

The contents of this book are, therefore, a combination of useful research results and well-tested schemes and protocols. It covers fundamental database topics that set the background for transition to the mobile database domain. The mobile database chapters contain a good mixture of fundamental topics and research findings. My main effort has been to illustrate how nicely database technology and wireless mobility have mingled together and produced this new exciting area. Two chapters are devoted to sensor technology—in particular, in sensor data stream processing—and one chapter discusses a number of case studies depicting the deployment of sensor networks to investigate and collect data from natural and manmade events.

The first exciting conversion took place when *E-commerce* became *M-commerce* and pervaded day-to-day activities of every user. Thus, instead of sitting in front of their desktops, they just began to turn on their mobile devices (e.g., cell phones, laptops, PDAs, etc.) to shop, turning conventional *window shopping* into exciting *mobile internet shopping*. However, our fascination with M-commerce was not without a lot of traffic hazards. I am not sure now how to distinguish between *drunk drivers* and *internut drivers*. Fortunately, this did not deter researchers and developers to continue to create complete mobile database systems, leaving the traffic police to deal with *internut drivers*.

Sensors, *the atomic computing particles*, and the wireless sensor networks (WSN) added another dimension to this pervasive discipline. WSNs went to the corners of the world where humans would not dare to venture. It captured the data stream that was crucial to understand the natural and manmade phenomena. Sensors have become important building blocks of nearly all gadgets that we use today, and today we cannot even imagine functioning without it.

The book begins with topics important for the development of mobile database systems. It discusses some basic concepts of database processing with reference to mobility whenever appropriate. It explains why conventional approaches to data processing on mobile systems would not work satisfactorily and makes a strong case for the development of new schemes. The book then covers mobile transaction models where execution of conventional transactions on mobile platforms and new transaction models for mobile database systems are discussed. None of these models have been implemented and validated in the real world mainly because commercial mobile database systems do not exist at the present time. A couple of chapters were devoted to sensor technology and sensor stream data processing. All other topics, such as concurrency control, database recovery, data broadcast, broadcast disks, data stream processing, and so on, have been discussed in a similar style.

I hope that most instructors will find this book useful in introducing the mobile discipline to their students. I believe that they will find that their understanding about the current status of mobile database systems will be greatly improved.

VIJAY KUMAR

University of Missouri—Kansas City
May 2013

ACKNOWLEDGMENTS

It gives me great pleasure to acknowledge the help I received from my students, co-researchers, and friends in writing this book. I am grateful to my Ph.D. students Nitin Prabhu and Debopam Acharya for letting me include their research works in the area of mobile databases and wireless data dissemination.

A large number of my friends and co-researchers provided me with useful material. Without their contributions, this book would not have been possible. I appreciate the generous help I received from Karl Abrer, EPL, Switzerland; Raman Adaikkalavan, Indiana University South Bend; Bharat Bhargava, Purdue University; Sharma Chakravarthy, University of Texas, Arlington; Panos Chryanthis, University of Pittsburgh; Margaret Dunham, Southern Methodist University; Tom Farley (Privateline.com); Sumi Helal, University of Florida, Gainsville; Qingchun Jiang, Oracle Corporation, CA; Sanjay Madria, Missouri University of Science and Technology; Evi Pitoura, University of Ionnina; Krithi Ramamritham, IIT Bombay, India; Indrakshi Ray, Colorado State University; Kyong-I Ku and Yoo-Sung Kim of INHA University, Korea; and Xing Xie, Colorado State University. I thank WirelessAdvisor.com for allowing me to use the terms for preparing the Glossary.

I thank John Wiley & Sons editor Simone Taylor for agreeing to publish the book, and I am grateful to Diana Gialo for her help with editorial issues. I thank Amy Hendrickson of Texnology Inc. for greatly needed help in preparing the manuscript. Thanks to Nancy Lorenz for carefully proofreading the contents and improving the presentation. I am thankful to IEEE for allowing me to use material from some published material.

V.K.

CHAPTER 1

MOBILE DATABASE SYSTEM

1.1 INTRODUCTION

This chapter presents an intuitive introduction to the architecture and basic components of a *mobile database system (MDS)*. Such an introduction is very helpful in preparing our readers to understand the complete architecture, its functionality, and research and development issues. The introduction briefly explains the objectives of MDS, describes the data organization, discusses the role of each component, explains how transactions are processed, describes the role of concurrency control mechanisms, and discusses database discovery issues.

1.1.1 Mobile Database System Architecture

An MDS is a distributed multidatabase client/server system built on a PCS (personal communication system) [1] or a GSM (global system for mobile communication) platform [2–4]. It provides complete database functionality to any user—mobile or stationary. End users, therefore, are unable to differentiate whether they are using an MDS or a conventional database system. A user can connect to the database from anywhere (driving, traveling on a plane, enjoying a roller-coaster ride, etc.) without having to go through the web. The connectivity between the user and the database system is established either through a cellular network or through satellite communication. There are some differences in GSM and PCS architectures; as a result, the architecture of MDS built on these platforms may differ slightly; however, it does not affect MDS functionality [5, 6].

Fundamentals of Pervasive Information Management Systems, Revised Edition. Vijay Kumar.
© 2013 John Wiley & Sons, Inc. Published 2013 by John Wiley & Sons, Inc.

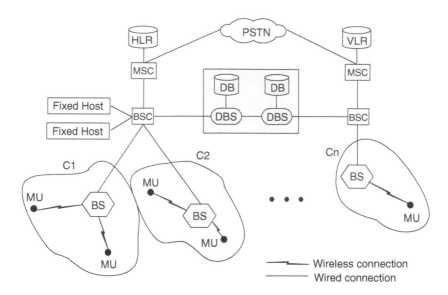

Figure 1.1 Reference architecture of a mobile database system.

Database functionality is provided by a set of DBSs (database servers) that are incorporated without affecting any aspect of the generic cellular network. A reference architecture of MDS is illustrated in Figure 1.1.

The architectures of GSM and PCS are discussed in detail in Chapter 2. The components of these systems are special-purpose computers (switches). The reference architecture of MDS is, therefore, described in terms of components of GSM/PCS such as *base station (BS)*, *fixed hosts (FHs)*, *base station controller (BSC)*, *mobile switching center (MSC)*, *home location register (HLR)*, and *visitor location register (VLR)*. These components are described in detail in Chapter 2. We refer to some of these components as workstations, PCs, PDAs, laptops, and so on, to better understand the architecture and functionality of MDS.

The reference architecture of our MDS that is discussed here is based on a GSM platform. In MDS, a set of general-purpose computers are interconnected through a high-speed wired network and categorized into *fixed hosts (FHs)* and *base stations (BSs)* or *mobile support stations (MSSs)*. FHs are not fitted with transceivers so they do not communicate with mobile units (laptop with wireless connectivity, PDAs, IPad, etc.) One or more BSs are connected with a *BSC* that is also referred to as the *cell site controller* [1, 4]. It coordinates the operation of BSs using its own stored software programs when commanded by the MSC. To coordinate with DBSs, some additional simple data processing capabilities are incorporated in BSs. Unrestricted mobility in PCS and GSM is supported by a wireless link between BS and mobile units. These mobile gadgets are referred to as *mobile hosts (MHs)* or *mobile units (MUs)* [1, 4]. BSs are fitted with transceivers and communicate with MUs through wireless channels and link wired and wireless parts of the MDS. Each BS serves one cell that is a well-defined geographical area. The size of a cell depends on the power of its BS. In reality, a high-power BS is not used because of a number of factors; rather, a number of low-power BSs are deployed for managing movement of MUs in various cells.

Database servers (DBSs) can be installed (a) inside BSs or (b) inside FHs. There are, however, a number of problems with this setup. BSs or FHs are switches and they have specific switching tasks to perform; incorporating database capability in them would interfere in their switching tasks. Besides, the size of a BS varies and inhibits incorporating complete database functionalities in smaller BSs, and the entire architecture of a BS (hardware and software) may have to be revised. Such a major change in a cellular platform would be unacceptable from a mobile communication viewpoint. In addition to this, the setup will not be modular and scalable because any change or enhancement in database components will interfere with data and voice communication. For these reasons, DBSs are connected to the system through a wired network as separate nodes as shown in Figure 1.1. Each DBS can be reached by any BS or FH, and new DBSs can be connected and old ones can be taken out from the network without affecting mobile communication. The set of MSCs and PSTN connects the MDS to the outside world.

A DBS communicates with MUs only through BSs. The duration a mobile user (MH or MU) remains connected to DBSs (through BSs) depends on the workload. On the average, it is actively connected for 2 to 4 hours during a day. At other times, when it is not engaged in transaction processing, it must save the battery power. To conserve the power, a mobile unit can be switched to stay in (a) powered off mode (not actively listening to the BS) or (b) an idle mode (doze mode—not communicating but continuously listening to the BS) or (c) an active mode (communicating with other parties, processing data, etc.) The unit can move from one cell to another in any of these modes. For example, a driver can switch its cell phone to save battery power while driving and may cross many cell boundaries. The total coverage area of an MH is the sum of all cell areas, that is $\{C_1 + C_2 + \cdots + C_n\}$ where C_i indicates a cell. As discussed in Chapter 2, the mobile unit encounters *handoff* only in active mode.

1.1.2 Data Distribution

The MDS has multiple DBSs and a database can be (a) partially distributed or (b) partitioned or (c) fully replicated [7–9]. However, in MDS, data distribution is architecture specific. An MDS can be either a federated or a multidatabase system; as a result, data distribution must follow the constraints of *location-dependent, location-aware*, and *location-free* data [10]. Under such constraints, unlike conventional data distribution, a data item can be replicated only at a certain DBS. For example, it does not make sense to duplicate or replicate the tax data of Kansas City to a DBS that serves the Dallas area. This implies that a global database schema may not be feasible in MDS. However, we will see later that under some situations, a full database replication is possible and highly useful. Generally, partial data replication is always possible.

1.1.3 Transaction Processing

A user initiates a transaction either at an MU or at a DBS. Since MDS is a distributed database system, the execution of a transaction follows a distributed transaction processing paradigm [11–13]. If the necessary data are available at the place of origin (mobile unit or DBS), then it either can be processed in its entirety as a single transaction or may be split into multiple *sub-transactions* and processed at multiple processing units (MU or DBS) for better throughput. On the other hand, if the place of origin does not have the entire data for the transaction, then it has to split into *sub-transactions* and is processed in a distributed manner. The process and mechanism of the transaction split, the mode of distributed processing, and so on, will be discussed in later chapters.

1.1.4 Concurrency Control Mechanism

Similar to conventional database systems, MDS also requires conventional concurrency control mechanisms to serialize the execution of concurrent or parallel transactions. There are a large number of serialization mechanisms developed for database systems such as two-phase locking, timestamping, multiversioning, and so on, but because of the unique requirements of MDS, they may not be satisfactory [14]. Conventional serialization mechanisms are process and communication intensive. MDS does not have a lot of *channels* and power to support the volume of communication it requires; as a result, new energy-efficient serialization mechanisms need to be developed or conventional schemes need to be revisited to make them energy-efficient. To provide better response and throughput, MDS needs serialization techniques that have (a) independent decision-making capabilities and (b) minimum locking and unlocking overheads. Later chapters explain the requirements and working of such concurrency control mechanisms and develops a few.

1.1.5 MDS Recovery

MDS has many unique requirements such as management of location-dependent data, transaction processing during handoff, etc. These requirements make recovery complex, compared to conventional database recovery. The complexity begins from log management. The main problem is the management of the log generated by mobile units [15]. Where and how to store the log, how to make the log available for recovery, how and where to recover, and so on, are some of the difficult issues that need efficient and cost-effective solutions. In the later chapters, we discuss all these issues in detail as well as their theoretical foundations and recovery protocols.

1.2 SUMMARY

This chapter presented a brief introduction to a reference architecture of a mobile database system (MDS) and explained how transactions are processed. The objective was to develop readers intuition so that they can get a clear understanding of unique and complex problems and issues of MDS. Since the backbone of MDS is wireless and mobile disciplines, we begin coverage of these topics in the next chapters.

EXERCISES

1.1 Explain the unique properties of mobile database systems and identify the similarities and differences between conventional distributed database and mobile database systems.

1.2 What is the difference between wireless communication and mobile communication? Explain your answer and give real-world examples to illustrate the difference.

1.3 Identify the the set of components that use wireless channels and identify the set of components that are connected with wired network. Explain the roles they play in mobile database systems.

1.4 Discuss the role of DBS in managing the database. Do you think DBSs should be made a part of BSs (housed in BSs)? First explain if it is possible to make them as a part of BSs and then comment on the benefits of this architecture. Suggest another location for DBSs that works fine without affecting functionality of the cellular system.

1.5 Design a database partition and distribution scheme that will improve transaction processing throughput and response time. Explain how transactions will be processed under your distribution scheme. (*Note*: This is a research-type question suitable for a graduate class project.)

REFERENCES

1. R. Kuruppillai, M. Dontamsetti, and F. J. Cosentino, *Wireless PCS*, McGraw-Hill, New York, 1997.

2. D. Barbara, Mobile Computing and Databases—A Survey, *IEEE Transactions on Knowledge and Data Engineering*, Vol. 11, No. 1, January 1999, pp. 108–117.

3. T. Imielinksi and B. R. Badrinath, Wireless Mobile Computing: Challenges in Data Management, *Communications of the ACM*, Vol. 37, No. 10, October 1994, pp. 18–28.

4. M. Mouly and Marie-Bernadette Pautet, *The GSM System for Mobile Communications*, Cell & Sys Publications, Palaiseau, France, 1992.

5. E. Pitoura and G. Samaras, *Data Management for Mobile Computing*, Kluwer Academic Publishers, Hingham, MA, 1998.

6. E. Pitoura and B. Bhargava, Building Information Systems for Mobile Environments. In *Proceedings of the Third International Conference on Information and Knowledge Management*, Washington, D.C., November 1994, pp. 371–378.

7. D. Barbara and H. Garcia-Molina, Replicated Data Management in Mobile Environments: Anything New Under the Sun? In *Proceedings of the IFIP Conference on Applications in Parallel and Distributed Computing*, April 1994, pp. 237–246.

8. Y. Huang, P. Sistla, and O. Wolfson, Data Replication for Mobile Computers. In *Proceedings of the 1994 SIGMOD Conference*, May 1994, pp. 13–24.

9. D. Lee, W.-C. Lee, J. Xu, and B. Zheng, Data Management in Location-Dependent Information Services, *IEEE Pervasive Computing*, Vol. 1, No. 3, July–September 2002, pp. 65–72.

10. V. Kumar and M. Dunham, Defining Location Data Dependency, Transaction Mobility and Commitment, Technical Report 98-cse-1, Southern Methodist University, Feb. 98.

11. P. K. Chrysanthis, Transaction Processing in Mobile Computing Environment. In *IEEE Workshop on Advances in Parallel and Distributed Systems*, October 1993, pp. 77–82.

12. M. H. Dunham, A. Helal, and S. Baqlakrishnan, A Mobile Transaction Model that Captures Both the Data and the Movement Behavior, *ACM/Balter Journal on Special Topics in Mobile Networks and Applications*, Vol. 2, No. 2, 1997, pp. 149–162.

13. E. Pitoura and B. Bhargava, Revising Transaction Concepts for Mobile Computing. In *Proceedings 1st IEEE Workshop in Mobile Computing Systems and Applications*, 8–9 Dec. 1994, pp. 164–168.

14. Kam-yiu, Lam, Tei-Wei Kuo, Wai-Hung Tsamg, and Gary C. K. Law, Concurrency Control in Mobile Distributed Real-Time Database Systems, *Information Systems*, Vol. 25, Issue 4, June 2000, pp. 261–286.

15. P. Krishna, N. H. Vaidya, and D. K. Pradhan, Recovery in Distributed Mobile Environment. In *Proceedings of the IEEE Workshop on Advances in Parallel and Distributed Systems*, October, 1993, pp. 83–88.

CHAPTER 2

MOBILE AND WIRELESS COMMUNICATION

2.1 INTRODUCTION

This chapter introduces the concept of fully connected information space and discusses how it can be achieved through mobile and wireless communications. It discusses different types of mobility, identifies essential hardware and software components, and explains how these can be combined to build a mobile database system (MDS).

2.1.1 Mobility—The Most Desirable Environment

Information retrieval by users with mobile devices such as cell phones, PDAs (personal digital assistant), MP3 music players, and so on, has become an everyday activity. Navigational systems in vehicles are now a standard accessory. These gadgets are quite useful and user-friendly because they can retrieve desired information from any information repository (database, web, cloud, etc.) from anywhere through wireless channels. However, they have a serious limitation: The information flow in these systems is only from the server to users. This limitation does not allow users to query or manipulate the information stored in a repository that can be located geographically anywhere in the fully connected information space. Consequently, users just have to contend with what information the server *pushes* that may not always be accurate or up to date. In database terminology, these systems are not capable of managing transactional activities.

Fundamentals of Pervasive Information Management Systems, Revised Edition. Vijay Kumar.
© 2013 John Wiley & Sons, Inc. Published 2013 by John Wiley & Sons, Inc.

Database researchers, practitioners, and commercial organizations have a common vision of building an information management system on a mobile platform that is capable of providing full transaction management and database functionality from anywhere and anytime. The recent advances in mobile discipline clearly indicate that reaching this ambitious goal is around the corner.

Traditionally, a database is processed by immobile processing units (servers and clients). The spatial coordinates of these processing units are fixed, and users go to them with their data processing requests. Under this information management model, both the processing units and their users are immobile at the time of data processing. This way of managing information has some inherent efficiency problems leading to unacceptably low productivity. In addition, it is not scalable because it is unable to grow with present-day information processing needs. The ever-changing social structure, the necessity to have desired connectivity among national and international communities, increasing spatial mobility, and fear of isolation have generated a very different class of information processing needs and demands. One of the important aspects of these demands is that a user must be free from *temporal* and *spatial* constraints in dealing with the desired information. Such a capability can only be achieved by geographical mobility during data processing. The inherent immobility of processing units of legacy systems was a serious impediment in achieving the desired objective.

Some of these limitations of the legacy systems began to disappear with the introduction of mobile gadgets (mobile phones, PDAs, etc.) as explained in the preface of this book. They managed to implement a part of *fully connected information space*. Thus, the "anytime, anyplace" connectivity paradigm for voice became very common, but the facility is becoming available for data too.

2.1.2 Fully Connected Information Space

We discuss the concept of *fully connected information space* and justify its importance in everyday activities of our workforce. Figure 2.1 illustrates a *fully connected information space*. It encompasses all objects of this real world, some of which could be stationary and are fully connected through wireless links. A component of this space can communicate and exchange information with any number of other components under the "anytime, anywhere paradigm." For example, a bank or a person is connected to conferences, buses, submarines, sharks, and so on, with a bidirectional wireless link. Thus, at any moment a person, or a bank, or a scuba diver could have complete information about all other objects (we are not considering data or person privacy here). Such connectivity has become essential for our highly mobile and dynamic workforce. Consider the case of working parents. Their children are in different schools, and each parent works at a different place. Each member of the family would like to have instant access to their children to reach them at a time of need. Similarly, the president of a company would like to have complete information about all activities of his company to manage it efficiently.

The fully connected information space, in addition to total connectivity through wireless communication, needs complete database functionality to satisfy today's

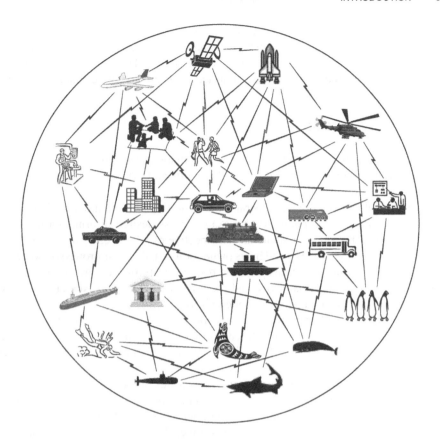

Figure 2.1   A fully connected information space.

workforce information processing needs. Users desire that a mobile unit (cell phone, PDA, etc.) should have transaction management capabilities so that, without going through the web, they should be able to access their accounts, execute fund transfer tasks, pay bills, buy and sell shares, allow a CEO to access his company's database, and offer salary raises to its employees while traveling in a car or on a plane, and so on. Today, each individual likes to have a facility to manage information related to him. For example, a user would like to change his personal profile for adding new call options on his cell phone service. The user would prefer to have editing capabilities to edit his profile and incorporate new options by himself, instead of having to reach out to the service provider. A customer would prefer to have a facility to execute his own fund transfer transactions (from anywhere) to pay for his purchases or to transfer money among his multiple accounts instead of requesting his bank to do so. Some of these facilities, for example, fund transfer facilities, are available, but they are through web services rather than MDS.

These demands and creative thinking laid down the foundation of the "ubiquitous information management system" or the "mobile database system," which in essence is a distributed client/server database system where the entire *processing environment* is mobile. The actual database may be static and stored at multiple sites, but the data processing nodes, such as laptops, PDAs, cell phones, and so on, may be mobile and can access the desired data to process transactions from anywhere and at any time.

2.2 TYPES OF MOBILITY

To implement mobility in a fully connected information space, the mobile framework defines two types of mobility: (a) *terminal mobility* and (b) *personal mobility*.

Terminal Mobility. Figure 2.2 illustrates the notion of terminal mobility. It allows a mobile unit (laptop, cell phone, PDA, etc.) to access desired information from any location, while in motion or stationary, irrespective of who is carrying the unit. For example, a cell phone can be used by its owner or it can also be borrowed by someone else to use. In terminal mobility, it is the responsibility of the wireless network to identify the communication device and process its request. A person at location C (longitude/latitude of *C*) uses the mobile unit to communicate with the car driver at location *A*. He can still establish communication with the driver from a new location *D*, irrespective of the movement of the car from *A* to *B*. The use of a phone card works on this principle. It can be used from different locations and from different machines such as pay phones, residential phones, and so on.

In terminal mobility, from a telecommunication viewpoint, the network connection point (referred to as the network access/termination point) is relevant (not the called party) in processing the request. Thus, the connection is established between two points and not between the two persons calling each other. This type of connection in a session allows the use of communication devices to be shared among anyone.

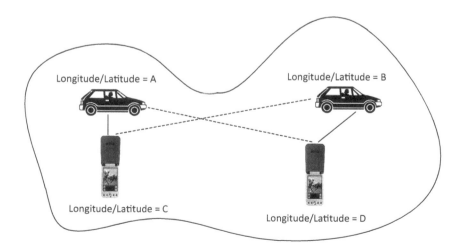

Figure 2.2   Terminal mobility.

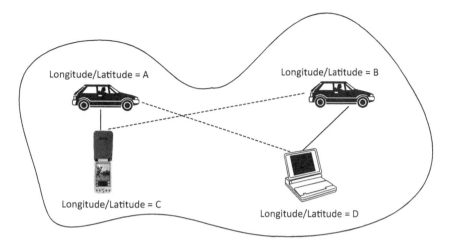

Figure 2.3   Personal mobility.

Personal Mobility. Figure 2.3 illustrates the notion of personal mobility. In terminal mobility, the mobility of a terminal is supported; that is, the same terminal can be used to connect to the other party from anywhere by any user. In personal mobility, this capability is provided to a human being. Thus, a user does not have to carry any communication device (laptop, PDA, etc.) with him; he can use any communication device for establishing communication with the other party. This facility requires an identification scheme to verify the person wishing to communicate. A person at location *C* communicates with the car at location *A* using his PDA, and from location *D* he also can communicate with the car at location *A* using his laptop. At present, personal mobility is available through the web. A user can log on to the web from different machines located at different places and access his e-mail. The mobile system extends this facility so that the user can use any mobile device for reaching the internet. In personal mobility, each person has to be uniquely identified; one way to do this is via a unique identification number.

There is no dependency relationship between terminal and personal mobility; each can exist without the other. In personal mobility the party is free to move, and in terminal mobility the communication unit is free to move. Voice or data communication can be supported by either type of mobility. However, to visualize a complete mobile database management system, both types of mobility are essential; the system does implement both.

2.3 MOBILE AND WIRELESS COMMUNICATIONS

In wireless communication, users communicate without wires. The communication link is established through radio frequencies (RFs). The telecommunication system has to perform a number of steps and go through a number of wired components for setting up a wireless communication session between two users. The current wireless technology is not advanced enough to eliminate these wired segments in setting up the link to make the process entirely wireless. The future wireless technology, such as iridium [1, 2], aims to extend the wireless connectivity to mobile systems to cover remote and sparsely populated areas. It also aims to provide emergency services in the event of failure of terrestrial wireless services due to natural events such as floods, earthquakes, and so on. It is possible that an iridium system may be successful in reducing the dependency on wired components, but it is highly unlikely that they could be completely eliminated. However, from the user side, it matters little how the wireless communication is set up; they will continue to enjoy complete mobility in talking to their partners but possibly with increased subscription cost.

2.3.1 Radio Frequency: Spectrum and Band

All forms of wireless communication use electromagnetic waves to propagate information from one place to another. To better understand the management of *radio frequencies (RFs)*, a number of terms are defined below.

Spectrum. The entire range of RFs is referred to as a *spectrum*. Theoretically, the range of this spectrum spans from zero to infinity. However, only a portion of this spectrum is suitable for voice or data communication for a variety of reasons including health hazards.

Band. A band refers to a range of RFs usable for a particular task that can transport data or voice. To describe the size of this band, the term *bandwidth* is used. For example, if a particular device can use RFs between 80 MHz and 180 MHz to perform a task, then it is said that the device has a bandwidth of $(180 - 80 \text{ MHz}) = 100 \text{ MHz}$. Sometimes bandwidth is expressed in percentages. For example, if some device can handle RFs from 80 MHz to 180 MHz, then the device can handle a 50% bandwidth. The percentage is calculated as follows:

  i. Calculate the bandwidth: $180 - 80 = 100$ MHz.
 ii. Compute the average frequency: $(80 + 180)/2 = 130$ MHz.
iii. Divide the bandwidth by the average frequency and multiply the result by 100: $(100 \div 130) \times 100 = 76.92\%$.

In a wide spectrum of RFs, the usable radio frequencies start from 3 Hz (hertz) to 3000 GHz (gigahertz). Higher frequencies that range from 3 THz (terahertz) to 3000 THz are under consideration for some use. This spectrum was originally categorized into 26 different bands, each representing some specific domain of use. The International Telecommunication Union (ITU) identified 11 bands for radio frequencies ranging from 3 Hz to 300 GHz. Table 2.1 identifies different frequency bands and their usage. The *Electronic Countermeasures (ECM)* refers to these bands with a different set of letters. Table 2.2 lists the ECM band identification.

Table 2.1   Electromagnetic Spectrum and Its Applications

Band	Frequency Range	Usage
ELF (extremely low frequency)	3 Hz–30 Hz	Metal detectors
SLF (super-low frequency)	30 Hz–300 Hz	Submarine communication
ULF (ultra-low frequency)	300 Hz–3000 Hz	Audio, telephone
VLF (very low frequency)	3 kHz–30 kHz	Navigation, sonar
LF (low frequency)	30 kHz–300 kHz	Aeronautical, maritime, radionavigation, and radio beacons
MF (medium frequency)	300 kHz–3 MHz	AM radio, direction finding, maritime, short-wave radio
HF (high frequency)	3 MHz–30 MHz	Amateur SW radio, citizen band radio, meter amateur radio
VHF (very high frequency)	30 MHz–300 MHz	Aircraft, amateur radio, cordless phones, FM radio, pagers, weather radio, etc.
UHF (ultra-high frequency)	300 MHz–3 GHz	Amateur radio, biomedical telemetry, pager, citizen band radio, walkie-talkie, TV, public service, mobile phone (AMPS, CDMA, TDMA, CDPD, GSM, military, radar, wireless, headphones, paging, PCS, etc.)
SHF (super-high frequency)	3 GHz–30 GHz	Microwave oven, Wi-Fi, Bluetooth, cordless phone, public safety, radar, etc.
EHF (extremely high frequency)	30 GHz–300 GHz	Automotive radar, LEOS (low earth-orbiting satellites), LMDS (local multipoint distribution system)

Table 2.2   ECM Bands

Band	Frequency Range
A	30 MHz–250 MHz
B	250 MHz–500 MHz
C	500 MHz–1 GHz
D	1 GHz–2 GHz
E	2 GHz–3 GHz
F	3 GHz–4 GHz
G	4 GHz–6 GHz
H	6 GHz–8 GHz
I	8 GHz–10 GHz
J	10 GHz–20 GHz
K	20 GHz–40 GHz
L	40 GHz–60 GHz
M	60 GHz–100 GHz

This defines the upper limit of the RF range. One important consideration is the selection of a subset of frequencies from this range for developing a wireless communication system. The selection of suitable communication frequencies is based on (a) health safety, (b) how far they can go without losing their energy to an unacceptable level, (c) the cost of their management, and (d) their availability for public use. Too high frequencies such as X-rays, gamma rays, and so on, have very high energy and could serve as excellent communication frequencies. Unfortunately, they present serious health hazards and can damage the ecosystem. In addition to this, they can be absorbed quickly by objects on their path. Low-frequency waves such as ultrasound, infrared, and so on, have poor immunity to interference and have a low data rate. They may be acceptable for short-distance communication such as activating radio, televisions, and other home appliances, but they require that the communication path be free from any obstacle. The optical waves have similar constraints. They can provide relatively high data rates but require a *line-of-sight* communication path and, therefore, they cannot be used reliably in the presence of foliage, dust, and fog. Then the question of a suitable antenna to capture and transmit necessary frequencies arises. The wireless industries, therefore, identified an RF spectrum from 100 MHz (UHF) to about 30 GHz for wireless communication. Out of this range, most wireless communication today uses a frequency range of 800 MHz to 3 GHz, which is allowed by the Federal Communication Commission (FCC).

The selection of 800 MHz for cellular communication is based on a number of factors. Initially, this band was not used for a long time; but industries, especially TV stations, did not want to relinquish their hold on this band because of its benefits. Some of these are

- It has a wavelength of about 12 inches ($12 \times 2.54 = 30.48$ cm), which is very short.
- It can be easily reflected by objects such as buildings, moving objects, and so on.
- Unlike short-wave radio, it does not easily skip or bounce off the ionosphere.
- The signal absorption is high, which allows us to achieve efficient *frequency reuse*. On the other hand, this absorption creates problems in major coverage points such as city centers, heavily wooded areas, and so on.

2.3.2   Cellular Communication

There is no radio frequency that can carry data or voice to long distances without serious attenuation. The entire communication is, therefore, achieved in multiple "communication slots" to overcome this limitation. A communication slot is a geographical area within which the RF can be used to set up communication. In cellular terminology, this communication slot is referred to as a *cell* and the entire communication infrastructure is known as *cellular communication*. The size of a cell is defined by keeping in mind the energy level of the RF to be used and the power of the transceiver. Thus, to cover an area of any shape that is larger than the RF frequency

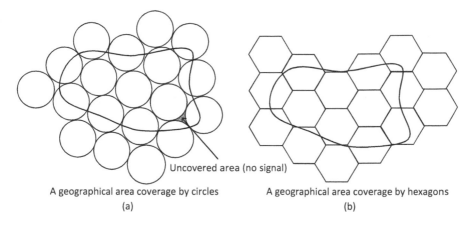

A geographical area coverage by circles   A geographical area coverage by hexagons
                    (a)   (b)

Figure 2.4 Cell coverage through circles and hexagons.

can support, for example, a city, it is logically divided into a set of cells. This logical division helps to identify the best position to install the transceiver for achieving the "best coverage", which means that a mobile device is able to receive communication from any geographical point of a cell. A mathematical model is used to identify the "best coverage" pattern. To understand what the meaning of the best coverage is, let us use a circle to develop a coverage pattern. Figure 2.4a illustrates an example of covering an area using circles. It is obvious from the figure that the entire area cannot be fully covered by using a circle of any size. The space at the junction of three circles will always remain uncovered. Thus, a cell phone will not receive any signal at this location. To eliminate all uncovered areas in a cellular structure, hexagons are used to create a coverage area. Figure 2.4b illustrates the coverage using hexagons that have no uncovered spaces.

A cell in real life is highly amorphous, and its actual radio coverage is referred to as a *footprint*. A real footprint is determined with some field measurement or through wave propagation prediction models, but in theory, a well-defined regular shape is required to compute the necessary parameter values.

One of the important factors for completely covering every point of a cell is the location of its "cell site." It is the point (geographical location) in the cell where the transceiver is installed. The transceiver is commonly referred to as a *base station (BS)*. The main objective here is to install the BS so that it can cover a maximum number of cells efficiently. Figure 2.5a shows the arrangement used in practice. The cell site is the smaller circle at the junction of three hexagons that represents cells. The transceiver covers a portion, referred to as the "sector" of each cell, and provides each sector with its own set of channels. This arrangement can also be visualized as shown in Figure 2.5b. It appears here that a cell site is located at the center of a cell. These architectural details are not that important for the topic of this book, so it is not further elaborated here. A useful site to visit for more up-to-date information is given in reference 3.

In a cellular architecture a number of wireless and wired components are required to establish the desired *point-to-point* or point-to-multipoint communication. A mobile

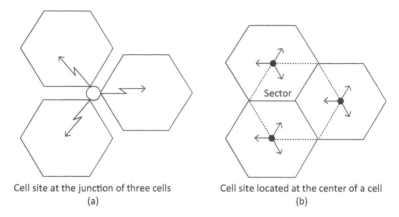

Cell site at the junction of three cells

(a)

Cell site located at the center of a cell

(b)

Figure 2.5 Location of a cell site.

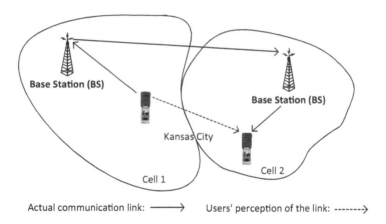

Actual communication link: ⟶   Users' perception of the link: -------⟶

Figure 2.6 Communication link between cells.

database system (MDS) is interested in the components that are directly connected through wireless channels with mobile devices. A BS is a component that functions under the supervision of a telecommunication switch called the *mobile switching center (MSC)* and is connected to it through a wired line. It is the MSC that connects the entire mobile system with a PSTN (public switched telephone network). Figure 2.6 illustrates a communication path. These components are discussed in detail later in this chapter.

2.4 CONTINUOUS CONNECTIVITY

Continuous connectivity during wireless communication is highly desirable for voice communication but essential for data exchange. A momentary disruption in voice communication is acceptable because the communicating parties can decipher the missing word. This, however, is not acceptable in data communication because it threatens the accuracy of the data.

A communication session uses a *channel* to exchange information. Continuous connectivity is affected by a variety of reasons, such as the absence of a free channel, signal fading, and interference.

2.4.1 Structure of a Channel

A channel is a communication path between any two devices such as computers, mobile units, base stations, and so on. In a mobile discipline, two frequencies are required to establish communication: one from the mobile to the base station and one from the base station to the mobile. For this reason, a channel is defined as a pair of radio frequencies, one to receive and one to transmit. The frequency that is used by a mobile unit for transmission to a base station is called an *uplink channel (reverse channel)*, and the frequency used by the base station to transmit to the mobile unit is called the *forward channel (downlink channel)*. Figure 2.7 illustrates the use of a channel for communication.

Figure 2.8 organizes the available frequencies in *AMPS (Advanced Mobile Phone Service)*, and Figure 2.9 presents the same distribution in a different way. In these figures, **A** represents a wireless carrier and **B** represents a wireline carrier. Channels repeat themselves, but frequencies do not because a channel is composed of two frequencies that are 45 MHz apart to avoid interference between them. For example, frequencies of 832.470 MHz and 877.470 MHz make up channel 249, which appears

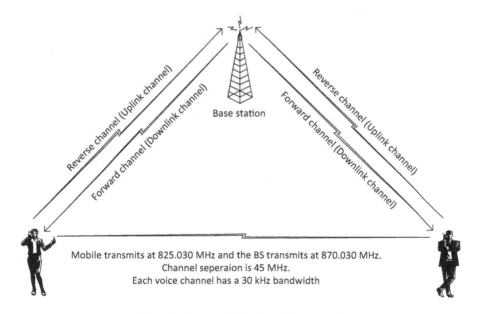

Figure 2.7 Downlink and uplink channels.

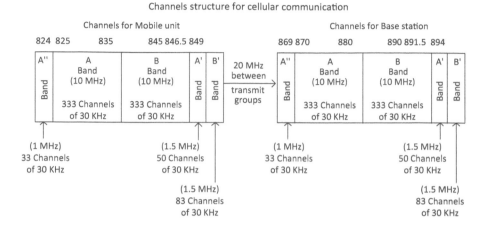

Figure 2.8   Channel structure.

at two places in the band. Cellular channels take up a total of 50 MHz, whereas the AM broadcast band takes up only 1.17 MHz. However, the difference is that cellular provides thousands of frequencies to carry voice and data, and an AM band provides only 107 broadcast frequencies [3].

Table 2.3 lists the frequencies that are commonly used by different systems. The list does not contain additional channels that have been released by the FCC.

2.4.2   Absence of a Free Channel

A cell has a fixed number of voice channels (usually around 25) available for communication. The mobile switching center (MSC) allocates (on demand) a channel through the base station to the mobile unit when it tries to make a call. During peak hours, there may not be a free voice channel for allocation to a new request and thus results in dropping the request. In some situations, the MSC may *borrow* a channel from the neighboring cell for use, but this is a temporary solution and besides, these two cells must be under the management of the same MSC. The lack of channels is caused by the limited bandwidth of cellular communication, and a solution could be to increase the available bandwidth. However, the problem is likely to persist because

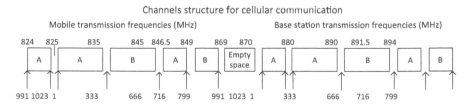

Figure 2.9   Alternate representation of channel structure.

Table 2.3   General Mobile Frequency Table

System	Frequency Range
American cellular (AMPS, N-AMPS, D-AMPS (IS-136) CDMA)	824 to 849-MHz Mobile unit to base station 869 to 894-MHz Base station to mobile unit
American PCS narrowband	901–941 MHz
American PCS broadband	1850 to 1910-MHz Mobile unit to base station 1930 to 1990-MHz Base station to mobile unit
E-TACS	872 to 905-MHz Mobile unit to base station 917 to 950-MHz Base station to mobile unit
GSM	890 to 915-MHz Mobile unit to base station 930 to 960-MHz Base station to mobile unit
JDC	810 to 826-MHz Mobile unit to base station 940 to 956-MHz Base station to mobile unit 1429 to 1441-MHz Mobile unit to base station 1477 to 1489-MHz Base station to mobile unit

of the continuously increasing ratio of the number of cell phones to the available number of channels.

2.4.3 Signal Fading

The strength of the communication channel reduces as the mobile unit moves away from the base station. Figure 2.10 shows how the strength (expressed in decibels (dB)) falls as the distance between the base station and the mobile unit increases. Signal fading affects speech audibility, video reception, and data loss.

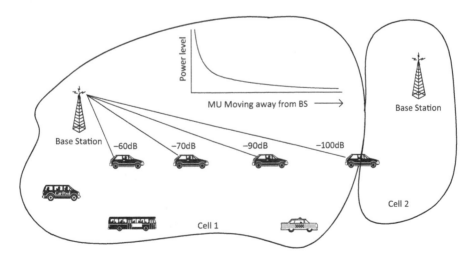

Figure 2.10 Strength of signal received by mobile unit from the base station.

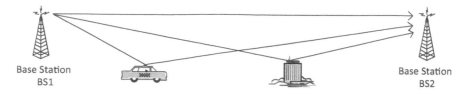

Figure 2.11   A typical mulipath absorption scenario.

Fading occurs mainly due to (a) *absorption*, (b) *free-space loss*, and (c) *multipath fading (Rayleigh fading)*. Absorption occurs when radio frequency hits obstacles such as buildings, trees, rain, hills, and so on. Different materials exhibit different absorption power; for example, organic material exhibits a relatively higher absorption effect. A good example is the absorption by heavy rain where it is possible that the radio frequency may completely be absorbed and the signal from the broadcasting station may not reach a home television at all. The signal fading can be minimized to some extent by utilizing higher gain antennas and smaller sized cells.

Free-space loss describes the absorption of signal power over a given distance between the source and the destination units. This information plays an important role in defining the size of a cell in cellular communication.

The reflection of a radio signal from the objects of its path of travel gives rise to multipath or Rayleigh fading. A radio signal may be divided into the main signal (direct) and a number of reflected signals (indirect). These direct and indirect signals travel different distances and reach the receiving antenna at different times where indirect signals could be out of phase with the direct signal. This situation affects the reception, and in satellite communication it creates ghost images in television reception. Figure 2.11 illustrates a typical multipath fading.

The decrease in the strength due to fading is not easy to compute precisely because it depends on a number of factors including the unpredictable movement of the mobile unit. When a mobile unit crosses its cell boundary and enters a neighboring cell, the system (MSC—mobile switching center) transfers the ongoing communication session to a new channel that belongs to the new base station. The migration of a mobile unit from one cell to another is managed by a process referred to as a *handoff*. A handoff makes sure that the mobile unit gets a channel in the new cell to continue its communication and relieves the channel it was using without any interruption. Figure 2.12 illustrates a typical handoff situation. The car from the cell of base station 1 enters the cell of base station 2 while either actively communicating with someone, being in a doze mode, or in a power-off mode.

One of the important points in a handoff is that it must be initiated and completed before the ongoing call is lost due to reduction in signal strength. To achieve this, an optimal signal level is defined and when this level is detected, the system initiates the handoff. This optimal level is higher than the minimum usable signal level, which is usually between −90 dBm and −100 dBm. Thus, the difference between the handoff threshold signal level and the minimum level should not be either too large or too small. If it is too small, then calls will be dropped before the handoff is complete,

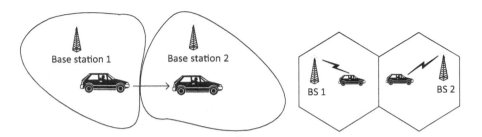

Figure 2.12 A typical handoff scenario.

and if it is too large, then there will be too many handoffs. Figure 2.13 illustrates the initiation of the handoff. Point **H1** identifies the handoff threshold for base station BS1 and **H2** for base station BS2 where handoffs are initiated for BS1 and BS2, respectively. The region covered by **H1** and **H2** is the handoff region, and to maintain continuous connectivity, the handoff process must be completed in this region. In particular, the handoff initiated at points **H1** and **H2** should be completed at point **H**.

The system has to cope with a situation called "false handoff," which occurs when the signal strength reaches the handoff threshold due to momentary fading caused by reflection or absorption by intermediate objects. To detect that the fading is actually due to the mobile unit moving away from the base station, the system measures the signal strength for a certain period of time and obtains a running average that is used to initiate the necessary handoff.

There are two types of handoffs: a *hard handoff* and a *soft handoff*. In a hard handoff, the mobile unit experiences momentary silence in voice communication when it relieves the old channel and acquires the new channel in the new cell. In a soft handoff, no such silence is experienced. The entire process of handoffs, hard and soft, is discussed in detail in Chapter 3. There are excellent books and reports available on these topics [3–5] for further information.

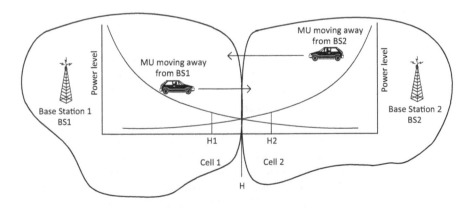

Figure 2.13 A typical handoff initiation.

2.4.4 Frequency Reuse

The continuous connectivity may also be affected by *interference* that can be defined as the interaction between two signals. The interference not only affects the communication but also is a major limiting factor in the performance of the entire system. Two communication sessions may interfere with each other if the frequencies they use are quite close to each other or even identical *(co-channel interference)*. It can also occur if the the base stations of two communicating mobile units are located closely, or if there is another active mobile unit in the vicinity, or if there is an active call in a nearby cell. The presence of an interference could give rise to *cross talk* where one party can hear the communication of the other party in the background. It may also occur between two control channels that may lead to blocked or missed calls. Theoretically, it is possible to have total silence if these frequencies are completely out of phase.

In cellular communication, the system has to deal with *co-channel interference* and *adjacent channel interference*.

Co-channel Interference. This occurs when the same frequency is used for communication in two nearby cells. To avoid *co-channel* interference, two frequencies are kept apart by least 45 Hz, but in the case of higher frequencies, the separation may be less. Each cell is usually assigned 25 to 30 channels for communication that depend on the expected traffic volume in the cell. This will support only 25 to 30 communication sessions. The number of channels for a cell is determined by a number of factors such as the density of callers, which indicates the number of callers per square meter, the average activity factors that relate to the average use of a phone in an hour, the probability of blocked calls, and so on. Co-channel interference could be tolerable in voice communication because humans can guess the words in the presence of noise with resonable accuracy. It is not acceptable in data communication because it can corrupt the data to an extent that cannot be recovered by the receiver. Co-channel interference is solved by keeping the cells, which plan to use the same set of frequencies, apart by a distance called the *frequency reuse distance*. A frequency reuse distance is the minimum safe distance between two cells that can reuse the same frequencies without interference. This distance is expressed in terms of intervening cells between the two cells where the same frequencies are reused.

Frequency reuse is implemented through *cell clustering*. A cell cluster is made up of a number of same-sized cells, and the cluster size depends on the entire coverage area, the frequency plan, acceptable co-channel interference, and mobile commerce (M-commerce) strategies. In M-commerce, it is important for a mobile user to know in which cluster he or she is currently residing. A cluster may be made up of 3, 4, 7, 9, 12, 13, 16, and so on, cells, but out of these, the 7-cell and 4-cell clusters are most commonly used to cover an area. Figures 2.14a through 2.14d illustrate the composition of clusters of sizes. In reality, an area is covered by a number of clusters, each one composed of different sized cells as illustrated by Figure 2.14e. This cluster organization was in fact used by the Vodafone company to provide communication service around the area covered by an M25 ringroad [6]. The inner area was populated

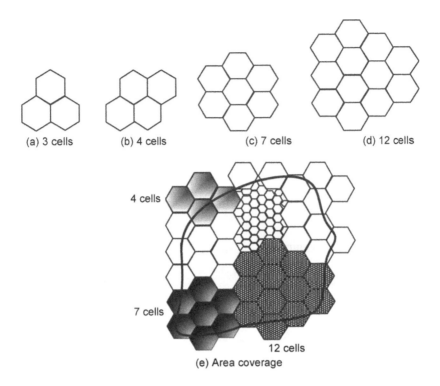

(a) 3 cells   (b) 4 cells   (c) 7 cells   (d) 12 cells

4 cells

7 cells

12 cells

(e) Area coverage

Figure 2.14   Clusters of different sizes.

by smaller-sized cells to manage high communication traffic from highly populated user communities.

To reuse the same set of frequencies in another cell, it must be separated by *frequency reuse distance* that is usually denoted by D. Figure 2.15 illustrates the separation of cells by frequency reuse distance in a cluster of seven cells. In order to derive a formula to compute D, necessary properties of a regular hexagon cell geometry are first discussed.

A regular hexagon can be split into 6 equilateral triangles as shown in Figure 2.16. It has a reflective symmetry about each of its three diagonals d_1, d_2, and d_3 and about lines joining the midpoints of opposite sides. It also has rotational symmetry about its center. A regular hexagon has inradius (r) and circumradius (R) as shown in Figure 2.16. The height H (apotham) of an equilateral triangle can be computed using the Pythagoras theorem as follows:

$$R^2 = \frac{1}{4}R^2 + H^2$$

$$H = \sqrt{R^2 - \frac{1}{2}R^2} = \frac{\sqrt{3}}{2}R \qquad (2.1)$$

Figure 2.17 illustrates the process of computing D. The initial cell is identified as "Start," and its corresponding reuse cell is identified as "End." To reach "End,"

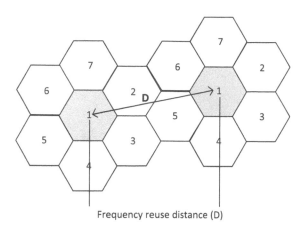

Frequency reuse distance (D)

Figure 2.15 Frequency reuse distance.

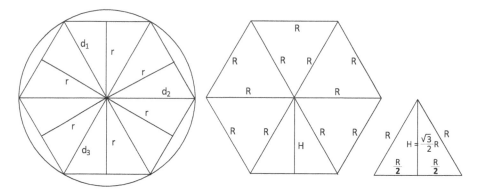

Circumradius = R, Inradius = r, and the Height of a triangle (apothem) = H

Figure 2.16 Properties of a regular hexagon.

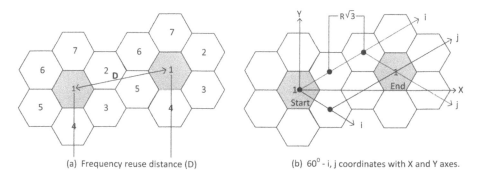

(a) Frequency reuse distance (D)

(b) 60^0 - i, j coordinates with X and Y axes.

Figure 2.17 Identification of frequency reuse cell.

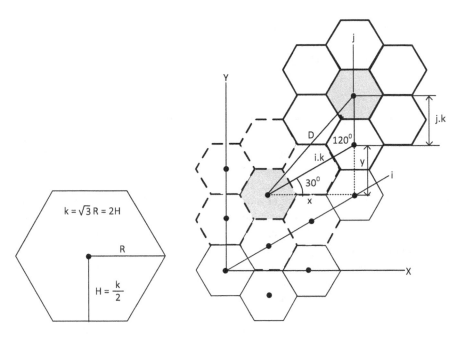

Figure 2.18 Computation of frequency reuse distance D.

multiple cell clusters are traversed always in the direction of H. So from the "Start" cell, travel on the i coordinate to some number of cells and then turn clockwise or counterclockwise and travel some number of cells on the j coordinate. How to get the correct value of i and j will be discussed later.

D is identified through the use of i and j coordinates. Thus, in the computation of D, the X and Y coordinates must be represented in terms of i and j. Figure 2.18 shows how this representation is achieved and gives the following values x and y for

$$x = i\sqrt{3}R\cos30 = \frac{3}{2}iR$$

$$y = i\sqrt{3}R\sin30 = \frac{\sqrt{3}}{2}iR$$

Thus,

$$D^2 = \left(\frac{3}{2}iR\right)^2 + \left(\frac{\sqrt{3}iR}{2} + \sqrt{3}jR\right)^2$$

$$= \frac{9}{4}i^2R^2 + 3R^2\left(\frac{i^2}{4} + ij + j^2\right)$$

$$= 3R^2(i^2 + j^2 + ij)$$

$$D = \sqrt{3R^2(i^2 + j^2 + ij)} \tag{2.2}$$

$$= R\sqrt{3\{(i+j)^2 - ij\}} \tag{2.3}$$

Distance D is closely related to the cell radius R and the cluster size N (number of cells in a cluster). Consider a cluster with C number of duplex channels for use and that are equally divided among N cells. Each cell of this cluster then will have

$$C = eN \qquad (2.4)$$

where e is the number of channels allocated to the cell.

The idea is to replicate this cluster a number of times to enhance the capacity of the system which refers to the number of users it can satisfactorily support. The degree of replication, which refers to the number of times a cluster is replicated, depends significantly on the cluster size. If the cluster size N is reduced without reducing the cell size, then a larger number of clusters will be required to cover the area. On the other hand, if it is increased, then a smaller number of clusters will be needed for coverage. A high degree of replication is able to support a larger number of users, but the probability of interference increases. Voice communication may be able to tolerate such interference but will not be acceptable for data communication. Figure 2.19 illustrates how degree of replication affects the coverage when cluster size is changed. In Figure 2.19a, the area is covered by one replication of a 7-cell cluster, and in Figure 2.19b it is covered by two replications of a 4-cell cluster. In Figure 2.19c, the cluster size is reduced to three; consequently, three replications of a 3-cell cluster are required. This provides a total number of $C \times 3$ effective channels for communication, assuming that each cell is separated by frequency reuse distance. This illustrates how the value of N depends on the degree of interference the base station can tolerate without affecting the quality of communication. In reality, from a system design viewpoint the smallest value of N that can support the largest number of users is used. This also means that only specific values of N can be used effectively and these values can be computed by

$$N = i^2 + ij + j^2 = (i + j)^2 - ij \qquad (2.5)$$

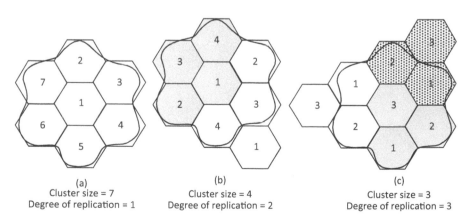

(a)	(b)	(c)
Cluster size = 7	Cluster size = 4	Cluster size = 3
Degree of replication = 1	Degree of replication = 2	Degree of replication = 3

Figure 2.19   Cluster replication.

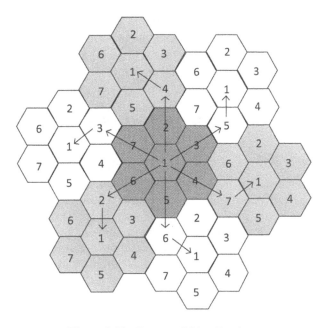

Figure 2.20   Reuse cell identification.

where i and j are non-negative integers and are referred to as *shift parameters*. They identify the direction of movement to find the cells that are located at the frequency reuse distance in the replication. Equation (2.5) indicates that the cluster can be constructed only with $N = 1, 3, 4, 7, 9, 12, 13, 16, 19, \ldots$, the most common values being 4 and 7.

It is easy now to identify the cells for frequency reuse using Eq. (2.5). The steps of the identification process can be illustrated using Figure 2.20, which is constructed with a cluster size of $N = 7$ using $i = 2$ and $j = 1$. Using Eq. (2.5), one must do the following: (a) Identify a starting cell; (b) from this cell move $i = 2$ cells in a straight line to reach the center of the third cell, (c) turn counterclockwise $60°$ in this cell, and (d) move $j = 1$ cell in a straight line to reach to the frequency reuse cell.

Adjacent Channel Interference.   This occurs in the region where energies of two adjacent channels overlap. The region between the points H1 and H2 (Figure 2.13) indicates a channel overlap area. The interference may become quite serious if multiple transmitters of different powers transmit close to each other. It becomes quite difficult in this scenario for the base stations to identify the right mobile user.

These interferences can be minimized by careful channel allocation to neighboring cells. The power of the base station (BS) of a cell is carefully controlled to make sure that the energy of its channels is confined to the cell and does not spill over to the adjacent cells. The main purpose of this control is to be able to reuse the same frequencies in nearby cells. A wireless channel, therefore, has a limited communication range, and mobile units (cell phones, laptops, etc.) are free to move from one cell to another during a wireless session. When a mobile unit leaves its initial cell and enters a neighboring cell, it must also relinquish the frequency it was using and acquire a new frequency in the cell it enters. It is not possible to increase the number of channels to support an increasing number of mobile users because of bandwidth limitations. The idea of *frequency reuse* is used to support a greater number of users. The frequency reuse allows the same frequency to be used in multiple cells, provided that the problems of the *co-channel* and *adjacent channel* are taken care of.

2.4.5 PCS and GSM

The cellular system was based on analog transmission. It experiences a rapid growth in Europe and in North America. However, because of its inherent limitations, it could not cope with the rapidly growing number of subscribers. This gave rise to the evolution of two mobile communication systems commonly known as *PCS (personal communication system)* and *GSM (global system for mobile communication)*. PCS evolved in North America, and GSM evolved in Europe. Both systems are based on digital transmission; however, PCS continued to support analog transmission mainly to service existing subscribers. The GSM system, on the other hand, is purely digital. As these systems evolved, they offered advanced services, and operational differences between them became somewhat blurred. In fact, NPAG (North American PCS 1900 Action Group) developed an American version of GSM, which is called PCS 1900.

Since their deployment, GSM was adopted by most of the countries of the world, capturing 75% of the world communication market, and PCS remained confined mostly to North America.

2.4.6 PCS—Personal Communication Service

Interim Standard-41 (IS-41) is a standard protocol for managing the voice communication in a mobile telecommunication network. It is produced by the Telecommunication Industry Association (TIA) as Revision 0 and since then has gone through three revisions: Revision A (IS-41A), Revision B (IS-41B), and Revision C (IS-41C). IS-41C describes components, protocols, and management of cellular technology that was introduced earlier in this chapter.

The IS-41C cellular system was originally introduced for use in moving vehicles, mainly cars, using analog communication. It had a number of limitations related to coverage size, clear reception, interference, and the degree of mobility. Very soon, subscribers of the IS-41C cellular system found these to be severe impediments in their working environment. Subscriber demands for improved services and facilities motivated investigation into PCS, leading to its deployment in 1996.

PCS is a more sophisticated and powerful wireless phone service that emphasized personal service and extended mobility. Unlike a cellular system, it used digital communication and smaller sized cells to enhance the quality of services and to support a larger number of subscribers. However, PCS did not reject the analog system completely and continued to support it. Thus, the older analog system can still work. FCC vaguely defines PCS as a mobile and wireless service that can be integrated with a variety of different networks to provide a wide variety of mobile and wireless services to individuals and business organizations. The commission allocated spectrum to PCS in three major categories: (a) *broadband*, (b) *narrowband*, and (c) *unlicensed*.

Broadband. The broadband category is designed to offer two-way voice, data, and video communications. It has been referred to as "the next generation of mobile telephone service." Broadband PCS is an allocated spectrum ranging from 1850 to 1910 MHz and 1930 to 1990 MHz. This 120 MHz of spectrum was divided into six frequency blocks A through F, where blocks A, B, and C are 30 MHz each and blocks D, E, and F are 10 MHz each. Different wireless services are provided under each of these bands.

Some C blocks were further divided into two sets: (a) C-1 (15 MHz) and C-2 (15 MHz) or (b) C-3 (10 MHz), C-4(10 MHz), and C-5 (10 MHz). These frequency blocks are used mainly for licensing. Table 2.4 lists the allocated frequencies in the broadband category [7].

Narrowband. The narrowband category is designed to offer advanced voice paging and messaging, acknowledgment paging, data and electronic messaging, two-way paging and other text-based services, and fax service. Narrowband PCS uses a smaller

Table 2.4   Broadband Spectrum

Frequency Block	Frequency	Frequency Range
A	30	1850.0–1865.0
		1930.0–1945.0
B	30	1870.0–1885.0
		1950.0–1965.0
C	30	1895.0–1910.0
		1975.0–1990.0
C-1	15	1902.5–1910.0
		1982.5–1990.0
C-2	15	1895.0–1902.5
		1975.0–1982.5
C-3	10	1895.0–1900.0
		1975.0–1980.0
C-4	10	1900.0–1905.0
		1980.0–1985.0
C-5	10	1905.0–1910.0
		1985.0–1990.0
D	10	1865.0–1870.0
		1945.0–1950.0
E	10	1885.0–1890.0
		1965.0–1970.0
F	10	1890.0–1895.0
		1970.0–1975.0

portion of the spectrum than broadband does, and it operates in the 901- to 902-MHz, 930- to 931-MHz, and 940- to 941-MHz bands. There are 32 channels, and the channel size is 12.5 kHz to 150 kHz.

Unlicensed. The frequency spectrum 1910- to 1930-MHz band has been allocated to the unlicensed PCS. It is designed to provide data networking within office buildings, wireless private branch exchanges, personal digital assistants, laptop computers, portable facsimile machines, and other kinds of short-range communications. An unlicensed system is particularly suitable for office-wide and campus-wide services. One of the advantages of this is that equipment manufacturers do not have to wait for the development of standards since they can design proprietary products for their clients.

Architecture of PCS. Figure 2.21 shows a generic architecture of PCS. It has two sets of components: (a) functional components, which are represented as rectangles, and (b) interfaces, which are represented as small circles between two functional components. The set of components in bold represent the standard as defined in IS-41-C. Since this is a reference architecture, it can be implemented and deployed in many different ways. In one implementation, multiple components may be integrated into a single physical unit without affecting their modularity.

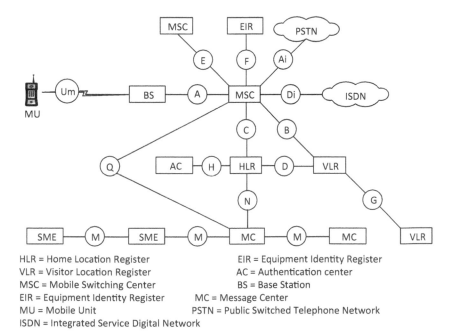

HLR = Home Location Register   EIR = Equipment Identity Register
VLR = Visitor Location Register   AC = Authentication center
MSC = Mobile Switching Center   BS = Base Station
EIR = Equipment Identity Register   MC = Message Center
MU = Mobile Unit   PSTN = Public Switched Telephone Network
ISDN = Integrated Service Digital Network

Figure 2.21   Generic PCS architecture. (Reproduced with permission from the Telecommunication Industry Association.)

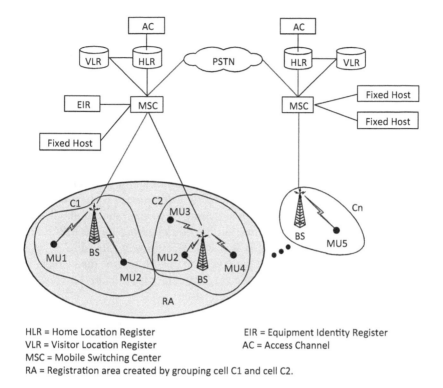

HLR = Home Location Register   EIR = Equipment Identity Register
VLR = Visitor Location Register   AC = Access Channel
MSC = Mobile Switching Center
RA = Registration area created by grouping cell C1 and cell C2.

Figure 2.22   A reference architecture of PCS.

A reference architecture of PCS is given in Figure 2.22, which shows the cellular components. This reference architecture is the basic platform for the development of the mobile database system (MDS) introduced later in the book.

The functional components of PCS are discussed below. The GSM system, which is discussed later, uses nearly the same set of components but with some difference in spectrum allocation.

Functional Components

Mobile Unit (MU). This is also called a *mobile host (MH)* or *mobile station (MS)*. It is a wireless device that is composed of (a) antenna, (b) transceiver, and (c) user interface. The antenna captures the signal, and the transceiver is responsible for receiving and sending signals. The user interface is responsible for interacting with the user by displaying graphics and text and receiving texts from the user. The audio interface component handles voice conversation.

A mobile unit is classified into Class I, which operates at 6 dBW (decibels); Class II, which operates at 2 dBW; and Class III, which operates at −2 dBW. The unit has its own permanent memory where it stores (a) a mobile identification number (MIN), (b) an electronic serial number (ESN), and (c) a station class mark (SCM). MIN is a

10-digit subscriber's telephone number. When a call arrives to a mobile unit, a paging message is sent by MSC with the subscriber's MIN to all base stations. When the mobile unit receives the page on a forward control channel, it sends a response with its own MIN using the reverse control channel. When the MSC receives the mobile unit's response with its MIN, it then directs the BS to assign a voice channel for setting up the communication. The ESN is a unique 32-bit number that is used by the cellular system to identify the unit. This number is hardwired, and any attempt to temper with it makes the unit inoperable. SCM identifies the power handling capability of a mobile unit and it is a 4-bit number.

Base Station (BS). The BS consists of a transmitter and a receiver. Each cell is managed by one BS only, and the size of the cell is determined by its power. In PCS architecture, the activities of a BS such as setting up a communication, allocating a channel for communication, and so on, are directly managed by the MSC. When a mobile subscriber dials a number, the BS of that cell reaches its MSC for a voice channel for establishing the call. At the end of the call it returns the channel to the MSC. Some BS are for indoor and some are for outdoor use. In GSM architecture, a BS is referred to as a BTS (base transceiver station).

Base Station Controller–BSC. This is a GSM component that manages the activities of a number of BSs, or BTSs. Its main functions are RF frequency administration, BTSs, and handover management. At one end, a BSC is connected to many BTSs and to a MSC on the other end.

Mobile Switching Center (MSC). This is a switch and is referred to by many names such as MTSO (mobile telephone switching office), mobile switch (MS), or mobile switching center (MSC). They all process mobile telephone calls. Large systems may have two or more MSCs and are connected with one or many base stations through a wired line.

Home Location Register (HLR). This is a large database that stores necessary information such as the geographical location of a subscriber, call processing, billing, service subscription, service restrictions, and so on. Its contents and structure are vendor-specific, but the schema developed by Lucent Technologies is used by almost all network companies. Lucent refers to their HLR as a stand-alone HLR because it is maintained at a central location and shared among all network elements. In a centralized scheme, HLR is usually stored at one MSC and in distributed approaches, it is distributed to multiple MSCs. Figure 2.23 illustrates a very small portion of the HLR as defined by Lucent Technologies.

Visitor Location Register (VLR). A VLR is a current subset of HLR for a particular cell. Whenever a subscriber enters a new cell, its current location is stored in VLR representing that cell. The entry is removed when the subscriber leaves that cell. The information about a subscriber is replicated in HLR and VLR to achieve a faster location search that begins from VLR and ends in HLR if the entry is not found in

Mobile Identification Number	----------	9135555555
Directory number		9135555500
International Mobile SubscriberID	100	
Electronic Serial Number		1054
Home service area		1
Traveler Service Area	01	
Primary Dialing Class	1	
Secondary Dialing Class		2
Primary Rate Center	1	
Routing Class		1
Mobile Type		2
Billing Type	1	
Primary Last Seen Location		3E7010H
Secondary Last Seen Location	000000	----------

Figure 2.23 Home location register (HLR) database.

the VLR. The VLR data is not used for any administrative purpose, it merely serves as a location identifier.

HLR and VLR are huge databases maintained by high-power servers, often a Unix workstation. Tandem, which is part of Compaq (a part of HP) made the server and called it HLR when it was used for cellular systems. A large number of mobile units use the same HLR and there are usually more than one HLR for nationwide cellular system. For example, Motorola uses more than 60 HLRs nationwide. The processing of HLR is not complex, so it does not need sophisticated database functionality. The recent trend is to distribute HLRs and use distributed processing approaches for their management.

Authenticating Center (AC or AUC). The AC is a processor system that authenticates subscribers. AC needs to access user information for authentication process so it is co-located with HLR. Thus, AC and HLR together are stored in MSC or at nearby locations. An AC may serve more than one HLR. A complete authentication process is performed only when the first call is made. In all subsequent calls from the same subscriber, if made within a system defined time period, the stored information is used for authentication. The authentication steps are as follows:

a. AC sends a random number to the mobile unit from where the call originates.
b. The authentication algorithm stored in SIM (subscriber identity module) manipulates this random number using a subscriber authentication key, which is also stored in SIM.
c. The result of this manipulation is sent to AC along with an encryption key (secured communication).

    d. Concurrent with the authentication computation at the mobile unit, AC performs identical computation using the random number and information stored in HLR.

    e. AC compares the result of its own computation and the result received from the mobile unit. In case of a successful comparison, it permits the subscriber to access the network and stores and sends the encryption key to BS to enable ciphering to take place.

Equipment Identify Register (EIR). This is a database that stores information for the identification of mobile units. For example, it maintains a database electronic serial number that is unique to a mobile unit that prevents its theft and malicious use. It helps the network to deny any service to a stolen mobile unit. To handle the use of questionable equipment (stolen or fraudulent), a GSM maintains three types of lists identified as white, black, and gray. A white list stores all clean equipment identities, which are allowed to use the network, a gray list contains a clean but semifunctional unit (malfunctioning) that has difficulty in making a call, and the black list contains the identities of stolen or fraudulent units. Any call originating from a black list unit is blocked by the network.

Public Switched Telephone Network (PSTN). This component refers to the regular wired line telecommunication network that is commonly accessed by landline calls.

Integrated Service Digital Network (ISDN). This is a wired line network that provides enhanced digital services to subscribers.

Short Message Entity (SME). This unit is added in the IS-41C to manage short text messages (200 bytes or less). This is a part of a system message service (SMS) that looks after text messages.

Message Center (MC). This unit stores and forwards short messages to a mobile destination. If the destination is unavailable for any reason, it stores the message for later dispatch.

2.4.7 Interface

A number of interfaces are required to establish links among functional units. This is especially true when components from different vendors with varied formats and structure are integrated together. These links could be one to one, one to many, many to many, and one to zero. As shown in Figure 2.21, the M, N, and Q interfaces were added to IS-41C, and they provide necessary signaling and bearer service communication to handle short messages. The A interface standards enable us to integrate the MSC and radio systems from different manufacturers and make sure that they function correctly. The A_i (analog) and D_i (digital) interfaces link the mobile side (cellular network) and wireline sides (PSTN and ISDN). The H interface links HLR and AC functionality and supports the authentication functions, and the D interface links HLR and VLR. This enables integration and support of their multiple formats. The interface A links MSC and BS, B links MSC and VLR, C links MSC and HLR, D links HLR and VLR, E links MSCs, F links MSC and EIR, and so on.

2.4.8 Call Processing

When a mobile unit is switched on, it goes through a set of validation steps before a call can be made, and then a channel is assigned to a mobile unit to initiate the call. The following list presents only a few essential steps, and the details can be found in references 4, 5, and 8:

a. Determine the type of home system from the stored parameter. The system types are referred to as A (A-license) and B (B-license), which are based on the number of assigned channels. Channels 1–333 (825.030–834.990 MHz) belong to A, and channels 334–666 (835.020–844.980 MHz) belong to B. Some new frequencies (667–799 and 991–1023) have been added to these types. If type A is identified, then the mobile unit begins scanning type A channels and tunes to the strongest signal. The mobile unit stores system identification (SID), which is a 15-bit number assigned to a cellular system by the FCC, and it stores paging channels and their range. It tunes to the strongest paging channel and receives an overhead message train. The mobile based on SID and being transmitted on the paging channel determines, its status (roaming or not) and sets the roam indicator accordingly.

b. The mobile enters the idle mode, where it periodically receives an overhead train message and captures system access information, system control information, and system configuration information. This information is used by the mobile unit for subsequent network access and for diagnostic purposes. The unit also monitors station control messages for page messages, and if a page is received, it matches the received and locally stored MIN (Mobile Identification Number). A successful match indicates that the page is for the unit and enters the system access task with a page response indicator. It also enters the system access mode for user-initiated call origination, registration, and other relevant information.

c. The mobile starts a timer for each operation. For example, it sets 12 seconds for call origination, 6 seconds for page response, and so on.

Mobile-to-Land Call. Figure 2.24 illustrates the message flow in call establishing. The following steps are performed to establish communication between a mobile and a land user.

a. The mobile user is in idle mode.
b. It dials the number that is stored in the memory. When the caller presses the SEND key, then only the numbers are transmitted.
c. The mobile unit goes into the system access mode as the call originator.

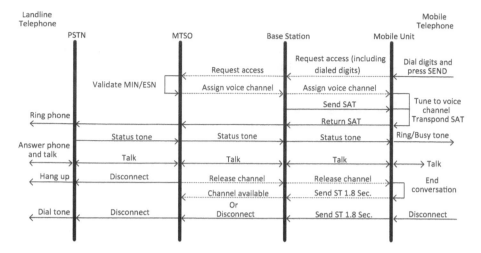

Figure 2.24 Mobile to land call setup. (Reproduced with permission from Wireless PCS, McGraw-Hill.)

d. The mobile unit tunes to the strongest control channel and attempts to send an origination message through this channel.

e. The base station receives the message, validates it, and sends a subset of fields for further validation to the MTSO (mobile telephone switching office). MTSO validates the user subscription type, service profile, etc., to make sure that the user is allowed to make this call.

f. After a successful validation, the MTSO sends a message to the BS to assign a voice channel to the user. In this assignment, the base station sends the channel number to the mobile unit via an IVCD (initial voice channel designation) message.

g. The base station transmits the SAT (supervisory audio tone) to the mobile unit. The unit tunes to the voice channel and returns the SAT on the reverse voice channel back to the base station.

h. The base station receives the SAT from the unit and sends it to the MTSO, which then dials the called number via PSTN.

i. The mobile user receives the ringing tone and begins conversation.

j. At the end of the session, it sends an ST (signaling tone) for 1.8 seconds and terminates the session.

k. The base station detects the ST and sends a disconnect message to MTSO. The MTSO releases the connection with PSTN and the land user.

l. If the land user terminates the call, then PSTN initiates the release process. The MTSO sends the base station a release message, and the base station sends a release message to the mobile unit. The mobil unit transmits ST for 1.8 seconds, and at the end of this time, the base station sends a channel available message to the MTSO.

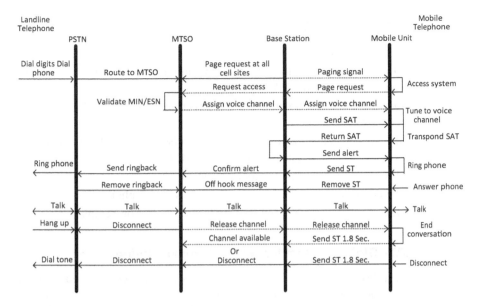

Figure 2.25 Land to mobile call setup. (Reproduced with permission from Wireless PCS, McGraw Hill.)

Land to Mobile call. Figure 2.25 illustrates the message flow in call establishing. The following steps are performed to establish communication between a land and a mobile user.

a. The land user keys in the mobile telephone number.

b. The MSC (mobile switching center) receives this number. First it has to make sure that the mobile unit is available to take this call, and it must also know the location. The MSC may have some information about the location of the unit from its recent registration, in which case it sends a page request to the BS of the registration area. After receiving this page request, the BS pages the MU through the paging channel. If the location of MU is not known, then a location manager is invoked.

c. The MU acknowledges the receipt of this page.

d. The BS informs the MSC that it has received the acknowledgment from the MU.

e. The MSC validates the user subscription type, service profile, and so on, to make sure that the MU is allowed to take this call.

f. After a successful validation, the MSC sends a message to the BS to assign a voice channel to the mobile unit. In this assignment the base station sends the channel number to the mobile unit via an IVCD (initial voice channel designation) message and asks the MU to tune to the channel

g. The base station transmits the SAT (supervisor audio tone) to the MU. The unit tunes to the voice channel and returns the SAT on the reverse voice channel back to the base station.

h. The base station receives the SAT from the unit and sends it to the MSC and sends an alert order to the MU.

i. In response to this alert order, the MU begins ringing to inform the user about the incoming call.

j. The MU generates a signaling tone on the reverse channel which BS detects, and it informs the MSC that MU has been alerted.

k. The MSC generates a ring-back tone for the land user.

l. The MU connects to the voice channel and answers the phone.

m. The MSC stops ringing the land user, and the conversation begins.

2.4.9 GSM—Global System for Mobile Communication

By the early 1990s the cellular communication system was widely used in many European countries. However, each country had their own system. For example, the TACS system, which was based on the AMPS system, was deployed in the United Kingdom in 1985. As of 1993, Austria had NETZ, Belgium, Cyprus, Estonia, Hungry, Luxembourg, and so on, had NMT (Nordic mobile telephone), Denmark, Finland, and so on, had GSM and NMT, and so on. System compatibility across multiple platforms was a major problem. Table 2.5 gives a summary of most of the European countries mobile systems that were in use as early as 1992. Handheld mobile gadgets began to appear around 1988, and only in 1990, did pocket-size devices begin to appear. At that time, a mobile gadget weighed about 400 g. These systems were based on analog technology, and they covered the entire country.

Table 2.5 European Mobile Systems

Country	Deployed in	System	RF Band
UK	1985	TACS	900 MHz
Norway, Sweden	1981	NMT	450 MHz
Denmark, Finland	1986	NMT	900 MHz
France	1985	Radiocom 2000	450, 900 MHz
France	1989	NMT	450 MHz
Italy	1985	RTMS	450 MHz
Italy	1990	TACS	900 MHz
Germany	1985	C-450	450 MHz
Switzerland	1987	NMT	900 MHz
The Netherlands	1985	NMT	450 MHz
Austria	1984	NMT	450 MHz
Austria	1990	TACS	900 MHz
Spain	1982	NMT	450 MHz
Spain	1990	TACS	900 MHz

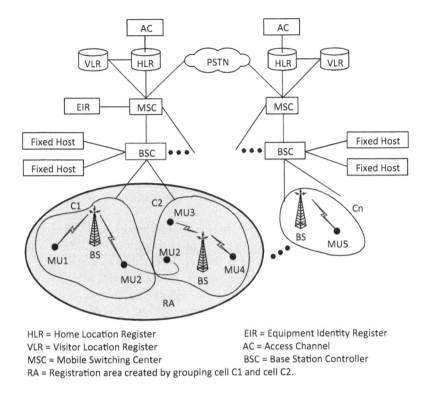

HLR = Home Location Register   EIR = Equipment Identity Register
VLR = Visitor Location Register   AC = Access Channel
MSC = Mobile Switching Center   BSC = Base Station Controller
RA = Registration area created by grouping cell C1 and cell C2.

Figure 2.26   A reference architecture of GSM.

To address the problem of compatibility and establish some standard in 1982, the Conference of European Posts and Telegraph (CEPT) created a study group called *Groupe Special Mobile (GSM)*. This was the beginning of a digital wireless system that later became known as GSM. Thus, right from the beginning, unlike in the United States, digital technology was used to develop a uniform European wireless communication infrastructure. With time, GSM became the most commonly deployed system across the world, and at present, GSM accounts for 75% of the world's digital and 64% of world's wireless market.

A reference architecture of GSM is shown in Figure 2.26. The architecture is basically similar to PCS. The main differences are that in GSM a base station is connected to MSC through a BSC (base station controller). Thus, the task of channel allocation, channel borrowing, and so on, is divided between BSC and MSC.

The BSC performs channel management for one or more base stations. In particular, it handles radio-channel, frequency-hopping, and other activities like handoff. The introduction of BSC between base stations and MSC is to ease the traffic through MSC for improving its performance. The MSC communicates to BSCs, which in turn, route calls to about 50 to 100 base stations.

The mobile unit of GSM has two components: (a) system hardware and software and (b) subscriber. The system hardware and software components are specific to the radio interface and deal with frequency allocation tasks. The subscriber component holds customer profile information that is called a SIM (subscriber identity module). A SIM is a small device (smaller than a credit card in dimension) and is highly potable, which offers personal and terminal mobility. A customer can remove the SIM card from his mobile device and carry it while mobile. He can plug this card into another device and continue to use it as if it were his own mobile device. In addition to storing the customer profile, it can also support a PIN (personal identification number, a 4- to 8-digit number), which is used to validate the owner of the SIM card. When the SIM card is removed from a mobile unit, then the unit can only make calls to emergency service providers such as police, hospitals, and so on.

GSM uses a combination of FDMA (frequency division multiple access) and TDMA (time division multiple access). The updated version of GSM is known as DCS 1800, which is also referred to as PCN. It works in a microcell environment and uses 1710–1785 MHz for uplink channels and 1805–1880 MHz for downlink channels. In the United States, the PCS 1900 system is deployed, which is structurally similar to the DCS 1800 system but uses 1850 to 1910 MHz for uplink and 1930–1990 for downlink channels with frequency separation of 80 MHz.

The FDMA part of GSM uses two 25-MHz frequency bands in the 900-MHz range. The mobile unit uses 890–915 MHz, and the base station uses the 935 to 960-MHz range. Here also the uplink and downlink frequencies are separated by 45-MHz frequency. Thus, the transmit frequency of the base station can be calculated just by adding 45 MHz to the mobile transmit frequency.

The enhanced version of GSM is known as DCS 1900 (also as PCN—personal communication network), which is mainly used in a microcell environment. This version uses two 75-MHz frequency bands and are separated by 95 MHz. The uplink channel range is 1710–1785 MHz, and the downlink range is 1805–1880 MHz. This provides 374 channels each with 200 kHz. As mentioned earlier, PCS 1900, which is deployed in the United States is architecturally similar to DCS 1800 but uses different frequency bands for communication. In PCS 1900, the uplink frequency ranges from 1850 to 1910 MHz and the downlink frequency ranges from 1930 to 1990 MHz with a frequency separation of 80 MHz.

The TDMA part of the GSM frequency spectrum is not broken down to individual radio channels; instead, a channel is shared among multiple users residing in the same cell. To share a radio channel among multiple users, it is divided into eight different time slots. These time slots are referred to as the *TDMA frame*. Each time slot supports user communication; consequently, each radio channel now can support eight different users. Each user is assigned a time slot for transmission, which is usually referred to as a *burst*. Each burst lasts for 577 μs which makes it 4.615 milliseconds ($8 \times 577\mu s$) in a frame. As soon as the time slot is over, a second user begins transmitting in that time slot. In this way, a round-robin scheduling is enforced and the first user gets the time slot again after the seventh user finishes.

The call processing, channel asignment, and so on, are similar to that of the PCS described earlier. Further technical and working details can be found in reference 8.

2.5 SUMMARY

This chapter covered the types of mobility necessary to visualize mobile infrastructure and envision the development of a fully connected information space where all functional units are fully connected with each other through wireless links. It presented the rationale for the development of a mobile database system necessary to manage all information management tasks in the information space.

The entire development can be looked at in terms of both analog and digital transmission and data transmission aspects. The first-generation wireless technology, which was basically analog, is usually referred to as *first generation (1G)*. 1G systems were deployed only in the business world in the 1980s. Mobile and cordless phones were introduced, and analog standards were defined. A number of wireless communication companies such as Nokia (Finland), Motorola (USA), and Ericsson (Sweden), to name a few, established their firm hold in the communication market.

The popularity of analog wireless technology motivated users to present new demands on the system, and soon the limitations of 1G infrastructure became known. In the early 1990s, therefore, the second-generation (2G) wireless technology was introduced, which was based on digital transmission. Digital technology provided a higher communication capacity and better accessibility. This marked the introduction of the global system for mobile communication—*Groupe Special Mobile* (GSM). Initially, the GSM was confined to Europe and gradually its standard spread to most other countries of the world. The 2G mobile units could send not only voice but also a limited amount of data as well.

The limited amount of data communication capability became one of the serious limitations of 2G system. A number of more powerful mobile phones were introduced in the early 2000s, which allowed higher voice and data transmission rates and improved connectivity. This was only a partial enhancement to 2G systems, so it was referred to as "2.5G" technologies. This allowed e-mails to be received and sent through 2.5G mobile phones that could be connected to a laptop or a PDA (personal digital assistant).

2.5G technology and systems were not quite capable of handling multimedia data transfers, unrestricted internet access, video streaming, and so on. These kinds of transfers became very important for the M-commerce (mobile commerce) community. The third-generation (3G) technology made it possible to achieve these capabilities. 3G made it possible to provide a variety of services through the internet, and the emphasis moved from a voice-centric to a data-centric environment. It also helped to establish a seamless integration of business and user domains for the benefit of the entire society. Thus, 3G technology made it possible to visualize *fully connected information space*.

The next chapters focus on a location management and handoff topics that are essential components of a continuous connectivity discipline.

EXERCISES

2.1 What is channel interference and how does it arise? How can you deal with the adjacent channel interference and co-channel interference? Explain your answer.

2.2 In real life, the actual radio coverage is called *footprint*, which is highly amorphous. In theory, however, a well-defined regular shape is used to identify the necessary parameters for mobility. Explain why such a regular shape is necessary, and discuss how it helps to define the coverages areas.

2.3 Define the following terms: (a) spectrum, (b) frequency band, (c) frequency, (d) downlink and uplink channels, and (e) frequency reuse. Establish a working relationship among them.

2.4 A cell size defines the reach of a wireless channel. The strength of a channel depends on the power of its base station. First explain the relationship among a base station, its cell size, and its channel strength and develop a rule of thumb that can quantify the value of a parameter (channel strength, base station power, cell size, etc.) if the value of the other two parameters are given. (*Hint*: Assume the power of a base station and then proceed to define the cell size.)

2.5 Experiment with different-sized cell clusters and discover why some cluster sizes are used more commonly than other sizes. Investigate and explain the advantages and disadvantages of different cell sizes. Derive the relationship $D = R\sqrt{3N}$, where D is the frequency reuse distance, R is the cell radius, and N is cell cluster size (number of cells in a cluster).

2.6 Create different-sized clusters with different R and find the frequency reuse distance (D) for each sample.

2.7 Prove that $N = i^2 + ij + j^2$, where N is the cell cluster size, i is the number of cells to be traversed in the i coordinate, and j is the number of cells to be traversed in the j coordinate from the originating cell. The j coordinate is $60°$ from the i coordinate.

2.8 Explain the difference between an ad hoc network and a cellular network.

2.9 At places such as inside a plane, inside a mine, in a forest, on a long metallic bridge, and so on, cell phone coverage is not very clear or is nonexistent. Explain the reasons for this limitation.

2.10 What do you understand by frequency reuse? Explain your answer. How does a cellular system make use of this option to support a large number of subscribers with limited a number of channels? Explain your answer.

2.11 Let a total of 33 MHz of bandwidth be allocated to a particular FDD cellular telephone system, which uses two 25-kHz simplex channels to provide full duplex voice and control channels. Compute the number of channels available per cell if the system uses (a) 4-cell reuse and (c) 12-cell reuse. If 1 MHz of the allocated spectrum is dedicated to control channels, determine an equitable distribution of control channels and voice channels in each cell for each of the three systems.

2.12 HLR and VLR are used in location management to find the geographical location of a mobile unit. Do you think VLR is necessary to locate a mobile unit, or this is just for reducing the search cost? Explain your answer.

REFERENCES

1. Raj Panda, *Mobile and Personal Communication Systems and Services*, Prentice Hall India, New Delhi, 2000.
2. John Walker (ed.), *Advances in Mobile Information Systems*, Artech House, Boston, 1999.
3. http://www.privateline.com
4. D. Agrawal and Q.-A. Zhang, *Introduction to Wireless and Mobile Systems*, Brooks Cole, Belmont, CA, 2003.
5. Wireless Intelligent Network (WIN), Lucent Technologies.
6. D. M. Balston and R. C. V. Macario (eds.), *Cellular Radio Systems*, Artech House, Boston, 1993.
7. http://wireless.fcc.gov/services/broadbandpcs/data/bandplan-table.html
8. R. Kuruppillai, M. Dontamsetti, and F. J. Cosentino, *Wireless PCS*, McGraw-Hill, New York, 1997.

CHAPTER 3

LOCATION AND HANDOFF MANAGEMENT

3.1 INTRODUCTION

The handoff process in mobile communication systems was briefly introduced in Chapter 2. In this chapter, the handoff process is discussed in detail with reference to transaction management in mobile database systems. The topic of location management is closely related to the handoff process, so the chapter also covers this topic in detail. Quite a few location management schemes have been proposed recently, but none has been implemented in any commercial system, so they are not discussed. We focus on the works of existing handoff and location mechanisms as explained in IS-41 [1–3].

3.1.1 Location Management

In cellular systems, a mobile unit is free to roam within the entire coverage area. Its movement is random, and therefore its geographical location, at any time, is unpredictable. This situation makes it necessary to locate the mobile unit and record its current location in the HLR (home location register), and maybe in the VLR (visitor location register), so that a call can be routed to it. Thus, the entire process of the mobility management component of the cellular system is responsible for two tasks: (a) location management—identification of the current geographical location or current point of attachment of a mobile unit (required by the MSC—mobile switching center) to route the call—and (b) handoff—transferring (handing off) the current

Fundamentals of Pervasive Information Management Systems, Revised Edition. Vijay Kumar.
© 2013 John Wiley & Sons, Inc. Published 2013 by John Wiley & Sons, Inc.

(active) communication session to the next base station to seamlessly resume the session using its own set of channels. The entire process of location management is a kind of directory management problem where its current location is continuously maintained.

One of the main objectives of efficient location management schemes is to minimize the communication overhead due to database updates (mainly HLR) [4]. The other related issue is the distribution of HLR to shorten the access path that is similar to the data distribution problem in distributed database systems. Motivated by these issues, a number of innovative location management schemes have recently appeared in the literature [5].

The current point of attachment or location of a subscriber (mobile unit) is expressed in terms of the cell or the base station to which it is presently connected. The mobile units (called and calling subscribers) can continue to talk and move around in their respective cells, but as soon as both or any one of the units moves to a different cell, then the location management procedure is invoked to identify the new location.

The unrestricted mobility of mobile units presents a complex dynamic environment, and the location management component must be able to identify the correct location of a unit without any noticeable delay. The location management performs three fundamental tasks: (a) location update, (b) location lookup, and (c) paging. In location update, which is initiated by the mobile unit, the current location of the unit is recorded in HLR and possibly in VLR databases. Location lookup is basically a database search to obtain the current location of the mobile unit. It finds its current location, and through paging the system, informs the caller the location of the called unit in terms of its current base station. These tasks are initiated by the MSC.

The cost of update and paging increases as cell size decreases. The cost becomes quite significant for finer granularity cells such as micro- or picocell clusters. The presence of frequent cell crossing, which is a common scenario in highly commuting zones, further adds to the cost. The system creates *location areas* and *paging areas* to minimize the cost. A number of neighboring cells are grouped together to form a location area, and the paging area is constructed in a similar way. In some situations, remote cells may be included in these areas. It is useful to keep the same set of cells for creating location and paging areas, and in most commercial systems they are usually identical. This arrangement reduces location update frequency because location updates are not necessary when a mobile unit moves in the cells of a location area. A large number of schemes to achieve low cost and infrequent updates have been proposed, and new schemes continue to emerge as cellular technology advances.

A mobile unit can freely move around in (a) *active mode*, (b) *doze mode*, or (c) *power down mode*. In active mode, the mobile unit actively communicates with other subscribers and may continue to move within the cell or may encounter a handoff that may interrupt the communication. It is the task of the location manager to find the new location and resume the communication. In doze mode, a mobile unit does not actively communicate with other subscribers but continues to listen to the base station and monitors the signal levels around it. In power down mode, the unit is not functional at all. When it moves to a different cell in doze or in power down modes, then it is neither possible nor necessary for the location manager to find its location.

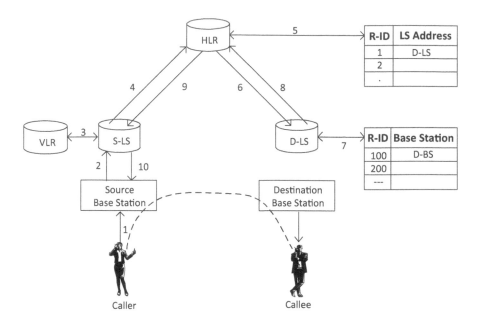

Figure 3.1 Location search steps.

The location management module uses a two-tier scheme for location related tasks. The first tier provides a quick location lookup, and the second tier search is initiated only when the first tier search fails.

Location Lookup. A location lookup finds the location of the called party to establish the communication session. It involves searching the VLR and possibly the HLR. Figure 3.1 illustrates the entire lookup process [6] that is described in the following steps.

Step 1: The caller dials a number. To find the location of the called number (destination), the caller unit sends a location query to its base station **source base station**.

Step 2: The source base station sends the query to the S-LS (source location server) for location discovery.

Step 3: The S-LS first looks up the VLR to find the location. If the called number is a visitor to the source base station, then the location entry is found in the VLR and the connection is set up.

Step 4: If the VLR search fails, then the location query is sent to the HLR.

Step 5: The HLR finds the location of the D-LS (destination location server).

Step 6: The search goes to the D-LS.

Step 7: The D-LS finds the address of the D-BS (destination base station).

Step 8: The address of the D-BS is sent to the HLR.

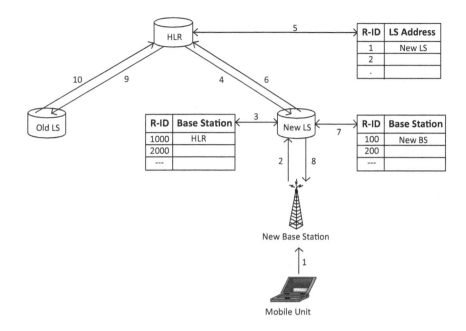

Figure 3.2 Location update steps.

Step 9: The HLR sends the address of the D-BS to the S-LS (source location server).

Step 10: The address of the D-BS is sent to the source base station that sets up the communication session.

Location Update. The location update is performed when a mobile unit enters a new registration area. A location update is relatively expensive, especially if the HLR is distributed. The frequency of updates depends on the intercell movement pattern of the mobile unit such as highly commuting subscribers. One of the tasks of a good location management scheme is to keep such updates to a minimum.

In the new registration area, the mobile unit first registers with the base station and the process of location update begins. Figure 3.2 illustrates the basic steps of the location update.

Step 1: The mobile unit moves to a new registration area that is serviced by a new location server (New LS). The mobile unit informs the new base station about its arrival.[*]

Step 2: The new base station sends the update query to the New LS.

Step 3: The New LS searches the address of the HLR in its local database.

Step 4: The new location of the mobile unit is sent to the HLR.

---

[*]This is a part of the registration process.

Step 5: The old location of the mobile unit is replaced by the new location.

Step 6: The HLR sends the user profile and other information to the New LS.

Step 7: The New LS stores the information it received from the HLR.

Step 8: The New LS informs the new base station that the location update has been completed.

Step 9: The HLR also sends a message about this location update to the Old LS. The Old LS deletes the old location information of the mobile unit stored in its database.

Step 10: The Old LS sends a confirmation message to the HLR.

The current location management scheme has very high search and update costs that increase significantly in the presence of frequent cell crossings, because every registration area crossing updates the HLR. These issues motivated researchers to find efficient and cost effective schemes. A number of new location management schemes have been proposed recently, and a partial list is given here [7–14]. A good survey of some of these schemes can also be found in [6, 15]. Instead of presenting a particular scheme, a general description of forwarding a pointer approach is discussed here to present the main idea [6, 11].

Forwarding Pointer Location Management Scheme. The objective of a forwarding pointer scheme is to minimize network overhead due to the HLR updates. Unlike conventional schemes, this scheme uses a pointer to the next location of the mobile user. Thus, instead of updating the HLR, the scheme just sets a pointer at the previous location of the mobile unit that points to its current location. The pointer is a descriptor that stores mobile unit identity and its current location. The scheme does reduce the HLR updates but introduces a number of other problems. We identify some of the issues of this setup. Consider the fact that the movement of a mobile unit is unpredictable, and therefore it is possible that the unit may visit a registration area multiple times during a communication session. If forward pointers are continuously created and maintained, then a revisit to a registration area creates a transient loop as illustrated in Figure 3.3. Initially, mobile units MU1 and MU2 were communicating in registration area **R1**. Unit MU2 makes its first move to R2, and then it moves back to R1 through R3 and R4. This type of movement creates a transient loop where the communication path is R1 $\rightarrow$ R2 $\rightarrow$ R3 $\rightarrow$ R4 $\rightarrow$ R1. However, even in the worst-case scenario, the transient loop does not last for long.

Updates Using Forward Pointers. When MU2 leaves registration area R1 and moves to R2, then (a) the user profile (MU2 profile) and the number of forward pointers created so far by MU2 is transferred from R1 to R2 and (b) a forward pointer is created at R1 that points to R2. This forward pointer can be stored in any BS data structure.

At some point, the current location of the MU needs to be updated in the HLR. Usually, a heuristic-based update approach is used. One scheme could be based on

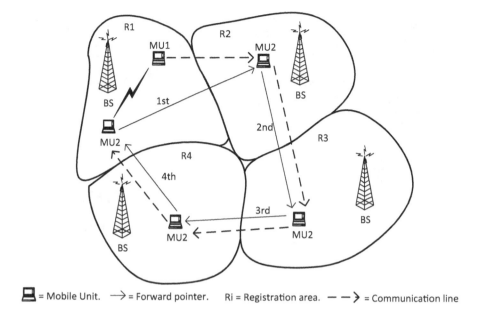

📟 = Mobile Unit. → = Forward pointer.   Ri = Registration area. — — ❯ = Communication line

Figure 3.3   Transient loop in forward pointer scheme.

the number of pointers created [6]. In this scheme, an upper limit of pointers can be predefined, and once this threshold is reached, the HLR is updated. Another scheme can be based on the number of search requests, yet another can be based on constant update time. Thus, the HLR is updated after so many hours or minutes have elapsed since the last update. The performance of these update schemes will very much depend on the user mobility.

Location Search Using Forward Pointers. The search scheme is illustrated in Figure 3.4. A user in the "Source" registration area wants to communicate with a user in the "Destination" area. The following steps describe the location discovery.

Step 1: The caller dials the number of the destination user. To find the location of the called number (destination), the caller unit sends a location query to its source base station.

Step 2: The source base station sends the query to the source LS (source location server) for location discovery.

Step 3: The source LS first looks up the VLR to find the location. If the called number is a visitor to the source base station, then the location is known and the connection is set up.

Step 4: If the VLR search fails, then the location query is sent to the HLR.

Step 5: The destination HLR finds the location of the destination location server (Dest-LS).

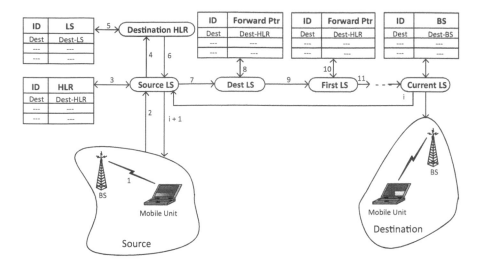

Figure 3.4   Location search using forward pointer.

Step 6: The destination HLR sends the location of the destination location server (Dest-LS) to the source LS.

Step 7: The source LS finds the first forward pointer (8) and traverses the chain of forward pointers (9, 10, 11, . . .) and reaches the destination location server (current LS).

Step i: The location of the current base station is forwarded to the source LS.

Step $i + 1$: The source LS transfers the address of the current base station to the source base station, and the call is set up.

Forward Pointer Maintenance. Pointer maintenance is necessary to (a) remove pointers that have not been used for some time and (b) delete dangling pointers. During movement, a mobile unit may create a number of pointers, including transient loops. In Figure 3.3, when the MU2 returns to R1, the forward pointers R2 → R3, R3 → R4, and R4 → R2, will not be referenced to locate MU2, so they can be safely removed from the search path. The identification of candidates for removal can be achieved in a number of ways. One way is to associate a timestamp with each forward pointer and define purge time slots. At a purge slot if *purge slot > a pointer timestamp*, then this pointer can be a candidate for removal. Another way is to keep a directed graph of pointers. If a loop is found in the graph, then all edges, except the last one, can be removed. It is possible that in a long path there may be a small loop. For example, in path *R2 → R3, R3 → R4, R4 → R3*, and *R3 → R5*, the small loop *R3 → R4 and R4 → R3* can be replaced by *R3 → R5*. Furthermore, a refinement path, *R3 → R5*, with R5 being the current location, can be replaced by *R2 → R5*.

A dangling pointer occurs if redundant pointers are not removed in a correct order. In the above removal process, if the path *R2 → R3* is removed first, then the path

$R2 \rightarrow R5$ cannot be set and paths $R3 \rightarrow R4$, $R4 \rightarrow R3$, and $R3 \rightarrow R5$ will create dangling pointers. This is a classical pointer management problem with a different effect in a mobile scenario.

The entire pointer management process must be synchronized with the HLR update. Note that the HLR may have been updated many times during the creation of forward pointers. Any reorganization must maintain the location consistency in the HLR. Further information about the performance of pointer maintenance schemes can be found in reference 6.

3.1.2 Handoff Management

The process of handoff was briefly discussed in Chapter 2. This section discusses how a handoff is managed to provide continuous connectivity. Figure 3.5 illustrates the presence of an overlap region between Cell 1 and Cell 2. A mobile unit may spend some time in this overlap area, and the value of this duration depends upon the movement speed of the mobile unit. The duration a mobile unit stays in this area is called the *degradation interval* [14]. The objective is to complete a handoff process while the mobile unit is still in the overlap area. This implies that the handoff must not take more than a *degradation interval* to complete the process. If for some reason the process fails to complete in this area or within the *degradation interval*, then the call is dropped.

A handoff may happen within or outside a registration area. If it happens within a registration area, then it is referred to as an intrasystem handoff where the same MSC manages the entire process. An intersystem handoff occurs between two separate

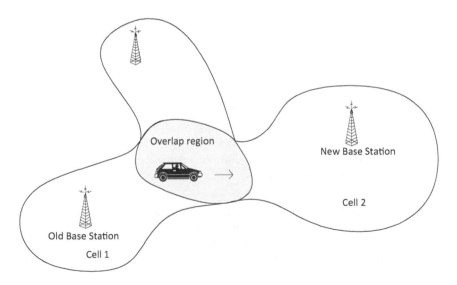

Figure 3.5 Cell overlap region.

registration areas where two MSCs are involved in handoff processing. In each of these cases, the handoff processing is completed in three steps:

- **Handoff detection**: The system detects when a handoff process needs to be initiated.
- **Assignment of channels**: During handoff processing, the system identifies new channels to be assigned for continuous connectivity.
- **Transfer of radio link**: The identified channels are allocated to the mobile unit.

Handoff Detection. Handoff processing is expensive, so the detection process must correctly detect a genuine and *False Handoff* (see Chapter 2) that also occurs because of signal fading. There are three approaches for detecting handoffs effectively and accurately. A brief description of these approaches, which are applied on a GSM system but also used in a PCS, is presented here and further details can be found in reference 14. They are called

- Mobile-assisted handoff (MAHO)
- Mobile-controlled handoff (MCHO)
- Network-controlled handoff (NCHO)

Mobile-Assisted Handoff (MAHO). This scheme is implemented in second generation systems where TDMA technology is used. In this approach, every mobile unit continuously measures the signal strength from surrounding base stations and notifies the strength data to the serving base station. The strength of these signals is analyzed, and a handoff is initiated when the strength of a neighboring base station exceeds the strength of the serving base station. The handoff decision is made jointly by the base station and the mobile switching center (MSC) or by the base station controller (BSC). In case the mobile unit (MU) moves to a different registration area, an intersystem handoff is initiated.

Mobile-Controlled Handoff (MCHO). In this scheme the mobile unit (MU) is responsible for detecting a handoff. The MU continuously monitors the signal strength from neighboring base stations and identifies if a handoff is necessary. If it finds that the situation requires more than one handoff, then it selects the base station with the strongest signal for initiating a handoff.

Network-Controlled Handoff (NCHO). In this scheme, the mobile unit (MU) does not play any role in handoff detection. The BS monitors the signal strength used by the MUs, and if it falls below a threshold value, the BS initiates a handoff. In this scheme, the BS and the MSC are involved in handoff detection. In fact, the MSC instructs BSs to monitor the signal strength occasionally, and in collaboration with the BSs, the handoff situation is detected. The MAHO scheme shares some detection steps of the NCHO.

Necessary resources for setting up a call or to process a handoff request may not always be available. For example, during a handoff, the following may occur: the destination BS may not have any free channels, the MU is highly mobile and has requested too many handoffs, the system is taking too long to process a handoff, the link transfer suffered some problem, and so on. In any of these cases, the handoff is terminated and the mobile unit loses the connection.

Assignment of Channels. One of the objectives of this task is to achieve a high degree of channel utilization and minimize the chances of dropping a connection due to unavailability of the channel. Such a failure is always possible in a high-traffic area. If a channel is not available, then the call may be blocked (*blocked calls*), and if a channel could not be assigned, then the call is terminated (*forced termination*). The objective of a channel allocation scheme is to minimize forced termination. A few schemes are presented in reference 14.

Nonprioritized Scheme. In this scheme, the base station does not make any distinction between the channel request from a new call or from a handoff process. If a free channel is not available, then the call is blocked and may subsequently be terminated. Figure 3.6 shows the entire channel assignment process.

Reserved Channel Scheme. In this scheme, a set of channels are reserved for allocating to a handoff request. If a normal channel is available, then the system assigns it to a handoff request; otherwise, the reserved channel is looked for. If no channels are available in either set, the call is blocked and could be dropped. Figure 3.7 shows the entire channel assignment process.

Queuing Priority Scheme. In this scheme, the channel is assigned based on some priority. If a channel is available, then the handoff request is processed immediately; otherwise, the request is rejected and the call is dropped. There is a waiting queue where requests are queued. When a channel becomes available, then one of the requests from the waiting queue is selected for processing. The queuing policy may

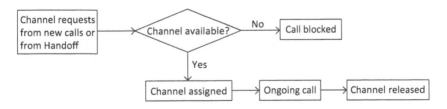

Figure 3.6 Nonprioritized scheme steps (Reproduced from *Wireless and Mobile Network Architectures* under written permission of John Wiley & Sons [13].)

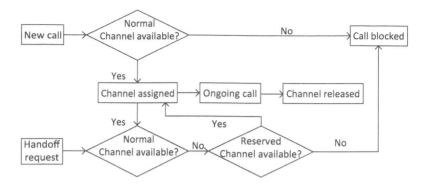

Figure 3.7 Reserved channel scheme steps (Reproduced from *Wireless and Mobile Network Architectures* under written permission of John Wiley & Sons [13].)

be *First in First Out (FIFO)*, or it may be *measured-based* or some other scheme. In the measured-based approach, the request that is close to the end of its degradation interval is assigned a channel first. In the absence of any free channel, the call is terminated. Figure 3.8 shows the entire channel assignment process.

Subrating Scheme. In this scheme, a channel in use by another call is subrated; that is, the channel is temporarily divided into two channels with a reduced rate. One channel is used to serve the existing call, and the other channel is allocated to a handoff request. Figure 3.9 shows the channel assignment process.

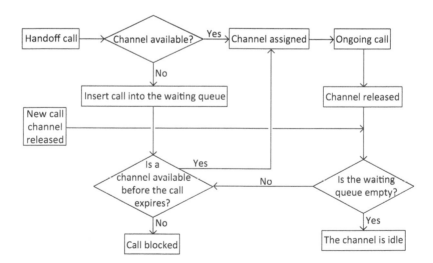

Figure 3.8 Queuing priority scheme steps (Reproduced from *Wireless and Mobile Network Architectures* under written permission of John Wiley & Sons [13].)

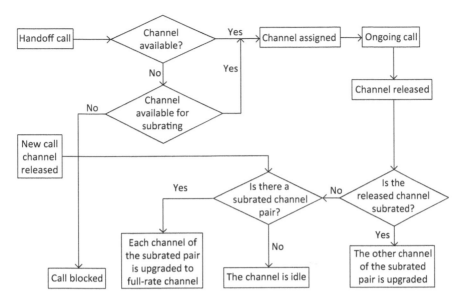

Figure 3.9 Subrating scheme steps (Reproduced from *Wireless and Mobile Network Architectures* under written permission of John Wiley & Sons [13].)

Radio Link Transfer. The last phase of handoff is the transfer of the radio link. The hierarchical structure of cellular system (PCS and GSM) presents the following five-link transfer cases for which a handoff has to be processed.

- **Intracell handoff:** Link or channel transfer occurs for only one BS. In this handoff, an MU only switches channels. Figure 3.10 illustrates the scenario.
- **Intercell or Inter-BS handoff:** The link transfer takes place between two BSs that are connected to the same BSC. Figure 3.11 illustrates the scenario.
- **Inter-BSC handoff:** The link transfer takes place between two BSs that are connected to two different BSCs, and the BSC is connected to one MSC. Figure 3.12 illustrates the scenario.
- **Intersystem or Inter-MSC handoff:** The link transfer takes place between two BSs that are connected to two different BSCs. These two BSCs are connected to two different MSCs. Figure 3.13 illustrates the situation.

As discussed in reference 14, typical call holding time is around 60 seconds. Some real-life data indicate that there could be around 0.5 inter-BS handoff, 0.1 inter-BSC handoff, and 0.05 inter-MSC handoff. The data also indicate that the failure rate of an inter-MSC handoff is about five times more than an inter-BS handoff. It is quite obvious that efficient processing of handoffs is quite important for minimizing the call waiting time.

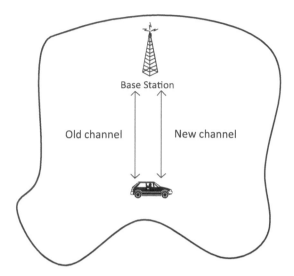

Figure 3.10 Channel transfer in intracell handoff.

There are two ways to achieve link transfer. One way is referred to as a *hard handoff*, whereas the other is called a *soft handoff*.

Hard Handoff. In this handoff process, the user experiences a brief silence or discontinuity in communication that occurs at any time the MU is attached to only one BS, and when the link is transfered, the connection is broken temporarily, resulting

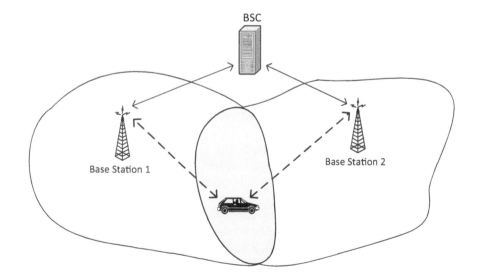

Figure 3.11 Channel transfer between two BSs with one BSC.

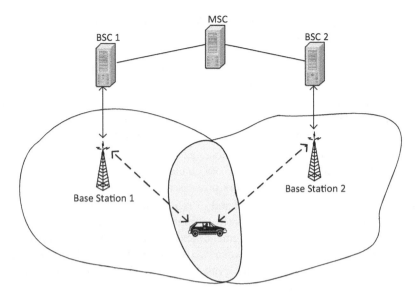

Figure 3.12   Channel transfer between two BSs connected to two BSCs.

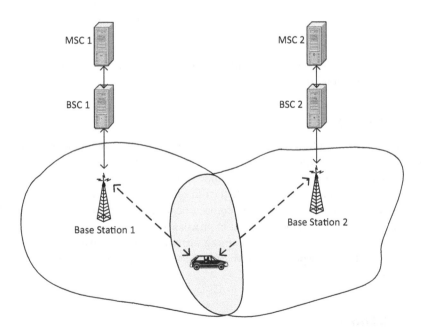

Figure 3.13   Channel transfer between two BSs with two BSCs connected to two MSCs.

in silence. The steps of the handoff for the MCHO link transfer is described below. Further detail is given in reference 14.

1. The MSC sends a "link suspend" message to the old BS that temporarily suspends the conversation (occurrence of silence).

2. The MSC sends a "handoff request message" to the network through the new BS. The new BS then sends a "handoff acknowledgment" message and marks the slot busy. This message indicates the initiation of the handoff process.

3. This acknowledgment message indicates to MU that the handoff process has started, and so MU returns to the old channel it was using and resumes voice communication while the network processes the handoff.

4. When the new BS receives the handoff request message, then two cases arise. One is (a) an intra-BS handoff or (b) an inter-BS handoff. In the former case, the BS sends a handoff acknowledgment message and proceeds with the handoff. In the latter case, since it is between two different BSCs, the BS must complete some security check. It gets the cypher key from the old BS and associates it with the new channel.

5. The MSC bridges the conversation path of the old and the new BSs.

6. On the command of the network, the MSC processes the handoff where it releases the old channel by sending an "access release" message to the old BS. In this process, the voice communication is briefly interrupted again.

7. The MU sends a "handoff complete" message through the new channel and resumes the voice communication.

A detailed discussion on hard handoffs for other kinds of link transfers and soft handoffs can be found in reference 14.

3.1.3 Roaming

In the presence of multiple wireless service providers, the continuous connectivity is provided through *roaming*. Thus, when a mobile unit moves from one GSM to another system (PCS or GSM) or some other system, the location of the MU must be informed by the new service provider to the old service provider. This facility is called roaming. These two service providers communicate with each other to complete the location management and the registration process as described earlier.

The other important aspects of roaming are the administrative issues related to billing. Multiple service providers have to come to some agreement about the charges and privileges.

3.2 SUMMARY

This chapter covered the topics of location management and the handoff process. They use a number of subsystems and databases such as a HLR and a VLR. The chapters described the structure and use of these subsystems and databases. It described the special role that VLR plays in speeding up the process of location identification.

This chapter completes the discussion of technology necessary to build a mobile database system. Subsequent chapters deal with information management issues beginning with the introduction to database management discipline.

EXERCISES

3.1 How is the geographical location of a mobile unit expressed? What is the reference point for identifying this location? Develop a simple scheme for identifying the geographical location of a mobile unit in a cell.

3.2 What do you understand by the term *location management*? Describe the steps of a location manager to identify the location of a mobile unit. (*Hint*: Assume that the HLR is stored at a central location.)

3.3 What do you understand by *handing over the channel*? When is this process necessary?

3.4 Explain the difference between a hard handoff and a soft handoff. Explain the different ways of processing them.

3.5 Explain in how many modes a cell phone may exist. Explain the energy consumption of each mode.

3.6 Explain different schemes of location management and explain their advantages and disadvantages.

3.7 What is a handoff process, and when does it happen? There are three strategies for detecting the presence of a handoff. Explain the working mechanism of any one of them. Discuss the difference between hard handoff and soft handoff. You must explain the difference at the working level, that is, in terms of channel allocation and deallocation.

3.8 Discuss the function of the HLR. Develop your own scheme of managing the HLR to improve search time and reduce update cost. (This can be a class project; single or group.)

3.9 Discuss the cost and performance of different ways of handling a handoff. Assume single and multiple MSCs.

3.10 Why is it expensive to manage roaming? Identify technical, as well as some business issues, that must be solved to implement roaming.

REFERENCES

1. S. Mohan and R. Jain, Two User Location Strategies for Personal Communications Services, *IEEE Personal Communications*, Vol. 1, No. 1, 1994, pp. 42–50.

2. R. Kuruppillai, M. Dontamsetti, and F. J. Cosentino, *Wireless PCS*, McGraw-Hill, 1997.

3. *Wireless Intelligent Network (WIN)*, Lucent Technologies.

4. J. Z. Wang, A Fully Distributed Locatioin Registration Strategy for Universal Personal Communication Systems, *IEEE Journal on Selected Areas in Communications*, Vol. 11, No. 6, August 1993, pp. 850–860.

5. C. Rose and R. Yates, Location Uncertainty in Mobile Networks: A Theoretical Framework, *IEEE Communication Magazine*, Vol. 35, No. 2, 1997, pp. 94–101.

6. P. Krishna, Performance Issues in Mobile Wireless Networks, Ph.D. dissertation, Texas A&M University, 1996.

7. I. F. Akyildiz and J. S. M. Ho, Dynamic Mobile User Location Update for Wireless PCS Networks, *ACM/Baltzer Wireless Network Journal*, Vol. 1, No. 2, 1995, pp. 187–196.

8. B. R. Badrinath, T. Imielinski, and A. Virmani Locating Strategies for Personal Communication Networks. In *IEEE Globecom 92 Workshop on networking of personal communications applications*, December 1992.

9. G. Cho and L. F. Marshal, An Efficient Location and Routing Schema for Mobile Computing Environments, *IEEE Journal on Selected Areas in Communications*, Vol. 13, No. 5, June 1995, pp. 868–879.

10. H. Harjono, R. Jain, and S. Mohan, Analysis and Simulation of a Cache-Based Auxiliary User Location Strategy for PCS. In *Proceedings of the 1994 International Conference on Networks for Personal Communications*, March 1994, pp. 1–5.

11. R. Jain and Y-B Ling, An Auxiliary User Location Strategy Employing Forward Pointers to Reduce Network Impacts of PCS, *Wireless Networks* Vol. 1 Issue 2, 1995, pp. 197–210.

12. S. Mohan and R. Jain, Two User Location Strategies for Personal Communication Services, *IEEE Personal Communications*, Vol. 1, No. 1, 1994, pp. 42–50.

13. S. Rajgopalan and B. R. Badrinath, An Adaptive Location Management Strategy for Mobile IP. In *Proceedings of the 1st ACM International Conference on Mobile Computing and Networking (Mobicom'95)*, Berkeley, CA, October 1995.

14. Y.-B. Lin and I. Chlamtac, *Wireless and Mobile Network Architecture*, John Wiley & Sons, Hoboken, NJ, 2001.

15. E. Pitoura and G. Samaras, Data Management for Mobile Computing, Kluwer Academic Publishers, Norwell, MA, 1998.

CHAPTER 4

FUNDAMENTALS OF DATABASE PROCESSING

The objective of this chapter is to introduce the conventional approach of data processing technology. It describes the fundamentals of database management systems and reviews available architecture. The limitations of current database technology to manage new types of information processing requirements are discussed in detail, which helps to make a case for mobile database systems.

4.1 CONVENTIONAL DATABASE ARCHITECTURE

A database is a repository of facts about the organization it models. The state of the organization continuously changes, and these changes must be incorporated in the database to preserve the facts. The system uses a transaction mechanism for incorporating these changes in the database in a consistency-preserving manner. The software module that manages transactions is called the database management system (DBMS). It also serves as an interface between users of the database and the database itself. A user interacts with the DBMS through a query language such as SQL (structured query language) that takes the user's data processing requests to the DBMS. The DBMS creates a transaction or a set of transactions that executes necessary operations under the *concurrency control mechanism* or *serialization mechanism* to process users requests. At the end of the execution of a transaction, the DBMS invokes a *commit* command that installs all transaction updates in the database and sends the user the final results.

Fundamentals of Pervasive Information Management Systems, Revised Edition. Vijay Kumar.
© 2013 John Wiley & Sons, Inc. Published 2013 by John Wiley & Sons, Inc.

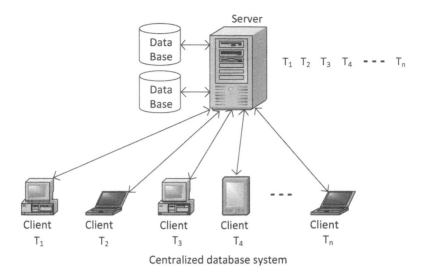

Figure 4.1 Architecture of centralized database systems.

There are two basic system architectures on which the entire DBMS is implemented: (a) centralized and (b) distributed.

Centralized DBMS. In a centralized database management system there is one processing node (server) and a number of intelligent terminals (clients) connected to the server through a wired network. A client accepts users' requests through a query language such as SQL. It may process the query (transaction) if it has the resources; otherwise, it sends it to the server for processing. The server sends the results to the client, and the client formats and sends them to the user. Figure 4.1 illustrates a reference architecture of a centralized database systems.

Distributed DBS. In a distributed database system a number of centralized database systems are connected together with a communication network. These servers can be configured as peers or as a set of dependent and independent, homogeneous and heterogeneous servers. Each configuration identifies a special type of distributed database system. A detailed categorization of a distributed database system is covered in references 1, 2. Figure 4.2 illustrates a reference architecture of a distributed database system.

There are two commonly known categories: (a) the Federated database system and (b) the Multidatabase system. This categorization is based on node autonomy, data processing, and the distribution of data. In a federated architecture, a subset of servers is partially autonomous in managing their activities. They are members of the federation and are willing to cooperate and participate with other members (servers) under a set of mutually agreed protocols. For example, in a big company each department may have their own servers and may participate among themselves to maintain the

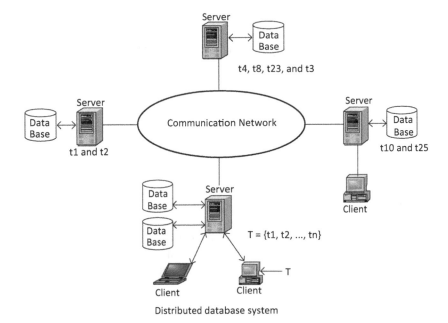

Figure 4.2   Architecture of distributed database systems.

consistent view of the entire company in its data warehouse. This federation could be: homogeneous, where each server may run the same database management system; or heterogeneous, where each has a different system. For example, one server may be using Oracle, the other may be DB2 or Sybase, and so on.

In a multidatabase architecture, all servers of the distributed database system have full autonomy. It is up to each server to cooperate or not to cooperate with any other server in the architecture. This kind of architecture can be found in a franchise setup. Each vendor operates under a franchise act independently with or without mutual cooperation.

4.1.1 Database Partition and Distribution

In centralized database systems there is only one server, so the question of data distribution does not arise. However, this is quite important in distributed database systems and must be managed carefully because it significantly affects system performance and availability.

In distributed systems, the database is distributed in three ways: (a) partitioned, (b) partially replicated, and (c) fully replicated to improve data availability, quality of service, and performance. The selection of a data distribution scheme depends on a large number of system and application parameters. One of the most important considerations is the local availability of necessary data to process user query efficiently and to minimize communication cost (data access latency).

Database Partition. Under this scheme, the entire database is divided into a number of partitions. Usually the number of partitions is the same as the number of processing nodes (servers). These database partitions are *allocated* to servers under a set of criteria. Some of the important criteria are as follows:

- The partition should support the highest database locality. This means that the majority of queries can be processed by the partition at that server.
- They should help to minimize the data communication cost (data access latency).
- They should help to minimize the cost of maintaining *global consistency*.
- They should help to localize the serialization of concurrent transactions.
- They should minimize the cost of recovery.

The partition scheme is less reliable and suffers from a center point of failure. If a server fails, then its partition becomes unavailable until it recovers from the failure. In addition to this, because of zero data redundancy, it is unable to provide adequate reliability. Some of these are taken care of by partial replication of the database.

Partial Replication. Under this scheme the database is partitioned and a subset of partitions is replicated at more than one server. The partial replication has nearly all the properties of the other two partition schemes and it further improves database locality and reliability. If a server fails, then the replicated copy of the partition is still available for processing queries. The recovery is easier because the replicated partition can be copied entirely to the server after it recovers from failure. To some extent, it is more time-consuming to maintain the global consistency because any change in a partition must be installed in all its replicas located at various servers. To further increase database locality, the database is fully replicated.

Full Replication. Under this scheme, the entire database is replicated at all servers. This has maximum locality and it also minimizes data communication costs during query processing.

The fully replicated scheme provides the highest reliability and availability on the cost of maintaining global consistency. This scheme is not used in reality because of a higher consistency and database storage cost. Table 4.1 summarizes the merits of the three data distribution approaches.

Table 4.1   Comparison of Data Distribution Schemes

Activity	Full Replication	Partial Replication	Partition
Data locality	Very high	Medium	Low
Serialization	Difficult	Moderate	Easy
Global consistency	Difficult	Moderate	Easy
Reliability	Very high	Moderate	Low
Recovery cost	Very high	Moderate	Low

4.2 DATABASE PROCESSING

The mechanism that facilitates consistency-preserving changes is called a *transaction*. A transaction, therefore, takes the database from an initial consistent state to the next consistent state by applying a set of operations on physical data items. This constrained transition involves a set of consistency constraints, the database, and an application program. Thus, a transaction structure can be viewed as

Transaction $=<$ *Set of Constraints, Database, Application program* $>$

The set of constraints can be implemented in two ways: (a) programmed in the application code and (b) as a part of a transaction structure. The first method is highly inefficient, unreliable, and not always possible. Programming each of these constraints in application code is prone to error. The programmer must have a good knowledge of the system architecture to avoid logical error. It is hard for any programmer to know when to initiate a test for what constraint. For these reasons, the second approach is used where these constraints are inherent in the transaction structure. With this association, a transaction acquires a unique place in the database system and is the only mechanism for database processing.

4.2.1 Transaction Structure

The structure of a transaction is best described in terms of the set of constraints mentioned earlier. The terms *atomicity, consistency, isolation,* and *durability* were introduced to represent these constraints and created the appealing acronym *ACID* [3–6]. To understand the significance of these properties or constraints, it is useful to review the types of actions one encounters in real life or in information management. The discussion given here follows the line of thoughts as explained in reference 7.

All possible actions, especially on data, can be categorized into (a) unprotected or free action, (b) protected or constrained action, and (c) real action.

Unprotected or Free Action. The partial result of a free action may be seen by other free actions, and the final outcome may not be consistency-preserving. An edit or sorting or searching operation on a file, writing to a disk or RAM, and so on, are examples of unprotected operation. This is because the intermediate result of a sorting process can be seen by another process. Database discipline requires that the actions performed on its data must not be unprotected.

Protected or Constrained Action. A partial result of a constrained action is not visible to another constrained or unprotected action. The availability of the final result implies that the action committed successfully. Since database processing must have this property, it was incorporated in transaction as an *atomicity* property. *Atomicity* requires that a constrained action can exist only in one of the two possible states: (a) successfully completed or (b) never started. The "never started" state is achieved by a *rollback* operation. Thus, a constrained action is atomic; either it successfully completes and the final result is available to other protected or unprotected action or if it fails in the middle, then its partial execution is rolled back to the initial state—that is, the partial effect is removed from the database. There is no guarantee that a constrained action will lead to data consistency. For this reason, especially for database processing, *Consistency* property is introduced. By incorporating the property of consistency, the definition of constrained action is refined.

Real Action. The completion of a real action cannot be undone by rollback operations. It can be a protected or unprotected action whose final results persist in the real world. For example, the result of firing a missile or cutting a finger cannot be undone. There is no such thing as "uncutting" the cut finger because once a real action is started, then the initial state is destroyed. The final result will be reached and may or may not be correct. For this reason, it cannot be called atomic. A real action would be useful in database management only if it could be guaranteed that starting the action will generate a consistency-preserving result. No such guarantee could ever be given, so they are not supported. It is obvious that a real action may be unprotected and may be acceptable if the final result does not affect real life.

Flat Transactions. The discussion on transaction mechanism begins with *flat transaction* leading to a more complex structure. A detailed discussion of transaction structure is necessary to understand its management on mobile database systems.

A *flat* transaction is the simplest type of mechanism that supports one level operation; that is, during its execution it does not trigger other *dependent* transactions. A transaction T_j is dependent on transaction T_i if T_j reads a data item modified by T_i. This can be described formally as follows:

A transaction T_j, reads data item x from T_i if the following conditions are satisfied:

- T_i is active (not yet committed) and it wrote into x.
- T_j reads x after T_i wrote into x but before T_i aborts or commits.
- Any transaction that writes into x after T_i wrote into x aborts before T_j reads x.

Some examples of flat transactions are *debit/credit* transactions, bill payment transactions, customer account statement transactions, and so on. These perform one-level operation.

Flat transactions are constrained operations with additional requirements that they must satisfy consistency property. The enforcement of atomicity and consistency need two additional properties that are included in the transaction structure. The essential properties of a transaction now can be defined as follows:

Atomicity. This is a protected action that supports only two mutually exclusive states: (a) *completed* and (b) *not started*. The *completed* state identifies the successful completion of an action, and the *not started* state identifies that the operation never started. The *not started* state is achieved with the help of a rollback operation which itself is atomic. The atomicity of a rollback action defines another property that is referred to as *idempotent*. The idempotent property guarantees that one or multiple rollback operations on the same action will produce the same final result. For example, the assignment operation $X := 5$ is idempotent because its multiple successful executions are equivalent to one successful execution. Thus, if an atomic operation is rolled back once or multiple times, its final result will be the same.

The atomicity of a transaction guarantees that its intermediate results do not exist for the user who initiated the transaction. This is also true for messages from the transaction. During execution, if the user receives a message from the transaction and if it is subsequently rolled back, then the received message cannot be taken back to indicate that no message was ever sent to the user. In fact, the message from the transaction *is* a partial result that under atomicity must not be visible to the user. This implies that during execution, a transaction does not generate any message; or if it does, it is not seen outside the transaction execution space.

Consistency. This property makes sure that the value of a data item represents the fact. If a user deposits $100 to his account with an existing balance of $500, then the database must show the final balance as $600. In terms of consistency constraints, the credit operation must satisfy

$$Previous\ balance\ =\ Current\ balance\ -\ Last\ credit\ amount$$

The next state of the database is consistent only if the last state was consistent. A transaction takes it for granted that it always manipulates a consistent database, and it also guarantees that it will produce a consistent database state.

The database does not care about the intermediate results of a transaction that is usually inconsistent. These results are confined to the execution space of the transaction and are not visible to the database or to any other transaction.

Isolation. This property makes sure that to preserve consistency, two conflicting operations (e.g., read and write or write and write) on the same data item by two different transactions are not allowed. As indicated earlier, the application program can check consistency constraints in the code. However, this approach not only is prone to error, difficult to program, and inefficient, but also burdens the programmer to know the system details as well. The isolation property was incorporated in the transaction model to move the enforcement of consistency from the programming level to modeling level. It was enforced through a separate system software module that is usually referred to as the *concurrency control mechanism* or *serialization mechanisms*, which are discussed in later sections.

Durability. This property guarantees that the final result (consistent by definition) of a transaction persists in the database, and it is not destroyed by any kind of system failure. The successful execution of a transaction indicates that it has satisfied *atomicity, consistency,* and *isolation,* and its results must be installed in the database. When the results are installed and the user of the transaction is notified, then it is said that the transaction "commits." The durability property guarantees that the effect of a transaction in the database cannot be undone. For example, a withdrawal transaction at an ATM commits only when the money is in customer's hand.

The property of durability is in fact not related to any of the other three properties (ACI). It merely makes sure that whatever is installed in the database persists despite any kind of failure. It does not differentiate between consistent and inconsistent data. However, the three properties make sure that the durability property deals only with consistent data.

4.3 SERIALIZATION OF TRANSACTIONS

In centralized database systems, transactions are processed entirely at one location. Many clients initiate transactions $(T_1, T_2, \ldots, T_n)$, and they all go to a central server for execution. The server dispatches the results to the client at the end of the commit of its transaction (see Figure 4.1). This way of processing concurrent transactions helps to keep the the cost of meeting ACID constraints and database recovery quite low, but, at the expense of system throughput. This is acceptable in an environment where the workload remains low and transactions are mostly short-lived. In a high-traffic environment, the use of distributed systems to manage the workload satisfactorily becomes necessary.

In a distributed system, depending upon the type of data distribution, a transaction (T) is divided into a number of subtransactions or fragments $(T = t_1, t_2, \ldots, t_n)$. These subtransactions are distributed to appropriate processing nodes or sites (servers), some of which are processed in parallel and some concurrently (see Figure 4.2). A distributed transaction processing is quite efficient and minimizes resource waste; however, managing the workload (concurrency control, recovery, etc.) becomes very complex and requires special approaches. This is especially true in multi-database or federated database environments.

A guaranteed way to achieve consistency preserving execution is through *serial* execution. A serial execution does not allow data sharing by making sure that the next transaction begins only when the last transaction terminates (commits or aborts); that is, an active transaction is not allowed to *read from* any other active transactions. Consistency is an inherent property of serial execution, but it suffers with poor resource utilization. Consequently, the efficiency (response time and throughput) of the database system suffers significantly, making the cost of achieving consistency in this way too high.

The only way out is then to run transactions concurrently (simultaneously). Unfortunately, concurrent execution cannot guarantee consistency-preserving execution if it is not managed properly. It amounts to achieving the consistency-preserving property of serial execution through concurrent execution without affecting database efficiency. This process is usually referred to as *serialization* of concurrent transactions that *mutually exclude* or *isolates* two transactions over the use of a common data item. The next few sections discuss the serialization process in detail.

4.3.1 Serializability-Based Correctness Criteria

A serial execution of transactions cannot achieve desirable efficiency, so they are executed concurrently. An uncontrolled concurrent execution of transactions gives rise to *interference* (arises in data sharing). Interference creates two types of problems: (a) *lost update* and (b) *inconsistent retrieval*. An inconsistent retrieval sometimes appears as *dirty read* and sometimes appears as *unrepeatable read*. These three problems of uncontrolled concurrent execution threatens database integrity.

When transactions are executed concurrently, then their basic operations (reads and writes) are interleaved. Interleaving of basic operations may interfere with each other, thereby producing inconsistent results; that is, either the output of the transaction is not consistent with the values of the objects in the database, or the effects of the transaction on the database destroy database consistency.

The database inconsistency, as a result of these three problems, can be illustrated through the execution of a set of concurrent transactions on a bank database using a checking account (identified as x) and a savings account (identified as y) that customers maintain. Overdrafts on these accounts are not permitted, so their values are never negative.

Lost Update: This occurs when a later transaction overwrites the updates installed by an earlier transaction. Consider two concurrent transactions T_1 and T_2 transferring money into the same account x. Initially, x has a balance of \$100. T_1 transfers \$50 and T_2 transfers \$100 into x. The correct final result should be \$250.

An interleaved execution of T_1 and T_2 is shown in Figure 4.3, where a and b are local variables. It is useful to represent the interleaved execution with a *schedule* that records the relative execution order of reads, writes, and commit or abort operations. It provides an easy way to see the precedence order of conflicting operations in a schedule that is needed in the serialization process. A read operation is defined by $r_i[x, v]$ that reads the initial value of x as v, and a write operation is identified as ($w_i[x, v]$) that writes the value v into x. The term c_i denotes the commit of transaction T_i. The schedule of the interleaved execution of T_1 and T_2 in Figure 4.3 can be written as

$$r_1[x, 100]r_2[x, 100]w_1[x, 150]w_2[x, 200]c_1c_2$$

In this schedule, T_1 and T_2 executed successfully and T_2 wrote \$200 as the final value of x. If T_1 and T_2 were run serially as $T_1 \longrightarrow T_2$ or $T_2 \longrightarrow T_1$, then the final value of x would have been \$250. Clearly, this is not the case and the \$50 deposit of T_1 is missing. The reason is that the value written by T_1 is overwritten by T_2, since T_2 read the initial value of x before T_1 wrote into it. This could not have happened in any of the serial executions $T_1 \longrightarrow T_2$ or $T_2 \longrightarrow T_1$. This is the case of interference from T_2 in the execution of T_1.

The above interleaved execution illustrates that the lost update did not violate the integrity constraint of the database even though it has potential of doing so. For instance, consider the interleaved execution of two concurrent transactions T_3 and T_4 that withdraw \$50 and \$90 from y, respectively, assuming that the balance in saving

Initial value of x = 100		Initial value of y = 90	
T_1	T_2	T_3	T_4
begin		begin	
	begin		begin
a = read (x)		a = read (y)	
(a = 100)		(a = 90)	
	b = read (x)		b = read (y)
	(b = 100)		(b = 90)
write (x, a + 50)		if (a ≥ 50), then	
(x = 150)		write (y, a – 50)	
		(y = 40)	
	write (x, b + 100)		if (b ≥ 90), then
	(x = 200)		write (y, b – 90)
			(y = 0)
commit		commit	
	commit		commit
		commit	
			commit
Final result x = 200. T_1's update is missing.		Final result y = 0. T_3's update is missing.	
Correct result x = 250.		Correct result y = 40.	
(a) Concurrent deposits		(b) Concurrent withdrawals	

Figure 4.3   Lost update problem.

account y is \$90. The schedule for this execution is shown in Figure 4.3b.

$$r_3[y, 90]r_4[y, 90]w_3[y, 40]w_4[y, 0]c_1c_2$$

The interleaved schedule processed both T_3 and T_4 successfully; but for a serial execution of $T_3 \longrightarrow T_4$, only one of the two withdrawals would have been executed since the second withdrawal that calls for $y \geq 90$ and would not have been permitted because it would have violated the integrity constraint (account value cannot be negative).

Unrepeatable Read: This problem occurs when a transaction T_i computes an average value of a set of data items stored in a buffer while T_j (i ≠ j) updates some of the items before T_i commits. When T_i reads them again, it finds different values for them. The problem can be compared with automatic web refresh. The last search finds a different values of the contents that it initially saved in the cache. This may be acceptable (even desirable) in web browsing; but in database processing, this may create inconsistency.

Dirty Read: This problem arises when T_j writes a data item that is subsequently read by T_i. If T_j fails, then the version of data item T_i read was not consistent. Thus T_j made T_i's data dirty.

Initial values of x = 200 and y = 100		Initial values of x = 40 and y = 38	
T_5	T_6	T_7	T_8
begin		begin	
	begin		begin
	c = read (x)	a = read (x)	
	(c = 200)	(a = 40)	
	d = read (y)		b = read (x)
	(d = 100)		(b = 40)
	write (x, c + 100)		c = read (y)
	(x = 300)		(c = 38)
			if (b > c + 1) then
a = read (x)			write (x, b – 1)
(a = 300)			(x = 39)
b = read (y)			commit
(b =100)			
	write (y, d – 100)	write (x, a – 1)	
	(y = 0)	(x = 39)	
	commit	commit	
output (a + b)			
(a + b = 400)			
commit			
Final result (a + b) = 400. T_6's update is missing from the final result. Correct result (a + b) = 300.		Final result x = 39 and y = 39. T_8's update is missing from the final result. Correct result x = 39 and y = 38.	
(a) Display combined balance		(b) Withdrawal from checking	

Figure 4.4   Inconsistent retrievals.

Unrepeatable Read vs. Dirty Read: Both problems create inconsistency. In an unrepeatable read, both transactions continue to execute; but in a dirty read, a transaction failure causes inconsistency. Thus, a dirty read is a consequence of transaction failure, while an unrepeatable read is a computational anomaly associated with interleaved execution. In some cases, unrepeatable reads are desirable—for example, in the case of computing running total of changing values (game points, changing temperature, etc.) The dirty read, on the other hand, is an incorrect execution that always leads to database inconsistency and, therefore, must be eliminated.

The following examples illustrate how interference gives rise to inconsistent retrieval, dirty read, and unrepeatable read. Consider the interleaved execution of transactions T_5 and T_6, shown in Figure 4.4a, in which a, b, c, and d are local variables. Transaction T_5 displays the sum of the balances of x and y, whereas transaction T_6 transfers $100 from y to x.

Assuming that the initial balance of x is $200 and that of y is $100, the execution of T_5 and T_6 is represented by the following schedule:

$$r_6[x, 200]r_6[y, 100]w_6[x, 300]r_5[x, 300]r_5[y, 100]w_6[y, 0]c_6c_5$$

In this execution, both x and y have been updated correctly (i.e., $x = \$300$ and $y = \$0$). Although the sum of the balance of x and y remains invariant and equals $300, T_5 outputs $400 (i.e., a + b = $300 + $100). In a noninterleaved execution of T_5 and T_6, in which T_5 and T_6 execute in any order, T_5 would have output a sum of $300. The reason for this discrepancy is that T_5 has observed partial effects of T_6 (i.e., T_6 read the value of x written by T_6 and it read the value of y before T_6 wrote it); hence, T_5 observed an inconsistent state of x and y. In this execution T_6 made T_5's data (i.e., y) dirty.

Although in the above execution no integrity constraint is violated, similar to lost updates, inconsistent retrievals can lead to a violation of database integrity, as the example shown in Figure 4.4b illustrates, assuming that $x = 40$ and $y = 38$. In addition, suppose we have the requirement that the balance of the checking account (x) should remain greater than the balance of the savings account (y) unless both have a zero balance ($x > y$ if $x \neq 0$ and $y \neq 0$). T_7 is a promoting transaction that sets the balance of the savings account to be a dollar less than the balance of the checking account. T_8 withdraws a dollar from the checking account. The schedule of Figure 4.4b can be written as follows:

$$r_7[x, 40]r_8[x, 40]r_8[y, 38]w_8[x, 39]c_8w_7[y, 39]c_7$$

The final result of this execution is $x = \$39$ and $y = \$39$, which violates the integrity constraint that calls for $x > y$ when x and y have a nonzero balance. This integrity violation was caused by interference from T_8 to the execution of T_7.

Figure 4.5 illustrates the occurrence of dirty read and unrepeatable read. Transaction T_5 reads dirty data of T_6 because the rollback of T_6 removes its updates to x and y. Thus, T_5 reads nonexistent data. In unrepeatable read, T_7 reads $x = 40$; but in the second read, it reads $x = 39$.

The preceding examples indicate the presence of interference and illustrate that the correctness of individual transactions is not sufficient to ensure the correctness of concurrent executions.

Intuitively, a correct execution of a set of transactions must be free from interferences. In all the examples above, we were able to conclude whether or not a concurrent execution of a set of transactions is acceptable by comparing its results to a non-interleaved or *serial* execution of the same set of transactions.

Serial executions are inherently interference-free, so they are consistency-preserving. Thus, if the result of a concurrent execution of a set of transactions is the same as one produced by one of the serial executions of the same set of transactions, then the concurrent execution is also consistency-preserving. Such concurrent executions, which are equivalent to serial executions, are called *serializable* and satisfy the isolation property.

Indeed, serializable executions are free from interferences, as the following schedule of execution of T_7 and T_8 illustrates (Figure 4.6)

$$r_7[x, 40]r_8[x, 40]w_7[y, 39]c_1r_8[y, 39]c_2$$

Initial values of x = 200 and y = 100		Initial values of x = 40 and y = 38	
T_5	T_6	T_7	T_8
begin		begin	
	begin		begin
	c = read (x)	a = read (x)	
	(c = 200)	(a = 40)	
	d = read (y)		b = read (x)
	(d = 100)		(b = 40)
	write (x, c + 100)		c = read (y)
	(x = 300)		(c = 38)
a = read (x)			if(b > c + 1) then
(a = 300)			write (x, b – 1)
b = read (y)			(x = 39)
(b =100)			commit
	write (y, d – 100)	a = read (x)	
	(y = 0)	(a = 39)	
	abort		
output (a + b)			
(a + b = 400)			
commit			
Final result (a + b) = 400. T_6 is rolled-back but its updates to x and y are read (dirty read) by T_5. Correct result (a + b) = 300.		The first read of x by T_7 gets 40 but its second read of x gets 39.	
(a) Dirty read		(b) Unrepeatable read	

Figure 4.5   Dirty read and unrepeatable read.

In this schedule, T_8 observes a consistent state of x produced by T_7; hence, T_8 does not violate the integrity constraint by avoiding withdrawal from x.

Several versions of serializability have been proposed, each based on different notions of equivalence of schedules. In most concurrency control protocols, serializability is based on the notion of conflicting operations and is called *conflict serializability*. Two operations conflict when their effect is order-dependent. Conflict serializability ensures that pairs of conflicting operations appear in the same order in two equivalent executions [8–11]. Whether an execution is conflict serializable can easily be determined, as discussed in the next section.

Different versions of serializability include *view* and *state* serializability [9, 12]. View serializability requires that each transaction reads the same values and that the final value of all data is the same, in two equivalent executions. State serializability requires that, under all possible interpretations of transactions' writes, two equivalent executions must be identical when viewed as mappings from one database state to another. Interpretation of a write is the relation of the value written in the database to the values read before the write from the database by a transaction. A write by a transaction can be potentially a function of some subset of the previously read values

Initial values of x = 40 and y = 38		Initial values of x = 40 and y = 38	
T_5	T_6	T_7	T_8
begin		begin	
a = read (x)			begin
(a = 40)		a = read (x)	
write (x, a - 1)		(a = 40)	
(x = 39)			b = read (x)
commit			(b = 40)
	begin	write (x, a - 1)	
	b = read (x)	(x = 39)	
	(b = 39)	commit	
	c = read (y)		
	(c = 38)		c = read (y)
	if (b > c + 1) then		(c = 38)
	write (x, b – 1)		if (b > c + 1) then
	commit		write (x, b – 1)
			(x = 39)
			commit
Final correct result x = 39 and y = 38.		Final Correct result x = 39 and y = 38.	
(a) Serial execution.		(b) Serializable execution.	

Figure 4.6 Correct execution.

by the same transaction. These different versions allow more concurrency than conflict serializability, but, unfortunately, they are not practical since it is NP-complete to test whether an execution is view or state serializable.

In the next section, the conflict serializability is formally defined followed by the definition of recovery correctness criteria.

4.3.2 Serializability Theory

Fundamental to the theory of serializability is the notion of *history*, which represents the concurrent execution of a set of transactions [13, 14]. As we discussed above, transactions are required to perform operations on objects in a certain manner to be considered correct. That is, correctness criteria can be defined as constraints on the ordering of concurrent operations and transaction primitives in histories. Similarly, correctness properties of different concurrency control protocols can be expressed in terms of the properties of the histories generated by these concurrency control protocols.

Although our focus here will be on conflict serializability, the theory can be used to reason about the other serializability criteria that are not as easy to realize. We begin with the notion of conflicts between operations on an object and then discuss how it induces dependencies between transactions.

Objects, Operations, and Conflicts. A database is the entity that contains all the shared objects in a system. A transaction accesses and manipulates the objects in the database by invoking operations specific to individual objects. The *state* of an object is represented by its contents. Each object has a type that defines a set of operations (create, change, read, etc.) to change and to examine the state of an object of that type. These operations are atomic, and an operation always produces an output (return value); that is, it has an outcome (condition code) or a result. Operations defined on an object are considered as functions from one object state to another object state. The result of an operation on an object depends on the state of the object. For a given state s of an object, we use $return(s, p)$ to denote the output produced by operation p, and we use $state(s, p)$ to denote the state produced after the execution of p.

Definition 4.1 *Two operations p and q conflict in a state s, denoted by* conflict(p, q), *iff*

$$
\begin{aligned}
(state(state(s, p), \ q) \ &\neq \ state(state(s, q), \ p)) \quad \vee \\
(return(s, \ q) \ &\neq \ return(state(s, p), \ q)) \ \vee \\
(return(s, \ p) \ &\neq \ return(state(s, q), \ p))
\end{aligned}
$$

Two operations that do not conflict are compatible *and* commute.

That is, two operations conflict if their effects on the state of an object or their return values are not independent of their execution order. Clearly, for this to be true (i.e., they conflict), both should operate on the same object and one of them modifies (writes) the object. On the other hand, two read operations on the same object commute and can be executed in any order. The conflicting operations on an object is represented in a table called *Compatibility Matrix*.

A *yes* entry in the matrix for (p, q) indicates that the operations p and q are compatible (i.e., do not conflict), and a *no* entry indicates that the two operations are incompatible (i.e., do conflict). Table 4.2 shows the compatibility matrix of an object such as a page that supports read and write operations.

It is now necessary to formally characterize transactions, histories, and a correct execution of a set of transactions in terms of the invocation of conflicting operations. Concurrent transactions may interfere with each other only if they invoke conflicting operations on the same object.

Table 4.2 Compatibility Matrix of Read and Write Operations

Operations	Read (x)	Write (x)
Read (x)	*Yes*	*No*
Write (x)	*No*	*No*

Histories of Transactions. During the course of their execution, transactions invoke operations on database objects and transaction management primitives. Invocation of an operation on an object or a transaction management primitive is termed as *event*. The set of operations and primitives invoked by a transaction T_i can be expressed as a partial order with an ordering relation "$\longrightarrow$," that denotes the temporal order in which the related events occur. The reason that a transaction is modeled as a partial order is because a transaction may invoke two or more nonconflicting operations in parallel. For example, two read operations on two different objects can be executed concurrently.

We use $p_i[ob]$ to denote the object event corresponding to the invocation of the operation p on object ob by transaction T_i. In general, we use ϵ_j to denote the invocation of an event ϵ by transaction T_j. The predicate $\epsilon \rightarrow_i \epsilon'$ is true if event ϵ precedes event ϵ' in transaction T_i. Otherwise, it is false. (Thus, $\epsilon \rightarrow_i \epsilon'$ implies that $\epsilon \in T_i$ and $\epsilon' \in T_i$.) We will omit the subscript in an ordering relation $\rightarrow$ when its context is clear.

Definition 4.2 *A transaction T_i is a partial order with ordering relation $\rightarrow_i$ where*

1. $T_i = \{p_i[ob] \mid p \text{ is an operation on } ob\} \cup \{\beta_i, \alpha_i, c_i\}$
   Operations in T_i can be operations on objects, begin (β), commit (c) and abort (α) primitives.

2. $\forall i \; \forall p \; \forall ob \;\; p_i[ob] \in T_i \Rightarrow (\beta_i \rightarrow_i p_i[ob])$
   All operations of a transaction follow its begin operation.

3. $\alpha_i \in T_i \Leftrightarrow c_i \notin T_i$
   A transaction can either commit or abort but not both.

4. *if ϵ is c_i or α_i,* $\forall i \forall p \forall ob \;\; p_i[ob] \in T_i \Rightarrow (p_i[ob] \rightarrow_i \epsilon)$
   All operations of a transaction precede its commit or abort.

5. $\forall i \; \forall p, q \; \forall ob$
   $p_i[ob] \in T_i \wedge q_i[ob] \in T_i \wedge \text{conflict}(p, q) \Rightarrow (p_i[ob] \rightarrow_i q_i[ob]) \vee (q_i[ob] \rightarrow_i p_i[ob])$
   The order of conflicting operations is defined.

Similar to transactions, a history of a set of transactions can be modeled as a partial order.

Definition 4.3 *Let $T = \{ T_1, T_2, \ldots, T_n \}$ be a set of transactions. A (complete) history H of the concurrent execution of a set of transactions T contains all the operations and primitives invoked by the transactions in T and indicates the partial order $\rightarrow_H$ in which these operations occur.*

1. $H = \cup_{i=1}^{n} T_i$
   Operations in H are exactly those in $T_1, \ldots, T_n$

2. $\forall i \; \forall p, q \; \forall ob \;\; (p_i[ob] \rightarrow_i q_i[ob]) \Rightarrow (p_i[ob] \rightarrow_H q_i[ob])$
   The order of operations within each transaction is preserved.

3. $\forall i, j \,\forall p, q \,\forall ob$
   $p_i[ob] \in H \wedge q_j[ob] \in H \wedge \text{conflict}(p, q) \Rightarrow (p_i[ob] \rightarrow_H q_j[ob]) \vee$
   $(q_j[ob] \rightarrow_H p_i[ob]).$
   The ordering of every pair of conflicting operations is defined.

H denotes a *complete* history. When a transaction invokes an event, that event is appended to the *current* history, denoted by H_{ct}. That is, H_{ct} is a *prefix* of a complete history, and is useful in capturing incomplete executions of transactions that contain active transactions. Incomplete executions may be a result of a system failure or describe a scheduler in execution. A complete history does not contain any active transactions.

The *projection* of a history H according to a given criterion is a sub-history (a part of a history) that satisfies the criterion. It is constructed by eliminating any events in H that do not satisfy the given criterion while preserving the partial ordering of the events in the projection. For instance, the projection of a history with respect to committed transactions, denoted by H_c, includes only those events invoked by committed transactions. The projection criterion can be formally specified as

$$\forall t \in T \; \epsilon_t \in H_c \Rightarrow c_t \in H$$

H_c is obtained from H by deleting all operations of noncommitted transactions in it. Note that H_c is a complete history with respect to committed transactions in T. Given that in H_c the effects of aborted transactions are nullified, serialization ordering requirements only consider operations invoked by committed transactions; hence, serializability criteria are expressed in terms of committed projection of histories.

Conflict Serializability. As mentioned in the previous section, the notion of equivalence between two histories needs to define, before being able to determine, whether a history is equivalent to a serial history and, hence, serializable. It is assumed here that any history H is over a set of committed transactions T_{comm} that is, $T = T_{comm}$ and $H = H_c$.

Definition 4.4   *Two histories H and H' are (conflict) equivalent* $(H \equiv H')$ *if*

1. $\forall i \,\forall p \,\forall ob, T_i \in T, p_i[ob] \in T_i p_i[ob] \in H \Leftrightarrow p_i[ob] \in H'$
   They are defined over the same set of transactions and have the same operations.
2. $\forall i \,\forall p, q \,\forall ob \, \text{conflict}(p, q) \wedge (p_i[ob] \rightarrow_H q_j[ob]) \Leftrightarrow (p_i[ob] \rightarrow_{H'} q_j[ob])$
   Any pair of conflicting operations p_i *and* q_j *belonging to committed transactions* T_i *and* T_j *is ordered in the same way in both histories.*

Definition 4.5   *A history* H_s *is serial if, for every pair of transactions* T_i *and* T_j *that appears in* H_s, *either all operations of* T_i *appear before all operations of* T_i *or vice versa; that is,*

$$\exists p_i[ob] \in T_i, q_j[ob] \in T_j(p_i \rightarrow_{H_s} p_j) \Rightarrow \forall r_i \in T_i, o_j \in T_j(r_i \rightarrow_{H_s} o_j)$$

Definition 4.6 *A history H is (conflict) serializable if its committed projection H_{comm} is (conflict) equivalent to a serial history H_s; that is, $H_c \equiv H_s$.*

Clearly, conflicting operations induce serialization ordering requirements between the invoking transactions. Specifically, if an operation $p_i[ob]$ invoked by transaction T_i precedes an operation $q_j[ob]$ invoked by T_j and with which it conflicts (*conflict*(p,q)), then T_i must precede T_j in a serializable history. We will denote this ordering dependency by C binary relation on transactions:

Definition 4.7 *Serialization ordering*
$$\forall t_i, t_j \in T_{comm}, t_i \neq t_j$$
$$(t_i \ C \ t_j) \ iff \ \exists ob \ \exists p, q \ (conflict(p, q) \wedge (p_i[ob] \rightarrow q_j[ob]))$$

Let C^* be the transitive-closure of C; that is,

$$(t_i \ C^* \ t_k) \ iff \ [(t_i \ C \ t_k) \vee \exists t_j \ (t_i \ C \ t_j \wedge t_j \ C^* t_k)]$$

It has been shown that serializability demands that the serialization ordering must be acyclic [13].

Definition 4.8 *Serializability Theorem*
$$H_c \ is \ (conflict) \ serializable \ iff \ \forall t \in T_{comm} \ \neg(t \ C^* \ t)$$

This means that given a history, it can be determined whether it is serializable by testing if its committed projection does not induce any ordering dependency cycles.

A simple way to recognize whether the induced ordering dependencies are acyclic is by constructing a dependency graph, called a *serialization graph* and search for cycles. A serialization graph is a directed graph in which nodes represent transactions in H, and an edge $T_i \longrightarrow T_j, i \neq j$, means that T_i has an ordering dependency on T_j (i.e., one of T_i's operations precedes and conflicts with one of T_j's operations in H). For example, Figure 4.7 shows the serialization graph of the following history:

$$H = r_1[x]w_1[x]r_3[x]w_2[y]c_1r_3[y]c_2w_3[y]c_3$$

A serialization graph that is acyclic can also be used in finding the equivalent serial history. This can be achieved by making a topological sorting of the serialization graph: Whenever an edge exists between two transactions, say $T_i \longrightarrow T_j$, then all operations of T_i must appear before all those of T_j in the equivalent serial history. Since histories are partial orders, several serial orders can be obtained by topological sorting. For example, the topological sorting of the serialization graph depicted in Figure 4.7 produces two equivalent serial histories:

$$H_s : T_1 T_2 T_3 \ or \ T_2 T_1 T_3$$

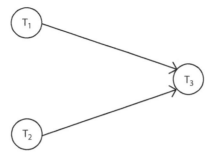

Figure 4.7   A serialization graph.

Another property of conflict serializability of practical significance is that it is *prefix commit-closed*[*] [13]. A prefix commit-closed property means that whenever it holds on history H, it also holds for any committed projection of a prefix H' of H. In other words, in an incomplete execution of transactions produced by a scheduler, transactions are allowed to commit if their corresponding history is serializable. Furthermore, it means that conflict serializability can be used as a correctness criterion in the presence of failures. After the recovery from a failure, the database reflects the execution of only those transactions that were committed before the failure. Such an execution corresponds to the committed projection of the prefix of the history, which includes all the aborted transactions and the active transactions at the time of the failure.

It should be pointed out that the serializability theory presented in this section does not assume that read and write are the only operations supported on the database. All the definitions in the theory depend on the notions of conflicts and hold for any pair of conflicting operations p and q defined on an object in a database. Hence, the theory is not limited to traditional database models, but it is also applicable to object-oriented ones.

Atomicity and Durability. In ensuring atomicity, transactions that read values written by some transaction that subsequently aborts must also be aborted. This situation is referred to as *cascading aborts*. Because of the *durability* property of transactions, once a transaction commits, it can neither subsequently be aborted nor can its effects be changed because of cascading aborts. An execution is *recoverable* if, once a transaction is committed, the transaction is guaranteed not to be involved in cascading aborts, and, hence, there will never be a need to nullify its effects.

Definition 4.9   *A transaction T_j reads from T_i in a history H, denoted ReadFrom(T_j, T_i), if*
$$\exists ob(w_i[ob] \to r_j[ob]) \land \neg(\alpha_i \to r_j[ob]) \land \exists T_k((w_i[ob] \to w_k[ob]) \Rightarrow (\alpha_k \to r_j[ob]))$$

---

[*]Note that neither view nor state serializability is prefix commit-closed.

In other words, a transaction T_j reads the value of ob written by T_i if T_i is the last transaction that has written into ob and had not aborted before T_j read ob.

Definition 4.10   *A history H is a recoverable iff* $\forall T_i, T_j \in T, T_i \neq T_j$
$$ReadFrom(T_j, T_i) \Rightarrow (c_i \rightarrow c_j)$$

That is, in a recoverable history, for every transaction T_j that commits, T_j follows the commitment of every transaction T_i from which T_j read a value.

Given a history H whose committed projection is serializable, it does not necessarily mean that H is *recoverable*. For example, the following history H' of transactions T_1 and T_2 is serializable with T_1 serialized before T_2, but not recoverable:

$$H' = w_1[x]r_2[x]w_1[y]w_2[x]c_2c_1$$

Hence, in the presence of both concurrency and failures, correct executions need to be both serializable and recoverable. Transaction executions often have additional properties in addition to serializability and recoverability. These simplify transaction management and minimize the amount of computation that may be lost due to failures.

An execution is said to be *cascadeless* if it ensures that every transaction reads only data values written by committed transactions; hence, the execution avoids cascading aborts [13, 15].

Definition 4.11   *A history H is cascadeless iff* $\forall T_i, T_j \in T, T_i \neq T_j$

$$(w_i[ob] \rightarrow r_j[ob]) \Rightarrow (c_i \rightarrow r_j[ob]) \vee (\alpha_i \rightarrow r_j[ob])$$

Strictness, a condition stronger than *cascadeless*, ensures that every transaction reads and writes only data values written by committed transactions.

Definition 4.12   *A history H is strict iff* $\forall T_i, T_j \in T, T_i \neq T_j \; \forall q \in \{r, w\}$

$$(w_i[ob] \rightarrow q_j[ob]) \Rightarrow (c_i \rightarrow q_j[ob]) \vee (\alpha_i \rightarrow q_j[ob])$$

The difference between Definitions 4.3 and 4.4 lies in $r_j[ob]$ becoming $q_j[ob]$ in the case of 4.4, implying that this is more general because it applies to both reads and writes. Thus, strictness implies cascadeless. Strict executions, besides avoiding cascading aborts, allow for efficient log-based recovery using *before images* [13, 15].

Serialization order does not necessarily correspond to the execution order of transactions as defined by their commit order. Given two *noninterleaving* transactions T_1 and T_2, with T_1 committing before T_2 starts execution, it is possible for T_2 to precede T_1 in the serialization order. *Order-preserving conflict serializable* execution is a serializable execution where all *noninterleaved* transactions have the same serialization order and execution order [16–18]. This property is useful for certain applications where a temporal relationship between noninterleaved transactions is important. Consider a stock trading application in which the order of the execution of different bids and sales affect the price of a stock. In an order-preserving conflict serializable execution, a stock report transaction submitted after the commitment of a bidding transaction T_b is guaranteed to return a stock price that reflects the effects of T_b. However, this property is not sufficiently strong to ensure that the serialization order and the execution order of all transactions in a set are the same. A property that guarantees that execution and serialization orders are the same is called *rigorousness* [19].

Definition 4.13   *A history history H is rigorous iff* $\forall T_i, T_j \in T, T_i \neq T_j \forall p, q \ \forall ob$

$$\text{conflict}(p, q) \wedge (p_i[ob] \rightarrow q_j[ob]) \Rightarrow (c_i \rightarrow q_j[ob]) \vee (\alpha_i \rightarrow q_j[ob])$$

A history is rigorous if no data item may be read or written until the transaction that previously invoked a conflicting operation on the data item either commits or aborts. The difference between Definitions 4.4 and 4.5 is in $w_i[ob]$ becoming $p_i[ob]$, meaning that $p_i[ob]$ applies to both reads and writes. Thus, rigorousness implies strictness and is more general. In addition, by disallowing the overwriting of data items read by a still-executing transaction, rigorous histories ensure reads are repeatable (i.e., a read by a transaction on a data item returns the same value as all the previous reads on the same data item by that transaction). Strictness does not ensure repeatable reads. Recall that repeatable reads is a requirement for serializability. In fact, by considering and controlling the ordering of all conflicting operations, rigorousness becomes a restricted form of conflict serializability [19].

Rigorousness simplifies transaction management, particularly in distributed databases, since it allows for the determination of a serialization order by controlling the order in which operations are submitted and executed.

Note that like order-preserving conflict serializability and rigorousness, recoverability, cascadeless, and strictness are all prefix commit-closed properties.

4.3.3 Degree of Isolation

This strict enforcement of consistency and isolation of ACID properties significantly affect database system performance. Consequently, such strict enforcement is an impediment in keeping with changing database processing trends as a result of new user requirements and changing system architecture. Consistency requirements appeared unnecessarily strict for many types of data modification. Consider, for example, the situation in statistical databases where the computation of average or mean value does not require strict enforcement of consistency. If one of the salary values, for example, is inconsistent, it did not create any problem in computing the acceptable salary average. Management of long-running transactions (execution time in days or weeks or months) became problematic too under a flat transaction model and it did not fit well with emerging mobile database systems.

A number of significant revisions and changes were introduced in the classic definition of transaction to resolve the efficiency (response time and throughput) and consistency issues. The notion of consistency was revisited and categorized into **Degree 0**, **Degree 1**, **Degree 2**, and **Degree 3** using the notion of *dirty data*, which is uncommitted data of an active transaction. Later on, to eliminate ambiguity, these degrees were introduced as *degree of isolation* [7]. In Chapter 5, degree of isolation is defined using the concept of the *two-phase* locking policy. In subsequent discussions, the letter T is used to represent a transaction.

- **Degree 0:** T_i observes degree 0 isolation if it does not overwrite dirty data of $T'_j s$, where $i \neq j$. Thus, T_i commits its writes before it ends. This means T_j may read or write T_i's write; and if T_i is rolled back, then T_j has to be rolled back too. From the recovery viewpoint, degree 0 transactions are not recoverable and also not cascade-free. The following example illustrates the use of degree 0 isolation.

■ **EXAMPLE 4.1**

Suppose T_i and T_j have the following operations:

$$T_i: write\ (x)$$
$$T_j: write\ (x)$$
History: $w_i(x)\ w_j(x)$

If T_i and T_j are run concurrently, then the final value of x is unpredictable; and in some situations, cascading may also occur. From the recovery point of view, degree 0 transactions are not recoverable, and for the serialization a short lock should be applied to x.

- **Degree 1:** T_i observes degree 1 isolation if
  - T_i does not overwrite dirty data of T_j and
  - T_i does not commit its write before it ends.

    This means T_j cannot overwrite T_i's write and T_j does not have to roll back if T_i is rolled back. However, T_j is allowed to read T_i's write before T_i completes; consequently, cascade rollback is still possible. From the recovery viewpoint, T_i can undo its execution without setting any lock and without erasing T_j's updates. This is the main reason that all commercial database management systems automatically provide degree 1 isolation.

■ **EXAMPLE 4.2**

$$T_i: write\ (x)$$
$$T_j: write\ (x)$$
History: $w_i(x)\ w_j(x)$

If T_i aborts, then it can restore x's value, which requires that under degree 1 a long write lock should be applied to x for serialization.

- **Degree 2:** T_i observes degree 2 isolation if
  - T_i does not overwrite dirty data of T_j,

- T_i does not commit any writes before it ends, and
- T_i does not read dirty date of T_j.

Thus, T_i isolates T_j's uncommitted data. Note that in degree 1 isolation T_i may read dirty data of T_j which cannot happen in degree 2. There is no cascading in degree 2 transactions, but unrepeatable reads may appear as shown below.

■ **EXAMPLE 4.3**

$$T_i: read\ (x) \qquad T_j: write\ (x)$$
History: $r_i(x)\ r_j(x)\ w_j(x)\ commit_j\ r_i(x)$

In this execution, T_i reads two different values of x. First, it reads the initial value of x and then it reads the value modified by T_j without violating any isolation condition. Under degree 2, therefore, T_i should apply a short read lock on x for serialization.

- **Degree 3:** T_i observes degree 3 isolation if
  - T_i does not overwrite dirty data of T_j,
  - T_i does not commit any writes before it ends,
  - T_i does not read dirty date of T_j, and
  - T_j does not read dirty data of T_i before T_i completes.

  Thus, T_i isolates dirty data of T_j for reads and writes. Note that in degree 2 isolation, T_i may read two different committed values of T_j. In degree 3 isolation, a long read lock should be applied on x for serialization.

The degrees of isolation allow decreasing data access flexibility with degree 3 having the least flexibility but offering true isolation of ACID properties. Such varied degrees of data access flexibility affect concurrency, leading to a lower performance. In fact, most commercial database systems do not support degree 3 isolation. Typically, they do not keep read lock until EOT to achieve higher concurrency [7].

In many transaction processing scenarios, lower degrees of isolation are acceptable. This is especially true in mobile database systems where waiting time of transactions affects the performance and costs expensive resources such as wireless bandwidth. In Chapter 5, degrees of isolation are discussed from serialization aspects, and their importance is evaluated for mobile database systems.

4.4 ADVANCED TRANSACTION MODELS

The flat transaction model quite faithfully managed database processing. It efficiently processed large and small units of work that existed at the time when flat transaction was introduced. However, its strict adherence to ACID properties became a severe impediment for managing emerging information processing requirements. The management of the large unit of processing, which became known as *workflow*, was too much for flat transactions to handle efficiently. The unit of work such as *travel planning*, *insurance claim processing*, *CAD/CAM tasks*, *utopia planning* [20], and so on, demanded significant freedom from ACID constraints that included redefining the concept of data consistency and isolation. This requirement motivated the development of more powerful and scalable transaction models. The main objectives of these models for advanced applications were to (a) increase the degree of parallelism in the execution of long running transactions, (b) redefine consistency to manage statistical database transactions, (c) handle failure cases in a confined way, and (d) redefine the conflict scenario. It became clear that flexible and scalable models were necessary for advanced systems like *multidatabase*, *federated database*, *data warehouse*, *web*, and so on.

A number of advanced transaction models were developed using flat transaction as the seed. In fact, all advanced transaction models are an extension of the flat transaction model. Since it has never been possible to build a system that would efficiently process all kinds of transactional requests, many different types of database systems evolved to satisfy user demands. The development of advanced transaction models followed this system evolution and new data processing requirements. As a result, a number of different models came into existence. This section introduces (a) nested transaction [21], (b) SAGA [22], (c) cooperative transaction [23], (d) ConTract [24], and (e) flex transaction [25]. The purpose of this discussion is to investigate their suitability for managing mobile database processing that has a number of unique requirements and constraints. All these transaction models support a common construct: finer granules unit of operations. The difference lies in the way each manages them for producing serializable history.

4.4.1   Nested Transaction Model

The nested transaction model was introduced in reference 21. The basic idea of this model is to organize a flat transaction in a tree with a set of semi-independent units of actions that are referred to as *subtransactions*. The root of the tree represents the parent (main) transaction, and the descendants of the root represent finer granularity *subtransactions* of the parent transaction. Theoretically, the height of the tree could be infinite. Figure 4.8 illustrates the nested transaction model. The parent transaction has two subtransactions, S1 and S2. Subtransaction S1 has two subtransactions, SS1 and SS2 and subtransaction S2 has two subtransaction, SS3 and SS4. Subtransaction SS1 has two subtransactions, SSS1 and SSS2, but SS2 has no subtransaction. Similarly, subtransaction SS3 has two subtransactions, SSS3 and SSS4, and subtransaction SS4 has two subtransactions, SSS5 and SSS6.

The relationship between the root and its descendants are clearly defined and used to manage consistency-preserving execution (commit, roll back, abort, etc.) of the entire transaction tree. The following list summarizes the relationship:

- Subtransactions at the leaf level are flat transactions that actually perform the necessary data processing. The parent of a set of subtransactions does not manipulate any data but invokes subtransactions and controls the flow of execution.

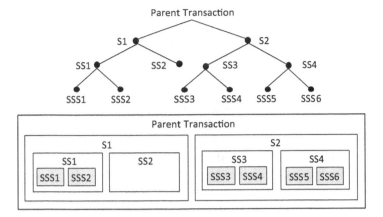

Figure 4.8 A nested transaction model.

- A subtransaction can commit or roll back independent of other subtransactions or the parent of the tree. However, such commit or rollback takes effect only if the parent commits or rolls back.
- A subtransaction has only A, C, and I properties because its durability depends only on its parent. If the parent rolls back, then all its subtransactions must also be rolled back.

Concurrent parent transactions conform to ACID properties; therefore, their execution must be serialized through some serialization scheme. From a transaction execution viewpoint, the nested transaction provides improved parallelism; and from the recovery viewpoint, it confines the transaction failure to a smaller unit of execution—that is, at the subtransaction level. The parent transaction has a number of options in dealing with the failure of a subtransaction which can be listed as follows. The parent can

- ignore the failure of subtransactions if it does not threaten database consistency.
- execute a special subtransaction (contingency subtransaction) to make up the failure of the subtransaction.
- reexecute the failed subtransaction.
- abort an active subtransaction.
- reschedule the execution of a set of subtransactions.

The original nested transaction model was further extended by removing some of the tight relationship between the parent and its subtransactions. To differentiate between the two models, the original model was referred to as the *closed-nested transaction*, and the extended model is referred to as the *open-nested transaction*. As the name suggests, the parent in an open-nested transaction does not enforce any restriction on the execution, rollback, and commitment of its subtransactions.

The parent transaction only invokes subtransactions, and then these subtransactions execute independently to each other and also to the parent. A *workflow* is a good example of an open-nested transaction model.

4.4.2 Saga

The saga transaction model [22] is based on *compensating transaction* [26] and *long-running transaction* [7]. If a long-running transaction is divided into a number of independent fine granularity transactions and are chained together, then each fine transaction can execute independently. For example, if a transaction updates 10 different accounts, then the entire transaction can be divided into 10 different subtransactions and can be executed independently of each other. It is also possible to remedy (compensate) the malfunctioning (rollback, abort, incorrect operation, etc.) of a subtransactions without affecting others.

The saga model can be formally defined as a set of fine granule transactions (subtransactions) (T) where each subtransaction is associated with a compensating transaction (C). The saga can be viewed as a unit of execution with two sequences: (a) sequence of subtransactions and (b) sequence of compensating transactions.

$$T_1, T_2, \ldots, T_n$$
$$C_1, C_2, \ldots, C_n$$

The saga model aims to achieve this kind of extension of long-running flat transactions; however, it does so by relaxing some of the ACID properties. The system either executes the first sequence successfully or, in case of some failure, executes sequence (a) and a part of sequence (b). During the execution of sequence (a), any subtransaction can commit or roll back independently; that is, it does not wait for other subtransactions of the same saga. In case of a failure, if forward recovery is not possible, then it uses the corresponding compensating transaction to remedy the situation. In this remedy, the compensating transaction may correct the error of the subtransaction or may undo all its operations on the database.

Saga achieves this kind of execution environment by relaxing some of the ACID properties as follows:

- **Atomicity:** Unlike a closed-nested transaction, saga allows other sagas to see the partial results of a transaction. As a result, saga cannot guarantee complete atomicity.
- **Consistency:** Unlike a flat transaction, saga allows interleaved execution of subtransactions where an active subtransaction can see the partial results of other active subtransactions. Under this execution, consistency may not be guaranteed.
- **Isolation:** Since consistency is relaxed, isolation cannot be guaranteed either.
- **Durability:** This is preserved because saga guarantees that the main transaction commits only when all its subtransactions are committed.

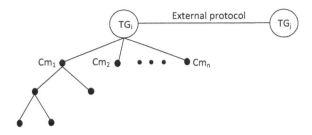

Figure 4.9   Cooperative transaction structure.

4.4.3 Cooperative Transaction

The cooperative transaction [23] is modeled as a rooted tree that is called the *cooperative transaction hierarchy*. The internal nodes of this tree are called *transaction groups*, and the leaves are called *cooperative transactions*. Figure 4.9 shows the hierarchy. TG is the transaction group, and Cm_is are cooperative transaction members.

Transaction Group (TG). A transaction group is a parent (root) for a number of cooperative transactions. A TG supervises the activities of its cooperative members. It may interact with other sibling TGs, and the interaction is managed by *external protocols*.

Every TG has its own version of a data item that is not accessible to any other TG. All of its cooperating members can access (read and write) this version. A TG does not take part in data processing unless it is itself a cooperative transaction.

When a member requires a data item, then it is automatically copied from the group to the requesting member. A new version of the data item is written back to to TG after the member has modified it. Thus, a TG plays the role of a server for its cooperating transaction members.

Cooperative Transaction Members. Cooperative transaction members are children of a TG and operate under *internal protocol*. They are like clients who issue reads and writes on data items that are performed by their TG. When an operation comes to TG from a cooperating transaction, then TG can either process it, refuse it, or queue it for later processing. The cooperation among members for serialization is monitored by their TG.

Members follow a familiar execution flow starting with the *begin transaction, end transaction*, and *commit*. A TG creates a new member with a *member begin* command. During execution, a member goes through checkpointing, rollback, commit, and so on; thus, from an execution viewpoint, the flow is identical to the execution of a lat transaction. However, this execution environment is developed in a different way than what is done in the concurrent execution of flat transactions.

The flexibility in achieving serializability is one of the main contributions of the cooperative transaction model. The freedom to define purpose-specific correctness criteria fits well in managing long-running transactions, but at the expense of consistency.

4.4.4 ConTract

The *ConTract* transaction model was proposed in reference 24. This model aims to develop a formal approach for developing, implementing, and managing a long-lived transaction that exists in a large number of environments such as CAD, office automation, manufacturing control, and so on. Similar to other advanced transaction models, *ConTract* also recognizes the limitations of ACID properties for dealing with long-lived transactions, especially in a distributed processing environment. The main idea of the *ConTract* approach is then to build a fault tolerant execution system to manage the execution of an arbitrary sequence of predefined actions, referred to as *steps*, according to a *script* (explicitly specified control flow description) [24]. Thus, from an application viewpoint, *ConTract* is a program that offers a parallel programming environment with persistent local variables and has well-defined error semantics for managing system recovery.

Step. A *step* is a basic unit of work that is executed strictly sequentially. It is similar to a *subtransaction* of other models. Some of the examples of steps are booking a hotel, crediting a bank account, and so on. A step is implemented as an ACID transaction. However, a step maintains only the local consistency of the data items it manipulates.

Script. It describes the flow of control that can be expressed in terms of recursion, loop, iteration, and so on, and manages the execution strategies of a long-running task. The *ConTract* model differs with the ACID structure as follows:

- **Atomicity:** Any time during execution, a *ConTract* step can be interrupted and its execution can be frozen, which can then be restarted from the point of interruption. In case of failure, to maintain atomicity, only roll-forward of a step that may use a different execution path than the original one is allowed.
- **Consistency:** A *ConTract* maintains system integrity on a larger scale.
- **Isolation:** A *ConTract*, for achieving a higher degree of concurrency, instead of locking, uses semantic isolation through predicates for the duration of a *ConTract*.
- **Durability:** A *ConTract* execution is durable in a conventional sense; however, a committed *ConTract* can be compensated (undone) only by running another *ConTract*. A compensation is a special case, so it is done only on a user's request.

4.4.5 Flex Transaction

This model is also an extension of the flat transaction and specially designed for managing transactions on multi and federated database systems. A flex transaction is a set of tasks where each task is composed of a set of functionally equivalent subtransactions. The objective of the model [25] is to minimize ACID constraints to allow more flexibility in processing concurrent transactions. One of the ways the flex model achieves this is by giving more freedom to users for defining their data processing preferences. The commitment requirement is also relaxed by allowing a flex transaction to commit even if some of its tasks did not complete. The main features of a flex transaction model can be described as follows [25, 27]:

Function Replication. A task, for example, renting a car, can be processed at any rental agency. It is left to the system to process this task as efficiently as possible. A user can also express his option for renting from a certain rental agency. The property is incorporated in this model to allow sufficient flexibility in composing and processing global transactions.

Mixed Transaction. A flex transaction is composed of *compensatable* and *non-compensatable* subtransactions and the construct is referred to as *mixed transaction*. A flex model allows for the execution of a compensating transaction so to semantically undo or redo the execution of a subtransaction. For example, a reserved seat can be cancelled or changed by running a compensating transaction.

Value Function. A value function denotes the completion time of each subtransaction. It also allows a user to define the order of execution of a subtransaction. For example, reserving a flight before or after reserving a hotel room at the destination. It can be formally defined as illustrated in references 25 and 27.

A flex transaction T can be represented as a 5-tuple (B, S, F, Π, f). Each member of this tuple is described as follows:

- $B = \{t_1(tp_1),\ t_2(tp_2), \ldots, t_n(tp_n)\}$. $t_i(tp_i)$ are typed subtransactions—that is, compensatable or noncompensatable.
- S is a partial order of B. It defines the success order (successful execution order) of two typed subtransactions. Thus, $t_i \prec t_j \in S$ indicates that t_i must successfully complete before t_j could be started.
- F is a partial order of B that is called the failure order of flex transaction T. The relationship $t_i \prec t_j \in F$ indicates that t_j is not completed if t_i fails.
- Π is a set of external predicates on B. It may contain cost functions, time constraints, and so on, on t_i.
- f is an n-ary boolean function that is called an *acceptability function* of T and describes all its acceptable states. For example, the success condition of a flex transaction can be defined over 4 transactions as $f(x_1, x_2, x_3, x_4) = (x_1 \wedge x_3) \vee (x_2 \wedge x_4)$, where x_i's are the execution states of t_i's. This states that the flex transaction can complete if any of the combinations $(x_1 \wedge x_3$, that is, transactions t_1 and $t_3)$ or $(x_2 \wedge x_4$, that is, transactions t_2 and $t_4)$ complete successfully.

4.5 SUMMARY

This chapter reviewed the consistency-preserving database processing through ACID transactions. To understand the mechanism of consistency preserving execution, it discussed the concept of serialization using different types of histories generated by the execution of concurrent transactions. The merit of strict enforcement of ACID properties was evaluated, and it presented some valid arguments against such strict enforcement. It then reviewed a number of advanced transaction models that relaxed ACID constraints for improving the performance of database processing.

The next chapter discusses mechanisms for serializing the execution of concurrent transactions. These mechanisms are commonly known as *concurrency control mechanisms*.

EXERCISES

4.1 Define transaction structure in terms of unprotected and protected actions.

4.2 Explain the ACID properties of transactions and identify which ACID property can be safely removed without affecting the consistency-preserving property of concurrent transactions.

4.3 Explain the serial execution of a set of transactions and their serializable execution. Identify their advantages and disadvantages. Give examples to illustrate their strengths and weaknesses.

4.4 Explain the degree of isolations and comments on their usefulness in managing database processing.

4.5 Compare the strengths and weaknesses of different transaction models.

4.6 Compare a conventional distributed database system with mobile database system and identify their difference from (a) architectural and (b) functional viewpoints.

4.7 Explain the ways of distributing a database and compare their advantages and disadvantages in terms of data access, serialization, consistency, reliability, and recovery.

4.8 Identify the problems that arise when the execution of concurrent transactions is not managed properly. Investigate and explain why these problems occur. Give suitable examples in support of your answer.

4.9 Explain the difference between a history and a schedule of the execution of a set of transactions. Formally define the history and their types. Give examples in support of your answer.

REFERENCES

1. T. Ozsu, and P. Valduriez, *Principles of Distributed Database Systems*, Prentice-Hall, Englewood Cliffs, NJ, 1999.
2. D. Z. Badal, Correctness of Concurrency Control and Implications in Distributed Databases. In *IEEE Proceedings of COMPSAC Conference*, November 1979, pp. 588–593.

3. T. Haerder and A. Reuter, Principles of Transaction-Oriented Database Recovery, *ACM Computing Surveys*, Vol. 15, No. 4, December 1983, pp. 287–317.

4. J. Gray, The Transaction Concept: Virtues and Limitations. In *Proceedings of the 17th International Conference on Very Large Databases*, Septempber 1981, pp. 144–154.

5. D. P. Reed, Implementing Atomic Actions on Decentralized Data, *ACM Transactions on Computer Systems*, Vol. 1, No. 1, February 1983, pp. 3–23.

6. P. K. Chrysanthis and K. Ramamritham, ACTA: A Framework for Specifying and Reasoning about Transaction Structure and Behavior. In *Proceedings of the ACM SIGMOD International Conference on Management of Data*, May 1990, pp. 194–203.

7. J. Gray and A. Reuter, *Transaction Processing Concepts and Techniques*, Morgan Kaufmann, San Francisco, 1993.

8. K. P. Eswaran, J. N. Gray, R. A. Lorie, and I. L. Traiger, The Notion of Consistency and Predicate Locks in a Database System, *Communications of the ACM*, Vol. 19, No. 11, November 1976, pp. 624–633.

9. C. H. Papadimitriou, The Serializability of Concurrent Database Updates, *Journal of the ACM*, Vol. 26, No. 4, October 1979, pp. 631–653.

10. J. N. Gray, R. A. Lorie, A. R. Putzulo, and I. L. Traiger, Granularity of Locks and Degrees of Consistency in a Shared Database. In *Proceedings of the First International Conference on Very Large Databases*, September 1975, pp. 94–121.

11. J. Gray, Notes on Data Base Operating Systems. In *Operating Systems: An Advanced Course, Lecture Notes in Computer Science*, R. Bayer, R. M. Graham, and G. Seegmuller, (eds.), Vol. 60, Springer Verlag, Berlin, 1978.

12. C. H. Papadimitriou *The Theory of Database Concurrency Control*, Computer Science Press, New York, 1986.

13. P. A. Bernstein, V. Hadzilacos, and N. Goodman, *Concurrency Control and Recovery in Database Systems*, Addison-Wesley, Reading, MA, 1987.

14. N. S. Barghouti and G. E. Kaiser, Concurrency Control in Advanced Database Applications, *ACM Computing Surveys*, Vol. 23, No. 2, September 1991, pp. 269–317.

15. V. Hadzilacos, A Theory of Reliability in Database Systems, *Journal of the ACM*, Vol. 35, No. 1, January 1988, pp. 121–145.

16. P. A. Bernstein, D. W. Shipman, and W. S. Wong, Formal Aspects of Serializability in Database Concurrency Control, *IEEE Transactions on Software Engineering*, Vol. 5, No. 5, May 1979, pp. 203–216.

17. W. Weihl, Distributed Version Management of Read-only Actions, *IEEE Transactions on Software Engineering*, Vol. 13, No. 1, January 1987, pp. 55–64.

18. C. Beeri, P. A. Bernstein, and N. A. Goodman, Model for Concurrency in Nested Transaction Systems, *Journal of the ACM*, Vol. 36, No. 2, April 1989, pp. 230–269.

19. Y. Breitbart, D. Georgakopoulos, M. Rusinkiewicz, and A. Silberschatz, On Rigorous Transaction Scheduling, *IEEE Transactions on Software Engineering*, Vol. 17, No. 9, September 1991, pp. 954–960.

20. N. A. Lynch, Multilevel Atomicity A New Correctness Criterion for Database Concurrency Control, *ACM Transactions on Database Systems (TODS)*, Vol. 8, No. 4, June 1983, pp. 484–502.

21. J. E. B. Moss, *Nested Transactions: An Approach to Reliable Distributed Computing*, MIT Press, Cambridge, MA, 1985.

22. H. Garcia-Molina and K. Salem, Sagas. In *Proceedings of the ACM Conference on Management of Data*, May 1987, pp. 249–259.

23. M. Nodine and S. Zdonik, Cooperative Transaction Hierarchies: A Transaction Model to Support Design Applications. In *Proceedings of the International Conference on Very Large Databases*, pp. 83–94, 1984.

24. A. Reuter, ConTracts: A Means for Extending Control Beyond Transaction Boundaries. In Advanced Transaction Models for New Appplications, Morgan Kaufmann, 1991.

25. A. Elmagarmid, Y. Liu, W. Litwin, and M. Rusinkiewicz, A Multidatabase Transaction Model for Interbase. In *Proceedings of the International Conference on Very Large Databases*, Brisbane, Australia, August 1990, pp. 507–518.

26. M. Chessell, C. Ferreira, C. Griffin, P. Henderson, D. Vines, and M. Butler, Extending the concept of transaction compensation, *IBM System Journal*, Vol. 41, No. 4, 2002, pp. 743–758.

27. E. Anwar, An Extensible Approach to Realizing an Extened Transaction Models. Ph.D. disertation, University of Florida, 1996.

CHAPTER 5

INTRODUCTION TO CONCURRENCY CONTROL MECHANISMS

This chapter introduces conventional schemes for serializing the execution of concurrent transactions in centralized and distributed database systems. These schemes are generally referred to as *concurrency control mechanisms (CCMs)*. The objective of this chapter is to prepare the readers to investigate the limitations of these conventional schemes for mobile database systems and present CCMs specifically for mobile database systems.

5.1 INTRODUCTION

In a multitasking environment, resource sharing is maximized to boost system performance. It is essential to achieve such sharing in database systems in a consistency-preserving manner, which requires that at any moment in time, only one activity has the resource for its exclusive use. In operating systems, a common way of sharing resources is through mutual exclusion, which is enforced using *semaphores* [1]. This mechanism, however, would not work efficiently for concurrent transactions because the granularity of mutual exclusion (critical section) is too fine to be used in databases. It would not be practical to treat transactions as critical sections because of their execution behavior and size. What is needed is a set of schemes that can work with coarser granularity for synchronizing the execution of concurrent transactions.

In database systems, data sharing is managed by *concurrency control mechanisms (CCMs)*. In database terminology, it is usually referred to as *serializing* the execution

Fundamentals of Pervasive Information Management Systems, Revised Edition. Vijay Kumar.
© 2013 John Wiley & Sons, Inc. Published 2013 by John Wiley & Sons, Inc.

of concurrent transactions that share database data. They achieve *serialization* by enforcing an execution order for conflicting operations from two different transactions in such a way that it is equivalent to a *serial* execution of these transactions. A CCM acts as a catalyst in the concurrent execution of transactions and maintains serializability either by *rolling back* or by *blocking* one of the conflicting transactions. It was recognized that the method of achieving serialization significantly affected the performance of database systems, and therefore, this problem has been intensively investigated. As a result, a large number of CCMs were developed and experimented on in order to identify the simple, yet efficient, CCM for a majority of transaction processing environments [2, 3]. An approach where the system had multiple CCMs to choose from and then selected the one most suitable for the workload in hand, was also tried [4]. It was observed from the experiment that a multiple choice scheme was too time-consuming to be efficient. Other investigations supported this observation and concluded that the basic scheme of *two-phase locking (2PL)* is the most favorable among all. Since then, almost all commercial database systems use some variation of the 2PL scheme without any serious performance problems.

Many researchers have extensively investigated the use of the two-phase locking approach in mobile database systems. The general agreement among them is that the two-phase locking approach is not a satisfactory solution to transaction serialization for mobile database systems. Some of the important constraints are related to lack of resources, limited channel bandwidth, channel availability, and the geographical location of mobile units. We discuss these issues in more detail in a separate section in this chapter. In particular, we discuss the nature of these constraints and their effect on transaction processing on MDS.

The available CCMs can be categorized into (a) locking and (b) nonlocking approaches. Locking approaches follow the *two-phase* locking protocol [5] to reserve (lock) data items for transactions and *rollback* and *blocking* operations to resolve conflicts over shared data items [2, 5]. These can be applied in a variety of ways with different combinations, and each way defines a new CCM. First, various ways of applying two-phase locking are discussed, and then multiple ways of resolving conflicts are explained.

5.1.1 Ways of Locking Data Items

Locking protocols support two atomic operations: (a) locking and (b) unlocking. A set of lock operations of a transaction defines its locking phase, which is also referred to as the growing phase; and a set of unlocking operations defines its unlocking phase, which is called the *shrinking* phase. The two-phase policy requires that these two phases must be mutually exclusive; that is, the unlocking phase begins only when the locking phase has ended. The policy also requires that a transaction must be *well-formed*. A well-formed transaction does not attempt to lock an item that is already locked and does not attempt to unlock a free item.

The execution life of a transaction under 2PL goes through three phases: (a) locking, (b) execution, and (c) unlocking. Under the two-phase policy, these three phases can be arranged in four different ways, each giving a unique concurrency control mechanism [2]. Each of these four concurrency control mechanisms are described below.

Simultaneous Locking and Simultaneous Release. This mechanism is also referred to as *static locking* in literature. In this scheme, locking, execution, and unlocking phases are applied atomically and serially. First, the locking phase begins and completes successfully, then the execution phase begins and completes, and finally the unlocking phase begins and completes. Thus, the *start and end of locking* ⟹ the *start and end of execution* ⟹ the *start and end of unlocking* defines the execution life of a transaction. The failure of the failure of the execution phase does not affect the locking phase. For example, if the execution phase does not complete for any reason, then the transaction can be restarted without restarting the locking phase.

This mechanism is simple to implement, but its mode of operation affects performance. A detailed explanation of issues related to this CCM can be found in reference 2. This mechanism locks data items that are referenced in transaction code; most of which may not be needed by the transaction during execution. For example, in the code *If x = 100, then read (a) else read (b)*, three data items are referenced. If this is executed, then the transaction will lock only two items (*x* and *a* or *x* and *b*), but since data items *x*, *a*, and *b* are referenced, the transaction will lock them in its locking phase statically. Such redundant locking is likely to generate an excessive wait for other transactions. Then there is the issue of a repeated restart that happens when the locking phase is not able to lock all referenced data items. The nature of static locking actually reduces the degree of concurrency drastically. Figure 5.1 illustrates the working of the protocol.

Incremental Locking and Simultaneous Release. In this scheme, the locking and execution phases are interleaved and precede the entire unlocking phase. Thus, the growing phase completes incrementally as *lock* → *process* → *lock* → *process*; consequently, unlike static locking, the transaction locks and processes only those data items it actually needs. Unfortunately, one of the side effects of incremental locking is the occurrence of *deadlock*. It has been observed [2] that deadlocks occur infrequently and there are a number of efficient ways to manage them that keeps the entire cost of deadlock detection and resolution quite low. Some systems do not

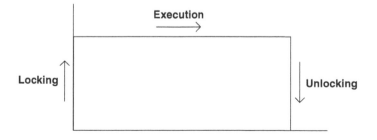

Figure 5.1   Simultaneous locking and simultaneous release protocol.

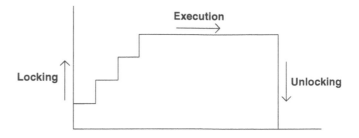

Figure 5.2   Incremental locking and simultaneous release protocol.

detect deadlocks but rather use the transaction blocking duration as an indication of a possible deadlock and take the necessary action (rollback) to resolve it. This approach works quite well because of their infrequent occurrences.

Once the execution phase is complete, locks are released simultaneously. The entire execution of a transaction can be stated as *lock → process → lock → process ⇒ unlock*. A CCM based on this scheme is also referred to as *General Waiting*. Nearly all database systems (reference and commercial) use this mechanism. The implementation may differ from system to system. Figure 5.2 illustrates the working of the protocol.

Simultaneous Locking and Incremental Release. In this scheme, the locking and the growing phases are mutually exclusive and the unlocking phase is interleaved with the execution phase. The entire transaction execution can be stated as *locking ⇒ execution → unlock → execution → unlock*. In addition to the problems of static locking, it suffers with *cascading* aborts. This happens when all dependent transactions need to be rolled back when the transaction on which they depend is aborted. Such aborts are expensive because the rollback operation of a transaction takes nearly the same amount of resources and time as its forward processing. It is far more expensive to manage cascading aborts than detecting and resolving deadlocks; as a result, it is always avoided. It gets worse in a processing environment where transaction dependency is quite high such as in a travel planning environment where a number of

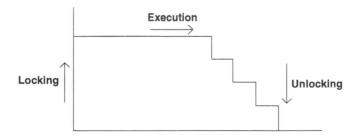

Figure 5.3   Simultaneous locking and incremental release protocol.

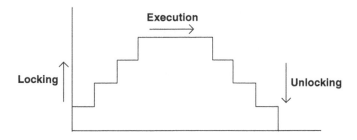

Figure 5.4   Incremental locking and incremental release protocol.

subtransactions of the main transaction are strongly linked to each other. This protocol is not used in any database system. Figure 5.3 illustrates the working of the protocol.

Incremental Locking and Incremental Release. In this scheme, the execution phase is interleaved with both locking and release phases. As a result, this protocol suffers from deadlock and cascading aborts. The objective is to minimize transaction waiting time. The scheme did manage to minimize transaction waiting time, but the benefit is too little compared to the cost of handling cascading. Figure 5.4 illustrates the working of the protocol.

CCMs based on a 2PL approach enforce an execution order among conflicting transactions *dynamically*. This means that when two transactions conflict over a data item, the underlying CCM decides which transaction should be blocked, or rolled back, to let the other transaction continue. Prior to a conflict, the conflicting transactions have no defined execution order; it is defined only when a conflict arises. This way of defining an execution order between conflicting operations provides significant freedom in scheduling concurrent transactions for execution.

5.1.2 The Phantom Problem

One of the aims of locking schemes is to achieve the highest degree of concurrency (number of transactions executed concurrently). The size of the locking unit (locking granularity) significantly affects the degree of concurrency. Coarse granularity (for example, an entire file or relation), reduces the locking overhead as well as the degree of concurrency where the finer granularity increases them. In addition, a finer granularity gives rise to a *phantom* problem. A lockable unit that is not present in the database, but is being entered, may give rise to this problem. Consider a case of adding a tuple to a relation. If a tuple is a locking granularity, then the concurrency control scheme will lock this new tuple to be added to the relation. Depending upon the progress of other concurrent transactions, some transactions would see this new tuple and some would not (a *phantom* problem). This may introduce database inconsistency. The following example illustrates the occurrence of a *phantom* problem. Two transactions T_1 and T_2 operate on relations *accounts* and *balance*. T_1 inserts a new tuple (*400 Lenexa 2000*) in the accounts table, and T_2 compares the sum of each account with the *sum* in the balance table. Figure 5.5 shows the current situation.

Accounts				Balance	
Account #	**Location**	**Amount**		**Location**	**Sum**
100	Kansas City	1000		Kansas City	1000
200	Lenexa	2000		Lenexa	5000
300	Lenexa	3000			

Figure 5.5   A bank database.

One of the possible concurrent execution of T_1 and T_2 could be

T_2: Lock 100, Lock 200, Lock 300
T_2: Read (Amount = 1000, Amount = 2000 and Amount = 3000)
T_1: Lock 400 (phantom record)
T_2: Sum = 2000 + 3000 ⇒ 5000
T_1: Insert (400, Lenexa, 4000) in Accounts table
T_2: Report the sum = 5000 *Does not included recent insert*
T_1: Unlock 400
T_2: Unlock 100, 200, and 300
T_2: Commit
T_1: Commit

Unfortunately, this execution schedule is not serializable. T_2 does not include the amount from the new record (*400   Lenexa   4000*), because at the time of reading the *Accounts* table, this record did not exist. If locking granularity is changed from a record to a table, then this problem would not arise for this example. The static locking approach also would not solve this problem. One way to take care of this problem is through the use of *Index locking*.

5.1.3 Index Locking

The idea of index locking is simple. Suppose an index *P* points to all instances of *Lenexa*. Now consider the case when T_1 locks index *P*, which effectively means T_1 locks all instances of *Lenexa* (including records yet to be inserted) and excludes all other transactions, including T_2, from accessing the *Lenexa* instance. T_2 can access the *Amount* value for *Lenexa* only after the insert is complete. This way, executing T_1 and T_2 generates a serializable schedule.

Index locking can be explained in terms of predicates. In the above example, T_1 locks those records that satisfy the predicate (*Location = Lenexa*). This idea gives rise to the scheme of *predicate locking*, where more complex predicates can be composed to precisely define the locking unit.

5.1.4 Multigranularity Locking

In reality, lockable unit could be of different sizes. It could be a disk block, a data page, a relation, an attribute of a relation, or a record of a file. This diversity defines a hierarchy of lockable granularity and suggests the scheme of multigranularity locking. In this scheme, a transaction T_i locks data items in a hierarchical manner (from coarser to finer granules) in different locking modes. This helps transactions that access and modify large volumes of data. For example, if a transaction modifies all tuples of a large relation, then it can just lock the entire relation for processing. On the other hand, if a transaction accesses only a couple of tuples of a large relation, then it can lock the entire relation in a sharable locking mode but lock the required tuples in an exclusive mode. This way of locking allows other concurrent transactions to access other tuples except the ones locked exclusively.

A total of five different lock modes are defined to manage multigranularity locking requirements. These lock modes are

- **Read:** This mode allows a transaction to read a data item.
- **Write:** This mode allows a transaction to write to a data item.
- **Intention Read—(ir):** A transaction applies an IR lock when it intends to read a data item. Thus, the transaction first applies an IR lock to ancestors of a data item (for example a relation) and then applies a read lock on the data item (for example its tuple) it wants to read.
- **Intention Write—(iw):** It is similar to an IR lock, only the operation is a write.
- **Read Intention Write—(riw):** This mode allows a transaction to read a set of records and modify a few of the records of this set.

Figure 5.6 shows a lock instance graph and a lock compatibility matrix that are used to define the steps of the protocol. Suppose transaction T_i wants to read *File 3* and T_j wants to write to $R3_2$. The execution of T_i and T_j goes as follows:

1. T_i intends to read *File 3* which is a node of the root *Database* so it applies an *ir* lock to *Database*.
2. It applies an *ir* lock to *Area 1*.

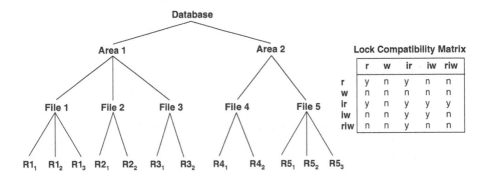

Figure 5.6 Lock instance graph and compatibility matrix.

3. Finally, it applies an *r* lock to *File 3*.
4. T_j applies an *iw* lock to *Database* successfully.
5. It applies an *iw* lock to *Area 1* successfully.
6. It cannot apply *iw* lock to *File 3* because the lock conflicts with T_i's *r* lock (see conflict matrix).
7. T_i releases the *r* lock from *File 3*.
8. T_j now sets *iw* lock on *File 3* and applies *w* lock on $R3_2$.
9. T_k wants to read *Area 1* so it successfully sets an *ir* lock on *Database*.
10. It tries to set an *r* lock on *Area 1* but it conflicts with T_j's *iw* lock (see conflict metrix).
11. It waits for T_j to release its *iw* lock on *Area 1*.

It is obvious from this execution that more transactions can work on the relation. As a result, the overall waiting time and the throughput increase significantly.

5.1.5 Nonlocking-Based Schemes

The purpose of the serialization process is to enforce consistency-preserving order in conflicting operations. Locking is one of the most effective and common ways of achieving this; however, it generates locking overhead. To lock and unlock a data item, a few thousand instructions have to be executed each time. In addition, some incremental locking approaches have to detect and resolve deadlocks that increase overhead. To eliminate or minimize such overhead, *timestamp-based* schemes were developed.

Timestamping. The timestamp approach for serializing the execution of concurrent transactions was developed to introduce more flexibility, to eliminate the cost of locking, and to cater for distributed database systems [2, 6]. In timestamping, the execution order of concurrent transactions is defined before they begin their execution. The execution order is established by associating a unique timestamp (usually an integer) to every transaction. When two transactions conflict over a data item, their timestamps are used to enforce serialization by rolling back one of the conflicting transactions. There are two timestamp-based CCMs: *simple timestamping* and *basic timestamping*.

Simple Timestamping Scheme. Under this scheme, each transaction is associated with a unique timestamp. When a transaction executes a read or a write over a data item, it attaches its timestamp to the data item to indicate which transaction operated on the data. Thus, to access a data item, a transaction first compares its timestamp with the timestamp of the data. If the timestamp of the transaction is smaller than the timestamp associated with the data, then it indicates that the transaction came too late and access is not allowed. The transaction is rolled back and restarted with the next higher timestamp. In some way, a timestamp appears to behave as a lock, but it does produce a serializable schedule that cannot be produced by a two-phase locking approach [6]. The algorithm goes as follows:

> *If timestamp (ts) of the data item < ts of the transaction, then*
> > *begin*
> > > *process the data item;*
> > > *overwrite the ts of the data item with transaction's ts*
> > *end*
> *Else roll back the transaction*

One of the problems with this simple scheme is that it cannot differentiate between a read and a write so it treats two reads, on the same data item from different transactions, as a conflict and rolls back the transaction. Consequently, two transactions cannot read a data item simultaneously, which severely restricts the degree of concurrency. This problem is eliminated in the *basic timestamping scheme.*

Basic Timestamping Scheme. This scheme associates two timestamps with each data item to allow read operations to go concurrently and to resolve read–write and write–write conflicts. When a transaction wants to read a data item, it compares its timestamp with the write timestamp of the data item to check the presence of a read–write conflict. The transaction is allowed to read the data item if its timestamp is larger than the write timestamp of the data. Note that this allows two transactions to read a data item that is not possible with only one timestamp. After reading the data item, the transaction overwrites the read timestamp of the data item with the larger of the two timestamps (data and transaction). The transaction is rolled back if this condition is not satisfied. Similarly, if a transaction wants to write to a data item then it compares its timestamp with the read timestamp of the data item. The transaction writes to the data item only if its timestamp is larger than the read timestamp of the data item and overwrites the write timestamp of the data with the larger of the two (data and transaction). In case of two consecutive writes (blind writes—write without reading the existing value of the data item) by two different transactions, the Thomas Write Rule (TWR) [6] is used to resolve write–write conflicts. The algorithm goes as follows:

Read operation

> *If write ts of the data item < transaction's ts then*
> > *begin*
> > > *overwrite read ts of the data by transaction's ts;*
> > > *read data item*
> > *end*
> *Else roll back the transaction*

Write operation

If the read ts of the data item < transaction's ts then
    begin
        overwrite write ts of the data item by transaction's ts;
        modify data item
    end
    Else roll back the transaction

Two consecutive writes

It is assumed that the last operation on the data item was a write.

If the write ts of the data < transaction's ts then
    begin
        modify the data item;
        overwrite write ts of the data with transaction's ts
    end
    Else roll back the transaction

Timestamping approaches manage to eliminate the locking and deadlock management costs, but they restrict conflict resolution options compared to two-phase locking schemes. In addition, they also add some new overhead such as timestamp maintenance, transaction rollback, and so on, that significantly affect system performance more than locking approaches [2, 7]. For these reasons, none of the timestamping schemes made its way into any commercial database systems.

5.1.6 Mixed Approaches

To exploit the dynamic aspects of two-phase locking and the static ordering of timestamping, a number of concurrency control mechanisms were developed using a combined approach. One of the main reasons for mixing these two approaches is to efficiently manage transaction execution in distributed database systems. The timestamping approach offers some freedom to the nodes of distributed database systems in making conflict resolution decisions with minimum consultation with other nodes participating in the execution of the transaction. In mixed approach schemes, locking is used to enforce isolation and timestamps are used to resolve conflicts. Two such well-known concurrency control mechanisms are *wound–wait* and *wait–die* [2, 8], which are explained below using transaction T_i as the holder and T_j as the requester of the data item.

5.1.7 Wound-Wait (WW)

In wound–wait (WW), a conflict is resolved by rolling back a younger (larger timestamp) holder. This is a preemptive algorithm since it rolls back the holder that might be under execution or waiting for a data item locked by an older (smaller timestamp) transaction. It avoids deadlock by not blocking the older requestor. When there is a conflict, then

If T_j's timestamp $> T_i$'s timestamp, then
* T_j waits for T_i to terminate (commit or abort)*
else T_i is wounded (T_j forces T_i to abort)

5.1.8 Wait–Die (WD)

In wait–die (WD), action is taken only on the requester. A requester is rolled back if it is younger than the holder, otherwise it is blocked. It is a non-preemptive algorithm because when a conflict over an entity occurs, it never takes away any resource from the holder (younger or older) in conflict. It avoids deadlock since it rolls back a younger requestor that only is capable of precipitating a deadlock.

If T_j's timestamp $> T_i$'s timestamp, then
* T_j dies (rolled back)*
else T_j waits for T_i to terminate (commit or abort)

5.1.9 Multiversion Approach

The main objective of the multiversion approach is to minimize the requester's waiting time by providing its requested data item [6]. Thus, the transactions' data requests are always immediately satisfied. To achieve immediate data allocation, every write operation generates a new version of the data. This creates a time series data item sequence of versions. The generation of this sequence can be illustrated by x_n, where x represents a data item and its subscript represents the time it was generated. Thus, x_1 is created by a write after x_0, x_2 is created after x_1, and so on. The generation of the temporal sequence of versions can be illustrated as follows:

$$x_0 \to w_1(x_1) \to x_1$$
$$x_1 \to w_2(x_2) \to x_2$$
$$\cdots$$
$$x_{n-1} \to w_n(x_n) \to x_n$$

This generates a time sequence of data item x as

$$\{x_1, x_2, \ldots, x_n\}$$

Suppose a transaction T_i requests data item x. The right version (the version that it would have accessed in a serial execution) of x for T_i is present in the sequence. The task of a multiversion scheme is first to identify the version and then reserve it for T_i. The multiversion approach can be implemented with a timestamp or with two-phase locking.

5.1.10   Optimistic Concurrency Control Mechanisms

Serialization of a concurrent transaction through locking is the most commonly used concurrency control scheme. It has, however, locking overhead that becomes significant for a high contention workload. It becomes unacceptable for a workload with a high percentage of read operations. The optimistic concurrency control approach tries to reduce locking overhead by delaying the lock operation until conflicting transactions are ready to commit. They hope that conflicts among transactions will not occur, as a result, the efficiency will improve. Since locks are not used during the execution life of transactions, the execution is deadlock-free. For these reasons, the scheme is called *optimistic* concurrency control or *certifiers* [6, 9].

The optimistic approach uses three phases for executing the transaction: (a) read, (b) validate, and (c) write.

Read.   A transaction reads the desired data item completely unrestricted and saves it in its local cache. The data valuer read is not returned to the user.

Validate.   In this phase, it is determined that the transaction will not generate inconsistent data and the result it returns will be correct.

Write.   In this phase, the transaction writes modified data items to the database and makes them available to other transactions if the validation is successful.

The optimistic approach can be implemented through timestamping, locking, or by graph testing [6]. The following example illustrates how the certification (validation) is performed at commit time. Suppose there are two concurrent transactions, T_i and T_j, that read and write data items. For each active transaction, the certifier maintains two queues to store its *read set* and *write set*. Thus, T_i maintains a queue R_i to store the data items it reads (read set) and a queue W_i to store data items it writes (write set) and so does T_j. When the certifier receives a request for data item x, that is, $r_i(x)$ or $w_i(x)$, from T_i, it adds x to R_i or to W_i depending upon the requested operation. When the certifier receives a commit operation from T_i, it tests for conflict by performing $R_i \cap W_j$, $W_i \cap R_j$, and $W_i \cap W_j$ with all active transactions. If any one of these produces an empty set, then the commit request is rejected and T_i is aborted; otherwise, the certifier commits the transaction and removes it from the active transaction queue.

The optimistic scheme does not apply lock; however, it does generate the effect of two-phase locking with the help of a transaction rollback. It eliminates locking overhead but replaces it with rollback overhead. Numerous performance investigations suggest that this scheme performs poorly in high contention transaction workloads [6].

5.2   HEURISTIC APPROACH IN LOCKING SCHEMES

The methods of resolving conflicts, that is, choosing which transaction to roll back and which to block, have a significant effect on the performance of CCMs. The main aim of an efficient CCM is to make the best possible selection, where the effects of rollbacks and blocking are minimal on the system throughput. Since the future conflicts of concurrent transactions are not known, usually conflict resolution methods select a victim (a transaction to rollback) either on an ad hoc basis or by applying some guesswork. It is possible to improve the conflict resolution method by taking into consideration some other aspects of the execution environment. A number of reports [2, 10–15] illustrate the detailed behavior of some two-phase locking CCMs and clearly show that some intelligence should be used in resolving conflicts more effectively. This motivated researchers and developers to use some heuristic approaches.

In the locking-based concurrency control mechanisms discussed so far, when a conflict occurs then the transaction requesting the data item is blocked. In incremental locking approaches this could create a *deadlock*, and one of the transactions is rolled back to resolve it. Thus, a rollback is to resolve a deadlock that is the result of a conflict and not to resolve the conflict. This unnecessarily increases the transaction waiting time. A scheme where the conflict is immediately resolved, instead of resolving its side effect, that is, deadlock, is more effective in minimizing the transaction wait time. This idea gave rise to some aggressive approaches where conflict was resolved immediately by rolling back or blocking conflicting transactions. It did prevent deadlock and achieved some performance gain. A number of such aggressive schemes are discussed below.

5.2.1 Cautious Waiting

The policy of cautious waiting is an improvement over *wound–wait (WW)* and *wait–die (WD)* mechanisms, and it can be further optimized. Under this mechanism, a conflict is resolved by rolling back or by blocking one of the conflicting transactions; however, unlike WW and WD mechanisms, a transaction to be rolled back is selected by examining the status of the conflicting transactions (blocked or running), thus eliminating the need for timestamps. When a requestor conflicts with a holder, the requestor is rolled back only if the holder is in a blocked state. If the holder is in execution, that is, not blocked due to a lock conflict, then the requestor is blocked and resumes its execution when the holder finishes, that is, commits or rolled back. If the holder is subsequently blocked, the previously blocked transaction remains blocked. CW kills (rolls back) only the requestor. It avoids killing the blocked holder that might have waited for a long time. The properties of the CW algorithm are summarized below:

- The algorithm is non-preemptive; that is, when conflict arises, it never aborts the holder of the entity in the conflict.
- The wait-for graph can have a queue length greater than one. This occurs when a transaction T_1 is blocked by a running transaction T_2 while T_2, in turn, is blocked by another running transaction T_3.
- It is deadlock-free. CW is also conceptually simpler since there is no externally imposed ordering.

- CW can be optimized if in the conflict resolution, the amount of resource utilized, that is, CPU, by conflicting transactions is taken into consideration. So in a conflict, if a transaction has to be rolled back, then the progress of the holder and the requestor (in terms of CPU utilization) can be compared and the transaction that has so far consumed the least amount of resources is rolled back. This way of selecting a transaction to be rolled back takes away the non-preemptive quality, but it may reduce the cost of rolling back.

5.2.2 Running Priority

The running-priority mechanism [16] blocks the requestor (transaction requesting the data) if the holder is running. But if the holder (transaction holding the data item) is blocked, then it is aborted. Thus, unlike cautious waiting, the running priority allows the requestor to continue execution by aborting all of its conflicting blocked holders. It is also possible, in running priority, that a blocked holder may remain blocked for a long time and could eventually get aborted.

Another algorithm similar to cautious waiting was proposed in reference 17. This algorithm limits the queue length of the waiting transaction to be one; that is, a transaction can wait, for at most, one blocked transaction.

Some concurrency control mechanisms tried to further reduce the cost of conflict resolution by more accurately selecting conflicting transactions for rolling back or for blocking. They select to roll back a conflicting transaction not only by examining the execution status of the holder–requestor pair, but also by analyzing their execution progress and resource utilization. One such concurrency control mechanism, called *Krishna*, reviews the progress of conflicting transactions in terms of locked data items and already executed *read*, *write*, and *abort* operations.

5.2.3 Krishna

This mechanism uses *dynamic attributes* [18] of conflicting transactions to resolve conflict. During their execution life, transactions inherit a number of *attributes*. Some of the examples of such attributes are *number of conflicts suffered by a transaction*, *number of entities locked by the transaction*, *duration the transaction waited for the desired data items*, *number of times the transaction was blocked*, *number of times the transaction was rolled back*, and so on. These attributes are called *dynamic attributes* of transactions, and a subset of them can precisely identify the execution status of a transaction. Since dynamic attributes acquire their values during execution, they can be used as a measure of the relative progress of a transaction in a concurrent environment. The values of a subset of these attributes can be used to identify the right transaction for resolving conflict efficiently. For example, if transactions T_1 and T_2 conflict, and if T_1 has acquired and processed a relatively larger number of entities, then an efficient way to resolve the conflict is to roll back or block (whichever is less expensive) T_2. It is possible that the values of all dynamic attributes of two transactions may match (identical progress in their execution). In this situation, any one of these transactions can be selected to roll back or to block for resolving a conflict. A dynamic Attribute Set (DAS) can be represented as

$$DAS = \{a_1, a_2, \ldots, a_n\}$$

where a_i is a dynamic attribute of a transaction. Theoretically, n can be very large; however, a small value of n with selected attributes may give us sufficient information for making a right conflict resolution decision.

Conflict Resolution Scheme. The scheme uses a subset of DAS to compute priorities of conflicting transactions and uses them to decide which transaction to roll back or to block. Whenever an operation is performed by a transaction, then the value of the dynamic attribute representing that operation is incremented. For example, if a transaction locks a data item, then the value of its *number of locks acquired so far* is incremented by one. This is done for all other attribute values, and as a result it makes the priority time-variant. It has a unique value at an instant of time, and it may either remain the same or increase with time but never decreases. The computation of priority of transactions T_j and T_k is computed as follows:

$$DAS_j = \{a_1, a_2, \ldots, a_n\}$$
$$DAS_k = \{b_1, b_2, \ldots, b_n\}$$
$$P_j \text{ and } P_k = Priorities \text{ of } T_j \text{ and } T_k$$

When these two transactions conflict, then the priorities are computed as follows:

If $(a_1 > b_1)$, then $P_j > P_k$
else if $(a_1 < b_1)$, then $P_j < P_k$
 else if $(a_1 = b_1)$, then
  if $(a_2 > b_2)$, then $P_j > P_k$
  else if $(a_2 < b_2)$, then $P_j < P_k$
   else if $(a_2 = b_2)$, then
    . . . .
    if $(a_n > b_n)$, then $P_j > P_k$
    else if $(a_n < b_n)$, then $P_j < P_k$
     else if $(a_n = b_n)$, then $P_j = P_k$

A *conflict resolution set (CRS)* is created to resolve conflict. An example of *CRS = {number of locks acquired so far, number of conflicts occurred so far, number of rollbacks so far, number of blockings occurred so far}*. Out of these, depending upon the transaction processing environment, an attribute—for example, the *number of locks acquired so far*—can be assigned the highest precedence since under the two-phase policy the progress of a transaction depends on successfully acquiring the desired locks. So the number of locks gives a measure of transaction maturity, that is, how far it has progressed in its execution, in terms of its data utilization.

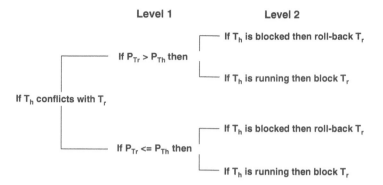

Figure 5.7 Conflict resolution in Krishna.

The algorithm can be defined as follows. Transaction T_r represents the requestor of the data item and T_h as the holder.

If the priority of T_r ≥ the priority of T_h, then
  if T_h is blocked then roll back T_h
  else block T_r
  else if the priority of T_r ≤ priority of T_h then
  if T_h is blocked then roll back T_r
  else block T_r

Figure 5.7 illustrates the conflict resolution steps of Krishna. A final decision is always reached at level 2. In the special case when $P_{Tr} = P_{Th}$, then a preemptive or non-preemptive decision can be taken. The introduction of the second level of tests make this algorithm deadlock-free.

5.2.4 Two-Phase Locking for Distributed Database Systems

Two-phase locking mechanisms were developed for centralized database systems, but they can be effectively applied to serialize distributed transactions as well. However, because of the different data distribution models, the implementation requires some modifications. There are three different ways a two-phase scheme can be applied to distributed database systems: (a) centralized two-phase locking, (b) primary copy locking, and (c) distributed two-phase locking.

Centralized Two-Phase Locking. In this scheme, one site (node) is responsible for managing all locking activities. This means that in the entire distributed database system, only one site has a lock manager. Any lock request from any node is directed to this site, which makes the decision and informs the requesting node. This approach is also called the *primary site* two-phase algorithm [19, 20]. A number of sites are usually involved in processing a transaction. One of these sites is called the *coordinating site,* which is also responsible for sending a node's locking request for the transaction to the central locking site. The other sites are called *participating sites* of that transaction. The centralized locking site only provides the locking service and does not send the operations (subtransactions) to participants, which is done by the coordinating site. In the case of partial and full database replication, the coordinator is responsible for selecting participating sites and completing updates for global consistency.

Primary Copy Two-Phase Locking. The centralized two-phase scheme suffers with a single point of failure and other performance problems [21, 22]. To minimize and eliminate some of these problems, the locking responsibility is distributed to multiple sites. Each lock manager is now responsible for a subset of data items. The node executing a part of the transaction sends lock requests to the appropriate lock manager. Once a copy of a data item is locked, then, in case of full or partial replication, all copies of the data item are implicitly locked. In this a way, the locked copy of the data item serves as the primary copy of the data item.

Distributed Two-Phase Locking. In this approach, all nodes can serve as a lock manager. In the case of a database partition, this algorithm degenerates to the centralized two-phase scheme. The coordinator sends lock requests to all participating sites that are responsible for managing the execution of their part of the transaction. As a result, all of the participants do not have to send a "lock granted" message back to the coordinator of the transaction. At the end of the execution, a participant just sends an "end of processing" message to the coordinator of the transaction. A distributed two-phase locking scheme was used in System R* [23] and in NonStoop SQL [24–26].

5.3 SUMMARY

This chapter introduced a number of concurrency control mechanisms for database systems to the readers. A two-phase locking scheme is most commonly used in centralized as well as distributed database systems, and all other schemes remain as topics of intensive investigation. The objective of the chapter is to encourage the readers to analyze the applicability of these schemes for mobile database systems. A detailed analysis of their applicability to mobile systems is presented in Chapter 6. Intuitively, because of their high communication and locking overheads, they would not perform satisfactorily in mobile database systems. The overhead generated by them cannot be handled by mobile databases that are highly resource-constrained systems.

EXERCISES

5.1 Explain the role of concurrency control mechanisms in managing serializable executions of concurrent transactions.

5.2 Prove that if the two-phase policy is violated, then it may not be possible to serialize the execution of concurrent transactions.

5.3 How many different types of lock modes are there in multigranularity locking, and what are they? Draw a compatibility matrix for these lock modes.

5.4 Explain the phantom problem. How does it arise? Why does it arise only in dynamic databases? Give a real-life example of a phantom problem and develop a scheme to handle it efficiently. Identify the phantom record in your example.

5.5 Do you think a lock conversion may give rise to a phantom problem? Explain your answer.

5.6 Consider developing your own concurrency control mechanism based on dynamic attributes of a transaction.

5.7 In the event of a conflict in a concurrent execution that is under a two-phase locking policy, if the requestor (transaction requesting a lock) or the holder (transaction has the lock on the data item) is immediately rolled back (no blocking), then deadlock cannot occur. First show with an example and then provide proof.

REFERENCES

1. A. Silberschatz, P. Galvin, and G. Gagne, *Operating System Concepts*, John Wiley & Sons, Hoboken, NJ, 2002.

2. V. Kumar, *Performance of Concurrency Control Mechanisms in Database Systems*, Prentice-Hall, Englewood Cliffs, NJ, 1996.

3. J. Robinson, Design of Concurrency Controls for Transaction Processing Systems, Ph.D. Thesis, Carnegie Mellon University, Pittsburg, 1982.

4. P. A. Bernstein, J. B. Rothnie, N. Goodman, Jr., and C. H. Papadimitriou, The Concurrency Control Mechanisms of SDD-1: A System for Distributed Databases (The Fully Redundant Case). *IEEE Transactions on Software Engineering*, Vol. 4, No. 3, May 1978, 154–168.

5. K. P. Eswaran, J. N. Gray, R. A. Lorie, and I. L. Traiger, The Notion of Consistency and Predicate Locks in a Database System. *Communications of the ACM*, Vol. 19, No. 11, Nov. 1976, 624–633.

6. P. A. Bernstein, V. Hadzilacos, and N. Goodman, *Concurrency Control and Recovery in Database Systems*, Addison-Wesley, Reading, MA, 1987.

7. V. Kumar, Performance Comparison of Some Database Concurrency Control Mechanisms based on Two-Phase Locking, Timestamping and Mixed Approach. *Information Sciences*, Vol. 51, No. 3, 1990, 221–261.

8. D. J. Rosencrantz, R. E. Sterns, and P. M. Lewis, System Level Concurrency Control for Distributed Database Systems, *ACM Transactions on Database Systems*, Vol. 3, No. 2, June 1978, 178–198.

9. H. T. Kung and J. T. Robinson, On Optimistic Methods of Concurrency Control, *ACM Transaction of Database Systems*, Vol. 6, No. 2, 1981, 213–226.

10. V. Kumar and N. Gaddipati, An Efficient CCM KRISHNA for High Contention Environment and Its Performance Comparison with WDL. *Data and Knowledge Engineering*, Vol. 34, 2000, 39–76.

11. V. Kumar, KRISHNA—An Efficient CCM Based on Dynamic Attributes of Transactions and Its Performance. *Data and Knowledge Engineering*, Vol. 21, 1997, 281–296.

12. V. Kumar and M. Hsu, A Superior Two-Phase Locking Algorithm and its Performance, *Information Sciences*, Vol. 54, No. 1, 2, 1991, 147–168.

13. V. Kumar, Concurrent Operations on Extendible Hashing and Its Performance, *Communications of the ACM*, Vol. 33, No. 6, June 1990, 681–694.

14. V. Kumar, Performance Comparison of Some Database Concurrency Control Mechanisms Based on Two-Phase Locking, Timestamping and Mixed Approach, *Information Sciences*, Vol. 51, No. 3, 1990, 221–261.

15. V. Kumar, Concurrency on extendible Hashing, *Information Processing Letters*, Vol. 30, No. 6, April 1989, 35–41.

16. P. Franaszek and J. T. Robinson, Limitations of Concurrency in Transaction Processing. *ACM Transactions on Database Systems*, Vol. 10, No. 1, March 1985, 1–28.

17. R. Balter, P. Berard, and P. Decitre, Why Control of Concurrency Level in Distributed Systems Is More Fundamental than Deadlock Management. In *Proceedings, ACM PODC*, Ottawa, Canada, August 1982, pp. 183–193.

18. A. Burger and V. Kumar, PRABHA—A Distributed Concurrency Control Algorithm. In *ACM Annual Computer Science Conference*, 1990, pp. 392–397.

19. P. A. Alsberg and J. D. Day, A Principle for Resilient Sharing of Distributed Resources. In *Proceedings, 2nd International Conference on Software Engineering*, 1976, pp. 562–570.

20. T. Özsu and P. Valduriez, *Principles of Distributed Database Systems*, Prentice-Hall, Englewood Cliffs, NJ, 1999.

21. T. Özsu, Performance Comparison of Distributed vs Centralized Locking Algorithms in Distributed Database Systems. In *Proceedings, 5th International Conference on Distributed Computing Systems*, May 1985, pp. 254–261.

22. T. M. Koon and T. Özsu, Performance Comparison of Resilient Concurrency Control Algorithms for Distributed Databases. In *Proceedings, 2nd International Conference on Data Engineering*, February 1986, pp. 565–573.

23. C. Mohan, B. Lindsey, and R. Obermarck, Transaction Management in R* Distributed Database Management System, *ACM Transactions on Database Systems*, Vol. 11, No. 4, December 1986, 378–396.

24. The Tandem Database Group. NonStop SQL—A Distributed High-Performance, High-Availability Implementation of SQL. In *Proceedings, International Workshop on High Performance Transaction Systems*, September 1987, pp. 60–104.

25. The Tandem Performance Group. A benchmark of NonStop SQL on the Debit Credit Transaction. In *Proceedings, ACM SIGMOD Conference on Management of Data*, June 1988, pp. 337–341.

26. A. Borr, High Performance SQL through Low-Level System Integration. In *Proceedings, ACM SIGMOD Conference on Management of Data*, June 1988, pp. 342–349.

27. M. Hsu and B. Zhang, Performance Evaluation of Cautious Waiting. *ACM Transactions on Database Systems*, Vol. 17, No. 3, 1992, 477–512.

CHAPTER 6

EFFECT OF MOBILITY ON DATA PROCESSING

This chapter discusses the effect of all aspects of mobility on data processing. First, we identify all types of mobility a data processor (cell phone, PDA, laptop, etc.) can experience, and then we discuss in detail the effect of each type of mobility on data processing. The relationship between mobility and data processing is useful in developing an efficient database partition and distribution schemes to improve data availability. A mobile database system must have the highest degree of data availability to minimize the cost of data processing and improve the response time. This chapter provides necessary information for developing efficient schemes for processing mobile transactions, recovering a database from any kind of failure, and improving quality of services.

6.1 INTRODUCTION

In recent years the work discipline has become highly dynamic with the introduction of "mobility in action." The concept "continuous connectivity in mobile space" allows the workforce to actively perform necessary tasks independent of its status (mobile or static). This is especially true for information management activities such as sending and receiving e-mails, web browsing, internet shopping, and so on. Personal and terminal mobility have become indispensable components of a highly efficient workforce and turn any location and situation into a job office. Thus, a manager, while traveling in a car, on a plane, or sitting on a beach, a person can create his job office

Fundamentals of Pervasive Information Management Systems, Revised Edition. Vijay Kumar.
© 2013 John Wiley & Sons, Inc. Published 2013 by John Wiley & Sons, Inc.

on the spot and can access necessary information to complete his tasks. It is quite obvious that this type of work environment provides increased productivity because the traveling time becomes available for completing the tasks at hand. For example, a manager on a plane can supervise the activities of his employees, can evaluate their performance, can decide their salary raises, can finalize the next leg of his travel plans, and so on.

The recent advances in wireless technology have made it possible to achieve "continuous connectivity in mobile space." The technology has managed to provide the convenience of smart phones, wireless web browsing, and use of e-mail facilities. Wireless networks are widely used within a business environment to connect laptops and other portables and have significantly increased the functionality of mobile devices. Laptops can now easily store and process large databases that were previously possible only by heavyweight stationary servers. The power and capacity of PDAs are continuously increasing, and they can perform a number of database tasks quite efficiently. As a result, more and more users have begun using wireless portable devices not only to communicate with each other but also to manage their day-to-day activities and information. These changing ways for interacting with the information space has formatted the business world and identified it with the name "Mobile Commerce (M-Commerce)." The following examples illustrate the existing power of mobility in action [1].

■ EXAMPLE 6.1

In busy city traffic, employees of companies spend a significant amount of time using public transportation. They can effectively use this time by connecting to their corporate database using mobile units and complete some of their tasks of the day. Managers can schedule their employees' tasks, supervisors can supervise ongoing activities, and so on. Since today's networks are quite reliable and provide satisfactory speed, the quality of task management will not suffer. In fact, real-time processes on the production floor can be managed during commuting time.

■ EXAMPLE 6.2

Automobiles of the future can use many mobility aware applications to access information like news, music, road conditions, and so on. Additionally, cars driving in the same area can build an ad hoc network for fast information exchange or to keep a safe distance from each other. A car can study the current road conditions and transmit this information to another car coming that way. In case of an emergency, the cars will have the capability to automatically call an ambulance or the police. Thus, a wireless notification system can be developed that will automatically notify agencies such as the police, a hospital, and so on, and prevents the occurrence of life-threatening events such as vehicle rollovers, farming accidents, and so on. A system called *NOW (Notification On Wireless)* [2] has been developed at the University of Missouri—Kansas City. NOW is very innovative, yet simple in design, using simple and currently existing components and technology to create a powerful system. NOW assures users that in the event of a vehicle rollover, the necessary information would be immediately and seamlessly transmitted through wireless channels to the appropriate emergency service provider. This kind of automatic notification is especially crucial for accident victims, trauma patients, and so on.

■ EXAMPLE 6.3

Users can access services depending on their actual location. For example, a user might query the local wireless network to find the whereabouts of a nearby restaurant, or his current geographical location; also a local network itself might advertise such data that the user can access and is similar to listening to music on a particular channel. A number of location services are being deployed to help travelers reach their destinations and find their friends using mobile gadgets.

■ EXAMPLE 6.4

Friends finder or location finder or tracker (services that track the movement of a known object such as a cell phone) are commonly available on nearly all mobile devices. This is a highly useful mobile facility that provides instant location information about the desirable objects.

■ EXAMPLE 6.5

In mobile commerce applications such as auctions, it is expected that a typical auction might bring together millions of interested parties. Updates based on bids must be disseminated promptly and consistently to appropriate data partitions located at various locations. A mobile system may use a broadcast facility to transmit the current state of the auction while allowing the client to communicate its updates using low bandwidth uplink channels. Broadcast-based data dissemination is likely to be the major mode of information transfer in mobile computing and wireless environments.

6.2 EFFECT OF MOBILITY ON THE MANAGEMENT OF DATA

The above set of examples illustrates issues related to data partition and their distribution that database systems have to deal with in real life. Unlike conventional distributed database systems, in mobile database systems (MDS), the entire database cannot be stored at any mobile node. An MDS, however, cannot function without the support of conventional systems. It is, therefore, important to understand how mobility affects conventional data processing approaches for achieving a seamless integration [3].

In conventional distributed database systems there is one common characteristic: all components, especially the processing units, are stationary. A user must go to a fixed location (personal mobility) to use the system. The entire database, or a part of it, can be stored at any node and may migrate from one node to another. The data partition (fragmentation) and distribution and its movement are usually coded in the underlying data distribution schema. In mobile database systems, because of the random movement of mobile devices, conventional data distribution schema would not work. Consider, for example, the Missouri tax database. There is no point in replicating it to Texas' tax database because these data are not required there.

In mobile database systems, we require both static and dynamic data distribution schema. The dynamic scheme is needed to move required data with the mobile unit when it goes from one cell to another while processing transactions. Consider the case of traveling salesmen who visit a number of states and sell a few items. When these salesmen get orders from customers, they update their databases. It is much easier and more efficient to update the local copy (fragment) of the database to maintain consistency. This can be achieved if the fragment follows the salesmen from one state to another. County appraisers usually go to other states for property appraisals, and the required portion of the database may go with their laptop (mobile unit).

6.2.1 Data Fragmentation

The integration of geographical mobility data processing capability is an excellent way to efficiently salvage time wasted in traveling. However, it gives rise to a number of problems related to the maintenance of ACID properties in the presence of personal and terminal mobility. A number of these problems are addressed in the following sections.

The ACID properties of a transaction must be maintained in all data management activities in the presence of mobility. In conventional systems, concurrency control mechanisms and database recovery schemes make sure that ACID is maintained. In mobile and wireless platforms, the nature of data processing remains the same but the situations under which the data are processed change. It is, therefore, important to understand the effect of mobility on data partition (fragmentation), data distribution, and its availability on ACID properties of transactions.

Conventional Database Partition. In conventional distributed database systems, the database is partitioned in three different ways [4]:

Horizontal Partition. A horizontal fragmentation of a relation provides the right subset of the relation for processing queries. The fragmentation is composed on the set of rows (tuples) that satisfies a set criteria. This type of fragmentation is appropriate where an organization needs information about a set of local customers. This fits well with mobile database requirements. The fragments must satisfy (a) completeness, (b) reconstruction, and (c) disjointedness.

Vertical Partition. In a vertical fragmentation, a set of attributes (columns) of a relation is created, depending upon the requirements of the application. This fragmentation is appropriate for an organization that maintains only a portion of its clients' information such as names, addresses, phone numbers, and account numbers.

Hybrid Partition. This is also referred to as *nested* or *mixed fragmentation*. In some cases, only a horizontal fragmentation or only a vertical fragmentation is not sufficient.

To create the required subset, therefore, a vertical fragmentation is followed by a horizontal fragmentation or vice versa. This fragmentation is appropriate for an organization that maintains a specific subset of information about its clients. In fact, nearly all organizations use this fragmentation. For example, a bank mainly keeps account and credit history information about its customers. It may not need their medical information to manage their financial assets.

A hybrid partition works well for MDS because it allows (a) a location-dependent partition, (b) selective full replication, and (c) caching of a part of a partition or the entire database dynamically. Caching may be pre-planned if the mobility of the mobile unit is known in advance (for example, local commuters or traveling salesmen), or may be ad hoc if the mobile unit roams randomly.

6.2.2 Data Distribution

In conventional distributed database systems, data distribution can be done in three ways: (a) partitioned, (b) partial replication, and (c) full replication.

Partitioned. The entire database is divided (fragmented) into multiple unique fragments, and each fragment is stored at a particular site (node). Thus, there is only one partition at one site, which means the distribution is dedicated to a particular node; as a result, the data availability is quite poor. If a node is not available for some reason (busy or failure, etc.), then that partition cannot be accessed. On the other hand, database recovery is easier than other cases (partial and full replication). In a conventional database, this kind of distribution may not be necessary. In mobile databases, however, some kind of database partition is required because of the processor mobility. It introduces the concept of *location-dependent data* (LDD) that restricts distribution flexibility. For example, the sales tax data of Kansas City may not be useful to replicate at Boston's tax database if these cities do not share the same tax policies and regulations. This leads to a selective replication of partitions for MDS, and a conventional full replication option may not be meaningful.

Partial Replication. In this distribution, a subset of fragments is replicated at more than one node. The selection of fragments to be replicated depends on a number of criteria such as frequency of access at that node, update frequency, and so on. This distribution can be effectively utilized in MDS, but it would be under a number of constraints.

Full Replication. In this distribution, the entire database is fully replicated at all nodes. This distribution mode offers maximum reliability and availability but significantly increases update and storage costs. Since the mobile nodes of MDS have processing and storage constraints, this replication type is not recommended.

Data Distribution for MDS. In MDS, database servers (DBSs) are fixed database nodes and mobile units serve as mobile nodes. A mobile node caches fragments on a needed basis because it continuously moves from one cell to another, generating needs for different location-dependent fragments. In one cell, it may need to cache one location-dependent partition; and in another cell, another partition. One or more mobile units may cache more than one fragment under the constraints of location-dependent data—for example, Kansas City's tax data and the geographical locations of its hotels. This becomes necessary if a mobile unit roams throughout the entire city that is covered by a number of cells. It is the most common scenario in MDS and models partial replication.

Location-Dependent Data (LDD). This is a class of data where data values are tightly linked to a specific geographical location. There is 1:1 mapping between a data value set and the region it serves. For example, a *city tax* data value is functionally dependent on the city's tax policy. It is possible that all cities may use the same city tax schema, but each city will map to a unique instance of the schema. Some other examples of LDD are zip codes, telephone area codes, and so on. In contrast, some classes of data have no association with any location; for example, social security numbers (SSN), street names, rainfall and snowfall totals, and so on. The value of an SSN or a street name do not identify any specific location. The same street names may exist in Boston, Seattle, or Kansas City. These are called location-independent data (LID), and the conventional data processing approach interprets all data as location-independent data.

Definition 6.1 *The geographic domain, G, is the entire area covered by the cells of a cellular network. Thus $G = \{C_1 + C_2 +, \ldots, + C_n\}$, where C_i is a cell. A mobile unit can freely roam in the entire G while remaining connected to the network through handoff.*

Definition 6.2 *A location is a precise point within the geographic domain (G). It represents the smallest identifiable position in the domain. It can be represented in terms of a latitude/longitude (L/L) pair. Each location is identified by a specific id, L. Also, $G = \bigcup L, \forall L$.*

Location-Dependent Query. LDD gives rise to *location-dependent queries (LDQ)* and *location-aware queries (LAQ)*. An LAQ needs LDD for computing the result. For example, *What is the distance to the airport from here?* is an LAQ because the value of the distance depends on the geographical location of the mobile unit that initiated the query. If the coordinates of the location "here" are not known then the query cannot be processed. Consider a situation when a person is driving to the airport to catch a flight. He is running late and so every 5 minutes he repeats the query, *How far is the airport now?* Each answer to this identical query will be different, but correct, because the geographical location of "here" is continuously changing. A similar situation arises in processing the query, *Where am I?* I will continuously ask this query after driving randomly to some direction and will receive different correct answers. (I may get completely lost, but this is a different matter altogether!). These kinds of situations exist only when the geographical coordinates of the origin of query continuously change with time. This is a common situation in everyday life.

If a traveler initiates the query, *What is the sales tax of this city?* while passing through that city, then the answer must be related to the current city and not to the next city where he arrives soon after initiating the query. A similar situation arises in listening to a radio station while traveling. When the traveler crosses the broadcast boundary, the same frequency tunes to a different radio station and the broadcast program changes completely.

In processing a location-dependent query, the necessary LDD and the geographical location of the origin of the query must be known. This requires that the system must map the location with the data to obtain the correct LDD. A number of service providers have location discovery facilities that can be used to access LDD.

Location Aware Query. This type of query includes references to a particular location either by name or by suitable geographical coordinates. For example, *What is the distance between Dallas and Kansas City?* is a location aware query because it refers to both locations, Kansas City and Dallas. The answer to this query, or any location aware query, does not depend on the geographical location where the query is initiated and, as a result, the mobility of the processing unit does not affect the result of the query.

6.2.3   Location Dependent Data Distribution

The 1:1 mapping between the data and its geographical location restricts the application of the three data distribution approaches that were discussed earlier. The horizontal fragmentation and vertical fragmentation of a relational database must implicitly or explicitly include the location information. The partition of the database, however, becomes easier because the decision is solely based on the location parameter. The concept of a *data region* is helpful to understand the distribution of database partitions in mobile databases.

Definition 6.3   *A data region is a geographical region or a geographical cell, and every geographical point of this region satisfies 1:1 mapping with data.*

Figure 6.1 illustrates data distribution for the data partition scheme. It assumes Kansas city as a data region for city sales tax. The entire data region is enclosed in a cell. Every location of Kansas City satisfies 1:1 mapping between the city tax value and the location. The entire Kansas City database is partitioned into subdivisions identified by P_1 through P_9. All subdivisions map to the same city sales tax and, as a result, all subdivisions charge the same city tax. If every subdivision maintains its own database, then at each subdivision a database partition can be stored. A mobile unit that moves among subdivisions will see the same consistent value of a data item.

■ EXAMPLE 6.6

A hotel chain or franchise can be used to demonstrate the problem of data replication and its consistency for mobile databases. A particular hotel has a number

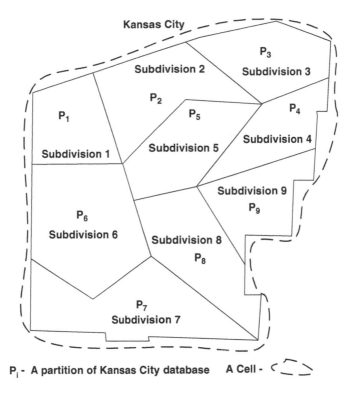

Figure 6.1 Database partition for LDD.

of branches across the nation. Each branch offers identical services; however, its room rent, policies, facilities, and so on, depend on the branch location. Thus, the same-sized suite may cost more in Dallas than in Kansas City. The data consistency constraints in Kansas City might be different than in Dallas, because of local taxes and environmental policies. Each branch may share the same schema, but their instantiations (values for the data) may differ.

In a partial replication approach, the same partition can be replicated at more than one subdivision. For example, at subdivision 1 and subdivision 2, P_1 and P_2 can be replicated without affecting the consistency. In a full replication, the entire database can also be replicated and used in all subdivisions in a consistent manner, but it may not be necessary if a subdivision does not need the partition of another subdivision.

The situation does not change if the data region is covered by multiple cells. A mobile unit can move from one subdivision to another and use the same data item in both subdivisions. However, the situation changes when a cell covers two or more data regions as shown in Figure 6.2. Data of one region cannot be replicated in another region. For example, the sales tax rate of Kansas City (region 1) cannot be replicated in Springfield (region 2). This constraint requires that a location-dependent query in

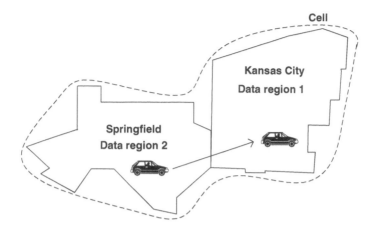

Figure 6.2   Database replication restriction.

Springfield must be processed in Springfield before the client enters Kansas City. This restriction also affects mobile data caching. A mobile unit must clear its cache before entering another data region to maintain global consistency.

Since the distribution of LDD is dependent on geographical locations, its distribution is defined as *spatial distribution* to distinguish it from the conventional distribution that is called *temporal distribution*. In spatial distribution, *spatial replication* is used; and in temporal distribution, *temporal replication* is used.

Definition 6.4   *Spatial replication refers to copies of data objects that may have different correct data values at any point in time. Each value is correct within a given location area. One of these copies is called a Spatial Replica.*

Definition 6.5   *Temporal replication refers to copies of data objects, all of which have only one consistent data value at any point in time. One of these copies is called a temporal replica.*

Temporal distribution mainly considers the local availability of data and the cost of communication; but for spatial distribution, geographical location must also be included. The identification of data as spatial and temporal affects the definition of consistency.

Figure 6.3 illustrates how the database is distributed among the DBSs and cached (replicated) at the MUs. Location-free data—for example, D_1, D_2, and D_4—can be replicated at all regions and have the same values (temporal replica). This is one of the reasons that temporal replicas can be processed using the *read-one write-all* version of distributed two-phase locking concurrency control mechanisms. A spatial replica, on the other hand, must be processed individually. For example, the schema of the location-dependent data, D_3, can also be replicated to all regions, but each region will have a different correct value. Three basic types of replications of the

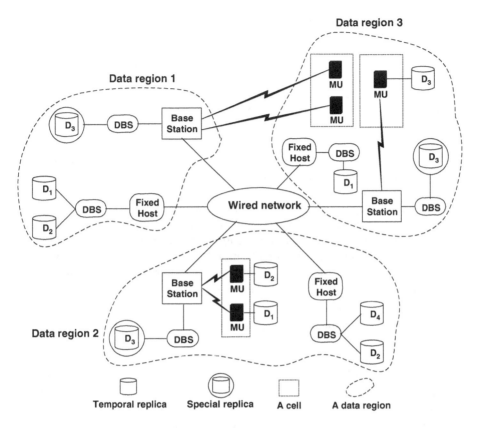

Figure 6.3 Different replication types.

database are shown in this figure: (a) "no replication," (b) "traditional distributed replication" (temporal replication), and (c) "location-dependent replication" (spatial replication). Data object D_4 has no replication, and data objects D_1 and D_2 are traditional replicas that are copied to data regions 1 and 2. The distributed replicas are copies of each other that may have different values temporarily, but there is only one correct value. The location-dependent data D_3 have multiple copies and multiple correct values. The correct value is determined by location (data region). It is replicated at all three regions. Each region has one correct value for D_3, and it may also have other temporal replicas in that region. The value of D_3 that exists at data region 3 is replicated at an MU, but it has the same value as that at the DBS. This is an example of temporal replication (caching) of location-dependent data. For example, information about phone numbers is spatially replicated where the data region granularity is associated with local phone company domains. Hotel information could have a data region granularity associated with postal codes (zip codes). Each data object uniquely determines the type of replication (none, temporal, spatial) and the data cell granularity (universe, zip code, metropolitan area as defined by counties).

Table 6.1   Summary of Data Replication in MDS

	Replication	Replication	Replication
Copies	One	Multiple	Multiple
Correct Values	One	One per time	One per location and time
Architecture	Centralized	Distributed	Mobile
Mobility	No	No	Yes

Table 6.1 summarizes the differences between the three types of data replication. Note that replicas at a cache at an MU are really temporal replicas; that is, there may be temporal replicas of spatial replicas (D_3 in Figure 6.3). That is, within a given area there may be temporal replicas of location-dependent data. For example, an MU could hoard a temporal copy of hotel information for Kansas City. This would allow a traveler to leisurely examine this location-dependent data while disconnected. Mobility has no effect on temporal replication but does on spatial replication. This means that as an MU moves from one data region to another, different values from the spatial replicas may be needed for processing queries.

6.2.4   Effect of Mobility on ACID Properties

Effect of Mobility on Atomicity. The property of atomicity guarantees that partial results of a failed or uncommitted transaction do not exist in the database. If a transaction fails to commit, then all its effects are removed from the database. The mobility does not alter the definition of atomicity but makes its enforcement quite difficult and time-consuming. Consider the situation where a mobile unit moves to multiple cells while processing a transaction T_i. In this situation, the execution history of T_i will contain the information of all the cells the mobile unit visited. Its log may reside at these cells and must be accessed to rollback T_i if it fails. This will require reaching out to base stations of these cells to unify the entire log. These steps make the entire rollback operation quite time-consuming. In a conventional system the log is stored at the server and is readily available for completing a rollback. In a mobile system, conventional logging approach does not work satisfactorily because a mobile unit gets connected and disconnected to several servers when it is mobile. There are a number of ways to manage the transaction log in mobile systems that are discussed in the recovery section.

Effect of Mobility on Consistency. In a centralized or distributed environment, there is only one correct value for each data object. The term *mutual consistency* is used to indicate that all values of the same data item converge to this one correct value [4]. A replicated database is said to be in a *mutually consistent state* if all copies have the exact same value [4]. In addition, a database is said to be in a *consistent state* if all integrity constraints identified for the database are followed [4]. In a mobile database system the presence of LDD defines two types of consistency: *spatial consistency* and *temporal consistency.*

Definition 6.6   *Spatial consistency indicates that the values of all data items of a spatial replication are associated with one and only one data region, and they satisfy consistency constraints as defined by the region. Thus, there is 1:1 mapping between the data value and the region it serves.*

Every mobile unit that initiates transactions in a region must get a consistent view of the data in that region, and the database must guarantee that the effect of the execution of the transactions is durable in that region. To achieve this state, the region must satisfy temporal consistency as well.

Definition 6.7   *Temporal consistency indicates that all data item values must satisfy a given set of integrity constraints. A database is temporally consistent if all temporal replicas (replication of data items at multiple sites) of a data item have the same value.*

Effect of Mobility on Isolation.   Transaction isolation ensures that a transaction does not interfere with the execution of another transaction. Isolation is normally enforced by some concurrency control mechanism. As with atomicity, isolation is needed to ensure that consistency is preserved.

In mobile database systems, a mobile unit may visit multiple data regions and process LDD and location-free data. The important thing is to ensure that execution fragments (subtransactions) satisfy isolation at the execution fragment level. It will do so under some concurrency control mechanism that must recognize the relationship between a data item and the transaction that uses it. The mechanism must enforce isolation in each region separately leading to the isolation for the entire transaction. This is quite different from a conventional distributed database system that does not recognize spatial replication and, thus, does not enforce regional isolation.

Effect of Mobility on Durability.   Durability guarantees the persistence of committed data in the database. In mobile database systems, the durability is regional as well as global. Global durability is enforced for temporal replicas and regional durability for spatial replicas. For example, if a customer has accounts at various banks in different cities, then each account will be subjected to its bank's policies. In this scenario, it is possible that a withdrawal transaction that withdraws money from these accounts may be subjected to location-dependent processing at some banks. This is a common scenario in international banking. The system then must guarantee durability at each bank that must lead to a global durability for maintaining consistency.

Effect of Mobility on Commit.   Transaction commitment is not affected by mobility; however, because of the presence of location-dependent data (LDD), a *location commit* is defined. A location commit binds a transaction commit to a region. For example, a department manager initiates the following transaction: *Reserve 5 seats in a vegetarian restaurant located 1 mile from here* on his mobile unit. This is a location-dependent update transaction and must be processed in the region where the restaurant is located. The confirmation must be sent back (on time) to the manager.

This notification becomes necessary if the manager is waiting for the confirmation. The database server, responsible for processing this transaction, must first map the location of the query and the location of the restaurant and then access the correct database for making the reservation. The entire execution remains confined to the region until the transaction commits. Thus, the process of commit is identical to the conventional notion of transaction commit; however, the requirements for the commit are different. It is called *location-dependent commit* to differentiate it from a conventional notion of commit.

Definition 6.8   *An execution fragment, e_i, satisfies a location-dependent commit iff the fragment operations terminate with a commit operation and a location to data mapping exists. Thus, all operations in e_i operate on spatial replicas defined on the location identified by location mapping. The commit is thus associated with a unique location L.*

Effect of Connectivity on Transaction Processing.   In a mobile environment an MU can process its workload in a *continuously connected* mode or in a *disconnected* mode or in an *intermittent connected* mode.

Connectivity Mode.   In this mode, an MU is continuously connected to the database server. It has the option of caching required data for improving performance or it can request data from the server any time during transaction processing. If necessary, it can enter into a doze mode to save power and become active again. However, this mode is expensive to maintain and is not necessary for processing transactions because they do not access data continuously or at every location. Once a transaction gets the desired data then the mobil unit can continue to process it locally.

Disconnected Mode.   In this mode an MU voluntarily disconnects from the server after refreshing the cache and continues to process workloads locally. At a fixed time, it connects and sends its entire cache to the server using wireless or wired link. The server installs the contents of the cache in such a way that global consistency is maintained. In real life, this kind of transaction processing exists at various *business-process* tasks. Consider the case of a department chairperson who downloads faculty and student evaluations on a laptop and processes faculty raises while traveling. Once the task is complete, the data are locally saved and the main database is updated when the chairperson returns to his/her office.

Intermittent Connected.   This mode is similar to the disconnected mode, but here the MU can be disconnected anytime by the system or voluntarily by the user. The disconnection by the system may be due to a lack of channels, a low battery, security, and so on. The user may disconnect the MU to save power or to process data locally because communication with a server is not required for some time. Unlike the disconnected mode, the intermittent mode does not have any fixed time for connecting and disconnecting the MU.

This type of connectivity is useful for agents dealing with customers—for example, insurance agents, UPS, or FedEx postal deliveries, etc. For postal delivery, the entire day's delivery can be defined as a long workflow. The agent delivers packages to a house and locally updates the cached database on the mobile device. At the end of the day or at a prescribed time, the agent connects and ships the entire cache to the server through a wired or wireless channel. It is possible that the agent may connect to the server to report the status of the high priority shipment. The stock evaluator in a supermarket also works in a similar manner. After recording the stock level, the agent connects to the server for updating the main database. Connection on demand is also a form of intermittent connectivity because a user's need for data is usually unpredictable.

The database consistency in a disconnected or intermittently connected mode is hard to define and maintain. This becomes relatively difficult in an e-commerce or m-commerce environment that can be explained with a simple example. Consider a company called Pani* Inc., which sells water purifiers aggressively. Two agents, Kumar and Prasad, go house to house in a subdivision, demonstrate the water filter and try to get the household's business. Suppose the company has 100 water purifier units in the warehouse and wants to sell them aggressively. Pani Inc. does not want to take a chance, so it asks each agent to download 100 units on his laptop and sell them in a day. In this way, if each agent sells 50 units, then the job is done. Now, suppose with a bit of luck and with some persuasion, Kumar and Prasad both sell 100 units without being aware of the other's success. This puts the database in a real mess. Pani Inc. handles the situation using a "back order" scheme and some reduction in the cost of the water purifiers. So in this situation, how can someone define the consistent state of the database? One way could be "existing inventory + back order", but this is quite risky. If Pani Inc. could not supply all back orders within the promised time, then some orders may have to be rolled back; as a result, it may be difficult to maintain ACID constraints.

Managing the processing of ACID transactions in a connected state is easy and can be handled in a conventional manner. However, their processing in disconnected and intermittent connected modes requires new caching consistency approaches, new locking approaches, new commit protocol, new rollback and abort schemes, and most importantly, a new transaction model or a new way of processing ACID transactions.

6.3 SUMMARY

This chapter discussed the effect of mobility on the management of data in terms of database partitions and their distribution and introduced the concepts of location-dependent data (LDD), location-free data, location-dependent query (LDQ), and location-aware query. It identifies different types of connectivity and linked these

---

*Pani is a Hindi word that means water.

concepts to explain the effect of mobility on ACID properties of transactions. A clear understanding of this relationship is necessary for the development of a mobile transaction model and its management. In the next chapter, various ways of executing ACID transactions on a mobile database system and on mobile transaction models are presented.

EXERCISES

6.1   Explain processor mobility from data management and transaction execution viewpoints and problems it creates.

6.2   Explain how data and transaction management are affected in the presence of processor mobility. Give examples in support of your answer.

6.3   Explain the difference among location-dependent, location-aware, and location-free queries and data. Do you think location-dependent data are always a temporal type? Explain your answer and give examples.

6.4   Discuss the effect of mobility on ACID properties. Do you think that all ACID properties are affected equally or some more than others? Explain your answer.

6.5   Discuss the problem of data consistency in intermittent connectivity. Do you think it is possible to define consistency in this type of connectivity? Explain and give examples.

6.6   Identify and explain the database partition and data distribution issues in mobile database systems. Why are the conventional database partition and distribution not suitable for mobile database systems? Explain and give examples.

REFERENCES

1. D. Barbara, Mobile Computing and Databases—A Survey, *IEEE Transactions on Knowledge and Data Engineering*, Vol. 11, No. 1, January 1999, 108–117.
2. D. Acharya, V. Kumar, G. M. Gaddis, and N. Garvin, SAVE: A Wireless Java Enabled Automobile Accident Reporting System, *International Journal of Intelligent Defense Support Systems*, Vol. 1, No. 3, 2008, 254–270.
3. E. Pitroura and B. Bhargava, Revising Transaction Concepts for Mobile Computing, *Proceedings of Workshop on Mobile Computing Systems and Application*, 1994, pp. 164–168.
4. M. Tamer Ožsu and P. Valduriez, *Principles of Distributed Database Systems*, Prentice-Hall, Englewood Cliffs, NJ, 1991.

CHAPTER 7

TRANSACTION MANAGEMENT IN MOBILE DATABASE SYSTEMS

This chapter discusses the management of transactions (processing, commit, correctness, etc.) in mobile database systems (MDS) using the reference architecture developed in Chapter 1. It was recognized in some of the earlier chapters that the conventional ACID transaction model is unable to satisfactorily manage mobile data processing requirements for successful execution of transactions. Some of the important reasons were the presence of *handoff*, which is unpredictable, the presence of *doze mode*, *disconnected mode*, and *forced disconnection*, the lack of necessary resources such as memory and wireless channels, the presence of location-dependent data, and so on. It was recognized that to manage data processing in the presence of these issues, a more powerful ACID transaction execution model that can handle mobility during data processing was highly desirable. A number of such execution models for executing ACID transactions were developed, and a few of them are discussed in this chapter. These execution models, unfortunately, are unable to handle location-dependent data satisfactorily; for this reason, mobile transaction models that included such a processing capability were developed. A few mobile transaction models are discussed in this chapter.

Concurrency control mechanisms (CCMs) or serialization mechanisms are essential for managing the execution of concurrent transactions correctly. A large volume of works on CCM for conventional database systems exists, but little work has been reported in this area for mobile database systems. This chapter discusses serialization techniques, transaction execution, and mobile transaction commitment. The chapter

Fundamentals of Pervasive Information Management Systems, Revised Edition. Vijay Kumar.
© 2013 John Wiley & Sons, Inc. Published 2013 by John Wiley & Sons, Inc.

also discusses a number of mobile database recovery issues and existing solutions in detail.

The topics covered in this chapter are highly research-oriented; and although a significant number of schemes have been proposed, none has been deployed yet. The chapter, therefore, identifies and presents the original scheme as described by the author(s) of the reports. The discussion clearly indicates the incremental understanding of mobile data processing and thinking trends. The chapter begins with a reference mobile database system.

7.1   MOBILE DATABASE SYSTEM

A reference architecture of a mobile database system (MDS) was presented in Chapter 1. We refer to the architecture to discuss the topic of this chapter.

A mobile database system provides full database and mobile communication functionalities [1]. It allows a mobile user to initiate transactions from anywhere and at anytime and guarantees their consistency-preserving execution. MDS does not use the web for accessing the database; the access is directly through wireless channels. In case of any kind of failure (transaction, system, or media), MDS guarantees database recovery. The reference architecture shown in Figure 7.1 provides the following essential properties.

- **Geographical mobility:** Clients (mobile units) are able to move around in the geographical space (G) without affecting their processing capability and continuous connectivity.

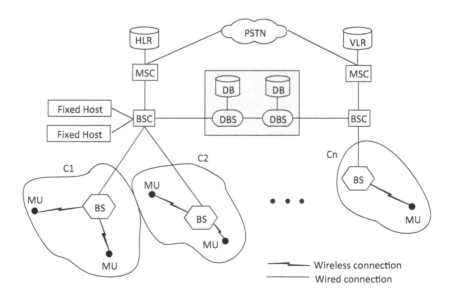

Figure 7.1   Reference architecture of a mobile database system.

- **Connection and disconnection:** A mobile unit (MU) is able to disconnect and reconnect with any database server (DBS) at any time through the base station (BS).
- **Data processing capability:** MUs have some database processing capability, and the database servers have full database processing capability.
- **Wireless communication:** An MU can communicate with the DBS and with any other client through a wireless network.
- **Transparency:** Although the mobility in data processing is introduced through cellular architecture, the data processing functions of MUs do not affect cellular communication.
- **Scalability:** At any time an MU can be added to, or an existing MU can be deleted from, the cellular network.

An MDS is a distributed multidatabase client/server system based on PCS or GSM. There are some differences in GSM and PCS architectures; however, they do not affect MDS functions. Database functionality is provided by a set of DBSs that are incorporated without affecting any aspect of the generic mobile network.

GSM and PCS systems were discussed in Chapter 2. The components of these systems are in fact, special-purpose computers responsible for connecting users with the system. The reference architecture of MDS is, therefore, described in terms of general-purpose computers such as personal computers, workstations, PDAs, cell phones, and so on.

In MDS, a set of general-purpose computers are interconnected through a high-speed wired network. These computers are categorized into *fixed hosts* (FHs) and *base stations* (BSs) or *mobile support stations* (MSSs). FHs are not fitted with transceivers, so they do not communicate with MUs. One or more BSs are connected with a base station controller (BSC) or cell site controller [2, 3] that coordinates the operation of the BSs using its own stored software programs when commanded by the mobile switching center (MSC). To coordinate with DBSs, some additional simple data processing capability is incorporated in the BSs. Unrestricted mobility in PCS and GSM is supported by a wireless link between BS and mobile units such as PDAs (personal digital assistants), laptop, cell phones, and so on. These mobile gadgets are referred to as mobile hosts (MHs) or mobile units (MUs) [2, 3]. BSs are fitted with transceivers and communicate with MUs through wireless channels. Each BS serves one cell whose size depends on the power of its BS. In reality, a high-powered BS is not used because of a number of factors (including health) [4]; rather, a number of low-power BSs are deployed for managing movement of the MUs.

To incorporate full database functionality, it is necessary to incorporate database servers (DBSs) to complete the MDS. They can be installed at the BSs or at FHs. There are, however, a number of problems with this setup. BSs and FHs are switches and perform specific switching tasks, which do not include database functions. In order to add database functions, the entire architecture of a BS (hardware and software) may have to be revised, which would be unacceptable from a mobile communication viewpoint. In addition to this, the setup will not be modular and scalable, and as a result, any change or enhancement in database components will interfere with data and voice communication. For these reasons, DBSs are connected to the mobile system through wired lines as separate nodes as shown in Figure 7.1. Each DBS can be reached by any BS or FH, and new DBSs can be connected and old ones can be taken out from the network without affecting mobile communication. The set of MSCs and the PSTN connects the MDS to the outside world.

A DBS communicates with an MU only through BSs. A mobile user remains connected on an average of 2 to 4 hours a day, and at all other times it must save battery power. To conserve power, a mobile unit can be switched to stay in (a) a powered off mode (not actively listening to the BS), (b) an idle mode (doze mode—not communicating but continuously listening to the BS), or (c) an active mode (communicating with another party, processing data, etc.) The unit can move from one cell to another in any of these modes. For example, a driver can switch its cell phone to save battery power while driving and may cross many cell boundaries. The total coverage area of an MDS is the sum of all its cell areas, that is, $\{C_1 + C_2 + \cdots + C_n\}$. As discussed in Chapter 2, the mobile unit encounters a handoff only in an active mode.

7.2 TRANSACTION EXECUTION IN MDS

A conventional distributed database system utilizes maximum parallelism in processing the workload to improve system performance. It implements parallel processing by fragmenting a transaction into a number of subtransactions, each of which is executed at a node. The entire execution requires a software module called *coordinator*, which manages the entire execution of the transaction leading to the termination of the transaction (commit or abort). The job of the coordinator is to distribute the fragments of a transaction to the processing nodes and to possibly provide resources to each fragment for execution and, finally, execute a protocol to commit the transaction.

There are mainly three ways to implement a coordinator: (a) centralized, (b) partially replicated, and (c) totally replicated. In the centralized approach, one of the nodes of the distributed database system serves as a coordinator for all transactions. In a partially replicated approach, a subset of nodes can serve as a coordinator; and in a fully replicated approach, all nodes can serve as a coordinator. In an MDS, because of resource limitations, only a centralized approach is feasible.

7.2.1 Identification of Coordinator in MDS

In an MDS, the identification of the coordinator nodes is not that well defined. A coordinator must have (a) direct and continuous communication with other nodes, (b) large storage, (c) a continuous power supply, and (d) high reliability and availability. Unlike conventional distributed database systems, there are several types of processing nodes in an MDS, but only some can play the role of a coordinator as discussed below:

- **MU:** An MU cannot provide continuous connectivity with the BS that it initially registered with because it is subjected to unpredictable *handoffs*, and it has a limited storage capacity and power supply source. Although it is a part of the cellular network, it is still a personal resource of a user who can disconnect it from the network at any time. Thus, an MU cannot serve as a coordinator.

- **DBS:** A *DBS* is continuously available and has sufficient storage capacity, but it has no direct communication with other nodes (DBSs and MUs) because it is not fitted with transceivers for wireless communication. Thus, a DBS cannot serve as a coordinator.

- **FH:** An FH is equipped with everything except transceivers. As a result, it cannot communicate with mobile devices that make it unfit to be a coordinator.

- **MSC:** An MSC seems to satisfy all the requirements of a coordinator. However, it has to use the services of a BS to reach a mobile unit. So this may not serve as a cost-effective coordinator.

- **BS:** A BS satisfies all the requirements of a coordinator. It is fitted with a transceiver, it can store and process data, it has direct communication with MUs and an MSC, and it can execute coordinator software. Furthermore, assigning it additional coordinator responsibilities through new applications is relatively easier. As a result, a BS is the ideal processing node to serve as a coordinator.

7.2.2 Transaction Initiation

A transaction in MDS can be initiated from a DBS or from an MU. It can be processed entirely at the MU where it was initiated (if the required data are available there) or it can be processed entirely at the DBS or at a combination of the two. If it is processed entirely at one node (origin node or any other) then the coordinator plays only a minor role in the execution and commitment of the transaction. When there is more than one node involved in the execution, then the following situations may arise.

- **Origin at MU:** Three processing scenarios are possible when a transaction originates at an MU: (a) The transaction executes at the MU and at a set of DBSs. The final result is sent to the MU, and updates are installed at the DBSs; (b) the transaction is processed only at a set of DBSs, and the final result goes to the MU; and (c) the transaction is processed entirely at the MU. It is important to note that no other MUs should be involved in the execution of this transaction because: (a) an MU is a personal processing resource of a user that can be disconnected or turned off by its owner any time, and (b) the owner of the MU may not like to share it with other users.

- **Origin at DBS:** A transaction originates at a DBS and executes either entirely at the DBS or at a number of DBSs. The involvement of other DBSs depends on the type of data distribution (partitioned, partial replication, or full replication). The final result goes to the DBS that initiates the transaction. Optionally, the result can go to the MU of the user who initiated the transaction.

7.2.3 Transaction Execution

When an MU initiates a transaction, it can be executed there (local execution) if it has the data required by the transaction. In this case, the MU executes and commits the transaction using its cached data. At the end of commit, the MU sends transaction updates to the DBSs that are installed by executing the same transaction there and sending the results to the user. If it cannot be entirely executed at the MU, then there are two options:

- **Transfer required data items from DBSs to the MU:** The MU identifies the set of data it requires to process the transaction. It communicates with its BS, which reaches the DBSs and moves these data items to the MU cache. The MU executes and commits the transaction and sends the final results to the user and the updates to the DBSs through its BS for installing them to the database. This scheme does not require the services of the coordinator but generates a significant amount of communication overhead.

- **Distribute transaction to a set of nodes:** The MU divides the transaction into a number of subtransactions. It keeps the subtransactions it can execute and with the help of the coordinator, it distributes the rest of them to a subset of DBSs for execution. The current BS of the MU becomes the coordinator of this transaction and manages the execution of all subtransactions, leading to either a commit or an abort of the main transaction. This scheme generates comparatively less communication overhead and incurs low database update costs.

The movement of the MU makes the job of the coordinator difficult. In addition to managing the processing, the coordinator has to manage the movement of the MU as well. In the presence of mobility, the following processing scenarios are possible:

- **MU does not move:** A transaction arrives and completes its processing entirely at the MU. The MU does not move during the execution of the transaction. This is a case of no movement of any kind and is similar to conventional centralized data processing.

- **MU moves:** A transaction arrives and can entirely complete its execution at the MU. Required data items are cached from other nodes if the MU does not have all the required data. During the transaction execution, the MU moves to different cells. This type of execution is called "local atomic", which is quite common in mobile computing. A typical example is of a traveling salesmen who usually processes all orders locally for efficiency and for minimizing message communication overhead. They cache the entire data they require from the DBS to the MUs before moving to their assigned sales site.

- **Distributed processing and MU moves:** A transaction originates at an MU and is fragmented. The subtransactions are distributed among the MUs and a set of DBSs. A coordinator is identified that manages the execution. The MU moves to different cells during the transaction execution.

7.2.4 Coordinating Service

A coordinator must be continuously available during the execution of a transaction and for managing the movements of MUs that are executing transactions. The link between

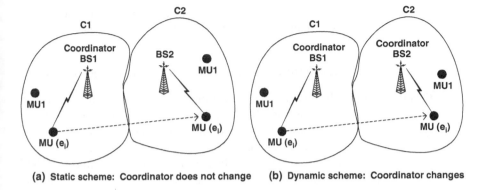

Figure 7.2 Change of coordinators due to mobility.

the coordinator and an MU may break when it crosses the current cell boundary and enters a different cell. This link can be maintained in two ways:

- **Static method:** When a transaction originates at an MU, then the BS of this MU becomes the coordinator of the transaction and remains the coordinator until the transaction terminates. The MU may continue to move from one cell to another while processing its subtransaction, but the coordinator does not change. This scheme is shown in Figure 7.2a. The MU moves from cell **C1** to **C2** with its subtransactions e_i leaving behind the coordinator at **BS1** that continues to manage the execution of e_i with the help of **BS2**.

  It is the responsibility of the MU to inform the new BS of the identity of its coordinator. This can be done when the MU registers with the new BS that communicates with the coordinator located at **BS1**, once it knows its identity. The problem with this simple method is that the coordinator and the MU each may have to go through a number of BSs to update each other. For example, **BS2** must communicate with the coordinator at **BS1** when the MU registers with **BS2**. This makes transaction termination and logging quite complex as discussed later in this book.

- **Dynamic method:** In this method, the role of coordinator moves with the MU. For example, as shown in Figure 7.2b, when the MU moves to cell **C2**, the coordinator moves to (**BS2**). Since a transaction is being processed by multiple DBSs, they must know when a new coordinator is assigned to an existing transaction. The new coordinator informs all DBSs of the identify of the new coordinator. For example, in Figure 7.2b, **BS2** is the new coordinator that informs all involved DBSs that **BS2** is the coordinator for this transaction.

  Although in the dynamic method a mobile unit is directly connected to its coordinator all the time, it becomes a problem for a highly mobile MU. Consider a situation where an MU rapidly moves between **C1** and **C2** many times. In this situation it is possible that the process of changing coordinators and the handoff process may go out of sync. As a result, BS2 may remain the coordinator while the MU is back in **C1**. In this highly mobile situation, the coordinator change is not desirable.

Two schemes can be applied to handle the coordinator for a highly mobile scenario:

- **Residency limit:** In this scheme, a maximum residency duration for a mobile unit—that is, how long an MU must stay in a cell before a coordinator is changed—is defined. Under this scheme, the coordinator migrates to the current BS only if the residency of the MU in a cell is longer than the predefined residency Limit. Thus, in Figure 7.2b, the coordinator moves from **BS1** to **BS2** if the residency of MU in **C2** is larger than the predefined limit. The value for a residency limit may be applied to all MUs or may be unique to a specific MU. A number of parameters such as movement behavior, traffic congestion, the time of the day, and so on, can be used to define a residency limit. Physical movement and traffic congestion may vary significantly; however, they probably exhibit some pattern. For example, in the morning during rush hour an MU may be highly mobile and the traffic volume on the network may be high. Thus, the residency value may be computed dynamically on a case-by-case basis. The residency duration is calculated from the time the MU registers with the new BS. Although the cost of coordinator change is not significant, it should not be allowed to happen frequently. The rate of change of coordinators can be controlled by the residency limit parameter.

- **Nonadjacent migration:** Under this scheme, the coordinator migrates only if the MU moves to a "nonadjacent cell." Nonadjacent cells are those that do not directly touch the cell in which the MU is currently residing. For example, in Figure 7.3, cells 2, 3, 4, 5, 6, and 7 are adjacent and all others such as 9, 10, 11, 12, 13, and 14 are nonadjacent cells to cell 1. The coordinator changes only if

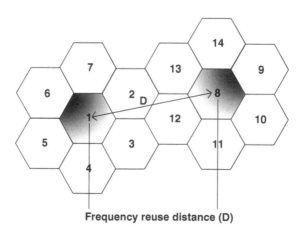

Figure 7.3 Adjacent and non-adjacent cells.

the MU moves to any of the 9 through 11 cells from cell 1. The idea is that an MU is likely to soon move back to cell 1 from an adjacent cell, and thus, there is no need to change the coordinator. This scheme is quite effective for local commuters.

7.3 MOBILE TRANSACTION MODEL

This section discusses the need for a new transaction model for mobile database systems. It was recognized in some of the earlier chapters that a conventional ACID transaction model was unable to satisfactorily manage mobile data processing tasks. Some of the important reasons were the presence of *handoff*, which is unpredictable; the presence of *doze mode*, *disconnected mode*, and *forced disconnection*; lack of necessary resources such as memory and wireless channels; the presence of location dependent data; and so on. To manage data processing in the presence of these new situations, a more powerful transaction model or ACID transaction execution model, which can handle mobility during data processing, was highly desirable. Two approaches to manage mobile databases were proposed, and the chapter discusses them in detail. Under each approach, a number of schemes were developed and each approach addressed some specific issues.

The entire topic of mobile transaction modeling is highly research-oriented, and although a significant number of schemes have been proposed, none has become a commonly accepted method. This chapter, therefore, identifies each execution model and presents the original scheme as described by the author(s) of the report. The discussion clearly indicates the incremental understanding of mobile data processing and how researchers address related issues with their execution models.

In Chapter 6, the effect of new parameters such as mobility, location information, intermittent connectivity, and so on, was investigated. It was illustrated that a basic ACID transaction model was unable to handle mobility aspect and location-dependent processing, which are now quite common in transactional requests.

There are basically two ways to handle transactional requests on an MDS: (a) develop an execution model of an ACID transaction for an MDS and (b) develop a mobile transaction model and its execution scheme. The first approach creates an execution model based on an ACID transaction framework. In the second approach, a user query is mapped to a mobile transaction model and executed under mobile ACID constraints. The execution model approach managed to handle mobility and location information, but its scope was somewhat limited. This gave rise to the development of mobile transaction models that captured and assimilated mobility and location property in its structure. These two approaches are discussed in detail in subsequent sections.

7.3.1 Execution Model Based on ACID Transaction Framework

The concept of an ACID transaction was introduced for consistency-preserving database processing. Informally, *"A transaction is a collection of operations on the physical and abstract application state"* [5]. The conventional transaction model makes sure that the ACID properties of a transaction are maintained during database processing [5]. The introduction of mobility significantly changed the database architecture and management paradigm, and it became clear that the strict enforcement of ACID properties was not necessary to maintain database consistency of mobile databases. As a matter of fact, mobility significantly changed the transaction processing discipline by relaxing or redefining the notion of consistency to accommodate the temporal and spatial (location) parameters in the geographical domain that is defined as follows:

Definition 7.1 *The geographic domain, G, is the total geographical area covered by all mobile units of a cellular system. Thus, $G = (C_1 + C_2 + \cdots + C_n)$, where C_i represent the area of a cell.*

Definition 7.2 *A location is a precise point within the geographic domain. It represents the smallest identifiable position in the domain. Each location is identified by a specific id, L. Also, $G = \cup L, \forall L$ and $C_i = \{L_i, L_2, \ldots, L_m\}$.*

In reality, a location of a mobile unit is identified with reference to the BS. If the geographic domain were on the earth, then one could think of a location as a *latitude/longitude* pair. However, the granularity of the location used may be larger. For example, the location could be an address, city, county, state, or country.

It is important to understand the complex relationship among the data, the operations to be performed on the data, and the termination of the execution for the development of an execution model. These issues were introduced in Chapter 6 and are further elaborated in this chapter.

Location-Dependent Query (LDQ). In legacy systems, it is the access frequency of data items and not their association with geographical locations that is used in data distribution (partition and partial replication). In an MDS, this association plays an important role in their processing as well as in their distribution. Figure 7.4 identifies some of the important points. Suppose a person is traveling by car from Dallas to Kansas City and asks, *"Tax rate please?"* The answer to this query will depend on where the query actually originated. If the location is Dallas, then it will give the tax rate of Dallas; and if it is Kansas City, then the tax rate will be of Kansas City. Now suppose that the query is repeated twice while traveling—once in Dallas and then in Kansas City. We will get two different correct values. Now suppose the traveler asks the query, *What is the temperature of Dallas?* The answer will not depend on the origin of the query. The result will be the same irrespective of the origin of the query or the location of the mobile unit that issued the query (Dallas or Kansas City).

Now consider the following query from the same agent. *Get the name and address of the least expensive hotel.* The answer to this query will depend on the characteristics of the place (e.g., city) where the hotel is located. Thus, in one city, the rent of the same hotel could be different compared to some other city.

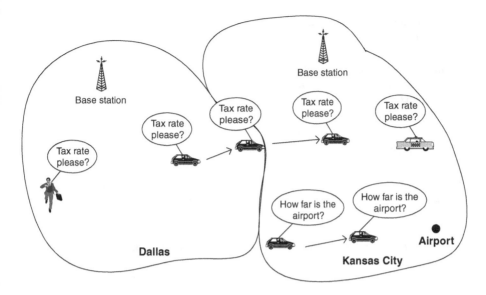

Figure 7.4   An example of LDD processing.

In every organization these types of data exist. For example, an insurance company may have a number of branches in different cities and in different states. At each branch, the premium, the coverage, and so on, will be different. These simple real-life examples suggest that the correct answer to a query depends on the geographical location of the query and the geographical location of the data required to answer the query.

A *location-dependent query (LDQ)* [6–8] is a query that processes LDD. To process an LDQ, the DBMS must first determine that it is an LDQ or a *location-aware query (LAQ)* or *location-independent query (LIQ)*. The location of the query must be determined and made available to the processor to obtain valid results. A process called *location binding* is used to bind the data required by the query with the location and to determine the correct results. The correct definitions of LDD and spatial replication can be viewed based upon a mapping from data to a location. Thus, given an object (data), this mapping identifies the correct data regions for that object. For a specific object, a subset of the powerset of $\mathcal{R}$ identifies the data regions for that object where $\mathcal{R}$ represents the set of all possible data regions.

Definition 7.3   *Given a set of data objects $\mathcal{D}$ and a set of data regions $\mathcal{R}$, a data location mapping (DLM) is a mapping $DLM : \mathcal{D} \rightarrow \mathcal{P}(R)$, where $DLM(D) = \{R_1, R_2, \dots, R_n\}$, $R_i \in \mathcal{R}$, $\bigcup_{i=1}^{n} R_i = G$, and $\forall i, j \; R_i \cap R_j = \emptyset$.*

Thus, the set of data regions for a data object is a partitioning of the geographic domain. In the case where no spatial replication of a data object exists, the number of data regions for that object is one. Given a specific location, L, in G each object is associated with a unique data region and any replication of this data adheres to the constraints discussed in Chapter 2.

Definition 7.4   *Given a set of data objects $\mathcal{D}$, a set of location ids $\mathcal{L}$, and a set of data regions $\mathcal{R}$, a data region mapping (DRM) is a mapping $DRM : \mathcal{D} \times \mathcal{L} \to \mathcal{R}$ where $DRM(< \mathcal{D},\mathcal{L}) >) \in DLM(D)$.*

A data region is identified by the data object and location. As an MU moves, each location uniquely identifies the data region to which each data belongs. This gives us the basis to perform location-dependent queries and transactions. A location-dependent query normally returns data values for the location from which it executes. Note that this approach is consistent with that in a centralized or distributed environment where only one data region exists for all data objects.

Effect of Mobility and LDD on Consistency. In a centralized or distributed environment there is only one correct value for each data object. The term *mutual consistency* is used to indicate that all the values converge to this same correct value. A replicated database is said to be in a *mutually consistent state* if all copies have the exact same value [9]. In addition, a database is said to be in a *consistent state* if all integrity constraints identified for the database are satisfied [9]. This basic idea of consistency is based only on temporal replication. The notion of spatial replication complicates the notion of consistency.

A conventional method of scheduling to ensure mutual consistency is called *one-copy serializability* [9]. Intuitively, this implies that the behavior of distributed transactions appear to provide values of replicas just as if there was no replication. Thus, the scheduling of update operations on the replicas ensures that mutual consistency is eventually achieved. In a snapshot database this would be the one correct value. In a temporal database this would be the mutually consistent value for that particular time point. Mutual consistency within temporal databases implies that the replicas for one time point must eventually have the same value. When spatial replication is added, the data location must also be added to this. Thus, mutual consistency with spatial replication implies that the spatial replicas for one location (data region) converge to the same value.

In MDS, a consistent view is obtained with reference to the geographical data location. A transaction may modify a data value that would be valid only for a specific data region. Thus, an identical update transaction (at a different location) may be subjected to different sets of consistency constraints that will depend upon the place of data manipulation. A hotel chain or franchise can be used to demonstrate the significance of spatial replication and its consistency. Hotel Luxury has a number of branches across the nation. Each branch offers identical services; however, the cost, policy, facilities, and so on, might depend on the place of the branch location. Thus, the same-sized suite at Hotel Luxury may cost more in Dallas than in Kansas City. The data consistency constraints in Kansas City might be different than that in Dallas, because of local taxes and environment policies. Even though each branch may share the same schema, their instances (data values) may differ. Any change in the rent of a

Kansas City suite by a transaction will not affect the Dallas suite rent and vice versa. This indicates that the conventional notion of global and mutual data consistency does not apply in MDS. The concept of *spatial* consistency is introduced here to distinguish this with conventional consistency, which is referred to as *temporal* consistency. We present the following examples of *location inconsistency* to further clarify the idea of location consistency.

■ EXAMPLE 7.1

Suppose that a driver, during his long trip in winter, plans to take a break according to the weather conditions. If the weather at the destination is bad, then he decides to book a hotel around X miles of his current location and eats at a nearby restaurant; otherwise, he decides to continue driving toward his destination and eat in a restaurant there. Suppose the destination is 20 miles from the starting point. He issues a transaction T from his MU that processes the following set of execution fragments.

- **T1**: Check weather at 20 miles from the current location.
- **T2**: Check into a hotel 20 miles from the current location.
- **T3**: Find a list of restaurants 20 miles from the current location.
- **T4**: Check into a hotel at X miles from the current location.
- **T5**: Get a list of restaurants at X miles from the current location.

If the weather at the destination is not bad, then the possible execution order is (T_1, T_2, and T_3); otherwise, the order is (T_1, T_4, and T_5). A bad weather scenario is used to analyze a possible execution order to illustrate how location inconsistency arises because of the mobility of the MU. Suppose the driver starts at X for destination Y (Figure 7.5). After traveling a few miles from X, he issues T_1 (what is the weather at Y?) while moving. He gets T_1's response, **Bad weather at Y** at A. In a mobile environment, even short transactions may run for longer periods of time (not long running in the conventional sense) because of resource constraints, bandwidth limitations, disconnections, and heavy traffic in the cell. Consequently, it is possible that by the time the MU receives the result of T_1, it might have traveled more than 10 miles. This also depends how fast the MU is moving. These are likely to create a location mismatch. At B, he issues T_4 (book a hotel within 5 miles) and then issues T_5 (list of restaurants within 5 miles of B). The following possibilities exist

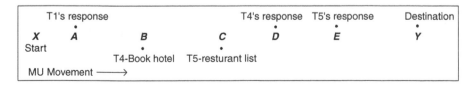

Figure 7.5   Transaction execution during mobility.

Figure 7.6   An example of location inconsistency.

a. The traveler gets the answer of T_4 (at D) when he is within 5 miles of B. This is consistent with the query.
b. The traveler gets the answer of T_4 beyond 5 miles of B (beyond D) in which case there is location inconsistency. In this case, the data region associated with the object (hotel) for the query is different from that of the current location of the MU.
c. If (b) exists, then the answer to T_4 will be inconsistent (location inconsistency).
d. Figure 7.6 shows an instance of location inconsistency. The result is that the hotel is booked at location D and the list of restaurants is from the current location of the user, which is beyond D. The MU has to go back to D where the hotel is booked and to location E for the restaurant.

A case of location consistency is illustrated in Figure 7.7. Here, the location where the hotel is booked and list of restaurants are the same. The current location of the traveler is beyond E, so he has to go back to D and eat at one of the restaurants at E.

A correct transaction execution model must address these issues. A number of execution models have been developed, and they are explained in detail below. These mobile execution models are based on existing basic and advanced ACID models

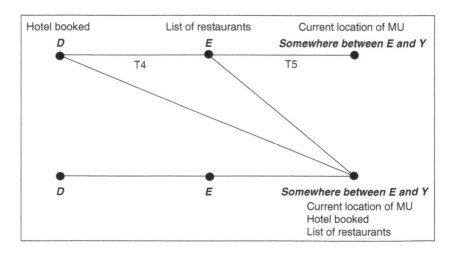

Figure 7.7   An example of location consistency.

such as ACTA, SAGA, and so on (see Chapter 4) and support distributed transaction execution. The underlying approach of these execution models is similar; that is, each support transaction fragmentation (subtransactions) satisfy ACID constraints to a large extent. However, they differ on how these fragments are executed and committed, leading to different execution models for mobile database processing. The important issues that each execution model considers are the resource constraints (wireless channel, memory and disk space, limited energy source, and channel bandwidth). Also the mobility of the processing units tries to create the same execution scenario that exists in conventional distributed database management systems. This is where these approaches differ from each other.

7.3.2 Execution Model with Reporting Transaction

A mobile execution model based on an *open-nested transaction* [10–12] approach is presented in reference 13. This execution model extends the semantic-based execution model presented in references 14 and 15. The execution model fragments data objects to facilitate semantic-based transaction processing in MDS. Each data fragment is cached separately but manipulated synchronously. The parent ACID transaction is a set of *component* transactions where each component transaction can be further fragmented into a number of lower-level (finer granule) components. Thus, the model can support arbitrary levels of nesting. Formally, the model can be defined as:

Definition 7.5 *Execution model* $= \{C_1, C_2, \ldots, C_n\}$, *where* C_i *is a component transaction.* $C_i = \{cc_1, cc_2, cc_m\}$, *where* cc_j *is a component transaction of* C_i.

A component transaction can commit or abort independent of other components; that is, it does not have to wait for other components to commit. However, its commit depends on the parent transaction. Thus, a component transaction that has not yet committed will be aborted if its parent transaction fails. A component transaction can be one of the following four types:

- **Atomic transaction:** This is an ACID transaction, and some of them may be compensated by a compensating transaction. Compensatable and compensating transactions are atomic transactions that have intertransaction dependencies. Like other open-nested transaction models, compensatable and noncompensatable components can be associated with contingency transactions. A contingency transaction is invoked to handle the abort of a component for which there is a contingency. A compensating transaction can be structured as {*Begin, Commit, Abort*}. An atomic transaction can be one of the children of a parent transaction and can commit before the parent commits and, if necessary, may be compensated.

- **Noncompensating component:** This is an atomic component but may not be compensated. For this reason, a noncompensating transaction can commit before the parent transaction commits, but its data updates cannot be installed in the final database. A noncompensating transaction (component of a parent transaction) delegates all its updates to its parent transaction that handles the final data updates leading to commit.

- **Reporting transaction:** A reporting component shares (reports) its updates with the parent transaction at any time during its execution. This transaction periodically reports to other transactions by delegating some of its current results. It continues to execute after it has reported its intermediate updates if it is not committed. Thus, reporting transactions are associated with the report transaction primitive in addition to the *Begin*, *Commit*, and *Abort* primitives. *Begin* is used to initiate a reporting transaction, and *Commit* and *Abort* are used for termination. The mode of this report depends on whether or not it is associated with a compensating transaction.

- **Co-transaction:** A co-transaction component also shares its results with the parent transaction, but unlike the reporting transaction, its execution is suspended when it reports to the parent transaction and resumes its execution from the point of suspension. Similar to the reporting transaction, a transaction delegates its current results to its co-transaction by invoking the *Report* transaction primitive. Because the co-transactions maintained their execution state, they could not be executed concurrently.

This scheme also identifies (a) vital and (b) nonvital components. The commitment of the parent transaction was dependent on the vital transaction; that is, the parent could commit only after its vital components are committed. On the other hand, the parent transaction could commit even if one of its nonvital components aborts, but it will do so only after the nonvital component is successfully aborted.

The reporting and co-transaction components are mainly responsible for all data modifications. Reporting components always execute on base stations where as co-transactions execute on mobile units. When a mobile unit, running a co-transaction, moves and registers with another base station, the corresponding reporting component also moves to the base station and the communication between reporting and the co-transaction remains active. They share their partial results so that the co-transactions get the most up-to-date values of data items and the reporting component receives updates to be installed in the database. The compensating components are invoked to repair any inconsistency that occurred during the execution of these components.

This execution model is based on an open-nested framework. It does not present a mobile transaction model, but it does present a scheme to execute an ACID transaction on an MDS. Furthermore, it does not address the location dependent data processing issues that are a vital component of an MDS.

In this approach, reporting transactions and co-transactions are treated as independent units of an action. These transactions support *delegation* between transactions.

7.3.3 Two-Level Consistency Model

This is not a transaction model, but rather a data consistency model that discusses how data consistency is maintained in the presence of mobility during transaction processing. The objective is to reduce the cost of data processing and maintain database consistency in the MDS, which is significantly high and undermines the benefits of the MDS. They achieve this cost reduction by introducing "weak operations" that support disconnected operations and save bandwidth.

In any database platform, centralized or distributed, the data distribution significantly affects database performance. A flexible transaction execution model is reported in reference 16, which considers the data distribution as a part of the execution model. It created clusters of semantically related or closely located data that were dynamically configured.

Data Cluster. A cluster is a set of data with a similar set of properties. Formally, a cluster C equals $\{d_1, d_2, \ldots, d_n\}$, where d_i is a data item. All d_i's of C are semantically related and are required to be fully consistent, while the set of data items at another cluster may exhibit bounded consistencies. The set of properties of a cluster may include the geographical location of data items; as a result, a cluster can be made up of data items that are stored at neighboring nodes such as neighboring base stations (if they are used to store part of the database). Clusters are created, revised, and merged dynamically, and their management is affected by connection and disconnection of mobile units.

The model also allows mobile users to specify conditions for creating clusters. This is especially useful for local commuters who frequently access a well-defined set of data items that are clustered to minimize the access latency. In this way, the model tries to satisfy the data needs of the mobile units for execution transactions. In terms of clusters, the database is defined as follows:

Definition 7.6 *A mobile database* MD *equals* $\{Cl_1, Cl_2, \ldots, Cl_n\}$, *where* Cl_i *is a cluster.* $Cl_i = \{x_1, x_2, \ldots, x_m\}$, *where* x_i *is a data item. An item* $x \in MD$ *iff* $x \in Cl_i$ *for some* $i \in N$.

Cluster Consistency. A data cluster is a unit of consistency. Since a database is a set of clusters, like conventional databases, two kinds of consistency exist (a) *intra-cluster* consistency and (b) *inter-cluster* consistency. Intra-cluster consistency refers to the consistency of data items of a cluster (local consistency), and inter-consistency refers to data item consistency across the clusters, similar to global consistency in conventional distributed systems. This type of consistency is defined by the model as follows:

Definition 7.7 *(m-consistency) A cluster state is consistent if and only if all intra-cluster integrity constraints hold. A mobile database state is m-consistent if and only if all cluster states are consistent and all inter-cluster integrity constraints are m-degree consistent [16].*

Data consistency was maintained at the cluster level (local) and at the database level (global). The model defines *weak transaction* and *strong transaction*. In addition to this, it defines *weak read* and *weak write* and refers to normal read as strict read and normal write as strict write to manage the entire database processing in the presence of mobility.

Strict Write. This writes and leaves the database in a consistent state.

Strict Read. This reads main database items that were written by the last strict writes.

Weak Write. Writes local data (data in a cluster). This data value becomes permanent only when installed in the main database.

Weak Read. Reads local data (data in a cluster) that is written by a weak write

Weak Transaction. A weak transaction is made up of only weak reads and weak writes.

Strict Transaction. A strict transaction is made up of only strict reads and strict writes; that is, it does not include any weak read or weak write operations.

When a transaction is initiated by a user, then it is fragmented into a number of weak and strong transactions.

7.3.4 Pro-Motion: Proactive Management of Mobile Transactions

This execution model focuses on the issues introduced by frequent disconnection, limited battery life, low-bandwidth communication, and limited resources [17, 18] in mobile units. The model manages transaction execution in the presence of these limitations. The Pro-Motion model makes use of object semantics for improving concurrency and site autonomy and *compacts* that encapsulate access methods, state information, and consistency constraints, to allow for the local management of database transactions. The model has a transaction management subsystem that consists of a *compact manager* at the database server, a *compact agent* at the mobile host, and a *mobility manager* located at an MSC (mobile switching center). The mobile database architecture assumes the presence of database servers located at fixed hosts and applications running on mobile units that can manipulate database stored on these servers.

Compacts. A compact is an *object* that is composed of (a) cached data (basic unit of caching), (b) cached data access methods, (c) information about the current state of the compact, (d) rules of maintaining global consistency, (e) obligations such as deadlines, and (f) an interface for the mobile unit to manage the compact. Figure 7.8a shows the complete structure and Figure 7.8b shows an instance of a compact.

The server comes to an agreement with the mobile unit where a transaction is to be executed through a compact. Under this agreement, the mobile unit is free to execute the transaction and makes its updates available to the server through the compact. If there *is* a need for changing some of the conditions in the execution of that transaction, then this change is renegotiated through the compact.

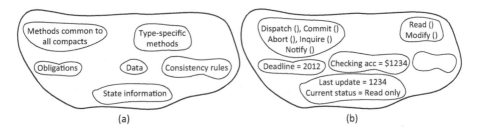

Figure 7.8 Compact object structure.

The server and the mobile unit together manage the compact. The creation and removal of a compact is handled by the database server. When a mobile unit begins transaction execution and needs data, then it sends the necessary request to the server. If the data are available, then the server creates a compact, initializes it with data and other necessary information, and sends it to the mobile unit. If a compact already exists for the execution of this transaction, then any further request from the mobile unit is satisfied by the updated compact. The arrival or modification of a compact is recorded in a data structure called the *compact registry*, which provides complete information about all open compacts initiated by a mobile unit.

The processing of a transaction on a mobile unit is managed by a *compact agent*. During its execution on a mobile unit, a transaction may generate a number of requirements. A compact agent, in addition to managing the set of compacts listed in the registry, is responsible for processing transaction requests. Its functions may be compared with the transaction manager of conventional database management systems. In particular, a compact agent is responsible for (a) enforcing a concurrency control mechanism, (b) logging, and (c) recovery. Since a compact is an independent object, a number of consistency constraints and data caching can be efficiently supported.

A compact agent has the following methods available for efficiently managing the execution of a transaction. In addition to these methods, a compact is also capable of supporting specialized methods that could be required by special concurrency control or specific data manipulation.

- **Inquire:** Inquires about the current status of a compact.
- **Notify:** Notifies the compact of any change in the status of the mobile unit.
- **Dispatch:** Processes operations on the compact issued by the transaction executing on the mobile unit.
- **Commit:** Commits the transaction executing on the mobile unit.
- **Abort:** Rejects or removes the changes made to the compact by the transaction.

The *compact manager* stores the status of each compact, and at predefined intervals the state of a compact is updated whenever the status of a compact changes. In this way, it acts as a front end to the database server and shields it from mobile units that execute transactions. The database server interacts with a compact manager as a client that executes the root transaction. The root transaction is fragmented under an open-nested model, and each mobile unit executes one or more fragments. The execution of these sibling fragments proceeds independently to one another without violating the consistency constraints defined in the compacts. The root transaction is committed by the compact manager.

The transaction processing under the Pro-Motion model has four basic steps that are performed by the compact agent. These steps prepare for (a) a disconnected execution, (b) a connected execution, and (c) server database updates. The four basic steps are as follows:

- **Hoarding:** The compact manager prepares and stores the required compacts to manage the disconnected execution of the transactions. The mobile unit may be disconnected from the network at any time.
- **Connected execution:** The mobile unit is connected to the network, and the compact manager processes the transactions.
- **Disconnected execution:** The mobile unit is disconnected from the network, and the compact manager processes the transactions locally.
- **Resynchronization:** The mobile unit, after completing the disconnected execution, is reconnected to the server and the compact agent reconciles local updates performed during the disconnected execution with the server database.

The entire execution is managed by the coordinated effort of the compact, compact manager, and compact agent. The task of the connected execution is simple and similar to any transaction processing on legacy distributed systems. The mobile process, the transaction, and updates are installed on the server database. The disconnected operation becomes complex in the presence of mobility. The other three steps are responsible for managing the disconnected execution and are explained in detail below.

Hoarding and Caching. A mobile unit requires a number of resources including data for transaction execution. Each resource request is implicitly or explicitly associated with a specific compact type. The compact agent, the mobile application, and the user, together build and maintain the resource list for a mobile unit in behalf of a transaction. The compact agent continuously monitors the additional resource needs and adds to the list as the execution progresses. If an application attempts to use the data that are not on the list, then the compact agents immediately adds them to the list and tries to obtain them. There are a number of ways hoarding steps can be performed, and the application developer has enough flexibility for implementing any scheme suitable for the mobile database platform.

It is possible in Pro-Motion to have multiple requests for the same resource with different access types. For example, an application A requires data item x with read and write permissions, and another application B only wants to read x. If application A is later removed from the MU, then x will still be required, but the access level may be downgraded to read-only. On the other hand, if B is removed, then the associated request from *B* is removed, and the compact is adjusted to comply with the requirements of the remaining requests.

When a conflict between a holder of a resource (MU) and a requestor occurs, the compact resolves it with the help of a server side compact. If the request can be satisfied, an MU-side compact, with appropriate constraints and obligation, is created and queued for transmission. Otherwise, a null compact is created and queued to be sent to the MU. If the resource is available, then the compact manager obtains data modification rights and finds the matching compact type. The compact manager creates an instance of the appropriate server-side compact type and forwards the request to the newly created compact. The server side compact creates an instance of matching the MU-side compact with the data and needed code and queues the new MU-side compact for transmission to MU. If the resource is held by a nonmobile transaction, then a null compact is created and queued for transmission to the MU. A null compact causes an operation attempted by an application to fail.

Disconnecting Transaction Processing. The compact agent on a mobile unit begins local processing when the communication link between the server and the unit is broken. In local processing, the compact agent and the compacts manage all the operations together. The compact agent maintains an event log to manage transaction processing, recovery, and resynchronization. The complete execution involves (a) transaction initiation, (b) transaction execution, (c) transaction completion, and (d) failure recovery.

Transaction Initiation. An application initiates a transaction on a mobile unit by issuing a *Begin* event. The compact agent then receives this event, assigns a unique transaction *ID*, and writes them (the event and the *ID*) in the event log. Pro-Motion allows a number of options to the *Begin* event to further specify transaction behavior. Two such options control the transaction's level of isolation and local commitment. A *Begin* event with a local option commits locally and makes its results available to other transactions with a possibility of failure at the server. A transaction without a local option does not commit locally until the updates have committed at the server.

A *Begin* event may also contain a group *ID*. In the absence of this *ID*, the compact assigns an *ID* and returns it to the new transaction. The application can pass this information to additional transactions, allowing them to join the active transactions, and these additional transactions receive the same group *ID* but different *ID*s for their transactions. All transactions with the same group *ID* are commit-dependent, that is, they terminate together.

Transaction Execution. When a transaction needs to access data during an execution, an OP event is sent to the compact agent with a compact ID, the operation to be performed, necessary parameters to complete the operation, the transaction *ID*, and group *ID*. The compact *ID* and OP event are used by the compact agent to invoke the compact's dispatch method. The compact determines the presence of a conflict between the new and any pending operations, and if there is one, then the OP event is returned to the compact agent with a *Conflict* code and a list of IDs of conflicting transactions. The agent then queues the OP event for dispatch to the compact when the compact event changes. The information saved in the queue is sufficient for deadlock detection and its resolution. In the absence of a conflict, the operation is performed by the compact.

Transaction Completion. Transaction commitment is performed using a two-phase commit protocol. Commitment is initiated when a commit is issued by the transaction. Unlike most transaction processing systems, Pro-Motion allows a contingency procedure to be attached to each commit event and logged with the event. When a commit event is received from a transaction, the compact agent coordinates and commits the transaction.

Further details about this approach can be found in references 17–19.

7.4 PREWRITE TRANSACTION EXECUTION MODEL

An ACID transaction execution model based on a *prewrite* operation was presented in reference 20. The approach of this execution model is to first execute and commit (pre-commit) a transaction on a "logical" level and make its data items available to other concurrent transactions. This, logical commit (pre-commit) is achieved through a *prewrite* operation. The results of this prewrite are not installed in the final database. The transaction finally commits (physically) only when it satisfies a set of predefined constraints.

A *prewrite* announces what value a data item will have after the commit of its write operation. In other words, it announces the *AFter IMage (AFIM)* of a data item before the application of a write. Thus the result of a *prewrite* can be announced as {*file-name, record number, field-name, new value*} for a simple database application. The notion of a virtual execution or *pre-commit* of a transaction can be expressed in terms of a *prewrite*. For example, a transaction can be called *pre-committed* if it has announced all its prewrite values, but the transaction has not been finally committed. Likewise, a *pre-read* returns a prewrite value of the data item whereas a conventional read returns the result of a write operation. A *pre-read* becomes a *weak-read* if it returns the result of a *prewrite* of a fully committed transaction. This is a different way of using *weak-read* than the way it was used in reference 21.

The proposed transaction execution model is based on these sets of operations. The model has the following features:

- Each *prewrite* operation of a transaction shows the AFIM value of a data item. The values of *prewrites* depend on the execution environments. In some cases, its value may be identical to what was produced by a conventional write, but in some cases it may differ. For example, the draft copy of a graphic (result of a prewrite) may be slightly different in color or dimension than the final copy (produced by a conventional write). Similarly, a prewrite may represent an abstract of the complete document.

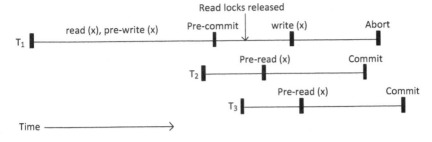

Figure 7.9 Execution of transactions with pre-read and prewrite.

- A transaction pre-commits after it has read or pre-read its required data items and prewrites are computed. After a transaction pre-commits, all its prewrite values are made available to other concurrent transactions. Since prewrites do not touch the final copy of the database, they are handled at the transaction manager level and conventional writes are handled by the data manager.
- The commit order of the concurrent transactions commit is decided at the pre-commit. This helps to detect conflict quite early.
- A transaction can only be aborted or rolled back before it pre-commits, and a rollback does not cascade. This is illustrated in Figure 7.9. Three transactions, T_1, T_2, and T_3, execute concurrently. T_1 begins and applies *read (x) and prewrite (x)* on data item *x*. T_2 begins and applies *pre-read (x)* after *pre-commit* but before *write (x)* and final commit of T_1. T_2 commits before T_1 is aborted. T_3 applies the same set of operations as T_2, but it commits after T_1 is aborted. Since T_2 and T_3 applied *pre-read (x)* after *prewrite (x)*, they are not rolled back because it is assumed that T_1 would write the result of *prewrite (x)* in the database. However, if a pre-committed transaction is forced to abort due to a system crash, then it is restarted after system recovery.
- Through the use of pre-read, prewrite, and pre-commit, the model relaxes the isolation constraints and a transaction makes its data items available to other transaction immediately after it pre-commits but before its final commit.

Prewrite Algorithm. The following steps describe the working of the algorithm. A Transaction Manager (TM) and Data Manager (DM) architecture is used for the execution of these steps. The algorithm uses the compatibility matrix given in Table 7.1.

Table 7.1 Compatibility Matrix

Operations	Pre-read	Read	Prewrite	Write
Pre-read	Yes	Yes	No	Yes
Read	Yes	Yes	Yes	No
Prewrite	No	Yes	No	Yes
Write	Yes	No	Yes	No

a. Transaction T_i arrives at the TM. The TM identifies read and write requests of T_i.

b. If T_i has reads and writes, then, if possible, locks are obtained for reads and data items values are read. If these values are generated by prewrites, then these reads become pre-reads.

c. Necessary locks are acquired for prewrites.

d. After T_i ends its execution, the pre-commit phase starts. In pre-commit, if there is no conflict, then the prewrite lock mode is converted to a write lock mode (Table 7.1).

e. The pre-commit of T_i is announced where all read locks are released.

f. The final commit begins where the database is updated with prewrite values (final write). All write locks are released and commit is announced.

7.4.1 Prewrite Execution in Mobile Database Systems

The prewrite execution model tries to work within resource constraints of a mobile database system. One of the important considerations is the speed of the CPU. For slow CPUs the execution model does not scale very well and MUs act as simple clients with no database processing capability. The following transaction execution example assumes a high-speed CPU.

MUs with high-speed CPUs store consistent data items to their local cache. When a transaction arrives at an MU, it uses cached data to process reads and returns the prewrite values. Those reads (for which cache does not have data) are sent to the server for processing. The server returns prewrite or write values. The transaction pre-commits when all values are returned by the server and the MU also has completed its processing. All locks are released and the pre-commit schedule is sent to the server for the final commit of the transaction.

In some data processing situations a tolerable difference between a prewrite version and a final write version may appear. Consider a transaction T_i that executes a pre-read on data item x which is produced by a prewrite of T_j. If T_j commits at the server. In some cases, T_i may have an old value of x, but it is tolerated. An example of this would be a draft and final versions of a graphic object or some average salary data. A minor difference in these versions is not likely to influence the outcome.

7.4.2 MDSTPM Transaction Execution Model

An execution model called a *Multidatabase Transaction Processing Manager (MDSTPM)* is reported in reference 22 that supports transaction initiation from mobile units. The model uses message and queuing facilities to establish necessary communication between mobile and stationary (base station) units. At each stationary unit, a personal copy of an MDSTPM exists that coordinates the connected and disconnected execution of transactions submitted at the mobile units.

The MDSTPM has the following components:

- **Global Communication Manager (GCM):** This module manages message communications among transaction processing units. It maintains a message queue for handling this task.
- **Global Transaction Manager (GTM):** This module coordinates the initiation of transactions and their subtransactions. It acts as a *Global Scheduling Submanager (GSS)* that schedules global transactions and subtransactions. It can also act as a *Global Concurrency Submanager (GCS)* that is responsible for the execution of these transactions and subtransactions.
- **Local Transaction Manager (LTM):** This module is responsible for local transaction execution and database recovery.
- **Global Recovery Manager (GRM):** This module is responsible for managing global transaction commits and their recovery in the event of failure.
- **Global Interface Manager (GIM):** This serves as a link between the MDSTPM and local database managers.

7.5 MOBILE TRANSACTION MODEL

In the last few sections, mobile execution models for ACID transactions were discussed in detail. An execution model provides a scheme to execute ACID transactions in resource-limited mobile platforms; however, they have some inherent limitations, especially in processing LDD (location-dependent data) and LDQ (location-dependent query). In these execution models, the location information must be provided either through a middleware or manually. Later mobile transaction models were developed to take care of these limitations. A number of such transaction models are discussed in this section.

7.5.1 HiCoMo: High Commit Mobile Transaction Model

This model was presented in reference 23. Although it has been presented as a mobile transaction model, in reality it is a mobile transaction execution model. The model is mainly for processing aggregate data stored in a data warehouse that resides in mobile units. Since the data warehouse resides in mobile units, *HiCoMo* transactions are always initiated on mobile units where they are processed in a disconnected mode. As a result, transaction commitments are quite fast. The main database is updated only when the mobile unit is reconnected. The results of the transaction (HiCoMo) are analyzed, and necessary updated transactions are initiated that install HiCoMo's updates to the main database. The update transactions are called *base* or *source* transactions. They are initiated at the fixed network to install updates of HiCoMo transactions. In this model there are some mismatches (data accuracy) between the results of HiCoMo and what are installed. In such cases, the model allows a reasonable error margin.

HiCoMo transactions achieve a high commit rate and are not affected by the frequent disconnection behavior of mobile units. This execution model is mainly suitable for aggregates, summary, statistical data, and so on, since they do not demand high data accuracy. The database (base tables) resides on the fixed network, and the aggregates of the data (warehouse) reside on the mobile hosts that mostly remain disconnected.

The execution model—in particular, HiCoMo transactions—makes the following assumptions:

- The data warehouse stores aggregate data of the following types: average, sum, minimum, and maximum.
- Operations such as *subtraction*, *addition*, and *multiplication* are allowed with some constraints on their order of application.
- The model allows some margins of error. These margins can be defined before allowed operations are initiated, and their value can be varied between a lower and an upper bound.

The structure of the *HiCoMo* transaction is based on the *Nested* transaction model. The database consistency is satisfied through *convergence* criteria. It is satisfied when the states of the base database and the data warehouse in mobile units are identical. This transaction model ensures that convergence is always satisfied.

As mentioned earlier, the base database at the server is updated by *source* transactions. This requires that the installation of the updates to the *HiCoMo* transactions, be converted to *source* transactions. This conversion is done by the *transaction transformation function* that works as follows:

- **Conflict detection:** A conflict is identified among other *HiCoMo* transactions and between *HiCoMo* and *base* transactions. The conflict resolution is made simple by only allowing addition and subtraction operations (division and multiplication are not allowed) by concurrent transactions. Since allowed operations commute, the execution schedule of conflicting transactions can be revised easily. If there is a conflict between *HiCoMo* transactions and any base transaction, then the HiCoMo transaction is aborted. The model uses timestamping to detect a conflict.
- **Base transaction generation:** In the absence of a conflict, initial *base* transactions are generated and executed as subtransactions on the base database at the server. The type of base transaction depends upon the *HiCoMo* transactions.
- **Alternate base transaction generation:** It is possible that some of these subtransactions may violate integrity constraints (may be outside the error of margin) and therefore are aborted. These updates are tried again by redistribution of error margin. In the worst-case scenario, the original *HiCoMo* transactions are aborted. If there is no integrity violation, then *base* transactions are committed.

The HiCoMo model does not have location-dependent parameters, so it cannot handle location dependent queries. An example illustrating the working of a HiCoMo transaction model is given in reference 23.

7.5.2 Moflex Transaction Model

A mobile transaction model called *Moflex*, which is based on the *Flexible* transaction model [24], is presented in reference 25. The structure of a *Moflex* has 7 components and can be defined as

$$\text{Moflex transaction} T = \{M, S, F, D, H, J, G\}$$

$M = \{t_1, t_2, \ldots, t_n\}$, where t_i are compensatable or noncompensatable subtransactions. Every compensatable t_i is associated with a corresponding compensating transaction.

S = a set of success-dependencies between t_i and t_j; $(i \neq j)$. This defines the serial execution order of these subtransactions. Thus, t_j has a success-dependency on t_i (i.e., $t_i <_s t_j$) if t_j can be executed only after t_i commits successfully.

F = a set of failure-dependencies that indicates that t_j can be executed only after t_i has failed. This dependency is represented as (i.e., $t_i <_f t_j$).

D = a set of external-dependencies that indicates that t_i can be executed only if it satisfies predefined external predicates. These predicates are defined on time (P), cost (Q), and location (L). With this parameter, a Moflex transaction model processes location-dependent and time-sensitive transactions. For example, if two time-sensitive transactions t_1 and t_2 must execute between 8 a.m. and 5 p.m., subtransactions t_2 and t_3 must not exceed \$100, and subtransactions t_1 and t_4 must execute at a certain location (location dependent) and then the external dependencies are identified as follows:

$D = \{P, Q, L\}$
$P = \{8 < time\ (t_1) < 17,\ 8 < time\ (t_2) < 17\}$
$Q = \{cost\ (t_2) < \$100,\ cost\ (t_3) < \$100\}$
$\{t_1, t_4\}$

H = a set of handoff control rules that manage the execution of subtransactions in the presence of a handoff. In this event a subtransaction may *continue* its execution or *restart* or *split-resume* or *split-restart*. These execution states (or modes) are related to the handoff and are explained later.

The Moflex model supports the handoff, process. In a handoff, if the parent subtransaction is compensable and it is processing location-dependent data, then the handoff rule forces the subtransaction to abort and restart in the new cell. A restart can be *split-restart* where the value of the partial execution of the subtransaction in the last cell is preserved. In the case of a location-independent subtransaction, it further splits into finer subtransactions. The subtransactions that represent the portion of the execution occurred in the last cell are free to commit.

J = a set of acceptable join rules that are used to determine the correct execution of a subtransaction.

G = a set of all acceptable states of T (*Moflex*).

A *Moflex* transaction can be (a) not submitted for execution (N), (b) currently executing (E), (c) successfully completed (S), or (d) failed (F). An execution of T is regarded complete if its current state exists in set G. When this is satisfied, then T can commit. Otherwise, if no subtransaction of T is executing nor can it be scheduled for execution, then T is aborted.

An Example of a Moflex. An emergency patient dispatch query can be stated as follows. The objective of this hypothetical transaction is to illustrate how the transaction fits into the *Moflex* transaction structure. *Find the right hospital or take the patient to the default hospital, then dispatch patient status to the emergency doctor for getting the correct treatment.* This can be expressed in a *Moflex* as

$$M = \{t_1(C), t_2(C), t_3(NC), t_4(C), t_5(C)\}$$
$$S = \{t_1 <_s t_3, t_2 <_s t_3, t_1 <_s t_4\}$$
$$D = \{t_1, t_4\}$$
$$H = \{\text{restart}(t_1), \text{continue}(t_2), \text{continue}(t_3), \text{split-resume}(t_4), \text{continue}(t_5)\}$$
$$J = \{\text{user}(t_4)\}$$
$$G = \{(S, —, S, S, S), (—, S, S, —, S)\}$$

In this example in set G, S indicates a successful execution of *Moflex* and "—" means that the execution state of the subtransaction does not have to be one of the predefined states. Further details about *Moflex* can be found in reference 25.

7.5.3 Kangaroo Mobile Transaction Model

In reference 26, a transaction model called *Kangaroo* is presented that captured both data and the movement of mobile units. The model is based on a split transaction model and enforces a majority of the ACID properties.

The structure of the Kangaroo transaction is based on the global transaction model. Since the global transaction model does not "hop" from one cell to another, the Kangaroo transaction (KT) model captures this property. A KT is composed of a number of subtransactions. Each subtransaction is similar to the ACID transactions that are composed of a set of reads and writes. These subtransactions are called a *Joey transaction (JT)* and define a unit of execution at a base station.

Upon initiation of a Kangaroo transaction, a base station creates a JT for its execution, which may be executed at mobile units. When these mobile units migrate to another cell, the base station of this cell takes control of the execution of this transaction.

Figure 7.10 shows the basic structure of a Kangaroo transaction. When a transaction is initiated at a mobile unit, the data accesss agent (DAA) that manages data access from the source (the associated base station) forwards the request to the base station that stores the required data. In fact, DAA manages (keeps track of the execution status of the mobile transactions, logging information, checkpointing, etc.) all mobile transactions through one of its components called the mobile transaction manager (MTM).

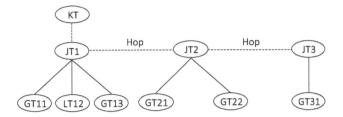

Figure 7.10 Basic structure of kangaroo transaction.

When a transaction is initiated at a mobile unit, the DAA at the base station of the mobile unit creates a KT and associates it with a unique identity. The KT, with its unique identity, is defined as

$$KTID = \text{base station ID} + \text{sequence number}$$

where ID represents the base station with a unique sequence number and + is a string catenation operation. When the mobile unit moves (hops) from one cell to another (handoff), the control of the KT is handed over to a new DAA of the receiving base station. The new DAA creates a new JT by splitting the old JT. In Figure 7.10, JT1 is split into JT2 and JT3. JT1 commits independently of JT2 and JT3; however, if JT1 fails to commit or abort, then the entire KT is undone (compensated).

The KT model supports transaction execution in *compensating* or *split* modes. When a failure occurs in a compensating mode, then all executions of the JT (preceding or following) are undone and previously committed JTs are compensated. It is difficult for the system to identify the compensating mode, so users provide useful input for creating compensating JTs. The default execution mode is a *split* mode. When a JT fails in a default mode, then no new local or global transaction is created from a KT and previously committed JTs are not compensated. As a result, in the compensating mode, JTs are serializable but may not be in a split mode. Further details on a KT can be found in reference 26.

Some other models have been reported in the literature that are briefly mentioned here. The semantics-based mobile transaction processing scheme [19] views mobile transaction processing as a concurrency and a cache coherency problem. The model assumes a mobile transaction to be a long-lived one, characterized by long network delays and unpredictable disconnections. This approach utilizes the object organization to split large and complex objects into smaller, manageable fragments. A stationary database server dishes out the fragments of an object on a request from a mobile unit. On completion of the transaction, the mobile units return the fragments to the server. These fragments are put together again by the merge operation at the server. If the fragments can be recombined in any order, then the objects are termed *reorderable* objects. Since a single database server is assumed, the ACID properties can be maintained.

Table 7.2 compares the various ACID transaction execution models and mobile transaction models based on the ACID property compliance and processing location.

Table 7.2 Summary of Previous Mobile Transaction Models and ACID Adherence

Model	A	C	I	D	Request	Execute
Kangaroo	No	No	No	No	MU	Fixed network
Reporting	No	No	No	No	N/A	N/A
Co-transaction	No	No	No	No	N/A	N/A
Clustering	No	No	No	No	MU	MU or fixed network
Semantics	Yes	Yes	Yes	Yes	MU	Restricted server/MU
MDSTPM	No	No	No	No	MU	MU or fixed network

These models do address some of the important issues of mobility; however, no single model captures or incorporates all issues at one place. In the Kangaroo model, a transaction initiated at one mobile unit can be fragmented so they can be executed at multiple mobile units. This is acceptable on a research level, but in reality this does not happen. A mobile unit is a resource dedicated to its own transactions and is not open for shared execution.

Due to the fact that the Kangaroo model assumes the autonomy of the underlying DBMS systems, subtransactions are allowed to commit/abort independently. Atomicity may be achieved if compensating transactions are provided. While the Semantics approach allows processing anywhere in the mobile platform, it is a restricted type of processing because it assumes the presence of only one server and all fragments processed at the MU must be returned to the server prior to commit. All but the Semantics-based approach may violate durability. This is because the local transactions that have committed may later be "undone" by a compensating transaction. It is debatable as to whether this really violates durability as the compensating transaction is a completely separate transaction. The request column indicates where the transaction is assumed to be requested. All but the Reporting model assume it is requested at the mobile unit. Since this model is more general than the others and not limited to a mobile computing environment, it does not assume the initial request is made from any particular site. The Execute column (Figure 7.2) indicates the sites where it is assumed that KT will execute. Again, this really does not apply to the Reporting approach. The KT limits processing to nodes on the fixed network, while the Semantics approach assumes that the execution at a server on the fixed network is limited to the creation and update of the fragments.

The location-dependent, location-aware, location-independent, intermittent execution, and so on, are some of the important issues that are interrelated and need a unified processing by a single model. A model called *Mobilaction* has tried to capture these into one model, and this is discussed next.

7.5.4 Mobilaction—A Mobile Transaction Model

In this section, a new mobile transaction model called *Mobilaction* is presented in reference 27. Mobilaction is capable of processing location-dependent queries. It is composed of a set of subtransactions that is also called *execution fragments*, and each fragment is a Mobilaction.

Mobilaction is based on the framework of an ACID model. To manage location-based processing, a new fundamental property called "location (L)" is incorporated into the ACID model, extending it to ACIDL. Thus, the capability of processing location-dependent queries is a part of the structure of Mobilaction. The "location (L)" property is managed by a location mapping function. Formally,

Definition 7.8   *A Mobilaction (T_i) equals $<F_i, L_i, FLM_i>$, where $F_i = \{e_i 1, \ldots, e_i n\}$ is a set of execution fragments, $L_i = \{l_i 1, \ldots, l_i n\}$ is a set of locations, and $FLM_i = \{flm_i 1, \ldots, flm_i n\}$ is a set of fragment location mappings where $\forall j, flm_i j(e_i j) = l_i j$. In addition, $\forall j, k, l_i j <> l_i k$.*

Definition 7.9   *Fragment Location Mapping (FLM): Each execution fragment, e_j, of a mobile transaction, T_i, is associated with a unique location. Given a set of execution fragments E, FLM is a mapping $FLM : E \rightarrow L$.*

■ EXAMPLE 7.2

Suppose a driver who is driving on an interstate asks a location-dependent query (LDQ) Which city am I in right now? It is an LDQ because the name of the city depends on the location (implied by "right now") of this query. To process this query, the FLM must first map the longitude and latitude of "right now" to a geographical location. Thus, if the lat-long of "right now" is 39.07-95.62, then the current location will be mapped to a point in the city of Topeka, KS.

The *FLM* identifies the location with respect to which execution fragment is executed and which spatial replica is to be used for each data object in that fragment. In addition, it is used to ensure spatial consistency of fragments within a transaction.

Atomicity for Mobilaction.   The purpose of atomicity is to ensure the consistency of the data. However, in a mobile environment we have two types of consistency. Certainly, atomicity at the execution fragment level is needed to ensure spatial consistency; however, transaction atomicity is not. We could have some fragments execute and others not.

Definition 7.10   *A mobile transaction, T_i, satisfies spatial atomicity iff each execution fragment, $e_i j$, of T_i is atomic. T_i is said to be spatially atomic iff each execution fragment, $e_i j$, is atomic.*

Isolation for Mobilaction.   Transaction isolation ensures that a transaction does not interfere with the execution of another transaction. Isolation is normally enforced by some concurrency control mechanism. As with atomicity, isolation is needed to ensure that consistency is preserved. Thus, we need to reevaluate isolation when spatial consistency is present. As with consistency, isolation at the transaction level is too strict.

The important thing is to ensure that execution fragments satisfy isolation at the execution fragment level.

Definition 7.11   *A mobile transaction, T_i, satisfies* **spatial isolation** *iff each execution fragment, $e_i j$, of T_i is isolated from all execution fragments of T_i or any other transaction.*

Note that Mobilaction will need to implement a concurrency control technique at the fragment level. Any concurrency control technique could be used. As a matter of fact, a different technique could be used for each fragment. The topic of concurrency control in a mobile database system is discussed later in this chapter.

Consistency and Durability for Mobilaction.   A conventional transaction commit satisfies the durability property. There is normally only one commit operation per T_i. However, to ensure spatial consistency, spatial isolation, and spatial atomicity, mobility requires that the commit must also change. We introduce the concept of a *location-dependent commit*.

Definition 7.12   *An execution fragment, $e_i j$, satisfies a location-dependent commit iff the fragment operations terminate with a commit operation and an FLM exists. Thus, all operations in $e_i j$ operate on spatial replicas defined by data region mapping on the location identified by the FLM. The commit is thus associated with a unique location, L.*

■ **EXAMPLE 7.3**

The commit of an LDQ at a location different than its origin may not be meaningful. Consider the LDQ, *Which city am I in right now?* The LDQ must complete and commit successfully in the city of Topeka (if Topeka is the origin of the LDQ) before the mobile unit moves to a different city. If it commits in a different city, then there will be a mismatch between the current location and the name of the city.

Definition 7.13   *An* **execution fragment** $e_i j$ *is a partial order $e_i j = \{\sigma_j, \leq_j\}$ where*

- $\sigma_j = OS_j \cup \{N_j\}$ *where* $OS_j = \cup_k O_j k$, $O_j k \in \{read, write\}$, *and* $N_j \in \{abort_L, commit_L\}$. *Here, these are a location-dependent commit and abort.*
- *For any $O_j k$ and $O_j l$ where $O_j k = R(x)$ and $O_j l = W(x)$ for a data object x, then either $O_j k \leq_j O_j l$ or $O_j l \leq_j O_j k$.*
- $\forall O_j k \in OS_j, O_j k \leq_j N_j$

The only difference between an execution fragment and a transaction is that either a location-dependent commit or abort is present instead of a traditional commit or abort. Every fragment is thus associated with a location. However, keep in mind that if the data object being updated is a temporal replica, then the fragment updates all replicas. Thus, it is not subjected to location constraints and appears as a regular transaction.

In traditional database systems, an ACID transaction is assumed to be a unit of consistency. Even with spatial atomicity, this is still the case with a Mobilaction. A Mobilaction is a unit of consistency. That is, given a database state that is both temporally and spatially consistent, a Mobilaction T_i converts this state into another temporally and spatially consistent state.

An Example of a Mobilaction

■ **EXAMPLE 7.4**

Suppose a driver who is driving on an interstate asks a location-dependent query LDQ, *Which city am I in right now and what is the distance to the Kansas City airport from here?* It is an LDQ because the name of the city and the distance to the airport depend on the location (implied by "right now") of this query. Two fragments will be created to process this query. LDQ1, *Which city am I in right now?*, and LDQ2, *What is the distance to the Kansas City airport from here?* They must be processed in the order LDQ1 then LDQ2 since LDQ2 needs the result of LDQ1. The FLM will first map the longitude and latitude of "right now" to a geographical location (Topeka, KS) and LDQ2 will use this location point to compute the distance. If the LDQ, *What is the distance to the airport from here?* or the LDQ, Where am I? is asked multiple times while the driver (the mobile unit in his car) is continuously moving, the FLM will have to map each "here" (this is embedded in the *where am I?* query) and point to a new current location to get the distance from each location.

7.6   DATA CONSISTENCY IN INTERMITTENT CONNECTIVITY

Mobile clients (mobile units) encounter *wide variations* in connectivity ranging from high-bandwidth, low-latency communications through wired networks, to a total lack of connectivity [28–30]. Between these two extremes, connectivity is frequently provided by wireless networks characterized by low bandwidth, excessive latency, or high cost. To overcome availability and latency barriers and reduce cost and power consumption, mobile clients most often deliberately avoid use of the network and thus operate switching between connected and disconnected modes of operation. To support such behavior, the *disconnected operation* (the ability to operate in a disconnected mode) is essential for mobile clients [29, 31–33]. In addition to the disconnected operation, the operation that exploits *weak connectivity*, that is, the connectivity provided by intermittent, low-bandwidth, or expensive networks—is also desirable [34]. Besides mobile computing, weak and intermittent connectivity also applies to computing using portable laptops. In this paradigm, clients operate in a disconnected mode most of the time, and they occasionally connect to an MDS through a wired telephone line or upon returning back to their working environment.

In the existing schemes, data located at strongly connected sites are grouped together to form clusters. Mutual consistency is required for copies located at the same cluster, while degrees of inconsistency are tolerated for copies at different clusters. The interface offered by the database management system is enhanced with operations providing weaker consistency guarantees. Such weak operations allow access to locally (i.e., in a cluster) available data. Weak reads access bounded inconsistent copies, and weak writes make conditional updates. The usual operations, called strict in this chapter, are also supported. They offer access to consistent data and perform permanent updates.

The scheme supports the disconnected operation since users can operate even when disconnected by using only weak operations. In cases of weak connectivity, a balanced use of both weak and strict operations provides for better bandwidth utilization, latency, and cost. In cases of strong connectivity, using only strict operations will reduce the scheme to the usual one-copy semantics. Additional support for adaptability is possible by tuning the degree of inconsistency among copies based on the networking conditions.

In a sense, weak operations offer a form of *application-aware adaptation* [35]. Application-aware adaptation characterizes the design space between two extreme ways of providing adaptability. At one extreme, adaptivity is entirely the responsibility of the application, that is, there is no system support or any standard way of providing adaptivity. At the other extreme, adaptivity is subsumed by the database management system. Since, in general, the system is not aware of the application semantics, it cannot provide a single adequate form of adaptation. Weak and strict operations lie in an intermediate point between these two extremes, serving as *middleware* between a database system and an application. They are tools offered by the database system to applications. The application can (at its discretion) use weak or strict transactions based on its semantics. The implementation, consistency control, and the underlying transactional support are the jobs of the database management system.

7.7 THE CONSISTENCY MODEL

The sites of a distributed system are grouped together in sets called *physical clusters* (or p-clusters) so that sites that are strongly connected with each other belong to the same p-cluster, while sites that are weakly connected with each other belong to different p-clusters. Strong connectivity refers to connectivity achieved through high-bandwidth and low-latency communications. Weak connectivity includes connectivity that is intermittent or low bandwidth. The goal is to support autonomous operations at each physical cluster, thus eliminating the need for communication among p-clusters, since such inter-cluster communication may be expensive, prohibitively slow, and occasionally unavailable. To this end, weak transactions are defined that access copies at a single p-cluster. At the same time, the usual atomic, consistent, durable, and isolated distributed transactions, called strict, are also supported.

7.7.1 The Extended Database Operation Interface

To increase availability and reduce inter-cluster communication, direct access to locally (e.g., in a p-cluster) available copies is achieved through *weak read (WR)* and *weak write (WW)* operations. Weak operations are local at a p-cluster; that is, they access copies that reside at a single p-cluster. We say that a copy or item is locally available at a p-cluster if there exists a copy of that item at the p-cluster. We call the standard read and write operations strict read (*SR*) and strict write (*SW*) operations. To implement this dual database interface, we distinguish the copies of each data item as core and quasi. *Core* copies are copies that have permanent values, while *quasi-copies* are copies that have only conditionally committed values. When connectivity is restored, the values of core and quasi-copies of each data item are *reconciled* to attain a system-wide consistent value.

To process the operations of a transaction, the database management system translates operations on data items into operations on copies of these data items. This procedure is formalized by a *translation function h*. Function h maps each read operation on a data item x into a number of read operations on copies of x and returns one value (e.g., the most up-to-date value), as the value read by the operation. That is, we assume that h, when applied to a read operation, returns one value rather than a set of values. In particular, h maps each $SR[x]$ operation into a number of read operations on core copies of x and returns one from these values as the value read by the operation. Depending on how each weak read operation is translated, we define two types of translation functions. The first is a *best-effort* translation function that maps each $WR[x]$ operation into a number of read operations on locally available core (or quasi-copies of) x and returns the most up-to-date value. The second type is a *conservative* translation function that maps each weak read operation into a number of read operations only on locally available quasi-copies and returns the most up-to-date value.

Based on the time of propagation of updates of core copies to quasi-copies, two types of translation functions are defined (a) an *eventual* translation function that maps an $SW[x]$ into writes of core copies only and (b) an *immediate* translation function that in addition updates the quasi-copies that reside at the same p-cluster with the core copies written. For an immediate h, conservative and best effort have the same result. Each $WW[x]$ operation is translated by h into a number of write operations of local quasi-copies of x. How many and which core or quasi-copies are actually read or written when a database operation is issued on a data item depends on the coherency algorithm used (e.g., quorum consensus) and ROWA [36]. Table 7.3 summarizes the semantics of operations.

Definition 7.14 *A transaction (T) is a partial order (OP, <), where OP is the set of operations executed by the transaction, and < represents their execution order. The operations include the following data operations: weak (WR) or strict reads (SR) and weak (WW) or strict writes (SW), as well as abort (A) and commit (C) operations. The partial order must specify the order of conflicting data operations and contains exactly one abort or commit operation which is the last in the order. Two weak or*

Table 7.3   Variations of the Translation Function

Weak Read (WR)	Reads local copies and returns the most recent value	
	Variations	Best effor h: Reads both core and local quasi-copies
		Conservative h: Reads only local quasi-copies
Strict Read (SR)	Reads core copies and returns the most recent value	
Weak Write (WW)	Writes local quasi-copies	
Strict Write (SW)	Variations	Eventual h: Writes only core copies
		Immediate h: Writes both core and quasi-copies at the corresponding p-clusters

strict data operations conflict *if they access the same copy of a data item and at least one of them is a weak or strict write operation.*

Two types of transactions are supported: *weak* and *strict*. A *strict* transaction (*ST*) is a transaction where *OP* does not include any weak operations. Strict transactions are atomic, consistent, isolated, and durable. A *weak* transaction (*WT*) is a transaction where *OP* does not include any strict operations. Weak transactions access data copies that reside at the same physical cluster and thus are executed locally at this p-cluster. Weak transactions are *locally* committed at the p-cluster at which they are executed.

After local commitment, their updates are visible only to weak transactions: in the same p-cluster, other transactions are not aware of these updates. Local commitment of weak transactions is conditional in the sense that their updates might become permanent only after reconciliation when local transactions may become globally committed. Thus, there are two commit events associated with each weak transaction, a local conditional commit in its associated cluster and an implicit *global commit* at reconciliation.

Other types of transactions that combine weak and strict operations can be envisioned; however, their semantics become hard to define. Instead, weak and strict transactions can be seen as transaction units of some advanced transaction model. In this regard, upon its submission, each user transaction is decomposed into a number of weak and strict subtransaction units (according to semantics), and the degree of consistency is required by the application.

7.7.2 Data Correctness

A database is a set of data items and a database *state* is defined as a mapping of every data item to a value of its domain. Data items are related by a number of restrictions called *integrity constraints* that express relationships among their values. A database state is consistent if the integrity constraints are satisfied [37]. In this paper, we consider integrity constraints being arithmetic expressions that have data items as variables. Consistency maintenance in traditional distributed environments relies on the assumption that normally all sites are connected. This assumption, however, is no longer valid in mobile computing, since the distributed sites are only intermittently connected. Similar network connectivity conditions also hold in widely distributed systems as well as in computing with portable laptops.

To take intermittent connectivity into account, instead of requiring maintenance of all integrity constraints of a distributed database, *logical clusters* are introduced as units of consistency. A logical cluster, l-cluster, is the set of all quasi-copies that reside at the same p-cluster. In addition, all core copies constitute a single system-wide logical cluster independently of the site at which they physically reside. Consistency is relaxed in the sense that integrity constraints are ensured only for data copies that belong to the same logical cluster. An intra-cluster integrity constraint is an integrity constraint that can be fully evaluated using data copies of a single logical cluster. All other integrity constraints are called inter-cluster integrity constraints.

Definition 7.15 *A mobile database state is consistent if all intra-cluster integrity constraints are satisfied and all inter-cluster integrity constraints are bounded inconsistent.*

In inter-cluster integrity constraints bounded inconsistency means that all copies in the same logical cluster have the same value while there is bounded divergence among copies at different logical clusters [38, 39]. Bounded divergence is quantified by a positive integer d, called a *degree of divergence*. Possible definitions of d are as follows:

- Maximum number of transactions that operate on quasi-copies
- Range of acceptable values that a data item can take
- Maximum number of copies per data item that diverge from a preassigned primary copy of the item, that is, the core copies
- Maximum number of data items that have divergent copies
- Maximum number of updates per data item that are not reflected at all database copies

A replication constraint for x (thus bounded) is called d-consistent. The degree of divergence among copies can be tuned based on the strength of the connection among the physical clusters, by keeping the divergence small in instances of high bandwidth availability and allowing for greater deviation in instances of low bandwidth availability.

Immediate Translation and Consistency. To handle integrity constraints besides replication, in the case of an *immediate* translation function h, h should be defined in order that the integrity constraints between quasi-copies in the same logical cluster are not violated. The following example is illustrative.

■ **EXAMPLE 7.5**

For simplicity, consider only one physical cluster. Assume two data items x and y, which are related by the integrity constraint $x > 0 \Rightarrow y > 0$, and a consistent database state $x_c = -1$, $x_q = -1$, $y_c = 2$ and $y_q = -4$, where the subscripts c and q denote core and quasi-copies, respectively. Consider the transaction:

```
x = 10
if y < 0
then y = 10
```

If the above program is executed as a strict transaction $SW(x)\ SR(y)\ C$, it sets the database state $x_c = 10$, $x_q = 10$, $y_c = 2$ and $y_q = -4$, in which the integrity constraint between the quasi-copies of x and y is violated. Note that the quasi-copies were updated because an immediate translation function was considered.

The problem arises from the fact that quasi-copies are updated to the current value of the core copy without taking into consideration the integrity constraints among them. Similar problems occur when refreshing individual copies of a cache [38]. Possible solutions include

a. Each time a quasi-copy is updated at a physical cluster as a result of a strict write, the quasi-copies of all data in this cluster (related to it by some integrity constraint) are also updated either after or prior to the execution of the transaction. This update is done following a reconciliation procedure for merging core and quasi-copies (as in Section 7.9). In the above example, the core and quasi-copies of x and y should have been reconciled prior to the execution of the transaction, producing, for instance, the database state $x_c = -1$, $x_q = -1$ $y_c = 2$, and $y_q = 2$. Then, the execution of the transaction would result in the database state $x_c = 10$, $x_q = 10$, $y_c = 2$ and $y_q = 2$, which is consistent.

b. If a strict transaction updates a quasi-copy at a physical cluster, its read operations are also mapped into reads of quasi-copies at this cluster. In cases of incompatible reads, again, a reconciliation procedure is initiated having a result similar to the one above.

c. Updating quasi-copies is postponed by deferring any updates of quasi-copies that result from writes of the corresponding core copies. A log of weak writes, resulting from strict writes is kept. In this scenario, the execution of the transaction results in the database state $x_c = 10$, $x_q = -1$, $y_c = 2$, and $y_q = -4$, which is consistent. The first two approaches may force an immediate reconciliation among copies, while the third approach defers this reconciliation and is preferable in cases of low connectivity among physical clusters.

7.8 WEAK CONNECTIVITY OPERATION

This section covers serializability-based criteria, graph-based tests, and a locking protocol for correct executions that exploit weak connectivity. In the operation represented by o_j, the subscript j indicates that o belongs to transaction j, while the subscript on a data copy identifies the physical cluster at which the copy is located. It is assumed that there was only one quasi-copy per physical cluster. This assumption can be easily lifted but with significant complication in notation. Since all quasi-copies in a physical cluster have the same value, this single copy can be regarded as their representative. Read and write operations on copies are denoted by *read* and *write*, respectively.

A complete intra-cluster schedule, IAS is an observation of an interleaved execution of transactions in a given physical cluster configuration, which includes (locally) committed weak transactions and (globally) committed strict transactions. Formally,

Definition 7.16 (Intra-cluster Schedule) *Let* $T = \{T_0, T_1, \ldots, T_n\}$ *be a set of transactions. A (complete) intra-cluster schedule, IAS, over T is a pair* $(OP, <_a)$ *in which* $<_a$ *is a partial ordering relation such that:*

1. $OP = h(\bigcup_{i=0}^{n} T_i)$ *for some translation function h. This condition states that the transaction managers translate each operation on a data item into appropriate operations on data copies.*

2. *For each* T_i *and all operations* op_k, op_l *in* T_i, *if* $op_k <_i op_l$, *then every operation in* $h(op_k)$ *is related by* $<_a$ *to every operation in* $h(op_l)$. *This condition states that the intra-cluster schedule preserves the ordering* $<_i$ *stipulated by each transaction* T_i.

3. *All pairs of conflicting operations are related by* $<_a$, *where two operations conflict if they access the same copy and one of them is a write operation. This states that the execution order of conflicting operations are also recorded.*

4. *For all read operations,* $read_j[x_i]$, *there is at least one* $write_k[x_i]$ *such that* $write_k[x_i] <_a read_j[x_i]$. *This condition states that a transaction cannot read a copy unless it has been previously initialized.*

5. *If* $SW_j[x] <_j SR_j[x]$ *and* $read_j(x_i) \in h(SR_j[x])$, *then* $write_j(x_i) \in h(SW_j[x])$. *This condition states that, if a transaction writes a data item x before it reads x, then it must write to the same copy of x that it subsequently reads.*

6. *If* $write_j[x_i] \in h(SW_j[x])$ *for some strict transaction* T_j, *then* $write_j[y_i] \in h(SW_j[y])$, *for all y written by* T_j *for which there is a* y_i *at physical cluster* Cl_i, *where* x_i *is a quasi-copy when h is conservative and any, quasi or core, copy when h is best effort. This condition indicates that for a strict transaction, if a write is translated to a write on a core copy at a physical cluster* Cl_i *then all other writes of this transaction must also write any corresponding copies at this cluster. This condition is necessary for ensuring that weak transactions do not see partial results of a strict transaction.*

A read operation on a data item x *reads-x-from* a transaction T_i, if it reads (i.e., returns as the value read) a copy of x written by T_i and no other transaction writes this copy in between. A transaction T_i has the *same reads-from* relationship in schedule S_1 as in schedule S_2, if for any data item x, if T_i reads-x-from T_j in S_1, then it reads-x-from T_j in S_2. Given a schedule S, the *projection of S on strict transactions* is the schedule obtained from S by deleting all weak operations, and the *projection of S on a physical cluster Cl_k* is the schedule obtained from S by deleting all operations that do not access copies in Cl_k. Two schedules are *conflict equivalent* if they are defined over the same set of transactions, have the same set of operations, and order conflicting operations of committed transactions the same way [36]. A *one-copy* schedule is the single-copy interpretation of an (intra-cluster) schedule where all operations on data copies are represented as operations on the corresponding data item.

7.8.1 Correctness Criterion

A correct concurrent execution of weak and strict transactions must maintain bounded-inconsistency. A weak form of correctness, in which the only requirement for weak transactions is that they read consistent data, is considered first. The requirement for strict transactions is stronger, because they must produce a system-wide consistent database state. In particular, the execution of strict transactions must hide the existence of multiple core copies per item; that is, it must be view-equivalent to a one-copy schedule [36]. A replicated-copy schedule S is *view-equivalent to a one-copy schedule* S_{1C}:

- If S and S_{1C} have the same reads-from relationship for all data items, and
- For each final write $WR_i(x)$ in S_{1C}, $write_i(x_j)$ is a final write in S for some copy x_j of x.

These requirements for the execution of strict and weak transactions are expressed in the following definition:

Definition 7.17 (IAS Weak Correctness) *An intra-cluster schedule S_{IAS} is weakly correct iff all the following three conditions are satisfied*

1. *All transactions in S_{IAS} have a consistent view; that is, all integrity constraints that can be evaluated using the data read are valid.*
2. *There is a one-copy serial schedule S such that: (a) it is defined on the same set of strict transactions as S_{IAS}, (b) strict transactions in S have the same reads-from relationship as in S_{IAS}, and (c) the set of final writes in S is the same as the set of final writes on core copies in S_{IAS},*
3. *Bounded divergence among copies at different logical clusters is maintained.*

The approach to enforce the first two conditions is discussed first. Protocols for bounding the divergence among copies at different logical clusters are outlined at the end of this section. A schedule is *one-copy serializable* if it is equivalent to a serial one-copy schedule. The following theorem defines correctness in terms of equivalence to serial executions.

Theorem 7.1   *Given that bounded divergence among copies at different logical clusters is maintained, if the projection of an intra-cluster schedule S on strict transactions is one-copy serializable and each of its projections on a physical cluster is conflict-equivalent to a serial schedule, then S is weakly correct.*

Proof: Condition (1) of Definition 7.17 is guaranteed for strict transactions from the requirement of one-copy serializability, since strict transactions get the same view as in a one-copy serial schedule and read only core copies. For weak transactions at a physical cluster, the first condition is provided from the requirement of serializability of the projection of the schedule on this cluster, given that the projection of each (weak or strict) transaction on the cluster satisfies all intra-cluster integrity constraints when executed alone. Thus, it suffices to prove that such projections maintain the intra-cluster integrity constraints. This trivially holds for weak transactions, since they are local at a physical cluster. The condition also holds for strict transactions. As long as a strict transaction maintains consistency of all database integrity constraints, then its projection on any cluster also maintains the consistency of intra-cluster integrity constraints, as a consequence of Condition (6) of Definition 7.16. Finally, one-copy serializability of the projection of strict transactions suffices to guarantee 2(b) and 2(c), since strict transactions read only core copies and weak transactions do not write core copies, respectively.

Inter-cluster integrity constraints, other than replication constraints among quasi-copies of data items at different clusters, may be violated. Weak transactions, however, are unaffected by such violations, since they read only local data. Although the above correctness criterion suffices to ensure that each weak transaction gets a consistent view, it does not suffice to ensure that weak transactions at different physical clusters get the same view, even in the absence of intercluster integrity constraints. This is illustrated by the following example.

■ EXAMPLE 7.6

Assume two physical clusters $Cl_1 = \{x, y\}$ and $Cl_2 = \{w, z, l\}$ with both quasi and core copies of the corresponding data items, and two strict transactions $ST_1 = SW_1[x]$ $SW_1[w]C_1$ and $ST_2 = SW_2 \, [y]SW_2[z]SR_2[x]C_2$. In addition, at cluster Cl_1 there is a weak transaction $WT_3 = WR_3[x]WR_3[y] \, C_3$, and at cluster Cl_2 the weak transactions are $WT_4 = WR_4[z] \, WW_4[l] \, C_4$, and $WT_5 = WR_5[w] \, WR_5[l] \, C_5$. For simplicity, the transaction that initializes all data copies is not shown. We consider an immediate and best-effort translation function h. For notational simplicity, no special notation for the core and quasi-copies have been used, since the copies that are read are inferred by the translation function.

Assume that the execution of the above transactions produces the following schedule, which is weakly correct:

$$S = WR_5[w]SW_1[x]WR_3[x]SW_1[w]C_1SW_2[y]SW_2[z]SR_2[x]C_2WR_3[y]C_3WR_4[z]$$
$$WW_4[l]C_4WR_5[l]C_5$$

The projection of S on strict transactions is $SW_1[x]SW_1[w]C_1SW_2[y]SW_2[z]C_2$, which is equivalent to the 1SR schedule: $SW_1[x]SW_1[w]C_1SW_2[y]SW_2[z]C_2$.

The projection of S on Cl_1: $SW_1[x]WR_3[x]C_1SW_2[y]SR_2[x]WR_3[y]C_3$ is serializable as $ST_1 \to ST_2 \to WT_3$.

The projection of S on Cl_2: $WR_5[w]SW_1[w]C_1SW_2[z]C_2WR_4[z]WW_4[l]C_4WR_5[l]C_5$ is serializable as $ST_2 \to WT_4 \to WT_5 \to ST_1$.

Thus, weak correctness does not guarantee that there is a serial schedule equivalent to the intra-cluster schedule as a whole—that is, including all weak and strict transactions. The following is a stronger correctness criterion that ensures that all weak transactions get the same consistent view. Obviously, strong correctness implies weak correctness.

Definition 7.18 (IAS Strong Correctness) *An intra-cluster schedule S is strongly correct iff there is a serial schedule S_S such that:*

1. *S_S is conflict-equivalent with S.*
2. *There is a one-copy schedule S_{1C} such that (a) strict transactions in S_S have the same reads-from relationship as in S_{1C}, and (b) the set of final writes on core copies in S_S is the same as in S_{1C}.*
3. *Bounded divergence among copies at different logical clusters is maintained.*

Lemma 7.1 *Given that bounded divergence among copies at different logical clusters is maintained, if the projection of an intra-cluster schedule S is conflict-equivalent to a serial schedule S_S and its projection on strict transactions is view equivalent to a one-copy serial schedule S_{1C} so that the order of transactions in S_S is consistent with the order of transactions in S_{1C}, S is strongly correct.*

Proof: It is necessary to prove that in S_{1C} strict transactions have the same reads-from and final writes as in S_S, which is straightforward, since strict transactions only read data produced by strict transactions and core copies are written only by strict transactions.

Since weak transactions do not conflict with weak transactions at other clusters directly, the following is an equivalent statement of the above lemma.

Corollary 7.1 *Given that bounded divergence among copies at different logical clusters is maintained, if the projection of an intra-cluster schedule S on strict* *transactions is view equivalent to a one-copy serial schedule S_{1C}, and each of its projections on a physical cluster Cl_i is conflict-equivalent to a serial schedule S_{S_i} such that the order of transactions in S_{S_i} is consistent with the order of transactions in S_{1C}, S is strongly correct.*

If weak *IAS* correctness is used as the correctness criterion, then the transaction managers at each physical cluster must only synchronize projections on their cluster. Global control is required only for synchronizing strict transactions. Therefore, no control messages are necessary between transaction managers at different clusters for synchronizing weak transactions. The proposed scheme is flexible, in that any coherency control method that guarantees one-copy serializability (e.g., quorum consensus, primary copy) can be used for synchronizing core copies. The scheme reduces to one-copy serializability when only strict transactions are used.

7.8.2 The Serialization Graph

To determine whether an *IAS* schedule is correct, a modified serialization graph that we call the *intra-cluster serialization graph* (IASG) of the *IAS* schedule is used. To construct the *IASG*, first a replicated data serialization graph (SG) is built that includes all strict transactions. An SG [36] is a serialization graph augmented with additional edges to take into account the fact that operations on different copies of the same data item may also create conflicts. Acyclicity of the SG implies one-copy serializability of the corresponding schedule. Then, the *SG* is augmented to include weak transactions as well as edges that represent conflicts between weak transactions in the same cluster and weak and strict transactions. An edge is called a *dependency edge* if it represents the fact that a transaction reads a value produced by another transaction. An edge is called a *precedence edge* if it represents the fact that a transaction reads a value that was later changed by another transaction. It is easy to see that in the IASG there are no edges between weak transactions at different clusters, since weak transactions at different clusters read different copies of a data item. In addition:

Property 7.1 *Let WT_i be a weak transaction at cluster Cl_i and let ST be a strict transaction. The IASG graph, induced by an IAS, may include only the following edges between them:*

- *a dependency edge from ST to WT_i*
- *a precedence edge from WT_i to ST*

Proof: Straightforward, since the only conflicts between weak and strict transactions are due to strict writes and weak reads of the same copy of a data item.

Theorem 7.2 *Let S_{IAS} be an intra-cluster schedule. If S_{IAS} has an acyclic IASG, then S_{IAS} is strongly correct.*

Proof: When a graph is acyclic, then each of its subgraphs is acyclic, and thus the underlying SG on which the *IASG* was built is acyclic. Acyclicity of the SG implies one-copy serializability of strict transactions, since strict transactions only read values produced by strict transactions. Let $T_1, T_2, \ldots, T_n$ be all transactions in S_{IAS}. Thus, $T_1, T_2, \ldots, T_n$ are the nodes of the IASG. Since IASG is acyclic, it can be topologically sorted. Let $T_{i_1}, T_{i_2}, \ldots, T_{i_n}$ be a topological sort of the edges in the IASG, then by a straightforward application of the serializability theorem [36], S_{IAS} is conflict equivalent to the serial schedule $S_S = T_{i_1}, T_{i_2}, \ldots, T_{i_n}$. This order is consistent with the partial order induced by a topological sorting of the SG; let S_{1C} be the serial schedule corresponding to this sorting. Thus, the order of transactions in S_S is consistent with the order of transactions in S_{1C}.

7.8.3 Protocols

Serializability. It is important to distinguish between coherency and concurrency control protocols. Coherency control ensures that all copies of a data item have the same value in the proposed scheme, where we must maintain this property globally for core and locally for quasi-copies. Concurrency control ensures the maintanance of the other integrity constraints and here, the intra-cluster integrity constraints. For coherency control, we assume a generic quorum-based scheme [36]. Each strict transaction reads q_r core copies and writes q_w core copies per strict read and write operation. The values of q_r, and q_w for a data item x are such that $q_r + q_w > n_d$, where n_d is the number of available core copies of x. For concurrency control we use *strict two phase locking*, where each transaction releases its locks upon commitment [36]. Weak transactions release their locks upon local commitment and strict transactions upon global commitment. There are four lock modes (*WR, WW, SR, SW*) corresponding to the four data operations. Before the execution of each operation, the corresponding lock is requested. A lock is granted only if the data copy is not locked in an incompatible lock mode. Figure 7.11 depicts the compatibility of locks for various types of translation functions and is presented to demonstrate the interference between operations on items. Differences in compatibility stem from the fact the operations access different kinds of copies. The basic overhead on the performance of weak transactions imposed by these protocols is caused by other weak transactions at the same cluster. This overhead is small, since weak transactions do not access the slow network. Strict transactions block a weak transaction only when they access the same quasi-copies. This interference is limited and can be controlled, for example, by letting in cases of disconnections, strict transactions access only core copies, and weak transactions access only quasi-copies.

Bounding Divergence among Copies. At each p-cluster, the degree for each data item expresses the divergence of the local quasi-copy from the value of the core copy. This difference may result either from globally uncommitted weak writes or from updates of core copies that have not yet been reported at the cluster. As a consequence, the degree may be bounded by either limiting the number of weak writes pending global commitment or by controlling the h function. Table 7.4 outlines methods for maintaining d-consistency for different ways of defining d.

	WR	WW	SR	SW
WR	X		X	X
WW			X	X
SR	X	X	X	
SW	X	X		

(a)

	WR	WW	SR	SW
WR	X		X	
WW			X	X
SR	X	X	X	
SW		X		

(b)

	WR	WW	SR	SW
WR	X		X	X
WW			X	
SR	X	X	X	
SW	X			

(c)

	WR	WW	SR	SW
WR	X		X	
WW			X	
SR	X	X	X	
SW				

(d)

Figure 7.11 Lock compatibility matrices. An X entry indicates that the lock modes are compatible. (a) Eventual and conservative h. (b) Eventual and best effort h. (c) Immediate and conservative h. (d) Immediate and best effort h.

Table 7.4 Maintaining Bounded Inconsistency

Definition of Divergence (d)	Applicable Method
The maximum number of transactions that operate on quasi-copies.	Appropriately bound the number of weak transactions at each phyical cluster. In the case of a dynamic cluster reconfiguration, the distribution of weak transactions at each cluster must be readjusted.
A range of acceptable values of a data item.	Allow only weak writes with values inside the acceptable range.
The maximum number of divergent copies per data item.	Writes local quasi-copies.
The maximum number of data items that have divergent copies.	Bound the number of data items that can have quasi-copies.
The maximum number of updates per data item not reflected at all copies.	Define h so that each strict write modifies the quasi-copies at each physical cluster at least after d updates. This, however, cannot be ensured for disconnected clusters since there is no way of notifying them for remote updates.

7.9 A CONSISTENCY RESTORATION SCHEMA

After the execution of a number of weak and strict transactions, for each data item, all its core copies have the same value, while its quasi-copies may have as many different values as the number of physical clusters. Approaches to reconciling the various values of a data item, so that a single value is selected, vary from purely syntactic to purely semantic ones [40]. In restoring the database state, syntactic approaches use serializability-based criteria, while semantic approaches use either the semantics of transactions or the semantics of data items. A purely syntactic (and thus application-independent approach) is adopted here. The exact point when reconciliation is initiated depends on the application requirements and the distributed system characteristics. For instance, reconciliation may be forced to keep inconsistency inside the required limits. Alternatively, it may be initiated periodically or on demand upon the occurrence of specific events, such as the restoration of network connectivity—for instance, when a PDA (personal digital assistant or palmtop) is plugged-back to the stationary network or a mobile host enters a region with good connectivity.

7.9.1 Correctness Criterion

The reconciliation approach is based on the following rule: *A weak transaction becomes globally committed if the inclusion of its write operations in the schedule does not violate the one-copy serializability of strict transactions.* It assumes that weak transactions at different clusters do not interfere with each other even after reconciliation; that is, weak operations of transactions at different clusters never conflict. A (complete) inter-cluster schedule, IES, models execution after reconciliation, where strict transactions become aware of weak writes; that is, weak transactions become globally committed. Thus, in addition to the conflicts reported in the intra-cluster schedule, the inter-cluster schedule reports all relevant conflicts between weak and strict operations. In particular:

Definition 7.19 (Intercluster Schedule) *An inter-cluster schedule (IES) S_{IES} based on an intra-cluster schedule $S_{IAS} = (OP, <_a)$ is a pair $(OP', <_e)$ where:*

1. *$OP' = OP$; and for any op_i and $op_j \in OP'$, if $op_i <_a op_j$ in S_{IAS}, then $op_i <_e op_j$ in S_{IES}. In addition:*
2. *For each pair of weak write $op_i = WW_i[x]$ and strict read $op_j = SR_j[x]$ operations, we have for all pairs of operations either $cop_i \in h(op_i)$ and $cop_j \in h(op_j)$, $cop_i <_e cop_j$, or $cop_j <_e cop_i$.*
3. *For each pair of weak write $op_i = WW_i[x]$ and strict write $op_j = SW_j[x]$ operations, we have for all pairs of operations either $cop_i \in h(op_i)$ and $cop_j \in h(op_j)$, $cop_i <_e cop_j$, or $cop_j <_e cop_i$.*

The reads-from relationship for strict transactions is extended to take weak writes into account. A strict read operation on a data item x *reads x from* a transaction T_i in an IES schedule, if it reads a copy of x and T_i, has written this or any quasi-copy of x and no other transaction wrote this or any quasi-copy of x in between. A weak write by a strict transaction is acceptable as long as the extended reads-from relationship for strict transactions is not affected; that is, strict transactions still read values produced by strict transactions. In addition, correctness of the underlying *IAS* schedule implies one-copy serializability of strict transactions and consistency of weak transactions.

Definition 7.20 (IES Correctness) *An inter-cluster schedule is correct iff:*

1. *It is based on a correct IAS schedule S_{IAS}.*
2. *The reads-from relationship for strict transactions is the same with their reads-from relationship in the S_{IAS}.*

7.9.2 The Serialization Graph

A modified serialization graph called an *inter-cluster serialization graph* (IESG) is defined to determine a correct *IES (inter-cluster schedule)* and to construct an IESG, and the IASG (intra-cluster serialization graph) of the underlying intra-cluster schedule is augmented. The following steps are induced to force conflicts among weak and strict transactions that access different copies of the same data item:

- First, a write order as follows: If T_i weak writes and T_k strict writes any copy of an item x, then either $T_i \rightarrow T_k$ or $T_k \rightarrow T_i$; and then
- A strict read order as follows: If a strict transaction ST_j reads-x-from ST_i in S_{IAS} and a weak transaction WT follows ST_i, we add an edge $ST_j \rightarrow WT$.

Theorem 7.3 *Let S_{IES} be an IES schedule based on an IAS schedule S_{IAS}. If S_{IES} has an acyclic IESG, then S_{IES} is correct.*

Proof: Clearly, if the IESG graph is acyclic, the corresponding graph for the IAS is acyclic (since to get the IESG we only add edges to the IASG) and thus the IAS schedule is correct. It can be shown that if the graph is acyclic, then the reads-from relationship for strict transactions in the inter-cluster schedule S_{IES} is the same as in the underlying intra-cluster schedule S_{IAS}. Assume that ST_j reads-x-from ST_i in S_{IAS}. Then $ST_i \rightarrow ST_j$. Assume, for the purpose of contradiction, that ST_j reads-x-from a weak transaction WT. Then WT writes x in S_{IES}; and since ST_i also writes x, either (a) $ST_i \rightarrow WT$ or (b) $WT \rightarrow ST_i$. Case (a), from the definition of the *IESG*, gives $ST_j \rightarrow WT$, which is a contradiction since ST_j reads-x-from WT. In case (b), $WT \rightarrow ST_i$; that is, WT precedes ST_i, which precedes ST_j, which again contradicts the assumption that ST_j reads-x-from WT.

Protocol. It is necessary to break potential cycles in the IES graph to get a correct schedule. There is always at least one weak transaction present in each cycle because the construction of the IESG starts from an acyclic graph where edges are added between a weak and a strict transaction. These weak transactions are rolled back. Undoing a transaction T may result in *cascading aborts* of transactions that have read the values written by T—that is, transactions that are related to T through a dependency edge. Since weak transactions write only quasi-copies in a single physical cluster and only weak transactions in the same cluster can read these quasi-copies, we have the following lemma:

Lemma 7.2 *Only weak transactions in the same physical cluster read values written by weak transactions in that cluster.*

The above lemma ensures that when a weak transaction is aborted to resolve conflicts in an inter-cluster schedule, only weak transactions in the same p-cluster are affected. In practice, fewer transactions ever need to be aborted. In particular, only weak transactions whose output depends on the exact values of the data items they read need to be aborted. These are called *exact* transactions. Most weak transactions are not exact, since, by definition, weak transactions are transactions that read local d-consistent data. Thus, even if the value they read was produced by a transaction that was later aborted, this value was inside an acceptable range of inconsistency and this is probably sufficient to guarantee their correctness.

Detecting cycles in the IESG can be hard. The difficulties arise from the fact that between transactions that wrote a data item an edge can have any direction, thus resulting in *polygraphs* [37]. Polynomial tests for acyclicity are possible, if it is assumed that transactions read a data item before writing it. Then, to get the IES graph from the IAS graph, only the following is needed to *induce a read order as follows: If a strict transaction ST reads an item that was written by a weak transaction WT, then add a precedence edge ST → WT.*

The reconciliation process can be expressed as follows:

```
Until there are no cycles in IESG
   roll back a weak transaction WT in the cycle
   roll back all exact transactions related with a dependency
edge to WT
If the final write is on a core copy, propagate this value to
all quasi-copies
else
   choose a value of a quasi-copy
   propagate this value to all core and quasi-copies
```

7.10 DISCUSSION

In the proposed hybrid scheme, weak and strict transactions coexist. Weak transactions let users process local data, thus avoiding the overhead of long network accesses. Strict transactions need access to the network to guarantee permanence of their updates. *Weak reads* provide users with the choice of reading an approximately accurate value of a datum; in particular, in cases of total or partial disconnections. This value is appropriate for a variety of applications that do not require exact values. Such applications include gathering information for statistical purposes or making high-level decisions and reasoning in expert systems that can tolerate bounded uncertainty in input data. *Weak writes* allow users to update local data without confirming these updates immediately. Update validation is delayed until the physical clusters are connected. Delayed updates can be performed during periods of low network activity to reduce demand on the peaks. Furthermore, grouping together weak updates and transmitting them as a block, rather than one at a time, can improve bandwidth usage. For example, a salesperson can locally update many data items, until these updates are finally confirmed, when the machine is plugged back into the network at the end of the day. However, since weak writes may not be finally accepted, they must be used only when compensating transactions are available, or when the likelihood of conflicts is very low. For example, users can employ weak transactions to update mostly private data and strict transactions to update frequently used, heavily shared data.

The cluster configuration is dynamic. Physical clusters may be explicitly created or merged upon a forthcoming disconnection or connection of the associated mobile clients. To accommodate migrating locality, a mobile host may join a different p-cluster upon entering a new support environment. Besides defining clusters based on the *physical location* of data, other definitions are also possible. Clusters may be defined based on the *semantics* of data or applications. Information about access patterns—for instance, in the form of a *user's profile* that includes data describing the user's typical behavior—may be utilized in determining clusters. Some examples follow.

■ EXAMPLE 7.7

Cooperative Environment: Consider the case of users working on a common project using mobile hosts. Groups are formed that consist of users who work on similar topics of the project. Physical clusters correspond to data used by people in the same group who need to maintain consistency among their interactions. Consider data that are most frequently accessed by a group as data *belonging* to this group. At each physical cluster (group), the copies of data items of the group are core copies, while the copies of data items belonging to other groups are quasi. A data item may belong to more than one group, if more than one group frequently accesses it. In this case, core copies of that data item exist in all such physical clusters. In each physical cluster, operations on items that do not belong to the group are weak, while operations on data that belong to the group are strict. Weak updates on a data item are accepted only when they do not conflict with updates by the owners of that data item.

■ EXAMPLE 7.8

Caching: Clustering can be used to model caching in a client/server architecture. In such a setting, a mobile host acts as a client interacting with a server at a fixed host. Data are cached at the client for performance and availability. The cached data are considered quasi-copies. The data at the fixed host are core copies. Transactions initiated by the server are always strict. Transactions initiated by the client that invoke updates are always weak, while read-only client transactions can be strict when strict consistency is required and weak otherwise. At reconciliation, weak writes are accepted only if they do not conflict with strict transactions at the server. The frequency of reconciliation depends on the user consistency requirements and on networking conditions.

■ EXAMPLE 7.9

Caching location data: In mobile computing, data representing the location of a mobile user are fast-changing. Such data are frequently accessed to locate a host. Thus, location data must be replicated at many sites to reduce the overhead of searching. Most of the location copies should be considered quasi. Only a few core copies are always updated to reflect changes in location.

7.11 RELATED WORK

One-copy serializability [36] hides from the user the fact that there can be multiple copies of a data item and ensures strict consistency. Whereas one-copy serializability may be an acceptable criterion for strict transactions, it is too restrictive for applications that tolerate bounded inconsistency and also causes unbearable overhead in cases of weak connectivity. The weak transaction model described in this chapter was first introduced in reference 21, while preliminary performance results were presented in reference 41.

Network Partitioning. The partitioning of a database into clusters resembles the *network partition problem* [40], where site or link failures fragment a network of database sites into isolated subnetworks called partitions. Clustering is conceptually different than partitioning in that it is electively done to increase performance. Whereas all partitions are isolated, clusters may be *weakly* connected. Thus, clients may operate as physically disconnected even while remaining physically connected. Strategies for network partition face similar competing goals of availability and correctness as clustering. These strategies range from *optimistic*, where any transaction is allowed to be executed in any partition, to *pessimistic*, where transactions in a partition are restricted by making the worst-case assumptions about what transactions at other partitions are doing. The model discussed here offers a hybrid approach. Strict transactions may be performed only if one-copy serializability is ensured (in a pessimistic manner). Weak transactions may be performed locally (in an optimistic manner). To merge updates performed by weak transactions, a purely syntactic approach has been adopted.

Read-Only Transactions. Read-only transactions do not modify the database state, thus their execution cannot lead to inconsistent database states. In the scheme discussed here, read-only transactions with weaker consistency requirements are considered a special case of weak transactions that have no write operations.

Two requirements for read-only transactions were introduced in reference 42: consistency and currency requirements. *Consistency* requirements specify the degree of consistency needed by a read-only transaction. In this framework, a read-only transaction may have (a) *no* consistency requirements; (b) *weak* consistency requirements, if it requires a consistent view (that is, if all integrity constraints that can be fully evaluated with the data read by the transaction must be true); or (c) *strong* consistency requirements, if the schedule of all update transactions, together with all other strong consistency queries, must be consistent. While the strict read-only transactions of this scheme always have strong consistency requirements, weak read-only transactions can be tailored to have any of the above degrees based on the criterion used for IAS correctness. Weak read-only transactions may have no consistency requirement, if ignored from the IAS schedule; weak consistency, if part of a weakly correct IAS schedule; and strong consistency, if part of a strongly correct schedule. *Currency* requirements specify what update transactions should be reflected by the data read. In terms of currency requirements, strict read-only transactions read the most-up-to-date data item available, that is, committed. Weak read-only transactions may read older versions of data, depending on the definition of the d-degree.

Epsilon-serializability (ESR) [43, 44] allows temporary and bounded inconsistencies in copies to be seen by queries during the period among the asynchronous updates of the various copies of a data item. Read-only transactions in this framework are similar to weak read-only transactions with no consistency requirements. ESR bounds inconsistency directly by bounding the number of updates. In reference 45, a generalization of ESR was proposed for high-level type specific operations on abstract data types. In contrast, our approach deals with low-level read and write operations.

In an *N-ignorant* system, a transaction need not see the results of at most N prior transactions that it would have seen if the execution had been serial [46]. Strict transactions are 0-ignorant, and weak transactions are 0-ignorant of other weak transactions at the same cluster. Weak transactions are ignorant of strict and weak transactions at other clusters. The techniques of supporting N-ignorance can be incorporated in the proposed model to define d as the ignorance factor N of weak transactions.

7.12 CONCURRENCY CONTROL MECHANISM

Consistency-preserving execution is necessary for maintaining database consistency. In Chapter 5, a number of commonly known concurrency control mechanisms were discussed. This section investigates if any of them would work satisfactorily in mobile database systems.

Any scheme or mechanism, such as sorting, searching, concurrency control mechanism, system recovery, and so on, has system overhead. In most cases, a mechanism with the least system overhead is preferred, even though it may not be efficient (moderate throughput and response). This is especially true for mobile database systems where system overhead can create serious performance problems because of low-capacity and limited resources. This is one of the main reasons for not considering conventional currency control mechanisms for serializing concurrent transactions for mobile database systems. However, they do provide a highly useful base for modifying conventional CCMs or for developing new ones, especially for MDS.

It is a common practice to categorize existing CCMs as (a) optimistic and (b) pessimistic. Optimistic CCMs aggressively schedule operations on data items with the assumption that the operation will not conflict with any other operation, and the transaction will commit correctly. If a conflict does occur, then one of the conflicting transactions is aborted. The pessimistic approach, on the other hand, assumes that the operation is likely to conflict with other operations and, therefore, takes the necessary action (such as locking), to safeguard the execution for a successful commit. The existing conventional CCMs can be further categorized under the following two categories:

7.12.1   Locking-Based CCMs

Two-phase incremental locking and simultaneous release is the most commonly used concurrency control mechanism. This scheme can be implemented on distributed database systems in three different ways: (a) centralized two-phase locking (primary site approach), (b) primary copy locking, and (c) distributed two-phase locking. It is useful to analyze if they are suitable for mobile database systems.

Centralized Two-Phase Locking.   In this scheme, one site (node) is responsible for managing all locking activities. Since the locking request traffic is likely to be very high, the central node should be almost always available. In a mobile database system, this requirement limits the choice of the central node. A mobile unit cannot be a central node because (a) it is a kind of personal processing unit, (b) it is not powerful enough to manage locking requests, (c) it cannot maintain the status (locked or free) of data items, (d) it is not fully connected to other nodes in the network, and (e) its mobility is unpredictable. Base stations are the next choice, but they also have a number of problems related mainly with functionality issues. A base station is a switch and is dedicated to providing services to mobile units. Adding transaction management functions is likely to overload them, which would not be recommended by wireless service providers. Theoretically, this may be the best choice, and many researchers have selected base stations for incorporating database functions; however, in reality, this is not an acceptable solution. A fixed host can be configured to act as a central node, but it is not equipped with a transceiver. As a result, it has to go through a base station to reach any mobile unit. No matter what component is identified as a central node, the problem of single-point failure cannot be avoided in this scheme.

Primary Copy Two-Phase Locking.   This scheme eliminates a single point of failure and minimizes other problems of the central node approach by distributing the locking responsibility among multiple sites. Each lock manager is now responsible for a subset of data items. The node executing a part of the transaction sends lock requests to the appropriate lock manager. This approach does not solve the problem of identifying suitable sites for distributing locking responsibility. The choices are either base station, fixed hosts, or both.

Distributed Two-Phase Locking. This scheme simply maximizes the extent of lock distribution. Here, all nodes can serve as a lock manager. In the case of a database partition, this algorithm degenerates to a centralized two-phase scheme. It is obvious that this scheme does not suggest a better selection of node for the lock manager.

The other acceptable option for a lock manager is to include separate database servers connected to base stations through a wired network. One of the database servers can be identified as the central node for managing transactions under a centralized scheme, a subset of them for a primary copy scheme, and all for a distributed scheme. Out of all the options, this seems to be the middle ground.

The communication overhead for managing locking and unlocking requests is another important problem to investigate. If a mobile unit makes a lock request on behalf of a transaction it is executing, then (a) it will send the request to the lock manager site (wireless message), (b) the lock manager will decide to grant or to refuse the lock and send the result to the mobile unit (wireless message), and (c) the mobile unit makes the decision to continue with forward processing or block or rollback, depending upon the lock manager's decision. Thus, each lock request will generate two wireless messages, which would become quite expensive with an increase in the workload. Furthermore, every rollback will generate additional message overhead by restarting the transaction.

The amount of overhead is closely related to the degree of consistency the database is programmed to maintain. To maintain a stronger degree of consistency requires more resources compared to maintaining a weaker degree of consistency. Thus, one way of reducing the cost is to maintain a weaker consistency level because in many data processing situations, a weaker consistency is acceptable. This is especially true for mobile database systems because mobile users are not likely to issue CPU-intensive large update transactions through their mobile units. If such a transaction is issued from a laptop, then it could be executed at the database servers with the strongest consistency level.

It would be hard to achieve maximum benefits only through a new CCM that maintains a weaker level of consistency. A new way of structuring and executing ACID transactions is also necessary. Very few CCMs for mobile database systems have been developed, and this section discusses a few of them.

Distributed HP-2PL CCM. In reference 47, a concurrency control mechanism called *Distributed HP-2PL (DHP-2PL)* is presented. This CCM is based on two-phase locking, and it is an extension of *HP-2PL* [48] CCM. It uses the conflict resolution scheme of a *cautious waiting* [49] mechanism to reduce the degree of transaction rollbacks.

In this scheme, each base station has a lock scheduler that manages the locking requests for data items available locally. Each transaction—that is, the holder of the data item (T_h) and the requestor of the data item (T_r)—is assigned a unique priority. Thus, when a requestor and a holder conflict, then their associated priority and their execution status (committing, blocked, etc.) are used to resolve the conflict. The steps are as follows:

- On a conflict, check the priority of the holder and the requestor.
- If *Priority (T_r) > Priority (T_h), then check the status of (T_h). If (T_h) is not committing (i.e., still active), then check if it is a local transaction.*
- *If (T_h) is a local transaction, then restart it locally. A local transaction accesses only those data items that are stored at the base station where the transaction originates.*
- *If (T_h) is a global transaction, then restart it globally. A global transaction accesses data at more than one base station. Rollback of a global transaction requires communicating with all those base stations where the global transaction has performed some update operations.*
- *If (T_h) is committing, then it is not restarted. Rather, the (T_r) is forced to wait until (T_h) commits and releases all its lock. Adjust the priority of (T_h) as follows: Priority (T_h) := Priority (T_r) + some fixed priority level.*
- *if Priority (T_r) ≤ Priority (T_h), then block (T_r) until (T_h) commits and releases its locks.*

A cautious waiting approach is incorporated in the above method to minimize the impact of disconnection and unnecessary blocking. The modified algorithm is given below:

```
If Priority (Tr) > Priority (Th) and Th is still active (not
    committing), then global or local restart (Th).
Else
    If Th is a mobile client, then
        If the time Th spent at mobile unit > threshold, then ping the
            mobile unit. (The ping is done by the base station to check
            if Th is active.)
        If there is no response, then restart Th
        Else
            Block Tr. This check is repeated at the end of a threshold.
        Endif
        Else block Tr. This checking is performed again when the time
            spent at
        the mobile unit is > threshold.
    Endif
    Else Block Tr
    Endif
Endif
```

The *threshold* is a function of average system performance that is used as a tuning parameter. This acts as a timeout value that helps to decide the status of a mobile unit. If the base station does not get a response from the mobile unit within the threshold value, then a disconnection is assumed. This may not be true, but its effect is similar to a disconnection. The holder T_h is restarted even though it has a higher priority. This may increase the chances of missing the deadline for T_r.

Two more CCMs are discussed below. One takes the approach of weaker consistency, and the other uses transaction restructuring for developing CCMs for an MDS.

7.13 MULTIVERSION CONCURRENCY CONTROL MECHANISM FOR MOBILE DATABASE SYSTEMS

A transaction execution model and a CCM based on a multiversion approach for a mobile database system are discussed in this section. Multiversion approaches have been shown to significantly improve concurrency, and a number of multiversion algorithms have appeared in the literature [36, 50–55]. Since many requirements of multiversion approaches are satisfied by an MDS, there is a general agreement that they are likely to work well in an MDS. Multiversion schemes can be implemented using timestamping and two-phase locking. The scheme presented in this section uses the two-phase locking approach to serialize the execution of concurrent ACID transactions on an MDS. There are two parts to the entire scheme: (a) a multiversion mobile transaction execution model (MV-T) and (b) multiversion concurrency control mechanisms (MCCM). First, the transaction-processing model is discussed followed by the locking-based MCCM.

7.13.1 A Multiversion Mobile Transaction Execution Model

A T in an $MV\text{-}T$ model goes through three steps during its entire execution: (a) start, (b) commit, and (c) terminate.

Start. This indicates the initiation of an $MV\text{-}T$. It is the same as a conventional *Begin Transaction* command, except there is no separate corresponding *End Transaction* command.

Commit. The commit of a T indicates its logical completion (T does not write its updates to the database). A T can start and commit at a mobile unit. At the end of this command, the mobile unit (executing the transaction) sends updates to the DBS.

Terminate. The termination of a T indicates the end of its execution where the DBS releases locks on the data items and installs all updates to the database (updates are durable). A T that committed successfully at the MU is assured of successful termination only at one DBS.

The $MV\text{-}T$ scheme synchronizes read and write lock requests on different versions of a data item in a constrained manner. The constraints are specified in terms of timestamps on the requested lock and on the lock held on the data item. The correctness of the execution of T is guaranteed if it can announce and submit its commit to the DBS. No separate validation phase is required. The model supports concurrent read and write operations without blocking. A read always gets the last committed or

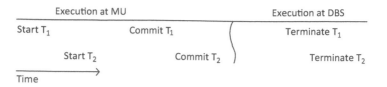

Figure 7.12 Concurrent transaction execution.

terminated version of the data and is never blocked; as a result, the data availability at the mobile unit and at the DBSs significantly increases. This makes T capable of supporting short and long transactions without incurring high blocking rates or aborting short-transactions.

The T partially executes at the mobile unit and then moves to a DBS to complete the execution (termination). We consider the following scenario: T may arrive concurrently at a DBS from multiple MUs and from other fixed hosts (other DBSs). Figure 7.12 illustrates a typical concurrent execution of Ts. Two transactions, T_1 and T_2, execute at two MUs controlled by the same DBS. T_2 starts as soon as T_1 commits, but before it terminates. Unlike some other schemes, T_2 does not wait for T_1 to start execution. This reduction in transaction waiting time significantly increases concurrency. By committing a transaction at the MU, the multiversion execution model reduces the locking time as well. The MU quickly sends its updates to the DBS, which installs them to the final database and makes them available to other Ts. A few examples demonstrate the application of the execution model in real-life data management scenarios.

■ EXAMPLE 7.10

In a mobile banking application, a bank agent may visit different regions to collect deposits/withdrawals of money at remote locations using a mobile device. When a credit T is executed, the balance gets updated (commit) locally. At the end of the commit at the MU, the account balance becomes available to the customer. The transaction terminates when the money is deposited in the bank (could be the next day), at which point the money becomes available to the account holder for further processing.

■ EXAMPLE 7.11

In a cellular network, an MU can broadcast the committed values along with the timestamp indicating the commit time. Ts at other MUs can listen to the broadcast and download desired data items. This helps to reduce the wait time for acquiring required data items and also reduces wireless communication overhead as other MUs will not send their read requests to the DBS. It is only when an MU wants to read, and subsequently writes, that locks need to be set by the DBS. The entire process reduces wait time and communication costs, leading to a higher throughput and a better response time.

7.13.2 Management of Multiple Versions of Data Items

Initially, a two-version (one committed and one terminated) approach of a data item is discussed to support the transaction execution model. The model is later extended to support more versions (many committed and one terminated).

When an MU requests a data item then (depending upon the specified constraints discussed later in the section) access is granted on one of the two versions. A version of a data item is represented as $X^i_{ts(i)}$, where X is the data item and $ts(i)$ is the current timestamp of the T that wrote to X (this is normal in any timestamp approach). Thus, $ts(i)$ becomes the timestamp of X that is used in version selection to process a read operation on X. It also implies that the T_i, which updated, X, has been successfully committed at the MU and awaits its termination at the DBS. The DBS assigns timestamps to X when a T accesses it and is used to synchronize the concurrent access across the system. Formally, the two versions of a data item X maintained at the DBS are X^j_0 and $X^k_{ts(k)}$, where X^j_0 is the data version written by T_j and successfully terminated at the DBS (subscript 0 indicates its successful termination at the DBS) and $X^k_{ts(k)}$ is the new version of X created at time $ts(k)$ by the committed T_k at the MU but is not yet terminated ($T_j < T_k$) in timestamp order at the DBS. There are two cases to deal with.

Case 1. Concurrent Read–Write to Increase Data Availability. An MV-T commit at an MU and its termination at a DBS increase concurrency among read and write operations. This is illustrated in Figure 7.13. Initially, the DBS has one version of X and two versions of Z. Versions X^i_0 and Z^i_0 represent the situation where T_i that updated X and Z has been most recently terminated. The version $Z^k_{ts(k)}$ indicates that the T_k is committed but not yet terminated. The data item versions present at the MU indicate that earlier, the transaction T_j being executed at the MU has requested a read operation on SZ and a write operation on data item X. The DBS assigned the most up-to-date version of data items to the read operation. Hence, the T_j read data item versions $Z^k_{ts(k)}$ (committed version) and X^i_0 (terminated version) are available at the DBS. After obtaining write-lock on X, it writes its version $X^j_{ts(j)}$. Version $Z^k_{ts(k)}$ at the DBS indicates that T_k that committed at the MU is not yet terminated. In the model, to maintain exactly two versions of a data item and to avoid the existence of more than one committed version of the same data item, two different transactions do not write lock the data item. If two writes are allowed, then it is possible that both transactions can simultaneously commit at the MU, leaving more than one committed version of the data item. Therefore, an MU cannot obtain a conflicting write lock on a version of Z, but it can read the version $Z^k_{ts(k)}$.

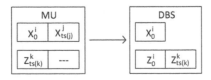

Figure 7.13   Case 1: Data versions at MH and DBS.

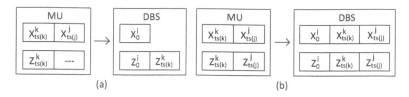

(a)   (b)

Figure 7.14   Case 2: Versions at MU and DBS (a) before and (b) after T_j commits at MU.

Case 2. Concurrent Write–Write to Increase Data Availability. In Figure 7.14a, two versions of data item X ($X_{ts(j)}^j$ and $X_{ts(k)}^k$) at the MU and one version of Z ($Z_{ts(k)}^k$) exist at the DBS. The data items $X_{ts(k)}^k$ and $Z_{ts(k)}^k$ indicate that T_k is committed but is yet to be terminated. The data items X_0^i and Z_0^i indicate that T_i most recently terminated at the DBS. Transaction T_j, being executed on the MU, reads the version $X_{ts(k)}^k$ at the MU. Contrary to the criteria discussed above, the DBS assigns the write lock to T_j at the MU on data item X even though there exists a committed (but yet to be terminated) transaction T_k at DBS that has a committed version $X_{ts(k)}^k$. This relaxation is possible because T_k is committed and, therefore, assured of successful termination. The versions of a data item written by such a transaction are up-to-date and can be used by another transaction. Since transactions can be terminated only at the DBS, it can keep track of the order in which transactions need to be terminated. As a result, the DBS can give a write lock on a data item when another transaction that is committed on the same data item but is yet to be terminated. For this reason, T_j at the MU was allowed to write lock version $X_{ts(k)}^k$ and then generate a version $X_{ts(j)}^j$, commits at the MH, and sends this version to the DBS to terminate.

It can be seen from the examples of these two versions that there can be more than one committed version of a data item present at a DBS resulting from transactions that have generated newer versions X and are successfully committed at an MU but yet to be terminated at a DBS (Figure 7.14b). The DBS terminates them in the order in which they were committed earlier. Thus, T_k terminates first and T_j is terminated next, and so on. If a new transaction T_l arrives at the DBS requesting a read or write operation on X when T_j holds a write lock, then it is blocked until T_j commits.

7.13.3 Locking Protocol

A new lock type, a verified lock, is required to manage the versions. A write lock is converted to a verified lock after a T commits. If there are conflicting lock requests, then one of the transactions is either blocked or aborted. To explain the locking protocol, a transaction is identified as a requestor (requesting a data item) or as a holder (holding the requested data item). The associated timestamp is used to resolve a conflict either by rolling back a transaction or by blocking it. In this protocol, a requestor is blocked if its timestamp is higher than the holder.

A T gets the latest version of the data item on a read request. This defines the Read Rule that is applied to all read requests. The scheduler rejects a lock request if it does

Table 7.5   Lock Compatibility Matrix for Case 1

	Read Lock (rl)	Write Lock (wl)	Verified Lock (vl)
Read Lock (rl)	✓	✓	✓
Write Lock (wl)	✓	X	X
Verified Lock (vl)	✓	X	X

not satisfy locking constraints. Since there is not any T blocked indefinitely, there is not any deadlock. The following two cases explain the locking protocol.

Locking Rules for Case 1. A transaction (requestor) may be initiated at an MU or at a DBS. The DBS is responsible for granting locks to requestors. There are two kinds of read locks (rl): (a) $rl^{=0}(X)$ indicates a read lock on the terminated (final) version (X_0^i) of X and (b) $rl^{\neq0}(X)$ indicates a read lock on the committed version ($X_{ts(k)}^k$) of X. $wl(X)$ indicates a write lock and $vl(X)$ indicates a verified lock that shows the transition of a T from its commit state at the MU to its termination state at the DBS.

A T at an MU acquires the required locks on data items before performing any read or write. The DBS assigns T_i at the MU if the appropriate version of the data item to read if it is not locked in a conflicting manner by T_j. A read lock does not conflict with a read or write or a verified lock. The write lock conflicts with write and verified locks because T_i may be aborted after it has acquired the write lock and if T_j has the write lock on the same data item. This may result in cascading aborts. More than one committed version of a data item may occur only when both T_i and T_j try to obtain a verified lock. But this situation will violate the following condition: *There can exist, at most, two versions of a data item at a DBS, one of which is the terminated version and the other is the committed (but yet to be terminated.)* This situation, therefore, will not occur in this protocol as discussed in Case 2 (Figure 7.14b) version the lock compatibility matrix of this protocol is given in Table 7.5.

There are two constraints that must be satisfied by any T for obtaining locks. The DBS checks the constraints before granting locks and it assigns the verified lock to a T when it has committed (completed all its reads and writes). An MU executes the following steps on a commit.

a. The new versions of a data item (if any) are sent to the DBS.
b. The write locks held by Ts are converted into verified locks at the DBS.
c. The committed version of data item $X_{ts(i)}^i$ written by the T is available to other Ts.

The DBS then executes a terminate command for T to end its execution after it is committed. The following steps complete a terminate operation.

a. All Ts holding read locks $rl^{\neq0}(X)$ on data item version $X_{ts(i)}^i$ are converted to $rl^{=0}(X)$.

Table 7.6 Lock Compatibility Matrix for Case 2

	Read Lock (rl)	Write Lock (wl)	Verified Lock (vl)
Read Lock (rl)	✓	✓	✓
Write Lock (wl)	✓	X	✓ (T_i Committed)
Verified Lock (vl)	✓	X ✓ (T_i Committed)	

    b. The previous committed and terminated versions of data item X_0^j are deleted, and data version $X_{ts(i)}^i$ is converted to X_0^i.

    c. All verified and read locks assigned to T_i are revoked.

    d. A T completes and leaves the system when locks are revoked, and the version of the data item is updated at the DBS.

Since the write and verified locks conflict, at any time only two versions of a data are available at the DBS. The compatibility matrix in Table 7.6 shows that no two T's can have write locks on the same data item simultaneously.

Locking Rules for Case 2. The constraint that at most only two versions of a data item at any instance of time are available to improve concurrency is relaxed. The compatibility matrix for this case is shown in Table 7.6, and the data versions scenario at the DBS and MU is shown in Figure 7.14b. In Table 7.6, if an MT holding the verified lock on a data item is committed but yet to be terminated, then it can assign the conflicting write lock or verified lock to another T at the MU. It does so by maintaining the order in which T's need to be terminated, as discussed earlier in Case 2 (Figure 7.14b). This is possible because the DBS can only assign locks to the MU and terminates a transaction. Thus, when T_j at MU requests a write or a verified lock on data item X, from the DBS the DBS can assign the write lock or verified lock to T_j, provided that the current lock held by T_i at the DBS is the verified lock. The DBS records the order of verified locks after assigning the lock to T_j. When T_j commits, the DBS performs termination in the order in which it has assigned the verified locks, that is, T_i and then T_j. If T_i cannot be terminated, then T_j is held from termination until T_i is terminated. In this way, the DBS preserves the correct serial order of T execution. Also, the value read by T_j is a correct value written by T_i since T_j gets the write lock only after T_i is committed but is yet to be terminated.

In an MDS, an MU can encounter a handoff randomly. This gets worse with highly mobile MUs, but a handoff (soft or hard) does not affect locking protocol but may affect its behavior. If a lock is not granted to a transaction, then it is blocked irrespective of its connection status and its geographical location. For example, if a transaction running at an MU requests a lock in the cell 1 and then moves to the cell 2, then the transaction will be blocked. Note that the change in the status of a transaction (blocked or aborted) is free from its movement and status of the MU where it is executing. It is possible that an MU may get disconnected before it receives a lock granted confirmation. The scheme treats this situation as a "lock not granted" if the disconnection is flowed with "doze mode". A network partition may have some effect on transaction execution; however, it is true only in a wired network. In a cellular network, such a network partition does not exist.

7.13.4 Constraints with Read and Write Operations

A read request is completed at the DBS using the read rule similar to the multiversion timestamp ordering the (MVTO) read rule [36]. Whenever a T wants to read a data item, then the committed version of the data item with the largest timestamp less than or equal to the timestamp of T is selected. For example, if there exist versions X_0^1 and $X_{ts(2)}^2$ exist at the DBS and transaction T_3 at the MU, or at the DBS requesting data item X with a timestamp $ts(T_3) > ts(T_2)$, then T_3 is given $X_{ts(2)}^2$, otherwise X_0^1. Read and write locks are granted as follows:

Read lock

- T_i requests a read lock on the data item X.
- The DBS grants $rl_i^{=0}(X)$ or $rl_i^{\neq 0}(X)$ corresponding to whether the version X_0^j or version $X_{ts(k)}^k$ (if it exists and is committed) is selected in accordance with the read rule and the read lock version satisfies the specified constraints.
- Transaction T_i reads the selected version of X.

Write lock

- T_i requests a write lock on data item X.
- The DBS grants $wl_i(X)$, if there are no conflicts.
- T_i creates a new version $X_{ts(i)}^i$ for data item X.

The following two constraints must be satisfied before the requested lock is granted.

Constraint 1. If T_j at DBS holding $wl_j(X)$ locks, then T_i gets read lock if $ts(T_i) > (T_j)$. This condition checks for the situation that no read request violates the read rule (if T_j is holding a write lock on the data item and has a timestamp less than $ts(T_i)$ (requesting a read lock), then granting a read lock might result in violation of serializability and also might result in cascading aborts). This constraint is automatically satisfied when serializing transactions at the DBS.

Constraint 2. The write lock request $wl_j(X)$ or verified lock request $vl_j(X)$ for T_i (at the MU or at DBS) must satisfy the following: (a) There should not exist any T at the DBS holding $wl(X)$ or $vl(X)$ and for all T_j at the MU holding $rl_j^0(X)$, the $ts(T_i) \geq ts(T_j)$; and (b) iff there is any other T_k at the DBS holding $vl_k(X)$ lock, then $ts(T_k) < ts(T_i)$, where T_i is requesting a verified or a write-lock on X. This constraint ensures that the transactions at the DBS with read locks on previous versions of data items are not made void by assigning a write lock or verified lock to another transaction that comes after these transactions, thus avoiding aborts.

7.13.5 Rules for Terminating a Transaction

The termination of a T_i may not be invoked immediately after it commits. The following rules must be observed for correct execution of transactions:

a. T_i at an MU will precede T_j at a DBS in commit order if T_i has read a previous version of a data item created by T_j or T_j has read the committed version of the data item written by T_i. This is because if T_i, and reads the previous version of a data item which has later been updated by T_j, then if T_j commits before T_i, it should have read the updated version. Note that a read-only transaction also needs to send the commit information to the DBS. Alternatively, such a read-only transaction can be switched back in the transaction history for the purpose of serialization . A second possibility is that if T_j has read the committed version written by T_i, then T_i should come before T_j in the serialization order.

b. T_j cannot terminate at a DBS until each transaction T_i at an MU that has either read X_0^k (for some k) or written a committed version $X_{ts(i)}^i$ that has been read by T_j has been terminated. This is because a transaction may be reading two data items; for one, it may get a data version written by the last terminated transaction, and the other version may be written by a committed transaction. Thus, there is no equivalent serial order because a read-only transaction reads one version of a data object at the initial state and reads an updated version of the second object in the next read.

c. T_i, executed at the MU, cannot terminate at a DBS until T_j, which has committed before T_i, terminates at the DBS.

Blocking Transactions. Deadlocks and subsequent aborts could be costlier in a mobile environment. Since wireless communication between an MU and DBS is expensive, MUs, as far as possible, should avoid contacting the DBS. In situations when a lock cannot be granted, a transaction can be blocked rather than aborted; and when the lock is available, it can be unicasted. Consider a case where a read transaction initiated at an MU does not satisfy constraint 1. It should then be blocked at the DBS rather than aborting it. When the write lock of a transaction is converted into the verified lock at the DBS, and the transaction blocked at the MU can read the committed version. DBS can unicast this message, and the MU needs not be contacted by the DBS again.

Deadlock Avoidance Rule. If T_i holds a write or verified lock on X, then the write lock request on X by T_j is rejected if $ts(T_i) > ts(T_j)$; otherwise T_j is blocked. Using this rule, along with the write lock request that failed to satisfy Constraint 2, can make the execution deadlock free. Since lock requests are blocked in asymmetric fashion, the only transaction with a higher timestamp may be blocked by a transaction with a lower timestamp; as a result, there will not be any deadlocks.

Table 7.7   Lock Compatibility Matrix for Case 2

	Read Lock (rl)	Write Lock (wl)	Verified Lock (vl)
Read Lock (rl)	✓	✓	✓
Write Lock (wl)	✓	X	$\Rightarrow$ (T_i Committed)
Verified Lock (vl)	✓	X $\Rightarrow$ (T_i Committed)	

7.13.6   Comparison with Constrained Shared Locking Model

The lock acquisition of this model has some similarity with the constrained shared locking model in reference 56. The lock acquisition rule in the constrained shared locking model states that: in a history H, for any two operations $p_i[x]$ and $q_j[x]$ such that $p_i[x] \Rightarrow q_j[x]$ is permitted if T_i acquires $pl_i[x]$ before T_j acquires $ql_j[x]$, then execution of $p_i[x]$ must precede the execution of $q_j[x]$. In this model, according to property 2a (given below), for any two transactions T_i and T_j at DBS, if the commit of T_i (c_i) < the commit of T_j (c_j), then $vl_i(x) < vl_j(x)$ and the termination of T_i (t_i) < the termination of T_j (t_i), then we state that the transactions obtain verified locks at the DBS and also terminate in the order they commit. That is, for two transactions T_i and T_j if there exists an ordering $c_i(x) \Rightarrow c_j(x)$, then:

a. They obtain verified locks in the same order, that is, $vl_i(x) \Rightarrow vl_j(x)$.

b. The corresponding termination operations have the order $t_i \Rightarrow t_j$.

There is an order for obtaining conflicting write locks and verified locks, given a condition that one of the two transactions is a committed transaction at the DBS. That is, for a T_i which is committed at the DBS and holding $vl_i(x)$ lock, if there is T_j requesting a write lock on X, it is assigned the write lock by maintaining an order between $vl_i(x)$ and $wl_j(x)$. Therefore, if $vl_i(x) \Rightarrow wl_j(x)$, then $vl_i(x) \Rightarrow vl_j(x)$ and $t_i \Rightarrow t_j$. The compatibility matrix shown in Table 7.6 is redrawn in Table 7.7 and illustrates the above cases where there is some similarity between the proposed model and the constrained shared locking model of [56].

7.13.7   Formal Proof of Correctness

A read operation T_i on a data object x is denoted as either $r_i(x^k_{ts(k)})$ or $r_j(x^j_0)$ depending on the read and write rules discussed in Section 7.13.3. A write operation is executed as $w_i(x^j_{ts(j)})$. The commit is denoted as c_i, an abort as a_i, and terminate as t_i. When a transaction is committed, its changes are updated at the DBS; and if it aborts, all the data versions that the transaction created are discarded. A transaction is correct if it maps the database at the DBS from one consistent state to another consistent state. Formally, a mobile transaction T_i is a partial order with ordering $<_i$ where

a. $T_i \subseteq \{r_i(x^k_{ts(k)})\}$ or $r_i(x^j_0, w_i(x^j_{ts(i)}) \mid x$ is a data object$\} \cup \{c_i, a_i, t_i\}$.

b. If $r_i(x^k_{ts(k)}) \in T_i$ iff $r_i(x^j_0) \notin T_i$.

c. If $a_i \in T_i$ iff $c_i \notin T_i$ and vice versa.

d. If t is c_i or a_i then for any operation $p <_i t$.

e. If $r_i(x_{ts(k)}^k)$, $w_i(x_{ts(i)}^j) \in T_i$, then $r_i(x_{ts(k)}^k) <_i w_i(x_i^i)$.

Let $T = \{T_0, T_1, T_2, \ldots, T_n\}$ be a set of transactions. The operations of T_i are ordered by $<_i$ for $0 \leq i \leq n$. To process operations of a T, a multiversion scheduler must translate T's operations on (single version) data items into operations on specific (corresponding) versions of those data items. This translation can be formalized by a function $\mathcal{F}$ that maps each $w_i(x)$ into $w_i(x_{ts(i)}^i)$, each $r_i(x)$ into $r_i(x_{ts(k)}^k)$ for some k, each c_i into c_i, and each a_i into a_i. A complete multiversion (MV) history [36] H over T is a partial order with order relation $<_H$ where

a. $H = \mathcal{F}(\cup_{i=0}^n T_i)$ for function $\mathcal{F}$, which is the combination of read and write rule constraints in our transaction model.

b. For each T_i and all operations p_i and q_i in T_i if $p_i <_i q_i$, then $\mathcal{F}(p_i) < \mathcal{F}(q_i)$.

c. If $\mathcal{F}(r_j(x)) = r_j(x_{its(i)}^i)$, then $w_i(x_{its(i)}^i) <_H r_j(x_{its(i)}^i)$.

d. If $w_i(x) <_i r_i(x)$, then $\mathcal{F}(r_i(x)) = r_i(x_{its(i)}^i)$.

e. If $\mathcal{F}(r_j(x)) = r_j(x_{its(i)}^i)$, $i \neq j$ and if $c_j \in H$, then $c_i <_H c_j$.

A committed projection of an MV history, H, (denoted as $C(H)$), is obtained by removing the operations of all but the committed transactions from H. $C(H)$ is a complete MV history if H is an MV history [36]. The two MV histories over a set of transactions are equivalent iff the histories have the same operations. Two operations in an MV history conflict if they operate on the same version and one is a Write. Only one pattern of conflict is possible in an MV history: If $p_i < q_j$ and these operations conflict, then p_i is $w_i(x_{its(i)}^i)$ and q_j is $r_j(x_{ts(i)}^i)$ for some data item SxS. The other type of conflicts [36] are not possible. Thus, conflicts in an MV history correspond to reads-from relationships.

A complete MV history is serial if for a pair of transactions T_i and $T_j \in H$, either all operations executed by T_i precede all operations executed by T_j or vice versa. Not all serial MV histories behave like ordinary serial 1V histories [36]. A serial MV history H is one-copy (or 1-serial) if for all i, j, and x, if T_i reads x from T_j then $i = j$, or T_j is the last transaction preceding T_i that writes into any version of x. An MV history is one-copy serializable (or 1SR) if its committed projection $C(H)$, is equivalent to a 1-serial MV history.

The serialization graph $SG(H)$ for an MV history is defined as for a 1V history. Given an MV history H and a data item x, a version order, $\ll$, for an x in H is a total order of versions of x in H. A version order for H is the union of version orders of data items. For example, for a history

$$H = w_0(x_{ts(0)}^0), \quad w_0(y_{ts(0)}^0), \quad w_0(z_{ts(0)}^0), \quad r_1(x_{ts(0)}^0), \quad r_2(x_{ts(0)}^0), \quad r_2(z_{ts(0)}^0), \quad r_3(z_{ts(0)}^0),$$
$$w_1(y_{ts(1)}^1), \quad w_2(x_{ts(2)}^2), \quad w_3(y_{ts(3)}^3), \quad c_1, c_2, c_3$$

the possible version orders are $x_{ts(0)}^0 \ll x_{ts(2)}^2$, $y_{ts(0)}^0 \ll y_{ts(1)}^1 \ll y_{ts(3)}^3$.

The Multiversion Serialization Graph for H and version order $\ll MVSG(H, \ll)$, is $SG(H)$ with the following version order edges added for each $r_k(x_{ts(j)}^j)$ and $w_i(x_{ts(i)}^i)$ in $C(H)$ where i, j, and k are distinct, if $x_{ts(i)}^i \ll x_{ts(j)}^j$, then include $T_i \rightarrow T_j$ otherwise include $T_k \rightarrow T_i$. An MV history H is $1SR$ and hence, conflict serializable, iff there exists a version order $\ll$ such that $MVSG(H, \ll$ is acyclic.

The MV-T schedular does produce a serializable history. This is illustrated through a number of histories produced by the scheduler. The execution of concurrent transactions starts with an initial correct and consistent database state (D_0) with a single version x_0^0 for each data item x_j^k in the database.

a. The history produced by the MV-T model is conflict serializable and is equal to a serial $1V$ history. Given $ts(1) < ts(2) < ts(3) < ts(4)$, consider the following simple history that conforms to both read and write constraints during obtaining locks:

$$rl_1^{=0}(x) \; r_1(x_0^0) \; rl_2^{=0}(x) \; r_2(x_0^0) \; c_2 \; wl_1(x) \; w_1(x_{ts(1)}^1) \; c_1 \; (wl_1(x) \rightarrow vl_1(x)) \; rl_3^{\neq 0}(x)$$
$$r_3(x)_{ts(1)}^1 \; wl_3(x) \; w_3(x_{ts(3)}^3) \; t_2 \; c_3 \; wl_3(x) \rightarrow vl_3(x) \; rl_4^{\neq 0}(x) \; r_4(x_{ts(3)}^3) \; c_4 \; t_1 \; t_3 \; t_4$$

The MVSG for the above history is $T_0 \ll T_2 \ll T_1 \ll T_3 \ll T_4$ (assuming that the version x_0^0 results from an earlier terminated T_0). It is acyclic. If we remove the versions of data items, then that would also result in

$$rl_1^{=0}(x) \; r_1(x) \; r1_2^{=0}(x) \; r_2(x) \; c_2 \; wl_1(x) \; w_1(x) \; c_1 \; wl_1(x) \rightarrow vl_1(x) \; rl_3^{\neq 0}(x) \; r_3(x)$$
$$wl_3(x) \; w_3(x) \; t_2 \; c_3 \; wl_3(x) \rightarrow vl_3(x) \; rl_4^{\neq 0}(x) \; r_4(x) \; c_4 \; t_1 \; t_3 \; t_4$$

It is clear that the above history is a serial $1V$ history with the execution order of $T_2 \rightarrow T_1 \rightarrow T_3 \rightarrow T_4$. It is now easier to show that if a transaction does not conform to either the rule or the write rule constraint, then it will not result in a serial $1V$ history.

b. A transaction cannot be assigned locks if there is some other uncommitted transaction at the DBS holding conflicting locks. Thus, the history is

$$rl_1^{=0}(x) \; r_1(x_0^0) \; rl_2^{=0}(x) \; r_2(x_0^0) \; c_2 \; wl_1(x) \; w_1(x_{ts(1)}^1) \; rl_3^{\neq 0}(x) \; r_3(x_{ts(1)}^1) \; c_1 \; wl_1(x) \rightarrow$$
$$vl_1(x) \; rl_3^{\neq 0}(x) \; r_3(x_{ts(1)}^1) \; wl_3(x) \; w_3(x_{ts(3)}^3) \; t_2 \; c_3 \; wl_3(x) \rightarrow vl_3(x) \; rl_4^{\neq 0}(x) \; r_4(x_{ts(3)}^3)$$
$$c_4 \; t_1 \; t_3 \; t_4$$

The above history is not possible since T_1 holds write locks and T_3 cannot apply the read lock $rl_3^{\neq 0}(x)$ without violating the locking constraint.

7.13.8 Proof of Correctness

In this section, the proof of correctness of the MV-T scheme using multiversion serializability theory discussed earlier, and confirming that all histories produced by it are $1SR$. To complete the proof of correctness, every operation of concurrent transactions must satisfy a number of properties given below.

Let H be a history over $T \{T_1, T_2, T_3, \cdots\}$ produced by $MV\text{-}T$ locking protocol. H must satisfy the following properties.

Property 1: For each T_i, there is a unique timestamp $ts(T_i)$ or simply $ts(i)$.

Property 2: For each T_i, its termination t_i follows after the commit action and after the verified lock $vl_i(x)$ acquisition, that is, $c_i < vl_i(x) < t_i$.

Property 3: For any two transactions T_i and T_j at a DBS, if $c_i < c_j$, then $vl_i(x) < vl_j(x)$ and $t_i < t_j$. This property states that if two transactions commit in the order they acquire and hold verified locks at a DBS and are terminated in the same order as they had acquired the verified locks, then they maintain the serializability of the transaction execution that allows the DBS to assign conflicting v_l and w_l locks.

Property 4: For each $r_k(x_0^j) \in H$, either $t_j < r_k(x_0^j)$ and $j > 0$ or $x_0^0 \in D_0$ (initial consistent state of database of data items at the DBS).

Property 5: For each $r_k(x_{ts(j)}^j) \in H$, either $c_j < r_k(x_{ts(j)}^j) < v_j(x) < t_j < vl_k(x) < t_k$ and $ts(x_{ts(j)}^j) < t_s(T_k)$ or $w_j(x_{ts(j)}^j) < r_k(x_{ts(j)}^j)$ and $j = k$.

Property 6: For each $r_k(x_{ts(a)}^l)$ and $w_k(x_{ts(k)}^k) \in H$ if $w_k(x_{ts(k)}^k) < r_k(x_{ts(a)}^l)$, then $a = k$ and $l = k$.

Properties 4 and 5 together say that every read $r_k(x)$ either reads a committed version or reads a version written by itself (T_k). In either case, it reads the version with the timestamp less than or equal to $t_s(T_k)$ $(t_j < t_k$ in Property 5 follows from the definition of unary relation) and *terminates*. Property 6 says that if T_k wrote x before the scheduler received $r_k(x)$, it translates the request to read the version written by T_k.

Property 7: For every $r_k(x_0^j)$ and $w_i(x_{ts(i)}^i) \in H$, either $t_i < r_k(x_0^j)$ or $r_k(x) < t_i$. This property says that $r_k(x_0^j)$, that is, a read on the version x_0^j, created by the terminated T_j at the DBS, is strictly ordered with respect to the terminate action of every transaction (either at the MU or DBS) that writes x. This is because each transaction T_i that writes and commits at the MU, making the version available for other transactions, holds a verified lock $vl_i(x)$ at the DBS. Each such T_i waits for each transaction that has read the existing version to terminate before it can terminate and release $vl_i(x)$ lock. Since the v_l and w_l locks conflict (according to Case 1) for each transaction T_k that reads, either T_i must have terminated before T_j even got the $wl_j(x)$ lock, that is, $t_i < wl_j(x) < t_j < r_k(x_0^j) < t_k$ or T_i must have terminated after T_k reading the version had terminated, that is $r_k(x_0^j) < t_k < t_i$.

Property 8: For every $r_k(x^j_{ts(j)})$ and $w_i(x^i_{ts(i)}) \in H$, if $w_i(x^i_{ts(i)})$, then either $vl_i(x) < r_k(x^j_{ts(j)})$ or $t_i < r_k(x^j_{ts(j)})$ else $r_k(x^j_{ts(j)}) < vl_i(x)$, $t_k < t_i$ and $t_s(k) < t_s(i)$. This property says that $r_k(x^j_{ts(j)})$, that is, a read on a committed version $x^j_{ts(j)}$ from T_j committed successfully at the MU but has yet to be terminated at the DBS, is strictly ordered with respect to every transaction that holds a verified lock $vl_i(x)$ at the DBS after committing at the MU and writing a version of data item x.

As discussed in Case 2 (Table 7.6), the DBS assigns conflicting v_l and w_l locks on data items depending on the condition that the transactions that have written a new version of a data item must be committed successfully at MU and hold a verified lock at the DBS in a strict complete order of execution. Therefore, T_i must have either successfully committed at the MU and have acquired $vl_i(x)$ or terminated and released the $vl_i(x)$ lock before T_j even got the $wl_j(x)$ lock; that is, either $c_i < vl_i(x) < wl_j(x)$ or $t_i < wl_j(x) < c_j < r_k(x^j_j)$.

By definition of the terminate action, t_j converts the version $x^j_{ts(j)}$ read by $r_k(x^j_{ts(j)})$ into x^j_0, converts the $rl_k^{\neq 0}(x)$ lock into rl_k^l, lock and then releases the $vl_j(x)$ lock. By Property 5, $t_j < t_k$; thus, after T_j terminated and before T_k terminates, if $t_s(k) > t_s(i)$, $wl_i(x)$ lock request must wait for T_k to terminate and release the lock $rl_k^0(x)$ in accordance with Constraint 2 $(r_k(x^j_{ts(j)}) < t_j < t_k < wl_i(x) < t_i$, otherwise $t_s(k) < t_s(i)$ and T_i obtains the $wl_i(x)$ lock, writes the version $x^i_{ts(i)}$, and then waits for T_k that has read the new version, to terminate, that is, $r_k(x^j_{ts(j)}) < t_j < wl_i(x) < t_k < t_i$.

Property 9: For every $r_k(x^j_0$ and $w_i(x^i_{ts)i})$, $i \neq j \neq k$; if $t_i < r_k(x^j_0)$, then $t_i < t_j$.

Property 10: For every $r_k(x^j_{ts(j)})$ and $w_i(x^i_{ts)i})$, $i \neq j \neq k$; if $t_i < r_k(x^j_{ts(j)})$, then $t_i < t_j$. This property says that $r_k(x^j_0)$ reads the most recently terminated version of x. Assume the contrary that $t_j < t_i$. But then, the version x^i_0 generated when T_j is terminated must have been deleted and replaced by x^i_0 when T_i terminates, and thus, $r_k(x)$ could not have accessed x^j_0.

Property 9 combined with Property 5 says that $r_k(x^j_{ts(j)})$ either reads the version written by itself or reads the most recently committed version $(x^j_{ts(j)})$. Since the v_l and w_l locks conflict if $t_i < r_k(x^j_{ts(j)})$ and $t_i < w_j(x^j_{ts(j)}) < c_j$ then with reference to property 5 $t_i < t_j$.

Property 11: For every $r_k(x^j_0$ and $w_i(x^i_{ts(i)})$, $i \neq j \neq k$, if $r_k(x^j_0) < t_i$, then $t_k < t_i$.

Property 12: For every $r_k(x^j_{ts(j)})$ and $w_i(x^i_{ts(i)})$, $i \neq j \neq k$, if $r_k(x^j_{ts(j)}) < t_i$, then $t_k < t_i$.

Properties 11 and 12 say that T_i cannot terminate until every transaction that has read the existing terminated version has terminated. Property 11 follows directly from the definition of unary relation *terminates*. Property 12 follows from Properties 8 and 3.

Property 13: For every $w_i(x^i_{ts)i})$ and $w_i(x^j_{ts(i)})$, either $t_i < t_j$ or $t_j < t_i$. This property says that the termination of every two transactions that write the same data item are atomic with respect to each other.

Theorem. Every history H produced is *1SR*.

Proof. By properties 2, 4, 5, and 6, H preserves reflexive reads-from relationship and is recoverable. Hence, it is an *MV* history. Define a version order $\ll$ as $x^i \ll x^j$ only if $t_i < t_j$. By Property 13, $\ll$ is indeed a version order. It can be shown that all edges in $MVSG(H, \ll)$ are in the termination order; that is, if $T_i \rightarrow T_j$ in $MVSG(H, \ll)$, then $t_i < t_j$.

Let $T_i \rightarrow T_j$ be in SG(H). This edge corresponds to a reads-from relation such as T_j reads x from T_i. By property 4, $t_i < r_j(x^i_0)$ and from Property 2, $r_j(x^i_0) < t_j$. Hence $t_i < t_j$. Similarly, by Properties 5 and 3 for any $r_j(x^i_{ts(i)})$, $t_i < t_j$.

Consider a version order edge induced by $w_i(x^i_{ts(i)})$, $w_j(x^j_{ts(j)})$ and $r_k(x^j_0)$ for $i \neq j \neq k$. There are two cases: (a) $x_i \ll x_j$ or (b) $x_j \ll x_i$. If $x_i \ll x_j$, then the version order edge is $T_i \rightarrow T_j$ and $t_i < t_j$ that follows from the definition of $\ll$. If $x^j \ll x^i$ then the version order edge is $T_k \rightarrow T_i$. Since $x^j \ll x^i$, $t_j < t_i$ follows from the definition of the version order. From Property 7, either $t_i < r_k(x^j_0)$ or $r_k(x^j_0) < t_i$. In the former case, Property 9 implies that $t_i < t_j$ contradicts $t_j < t_i$. Thus, $r_k(x^j_0) < t_i$. From Property 11, $t_k < t_i$ that is, $T_k \rightarrow T_i$, as desired. The case of the version order edge induced by $w_i(x^i_{ts(i)})$, $w_j(x^j_{ts(j)})$, and $r_k(x^j_{ts(j)})$, where $i \neq j \neq k$, can be proved in a similar manner by applying Properties 8, 10, and 11 in place of Properties 7, 9, and 11 as used above.

This proves that all edges in the $MVSG(H, \ll)$ are in termination order. Since termination order is embedded in a history, which is acyclic by definition, $MVSG(H, \ll)$ is acyclic too. Thus, from the definition of multiversion conflict serializable history, H is *1SR*.

7.13.9 CCM Based on *Epsilon* Serializability

A CCM based on *epsilon* serializability (ESR) [57] is presented here, which tolerates a limited amount of inconsistency. The mechanism is based on a two-tier replication scheme [58] that produces an epsilon serializable schedule. The scheme provides availability, accommodates the disconnection problem, and is scalable. It reduces transactions commit time and number of transaction rejections. The ESR approach keeps the amount of inconsistency within a limit specified by *epsilon*. When *epsilon* $\rightarrow$ 0, ESR reduces to a conventional serializability situation. For example, in a banking database, a report that prints a total summary in units of millions of dollars can tolerate inconsistency of a few hundred dollars. Divergence control methods guarantee ESR the same way as concurrency control guarantees serializability.

The concurrency control method that is presented here is a divergence control method to maintain ESR that can be applied to a database whose state space is *metric*. Database state space depends on database semantics. Many practical applications with different semantics such as bank accounts and seats in airline reservations are examples of metric state space. A bank database contains client names, addresses, account numbers, and account amounts, but updates happen only to the amount. Metric space S is defined as a state space having the following properties:

- A distance function $dist(u, v)$ is defined over every $u, v \in S$ on real numbers; $dist(u, v)$ is the difference between u and v, which represents database states.
- Triangular inequality, that is, $dist(u, v) + dist(v, w) = dist(u, w)$.
- Symmetry, that is, $dist(u, v) = dist(v, u)$.

In the mechanism, ESR [57, 59] is used to achieve acceptable reduction in consistency. ESR is an abstract framework and an instance of ESR is defined by concrete specification of tolerated inconsistency. The CCM that is discussed here can also be applied on fragmentable, reorderable objects [19] that include aggregate items, such as sets, queues, and stacks.

The two-tier replication does not use traditional mechanisms (like two-phase locking or time stamping), but it provides availability and scalability, accommodates the disconnection problem, and achieves convergence. The basic idea of a two-tier replication is first to allow users to run *tentative* transactions on mobile units that make tentative updates on the replicated data locally. When the mobile node connects to the database server, then these transactions are transformed to corresponding *base* transactions and re-executed at the servers. The base transactions are serialized on the master copy of the data, and mobile units are informed about any failed base transactions. However, the problem with this approach is that the mobile unit executes a transaction without the knowledge of what other transactions are doing. This situation can lead to a large number of rejected transactions [60]. Another drawback is that the transaction commit at the MU tends to be large because these transactions know their outcome (i.e., committed or rejected) only after base transactions have been executed and the results are reported back to the MU. The two-tier replication scheme [58] that the CCM discussed here is modified to reduce the number of rejected transactions and to reduce the commit time of transactions executed at the MU. The BS can broadcast information to all the MUs in its cell.

A central server holds and manages the database $D = \{D_i\}$, where $i \in N$ is a set of natural numbers and $D_i \in S$, where S is a metric space. Let d_i be the current value of the data object D_i. The data objects are replicated on the MUs, and let n_i be the number of replicas of D_i in the MDS. A limit Δ indicates the amount of change that can occur on the replica at each MU; thus Δ_i denotes the change allowed in each replica of data object D_i on any MU. If the transaction changes the value of the data item by at most Δ_i in an MU, then they are free to commit and they do not have to wait for the results of the execution of the base transaction on the DBS. This reduces the commit time of the transactions and also the number of rejected transactions, which could happen due to the base transaction not being able to commit. To control the validity of Δ_i, a timeout parameter is defined whose value indicates a duration within which the value of Δ_i is valid. Timeout values of the data item should be some multiple I of broadcast cycle time T. The value I depends on the frequency of the incoming updates for the data item, and it should also be sufficiently large so that the MUs can send their updates within duration $I \times T$. The server will not update the value of the data item until time $I \times T$ has elapsed. It is assumed that the MUs take into consideration the uplink time and send their updates before the timeout expires at the server. The client can disconnect from the MDS during the timeout period and can perform updates. If the client disconnects for a period longer than the timeout, then when it reconnects it should read the new values of Δ. If the updates are within the new limit set by Δ, then the MU can send the updates to the server; otherwise, the MU will have to block some transactions so that the total updates are within Δ. The blocked transactions will have to wait until the new values of Δ arrive at the MU. The steps of the algorithm are as follows:

At a DBS

1. Δ_i is calculated for each data object D_i. Δ_i is calculated using the function $\Delta_i = f_i (d_i, n_i)$. A function $f_i(d_i, n_i)$ is associated with each data object D_i and it depends on the application semantics.
2. A timeout value τ is linked with Δ_i values of the data item.
3. DBS broadcasts the values of (d_i, Δ_i) for each data item and a timeout τ for these values at the beginning of the broadcast cycle.
4. Either the DBS receives pre-committed transactions (transactions that have made updates to the replicas on the MU and committed) or it can receive request transactions (transactions which are directly sent to the DBS by the MU). A transaction that violates the limit is not executed at an MU, because it could change the value of replica D_i by more than Δ_i at the MU. It is sent to the DBS as a request transaction for execution on the master database.
5. The DBS serializes the pre-committed transactions according to their order of arrival. After the timeout expires, the DBS executes the request transaction, reports to the MU whether the transaction was committed or aborted, and repeats procedure from the first step.

At MU

- The MU has the value of (d_i, Δ_i) and timeout τ for every data item D_i it has cached.
- The MU executes transaction t_i. It changes the current value of D_i by Δ_{i-t_i}. Let $\Delta_{i-c}i$ be the current value of D_i after the total change in D_i since its last broadcast of value Δ_i.
- The value Δ_{i-t_i} is added to Δ_{i-c}. The following cases are possible depending on the value of Δ_{i-t_i} and Δ_{i-c}:

1. If $\Delta_{i-t_i} \leq \Delta_i$ and $\Delta_{i-c} \leq \Delta_i$, then t_i is committed at MU and it is sent to the DBS for re-execution as a base transaction on the master copy.
2. If $\Delta_{i-t_i} \leq \Delta_i$ and $\Delta_{i-c} > \Delta_i$, then t_i is blocked at the MU until new set of (D_i, Δ_i) is broadcasted by the server.
3. If $\Delta_{i-t_i} > \Delta_i$, then t_i is blocked at the MU and submitted to the server as a request transaction.

7.13.10 Relationship with ESR

The mechanism for maintaining ESR has two methods: (a) *divergence control (DC)* and (b) *consistency restoration*. This section discuses these methods and shows their use in developing the concurrency control mechanism.

A transaction imports inconsistency by reading uncommitted data of other transactions. A transaction exports inconsistency by allowing other transaction to read its uncommitted data. Transactions have *import* and *export* counters. The following example shows how these counters are maintained.

$t_1: w_1(x), w_1(z);$ $t_2: r_2(x), r_2(y);$ $t_3: w_3(y), r_3(z)$
Schedule: $w_1(x), r_2(x), r_2(y), w_3(y), r_3(z), w_1(z)$

In the above execution, t_2 reads from t_1. So it is counted as t_1 exporting one conflict to t_2 and t_2 importing one conflict from t_1. So export counter of t_1 is incremented by 1 and import counter of t_2 is incremented by 1. Transaction t_3 does not import or export any conflicts. The divergence control (DC) method sets a limit on conflicts by using import and export limits for each transaction. Thus, update transactions have an export limit and query transactions (read-only) have an import limit, which specifies the maximum number of conflicts they can be involved in. When import limit is less than 0 and export limit is greater than 0, then successive transactions may introduce unbounded inconsistency. For example, t_1 may change the value of a data item by a large amount and t_2 will read this value and operate on it as import and export counters are not violated. Later if, t_1 aborts, t_2 would have operated on a value that was deviated from the consistent value by a large amount. This situation requires consistency restoration that is done by consistency restoration algorithms.

In this concurrency control mechanism, the DC sets limits on the change allowed in each data item value at the MU and does not allow transactions to violate this limit. If it does, then it is sent as a request transaction to the DBS for execution. In this scheme, a transaction at the MU will see an inconsistent value of a data item for a maximum period of τ (the timeout period) after which it receives new consistent values of the data items. During τ, the value of data item d_i may diverge from the consistent value by a maximum of $N_i \times \Delta_i$, where N_i is the number of replicas of d_i. In this way, transactions are allowed to execute on an inconsistent data item, but the inconsistency in the data value is bounded by $N_i \times \Delta_i$. So in this CCM, the DC includes the function $fi(d_i, n_i)$ that calculates Δ_i for each d_i and also for the algorithm executed at the MU

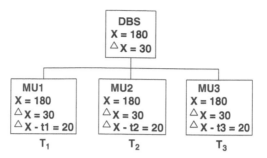

Figure 7.15   Concurrency control mechanism.

to execute transactions. Thus, the consistency restoration includes the execution of the request and pre-committed transactions at the DBS and the broadcasting of the consistent value of the data item to the MU.

■ **EXAMPLE 7.12**

This example explains the working of the CCM discussed in this section. Figure 7.15 illustrates the execution of concurrent transaction under this CCM. Suppose a data item X represents the total number of movie tickets. X belongs to metric state space. Let N_x be the number of replicas of X. Initially, suppose $X = 180$ and $N_x = 3$ and X is replicated at MU1, MU2, and MU3. The functions $f_x(X, N_x)$ that calculates Δ_x is $\Delta_x = f_x(X, N_x) = (X/2)/N_x = X/2N_x = 30$. Here X is divided by 2 to keep some tickets for the request transaction, which cannot be executed at the MU. This function depends on the application semantics and the policy the application developer wants to follow. Each data item will have a different function, depending on its semantics. (Δ_x, X, τ), where τ is timeout within which the MU should send a committed transaction for re-execution at the server, is broadcasted by the DBS server to the MUs. The following three cases arise

Case 1. Transactions t_1, t_2, and t_3 arrive at MU1, MU2, and MU3, respectively. Consider the case where t_1 books 20 tickets, t_2 books 30 tickets, and t_3 books 40 tickets. Figure 7.16 shows the state of the system at this instant. Suppose Δ_x represents change in the value of data item X; each MU that has a replica of X will maintain the value Δ_{x-c}.

At MU1: Initially $\Delta_{x-c} = 0$.

> t_1 books 20 tickets, so $\Delta_{x-t_1} = 20$ and $\Delta_{x-c} = \Delta_{x-c} + \Delta_{x-t_1} = 20$. As $\Delta_{x-c} < \Delta_x$, t_1 is committed at MU1 and so X is updated to 160 and t_1 is sent to the DBS for re-execution on the master copy.

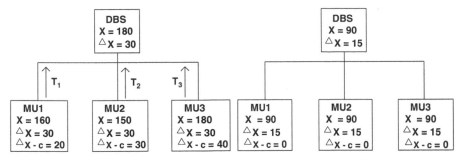

(a) **Transactions are sent to the server**   (b) **New values of △ and X are broadcasted**

Figure 7.16   Intermediate state in CCM.

At MU2: Initially $\Delta_{x-c} = 0$

t_2 books 30 tickets, so $\Delta_{x-t_2} = 30$ and $\Delta_{x-c} = \Delta_{x-c} + \Delta_{x-t_2} = 30$. As $\Delta_{x-c} \le \Delta_x$, t_2 is committed at MU2 and X is updated to 150 and t_2 is send to the DBS for re-execution.

At MU3: Initially $\Delta_{x-c} = 0$.

t_3 books 40 tickets and makes $\Delta_{x-t_3} = 40$ and $\Delta_{x-c} = \Delta_{x-c} + \Delta_{x-t_3} = 40$. Since $\Delta_{x-c} < \Delta_x$, t_3 is not executed at MU3 and is sent as a request transaction to DBS for execution.

The DBS receives t_3, t_2, and t_1 in this order. Since t_3 is a request transaction, it is executed after timeout τ has expired and after the execution of t_2 and t_1 on the master copy. So the execution at the DBS is: $X = 180$, t_2, $X = 150$, t_1, $X = 130$, t_3, $X = 90$; and after the execution, Δ is recomputed using the function $f_x(X, N_x)$. Thus, $\Delta_x = f_x(X, N_x) = X/2N_x = 15$. The DBS broadcasts $(X = 90, \Delta_x = 15, \tau)$ and each MU now can update the value of X (by not more than 15) and send the transaction for re-execution within τ. Figure 7.16 illustrates Case 1.

Transactions on the MU see an inconsistent value of the number of tickets only for period τ; after that, the DBS sends their consistent value. The transactions that want to know the number of tickets available will get the approximate value of the number of tickets. Inconsistency in the value of data objects is bounded by refreshing the data object value at a regular interval of τ and setting a limit on Δ on the maximum update that can be made during that period.

Case 2. MU3 receives the values $(X = 90, \Delta_x = 15, \tau)$ from the DBS. For every new timeout value, Δ_{x-c} is reset to zero. Transactions t_4 and t_5 arrive at MU3. t_4 books 10 tickets and t_5 books 8 tickets. Suppose the execution order is t_4, t_5. After the execution of t_4, $\Delta_{x-t_4} = 10$ and $\Delta_{x-c} = \Delta_{x-c} + \Delta_{x-t_4} = 10$. As $\Delta_{x-c} = \Delta_x$, t_4 is executed at MU3 and is sent to the DBS for re-execution. Before τ expires, transaction

t_5 arrives at MU3 where $\Delta_{x-t_5} = 8$ and $\Delta_{x-c} = 8$. This makes $\Delta_{x-c} = \Delta_{x-c} + \Delta_{x-t_5} = 18$. As $\Delta_{x-c} = \Delta_x$, t_5 is not executed at MU3 and is sent to the DBS for execution as a request transaction.

Case 3. The MUs receive values $(X = 80, \Delta_x = 0, \tau)$ from the DBS. t_6 arrives at MU2 and books 2 tickets. At MU2 initially $\Delta_{x-c} = 0$. t_6 books 2 tickets and makes $\Delta_{x-t_6} = 2$. At this point, $\Delta_{x-c} = \Delta_{x-c} + \Delta_{x-t_6} = 2$. As $\Delta_{x-c} = \Delta_x$, t_6 is not executed at MU2 but is sent as a request transaction to the DBS.

All update transactions that arrive at the MU will be sent to the DBS as a request transaction because no change is allowed to the replica at the MU since $\Delta_x = 0$. Only read transactions at the MU can access data item X.

7.14 TRANSACTION COMMITMENT

The distributed execution of a transaction requires collaboration among nodes to commit the transaction. The collaboration is initiated and managed by the coordinator that makes sure that every subtransaction is executed successfully and ready to commit. If any of its subtransactions cannot commit, then the parent transaction is aborted by the coordinator.

The entire process of commit has two phases: (a) checking the intention of each node participating in the execution of a transaction (participants) and (b) collecting the intensions of participants and committing the transaction. The entire process is atomic and the commit protocol is referred to as the *Atomic Commitment Protocol (ACP)*.

The most common ACP used in conventional distributed database systems is called the *Two-Phase Commit* (2PC) protocol. There is a *Three-Phase Commit* (3PC) protocol [36] that claims to be more efficient than the 2PC but requires a higher number of messages compared to the 2PC for making a commit decision. So far, no system has implemented a 3PC, but it continues to be an interesting research topic.

7.14.1 Two-Phase Commit Protocol—Centralized 2PC

A distributed database system with multiple nodes is assumed to describe a 2PC. A transaction T_i originates at a node that assumes the role of coordinator for T_i. The coordinator fragments T_i and distributes them to a set of participants. The coordinator may or may not keep a fragment for itself. Thus, a coordinator and a set of participants together execute T_i leading either to a commit or to an abort as decided by the coordinator. The protocol makes sure that:

- **Participants' decision:** All participants reach a decision for their fragments. All decisions can be either Yes or No.
- **Decision change:** A participant cannot change its final decision.
- **Coordinator's decision:** The coordinator can decide to commit T_i only if all participants and the coordinator agree to commit their subtransactions. In this

situation, it is not that the coordinator has no other option than to decide commit; it can still abort the transaction.

When the failure scenario is included, then the following additional steps are required for making some decision.

* **No failure:** In the absence of any failure and if all processing nodes (participants and coordinator) agree to commit, then the coordinator will commit T_i.
* **With failure:** Failure of one or more participants (or the coordinator), may delay the decision. However, if all failures are repaired within an *acceptable* time then the coordinator will reach a decision. This identifies the *nonblocking* property of centralized 2PC. The nonblocking property is essential for any APC. However, it may not be strictly enforced; that is, a failure may generate an infinite blocking situation.

The working of a centralized 2PC is described in the following steps [36].

1. **Transaction fragmentation and distribution:** A transaction T_i arrives to a node. This node serves as the coordinator for T_I. The coordinator fragments T_i into subtransactions and distributes these fragments to a set of participants. These nodes begin executing their subtransactions of T_i.
   First phase of centralized 2PC—Voting phase
2. **Voting:** The coordinator multicasts a message (vote request—VR) to all participants, asking them to vote if they can commit their subtransaction of T_i.
3. **Participants' vote:** When a participant receives a VR message from the co-ordinator, it composes its response (vote) and sends it to the coordinator. This response can be a *yes* or a *no*. If the vote is *yes*, then the participant enters into an "uncertainty" period after sending it to the coordinator . During this period, a participant cannot proceed further (make any unilateral decision on behalf of its subtransaction of T_i) and just waits for an abort or commit message from the coordinator. If the vote of the participant is *no*, then it does not wait for the coordinator's response and aborts its subtransaction and stops.

   Second phase of centralized 2PC—Decision phase

4. **Commit decision and dispatch:** When the coordinator receives votes from all participants and has its own vote, it performs an AND operation among these votes. If the result is a *yes*, then the coordinator decides to commit; otherwise it decides to abort T_i. It multicasts the decision to all participants and stops.
5. **Participants decision:** All participants receive the coordinator's decision and act accordingly. If the decision is to abort, all participants abort their fragments and stop.

7.14.2 Node Failure and Timeout Action

In order to make sure that the nonblocking property of centralized 2PC is effectively implemented, the possible occurrences of infinite wait may occur because of node failure and must be dealt with. One of the schemes to enforce a nonblocking property is to use a timeout action. A timeout value identifies how long a participant should wait for the anticipated message before it takes some action.

In the description of the centralized 2PC, participants wait for a VR message from the coordinator in the beginning of step 3, and the coordinator waits for the participants' *yes* or *no* decision at the end of step 3. Similarly, all participants wait for the coordinator's commit or abort message in step 5. If a participant times out in the beginning of step 3, then it can unilaterally decide to abort because it is not in its uncertainty period. At the end of step 3, the coordinator may time out waiting for *yes* or *no* messages from some or all participants. It may decide to abort and send abort messages to those participants that did not send their vote and that sent *yes* votes.

The timing out of participants at the beginning of step 4 is more involved because participants are in their uncertainty period and they cannot change their vote from *yes* to *no* and abort their subtransactions. It is possible that the coordinator might have sent the commit message and it reached only a subset of participants. If a participant times out in its uncertainty period and decides to abort then, it would be a wrong action. To take care of this immature abort by a timed-out participant, a *cooperative termination protocol* can be used. A cooperative termination protocol helps a participant to gather information about the last message from the coordinator that this participant missed and timed out.

Cooperative Termination Protocol. When a participant in an uncertainty period fails to receive a commit or abort message from the coordinator, then it has two options: (a) ask the coordinator about its last message or (b) ask one of is neighbor participants. In case (a), if the coordinator is available to respond, then it can get the desired information and decide accordingly. To use (b), every participant must know the identity of all other participants. This can be easily provided by the coordinator at the time of sending the VR message in step 2. The following three cases arise when (b) is used.

1. Participant P1 asks P2 about the final outcome. If P2 has decided to commit or abort (it did receive coordinator's decision message), then it can inform P1 about its decision and P1 can act accordingly.
2. P2 is not in the uncertainty period and has not voted. It decided to abort and informs P1. P1 also aborts.
3. P2 has voted *yes* but has not received a decision from the coordinator either. P2 is in a similar situation; that is, it timed out in its uncertainty period as P1 and cannot help.
4. P1 and P2 can continue to ask other participants, and hopefully at least one participant might have received the coordinator's decision. It informs P1 and P2 and they act accordingly. If all participants are timed out and did not get the coordinator's decision, then the coordinator has possibly failed and they can abort and stop.

The performance of a commit protocol largely depends on the number of messages it uses to terminate (abort of commit) a transaction. To evaluate the cost of communication, two parameters are used (a) time complexity and (b) message complexity.

Time Complexity. This parameter evaluates the time to reach a decision. It includes the time to complete a number of other necessary activities such as logging messages, preparing messages, and so on. A smaller value is highly desirable. The decision time in the absence of any kind of failure (coordinator or participants of both) is obviously smaller compared to the time with failures. In the absence of failures, the protocol uses three message *rounds*. A message round is the total time the message takes to reach from its source to the destination. The first message round is the broadcast of VR messages to the participants from the coordinator; in the second round, all participants send their vote; and in the third round, the coordinator broadcasts its decision (commit or abort). In the presence of failures, two additional rounds are required (a) a timed-out participant enquires about the coordinator's decision and (b) a response from a participant who received the coordinator's decision (this participant is out of its uncertainty period). Thus, with no failure of any kind, three message rounds and five message rounds with failure are required to terminate a transaction.

Message Complexity. Message complexity evaluates the number of messages exchanged between destinations and sources to reach a decision. In a centralized 2PC, message exchange takes place between one coordinator and n participants when there is no failure. The total number of messages exchanged is $3n$ in the three steps of the protocol are as follows:

- The coordinator sends a VR message to n participants $= n$ messages.
- Each participant sends one vote message (Yes or No) to the coordinator $= n$ vote messages.
- The coordinator sends the decision message to n participants $= n$ messages.
  In the presence of failure, each timed out participant who voted *Yes* initiates a cooperative termination protocol. In the worst case scenario, all participants could be timed out and initiate the protocol. If there are m such timed-out participants with *Yes* vote, then $m \leq n$.
- m participants will initiate the protocol and send $n - 1$ decision request messages. The requestor participant m_i will get a response from at least one of the n participants and would come out of its uncertainty period. This cycle will continue until m participants come out from their uncertainty period. The total number of messages used in this entire process will be

$$m(n - 1) + \sum_{i=1}^{m}(n - m + i) = 2m(n - 1) - m^2/2 + m/2$$

To minimize the time or message complexity or both, two variations of 2PC exist: (a) *decentralized 2PC* and (b) *linear or nested 2PC*.

7.14.3 Decentralized 2PC

In this scheme, the coordinator minimizes the message complexity by sending its vote along with the VR message to the participants. If the coordinator's vote is *No*, then participants know the decision and abort their subtransactions and stop. If the coordinator's vote is *Yes*, then each participant sends its vote to all other participants. After receiving all votes, each participants decides. If all votes are *Yes*, then the transaction commits; otherwise, it is aborted.

Time Complexity. In the decentralized 2PC there are two message rounds: (a) the coordinator sends the VR message and its vote, and (b) the participants send their *Yes* votes and transaction commits. When the coordinator sends its *Yes* vote to the participants, it implies that "I am ready to commit and if you are also, then go ahead and commit" and, therefore, there is no need for the coordinator to send a commit vote. This reduces one message round compared to the centralized 2PC.

Message Complexity. The reduction in time complexity unfortunately increases the message complexity. In the centralized 2PC, the coordinator makes the final decision, but in the distributed 2PC, everybody participates in the decision process. This requires that each participant communicates with all other participants to know their votes. If there are n participants, this process requires n^2 messages. Thus, the total number of messages to commit a transaction in failure, as well as in no failure cases, is n^2 (participant to $n-1$ participants) $+ n$ (coordinator to n participants) . In case of $n > 2$, the decentralized 2PC always takes a greater number of messages than centralized 2PC.

7.14.4 Linear or Nested 2PC

In the linear 2PC, the message complexity is reduced by collecting votes serially. All participants and the coordinator are ordered linearly. Each participant has a left and a right neighbor and a coordinator has only one neighbor. Figure 7.17 illustrates the setup.

The protocol works as follows:

1. The coordinator sends its Yes or No vote to participant P_1.
2. P_1 performs *Coordinator's vote* $\bigwedge$ P_1's *vote* $= X$. $X =$ Yes or No.
3. P_1 sends X to P_2 and the process continues until the result reaches to P_n.
4. If the outcome of P_n computation is Yes, it decides to commit and sends this message to P_{n-1}.
5. The return message containing the commit decision finally reaches to the coordinator and completes the commit process.

| Coordinator | P_1 | P_2 | P_n |

Figure 7.17 Linear ordering of participants and coordinator.

Table 7.8 Message and Time Complexity in Various 2PC

Protocols	Messages	Rounds
Centralized	$3n$	3
Distributed	$n^2 + n$	2
Linear	$2n$	$2n$

Time Complexity. There is no message broadcast in the linear 2PC, so it requires the same number of rounds as the number of messages to make the final decision. Thus, with n participants it will require $2n$, rounds, which are much larger than the centralized and decentralized 2PC.

Message Complexity. With n participants, this protocol requires $2n$ messages: n forward messages and n return messages, which are much smaller than the message complexity of the decentralized and centralized 2PC.

Table 7.8 compares the message and time complexity of the centralized, decentralized, and linear 2PC with no failure. It is hard to identify the most efficient protocol for all systems because of the wide ranging values of parameters such as message size, communication speed, processing delay, and so on, which are highly system-dependent. However, it can be seen that the centralized 2PC offers a good compromise.

7.15 COMMITMENT OF MOBILE TRANSACTIONS

7.15.1 Commit Protocols for Mobilaction

The mobility and other characteristics of *MUs* affect Mobilaction processing, especially its commitment. Some of the common limitations are as follows: (a) an *MU* may cease to communicate with its *BS* for a variety of reasons, (b) it may run out of its limited battery power, (c) it may run out of its disk space, (d) it may be affected by airport security, (e) physical abuse and accident, (f) limited wireless channels for communication, and (g) unpredictable *handoffs*.

A mobile computing environment creates a complex distributed processing environment and, therefore requires a distributed commit protocol. We have assumed the two-phase commit approach as the basis of developing our mobile commit protocol. One of the essential requirements of distributed processing is that all subtransactions of T_i must be ready to commit. In an MDS, a complete knowledge of this state becomes relatively more complex because of mobility. It is crucial that the scheme to acquire this knowledge must use minimum message communication and it is also important that this scheme should not be dependent on the mobility of the involved *MUs*.

The different types of data (temporal and spatial) in mobile computing provide more freedom in designing commit protocols. Like conventional distributed database systems, a transaction in an MDS may be processed by a number of *DBSs* and *MUs*;

therefore, some commit protocol is necessary for their termination. Legacy commit protocols such as *2PC (two-phase commit)*, *3PC (three-phase commit)* [36], and so on, will not perform satisfactorily mainly because of limited resources, especially wireless channel availability. For example, the most commonly used *2PC* uses three message rounds in case of no failure and five in case of failure for termination [36]. Note that it requires additional support (use of timeout) for termination in the presence of blocked or failed subtransactions. Thus, the time and message complexities are too high for the MDS to handle and must be minimized to improve the utilization of scares resources.

The mobility of an *MU* adds another dimension to these complexities. It may force the MDS to reconfigure the initial commit setup during the life of a transaction [61]. For example, a proper coordination among the subtransactions of a transaction under the *participants–coordinator* paradigm may be difficult to achieve with the available resources for its commitment. Mobile database systems, therefore, require commitment protocols that should use a minimum number of wireless messages, and the *MU* and *DBSs* involved in T_i processing should have independent decision-making capabilities, and the protocol should be *nonblocking* [36].

7.16 TRANSACTION COMMITMENT IN MOBILE DATABASE SYSTEMS

The mobility and other characteristics of MUs affect transaction processing, especially its commitment. Some of the common limitations are as follows: (a) an MU may cease to communicate with its BS for a variety of reasons, (b) it may run out of its limited battery power, (c) it may run out of its disk space, (d) it may be affected by airport security, (e) physical abuse and accident, (f) it has limited wireless channels for communication, and (g) unpredictable *handoff*.

Like conventional distributed database systems, a transaction in MDS may be processed by a number of nodes such as the DBSs and MUs; therefore, some commit protocol is necessary for their termination. Conventional commit protocols such as 2PC, 3PC [36], and so on could be molded to work with the MDS; however, they will not perform satisfactorily mainly because their resource requirements may not be satisfied by the MDS on time. For example, the most commonly used centralized 2PC uses three message rounds in case of no failure and uses five in case of failure for termination [36]. It requires additional support (use of timeout) for termination in the presence of blocked or failed "subtransactions." Thus, the time and message complexities are too high for the MDS to handle and must be minimized to improve the utilization of scares resources (wireless channel, battery power, etc.)

The mobility of the *MU* adds another dimension to these complexities. It may force the MDS to reconfigure the initial commit setup during the life of a transaction [61–63]. For example, a proper coordination among the subtransactions of a transaction under the *participants–coordinator* paradigm may be difficult to achieve with the available resources for its commitment. For example, a mobile unit may not receive the coordinator's vote request and commit messages, and it may not send its vote on time because of its random movement while processing a subtranaction. This may generate unnecessary transaction aborts. These limitations suggest that the MDS commit protocol must support an independent decision-making capability for the coordinator and for the participants to minimize the cost of messages. A new commit protocol is required for the MDS that should have the following desirable properties:

- It should use a minimum number of wireless messages.
- The *MU* and *DBSs* involved in T_i processing should have independent decision-making capabilities, and the protocol should be *nonblocking*.

An analysis of conventional commit protocols indicates that a timeout parameter could be used to develop a commit protocol for an MDS. In conventional protocols, a timeout parameter is used to enforce a nonblocking property. A timeout identifies the maximum times a node can wait before making any decision. The expiration of timeout is always related to the occurrence of some kind of failure. For example, in a conventional 2PC, the expiration of timeout indicates a node failure and it allows a participant to take a unilateral decision.

If a timeout parameter can identify a failure situation, then it can also be used to identify a success situation. Under this approach, the end of timeout will indicate a success. The basic idea, then is to define a timeout for the completion of an action and assume that at the end of this timeout, the action will be completed successfully. For example, a participant defines a timeout within which it completes the execution of its subtransaction and sends its update through the coordinator to the DBSs for installing it in the database. If the updates do not arrive within the timeout, then it would indicate a failure scenario. The coordinator does not have to query the participant to learn about its status.

Recently, timeout parameter has been used in a nonconventional way for developing solutions to some of the mobile database problems. This section presents a commit protocol that is referred to as *Transaction Commit on Timeout (TCOT)* [61, 62]. It uses the timeout parameter to indicate a success rather than a failure.

The TCOT protocol is discussed below in detail. A transaction T_i is fragmented, and they are distributed for execution among a number of DBSs and the MU where T_i originated. These nodes are defined as *Commit Set* of T_i; the MU where T_i originates is referred to as *Home MU* (MU_H), and the BS of MU_H is referred to as Home BS (BS_H).

Definition 7.21 *A **commit set** of a T_i is defined as the set of DBS and the MU_H that takes part in the processing and commit of T_i. A DBS is identified as a static member, and the MU is a mobile member of a commit set.*

TCOT strives to limit the number of messages (especially uplink). It does so by assuming that all members of a commit set successfully commit their fragments within the timeout they define after analyzing their subtransactions leading to commit of T_i. Unlike 2PC or 3PC, no further communications between the CO and participants take place for keeping track of the progress of fragments. However, the failure situation is immediately communicated to the CO to make a final decision.

It is well known that finding the most appropriate value of a timeout is not always easy because it depends on a number of system variables, which could be difficult to quantify. However, it is usually possible to define a value for timeout that performs well in all cases. An imprecise value of timeout does not affect the correctness but affects the performance of the algorithm.

Every CO (new or existing) must know the identity of each member of a commit set. Every MU_H stores the identity of its current CO for each transaction requested there. When MU_H moves to another cell, then during registration it also informs the BS about its previous CO. As soon as MU_H sends T_i to BS_H, the latter assumes the role of CO for T_i. Also in the dynamic approach, the transfer of CO does not require extra uplink or downlink messages because the notification process is a part of the registration.

Types of Timeout. TCOT protocol uses two types of timeout: *execution timeout* (E_t) and *update shipping timeout* (S_t).

Execution Timeout (E_t). This timeout defines a value within which a node of a commit set completes the execution (not commit) of its execution fragment or sub-transaction e_i. It is an upper bound of the time a DBS or the MU_H requires to complete the execution of e_i.

The CO assumes that the MU_H or a DBS will complete the execution of its e_i within E_t. The value of E_t may be node-specific. It may depend on the size of e_i and the characteristics of the processing unit; thus $E_t(MU_i)$ may or may not be equal to $E_t(MU_j)$, $(i \neq j)$. We identify MU_H's timeout by $E_t(MU)$, and we identify the DBS timeout by $E_t(DBS)$. The relationship between these two timeouts is $E_t(MU) = E_t(DBS) \pm \Delta$. The Δ accounts for the characteristics such as poor resources, disconnected state, availability of wireless channel, and so on, compared to the DBS. It is possible that an MU may take less time than its E_t to execute its e_i. We also do not rule out the possibility that in some cases $E_t(DBS)$ may be larger than $E_t(MU_H)$. E_t typically should be just long enough to allow a fragment to successfully finish its entire execution in a normal environment (i.e., no failure of any kind, no message delay, etc.)

Shipping timeout (S_t). This timeout defines the upper bound of the data shipping time from MU_H to the DBS.

In E_t, the cached copy of the data is updated at the MU. To maintain global consistency, all data updates done by the MU_H must be shipped and installed at the database located at the DBS. Thus, at the end of E_t the CO expects the updates to be shipped to the DBS and logged there within S_t.

7.16.1 TCOT Steps—No Failure

In TCOT three components, MU_H, CO, and DBSs, participate. The steps in the absence of any kind of failure are as follows:

- *Activities of MU_H:*
  - A T_i originates at MU_H. The BS_H is identified as the CO. MU_H extracts its e_i from T_i, computes its E_t, and sends $T_i - e_i$ to the CO along with the E_t of e_i. MU_H begins the processing of e_i.
  - While processing e_i, MU_H updates its cache copy of the database, composes an update shipment, and appends it to the log.
  - During processing, if it is determined that e_i will execute longer than E_t, then MU_H extends its value and sends it to the CO. Note that this uses one extra uplink message. The frequency of such extension requests can be minimized with a careful calculation of $E_t(MU_H)$.
  - If the local fragment e_i aborts for any reason, then MU_H sends an abort message to CO (failure notification).
  - After execution of e_i, MU_H sends the updates to the CO. The updates must reach the CO before S_t expires. It could be possible that updates may reach the CO much earlier, in which case it may decide to commit sooner.
  - In the case of read-only e_i, MU_H sends a commit message to the CO. This is not an extra message, it just replaces the shipping update message.
  - Once the updates are dispatched to the CO, MU_H declares commit of e_i. Note that the underlying concurrency control may decide to release all the data items to other fragments. If for some reason T_i is aborted, then fragment compensation may be necessary.
  - If MU_H fails to send updates to the CO within S_t and it did not extend E_t, then the CO aborts e_i.
- *Activities of the CO:*
  - Upon receipt of $T_i - e_i$ from MU_H, the CO creates a *token list* for T_i that contains one entry for each of its fragments. (Figure 7.18) shows a token list entry for e_i of T_i. In the case of a CO change, a token is used to inform the new CO the status of fragment and commit set members. The CO splits $T_i - e_i$ into e_j's $(i \neq j)$ and sends them to the set of relevant DBSs.
  - After receiving E_t from a DBS, the CO constructs a token for that fragment and keeps it for future use.
  - If a new E_t (extension) is received either from MU_H or from a DBS, then the CO updates the token entry for that fragment.
  - The CO logs the updates from MU_H.
  - If the CO has MU_H's shipment before S_t expires and commit messages from other DBSs of the commit set, then the CO commits T_i. At this time, the

e_i	E_t (MU_i) or E_t (DBS_j)	Coordinator ID	Commit set

Figure 7.18   An entry of a token list.

updates from the MU_H are sent to the DBSs for updates to the primary copy of the databases. Note that no further message is sent to any member of the commit set of T_i.

- If the CO does not receive updates from MU_H within the timeout or does not receive commit message from any of the DBSs of the commit set, then it aborts T_i and sends a global abort message (wired message to the DBSs and wireless to the MU) to those members of the commit set who committed their fragments.

- *Activities of the DBS*:
  - Each *DBS*, upon receiving its fragment, computes E_t and sends it to the CO. *DBS* begins processing its fragment and updates its own database.
  - If it is determined that the fragment will execute longer than E_t, then this value is extended and the new value is sent to the CO.
  - At the end of e_j it sends a "commit message" to the CO.
  - If the *DBS* cannot complete the execution of its e_j for any reason and did not extend E_t, then it sends an abort message to the CO.

Discussion. One may argue that either E_t or the "commit message" from a DBS is sufficient for making a commit decision. This is not entirely correct. E_t identifies when a fragment will finish its execution and will be ready to commit. Thus, at the end of E_t, CO will assume that the *DBS* has committed its fragment, which may not be true (fragment may not have been processed because of the failure of the *DBS*). Since a *DBS* does not ship updates, it must use a message for informing the status of the fragment. On the other hand, if there is only a "commit message," then for some reason the CO could never get this message from a *DBS* and waits forever to make the final commit decision. Thus, for making the final decision and doing it efficiently, both E_t and the "commit message" are necessary. Note that a *DBS* communicates with the CO through a wired channel and any extra messages do not create any message overhead.

TCOT, unlike 2PC, has only one-phase commit operation. No vote-request or commit message is sent to commit set members. The task assignment message to these members provides necessary information and directives for completing commit. Only in the case of abort, one extra wireless message is used. In reality, not many transactions are aborted and this extra message is not likely to generate noticeable overhead.

In the case of a read-only fragment, MU_H does not send any update to the CO, but similar to a DBS, it sends only a "commit" message.

7.16.2 Node Failure—Fragment Compensation

The process of compensation is not related to commit; rather, it comes under recovery [64], but it becomes an issue for a long-running transaction. In TCOT, a member of T_i's commit set may commit its fragment and the underlying concurrency control (two-phase locking scheme is assumed) may decide to release its data items to other concurrent fragments before the CO declares the commit of T_i. For example, if $e_i(T_i)$

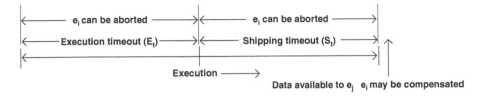

Figure 7.19 Relationship between E_t and S_t, abort, and compensation.

is committed by MU_H, but T_i is aborted, then e_i must be compensated. When MU_H receives a message to abort e_i from the CO, then if possible [64] a compensating transaction for e_i is executed. At the end of compensation, MU_H informs the CO and sends new updates if there are any. Figure 7.19 illustrates the relationship among E_t, S_t, abort, and compensation. After S_t, the MU_H can make data items available to e_j ($i \neq j$). This means that after S_t, an e_i may be compensated.

7.16.3 TCOT with Handoff

In the case of a handoff, updates from MU_H and a dispatch of a commit message from the DBSs must be sent to the right CO if it changes. The change in the CO is notified using a *token*. The following steps define the commit process in the presence of a handoff.

- MU_H moves to a different cell and registers with the new BS.
- If MDS employs a dynamic selection of the CO, then the MU_H sends the identity of its last CO in the registration process and accepts the new BS as its next CO. The new BS gets the *token* from the last CO, which provides necessary information.
- The new CO identifies other members of the commit set from the *token* and notifies them about the change of the CO. Note that the communication between the new CO and DBSs is through a wired channel. The processing of T_i resumes normally.

A doze mode of MU_H will mainly affect its E_t. MU_H may not be aware of its movement, but it knows when it enters into the doze mode. Therefore, before going into the doze mode, MU_H can always request an extension to its E_t. If granted, then the fragment will not be aborted; otherwise, a global abort will be initiated.

7.16.4 Special Cases

A number of special cases may arise during commit and TCOT manages them as follows.

- S_t **expires before DBSs send commit message:** It is possible that MU_H commits its e_i and sends its updates to the CO before the DBSs send their commit messages to the CO. In this case, the CO will wait for the commit messages.

- **The DBSs send commit messages before S_t expires:** The CO will wait for S_t to expire before making any decision.
- **S_t expires but no updates or no commit message:** The CO will send an abort message to the members of the commit set.

Note that the abort could be received at any time. If it is received prior to the commit, then a local abort with a corresponding undo is needed. If, however, it is received after the local commit, then compensation is needed. Further, when a fragment is executed, the decision to commit or abort is made locally. However, the implicit assumption is that a global commit occurs.

7.16.5 An Alternate TCOT Protocol

In the first version of TCOT, MU_H is responsible for extracting e_i from T_i, computing E_t, and sending $T_i - e_i$ to the CO. In this approach, every T_i is examined by MU_H, which is not necessary. This can be improved by sending the entire T_i to the CO and by letting the CO do the fragmentation, estimate E_t, and send the information back to MU_H. This will use one extra wireless downlink message, but reduces the workload of MU_H since many T_i's may not be processed by MU_H. The other advantage of this is related to *token* passing. The CO can send the *token* to MU_H, which in turn can send it to the new CO during registration. The steps, which differ from the first version of TCOT, are

- MU_H forwards T_i to the CO.
- The CO fragments T_i, computes $E'_t s$ of all the fragments, creates *tokens*, and sends them to the members of the commit set. (This step uses one extra downlink message.)
- MU_H computes S_t for its fragment.

7.16.6 Correctness

A commit decision by a CO is said to be "correct" if the decision to commit is unanimous. Suppose the CO decides to commit T_i when at least one member of the commit set is undecided. This is possible only if the CO declares commit before either the expiration of S_t or the absence of a commit message from at least one DBS. This, however, cannot happen. Further, suppose that the MU_H failed and could not send updates to the CO within S_t or that the "commit message" is not received by the CO. In this situation, the CO will abort T_i. Since our algorithm is based on timeout, it is not possible that at any stage the CO will enter into an infinite wait.

7.17 SUMMARY

This chapter introduced a reference architecture of a mobile database system and discussed a number of transaction management issues. It identified a number of unique properties of a mobile database system and discussed the effect of mobility on its functionality.

It demonstrated that location of the database and the location of the origin of the query must be considered to enforce ACID properties of transactions. To handle these requirements, the concept of *Location-Dependent Data* and *Location-Dependent Commit* were introduced. Thus, in a mobile database system, a user initiates (a) a location-dependent query, (b) a location-aware query, or (c) a location-independent query. The concept of *data region* was introduced to accommodate cellular structure in mobile database processing and transaction commit.

It identified unique system requirements for concurrency control mechanisms and transaction commitment. First it analyzed the relationship between mobility and transaction processing. A clear understanding of this relationship is necessary for the development of mobile transaction model and its management.

It argued that conventional 2-phase or 3-phase commit protocols were not suitable for mobile database systems and illustrated that a commit protocol that uses the least number of messages and offers independent commit decision capability was highly desirable. It introduced the one-phase commit protocol with the above properties.

A data replication scheme for connected and disconnected operations was discussed for mobile database system. Under this scheme, data located at strongly connected sites are grouped in clusters. Bounded inconsistency was defined by requiring mutual consistency among copies located at the same cluster and controlled deviation among copies at different clusters. The database interface is extended with weak operations.

This chapter provided necessary material for the development of a mobile database system framework and a mobile transaction model.

EXERCISES

7.1 Explain the main differences between mobile database systems and conventional distributed database systems from a transaction execution viewpoint. Discuss the role of a coordinator in executing transactions in a distributed system. Why is it difficult to select a coordinator in mobile database systems? Explain.

7.2 Investigate the role of the coordinator in mobile database systems and develop a scheme (other than what is given in the book) for coordinator selection and their management.

7.3 Investigate the issues in processing location-dependent data. Give a real-life example to illustrate the occurrence of location inconsistency. Why does this problem not occur in conventional distributed database system? Explain.

7.4 Consider the architecture of a given mobile database system. What issues may one encounter during the execution of a transaction related to mobility and data distribution? Investigate and develop your own scheme of managing these issues successfully.

7.5 A number of transaction execution models are there that execute ACID transactions on mobile database systems. There are some transaction models defined specifically for mobile database systems such as Kangaroo, Mobilaction, and so on. Investigate and develop a mobile transaction model of your own that will successfully process location dependent data.

7.6 Discuss the job of location mapping function in Mobilaction. Clearly indicate (with appropriate examples) when this function is required to process a location-dependent query. Is this mapping function required for processing a location-aware query? Explain.

7.7 Discuss the problems you would encounter if you use a version of two-phase locking concurrency control mechanisms to serialize the execution of concurrent transactions on an MDS. First explain the version of two-phase locking protocol and then explain the problems.

7.8 In TCOT (Transaction Commit On Timeout) commit protocol a number of timeouts are defined. Explore the relationship among these timeouts and discuss their effect on the others if the value of a timeout parameter is changed and vice versa. Investigate what will happen to the performance if their values are made (a) too large and (b) too small. Give examples.

7.9 Implement a version of a two-phase locking mechanism in a mobile database system and count the total number of messages it requires to (a) execute a transaction, (b) roll back a transaction, and (c) commit a transaction.

7.10 Investigate and modify TCOT protocol to manage transaction failure more efficiently.

7.11 Caching is supposed to speed up getting required data. Consider several activities of mobile database systems including location management and identify those activities that you think could benefit with caching. Explain your answer and give examples.

7.12 When a transaction arrives at a mobile unit, then it is fragmented because the mobile unit does not have all the data to process it locally. Develop a scheme to fragment this transaction appropriately so that its fragments can be assigned to appropriate processing units (DBSs). Explain your splitting criteria and the workings of your scheme.

REFERENCES

1. E. Pitoura and B. Bhargava, Building Information Systems for Mobile Environments. In *Proceedings of 3rd International Conference on Information and Knowledge Management*, Washington, D.C., November 1994, pp. 371–378.

2. R. Kuruppillai, M. Dontamsetti, and F. J. Cosentino, *Wireless PCS*, McGraw-Hill, New York, 1997.

3. M. Mouly and M.-B. Pautet, *The GSM System for Mobile Communications*, Cell & Sys France, 1992.

4. http://hps.org/publicinformation/ate/faqs/cellphoneqa.html.

5. J. Gray and A. Reuter, *Transaction Processing: Concepts and Techniques*, Morgan Kaufmann, San Francisco, 1993.

6. E. Pitoura and G. Samaras, Locating Objects in Mobile Computing, *IEEE Transaction on Knowledge and Data Engineering*, Vol. 13, No. 4, 2001, 571–592.

7. E. Pitoura and I. Fudos, Distributed Location Databases for Tracking Highly Mobile Objects, *The Computer Journal*, Vol. 44, No. 2, 2001, 75–91.

8. A. Y. Seydim, M. H. Dunham, and V. Kumar, Location Dependent Query Processing. In *Proceedings of MobiDE*, 2001, pp. 47–53.

9. M. T. Ozsu and P. Valduriez, *Principles of Distributed Database Systems*, Prentice-Hall, Englewood Cliffs, NJ, 1991.

10. C. Pu, G. Kaiser, and N. Hutchinson, Split-Transactions for Open-Ended Activities, In *Proceedings, Fourth International Conference on VLDB*, September 1988, pp. 26–37.

11. G. Weikum and G. Vossen, Transactional Information Systems. Morgan Kaufmann, San Francisco, 2002.

12. B. E. Moss, Nested transactions. The MIT Press, Cambridge, Massachusetts, 1985.

13. P. K. Chrysanthis, Transaction Processing in a Mobile Computing Environment. In *Proc. of the IEEE Workshop on Advances in Parallel and Distributed Systems*, Princeton, NJ, October 1993, pp. 77–82.

14. K. Ramamritham and P. K. Chrysanthis, A Taxonomy of Correctness Criterion in Database Applications, *The VLDB Journal The International Journal on Very Large Data Bases*, Vol. 5, No. 1, January 1996, 85–97.

15. N. Barghouti and G. Kaiser, Concurrency Control in Advanced Database Applications, *ACM Computing Surveys*, Vol. 23, No. 3, 269–317.

16. E. Pitoura and B. Bhargava, Maintaining Consistency of Data in Mobile Distributed Environments. In *Proceedings of 15th International Conference on Distributed Computing Systems*, 1995, pp. 404–413.

17. D. G. Walborn and P. K. Chrysanthis, Pro-Motion: Support for Mobile Database Access. *Personal Technologies*, Vol. 1, No. 3, September 1997, 171–181.

18. D. G. Walborn and P. K. Chrysanthis, Pro-Motion: Management of Mobile Transactions. In *Proceedings 12th ACM Annual Symposium on Applied Computing*, San Jose, CA, February 1997, pp. 101–108.

19. D. G. Walborn and P. K. Chrysanthis, Supporting Semantics Based Transaction Processing in Mobile Database Applications. In *Proceedings 14th IEEE Symposium on Reliable Distributed Systems*, September 1995, pp. 31–40.

20. S. K. Madria and B. Bhargava, A Transactional Model to Improve Data Availability in Mobile Computing, *Distributed and Parallel Databases*, Vol. 10, No. 2, September 2001, 127–160.

21. E. Pitoura and B. Bhargava, Maintaining Consistency of Data in Mobile Distributed Environments. In *Proceedings of the 15th IEEE International Conference on Distributed Computing Systems*, May 1995, pp. 404–413.

22. L. H. Yeo and A. Zaslavsky, Submission of Transactions from Mobile Workstations in a Cooperative Multidatabase Processing Environment. In *Proceedings of 14th Distributed Computing Systems*, 1994, pp. 372–379.

23. D. Lee, W.-C. Lee, J. Xu, and B. Zheng, Data Management in Location-Dependent Information Services, *IEEE Pervasive Computing*, Vol. 1, No. 3, July–September 2002, 65–72.

24. A. K. Elmagarmid, Y. Lie, and Marek Rusinkiewicz, A Multidatabase Transaction Model for INTERBASE. In *International Conference on Very Large Databases (VLDB)*, Brisbane, Australia, August 1990, pp. 507–518.

25. K. I. Ku and Y.-S. Kim, Moflex Transaction Model for Mobile Heterogenous Multidatabase Systems. In *Proceedings of the 10th International Workshop on Research Issues in Data Engineering*, 2000, pp. 39–45.

26. M. H. Dunham, A. Helal, and S. Balakrishnan, A Mobile Transaction Model that Captures Both the Data and the Movement Behavior, *ACM/Balter Journal on Special Topics in Mobile Networks and Applications*, Vol. 2, No. 2, 1997, 149–162.

27. V. Kumar, M. H. Dunham and N. Prabhu, Mobilaction: A Mobile Transaction Framework Supporting Spatial Replication and Spatial Consistency", *Special Issue on Mobile Databases International Journal of Computer Systems Science & Engineering*. Vol. 20, No 2. March 2005, 117–131.

28. G. H. Forman and J. Zahorjan, The Challenges of Mobile Computing, *IEEE Computer*, Vol. 27, No. 6, April 1994, 38–47.

29. T. Imielinksi and B. R. Badrinath, Wireless Mobile Computing: Challenges in Data Management, *Communications of the ACM*, Vol. 37, No. 10, October 1994, 18–28.

30. E. Pitoura and G. Samaras, *Data Management for Mobile Computing*, Kluwer Academic Publishers, Norwell, MA, 1998.

31. J. J. Kistler and M. Satyanarayanan, Disconnected Operations in the Coda File Systems, *ACM Transactions on Computer Systems*, Vol. 10, No. 1, February 1992, 3–25.

32. M. Satyanarayanan, J. J. Kistler, L. B. Mummert, M. R. Ebling, P. Kumar, and Q. Lu, Experience with Disconnected Operation in a Mobile Computing Environment. In *Proceedings of the 1993 USENIX Symposium on Mobile and Location-Independent Computing*, Cambridge, MA, August 1993, pp. 537–570.

33. E. Pitoura and B. Bhargava, Building Information Systems for Mobile Environments. In *Proceedings of the Third International Conference on Information and Knowledge Management*, Washington, D.C., November 1994, pp. 371–378.

34. L. B. Mummert, M. R. Ebling, and M. Satyanarayanan, Exploiting Weak Connectivity for Mobile File Access. In *Proceedings of the 15th ACM Symposium on Operating Systems Principles*, December 1995, pp. 143–155.

35. B. D. Noble, M. Price, and M. Satyanarayanan, A Programming Interface for Application-Aware Adaptation in Mobile Computing, *Computing Systems*, Vol. 8, No. 4, Winter 1995, 345–363.

36. P. A. Bernstein, V. Hadzilacos, and N. Goodman, *Concurrency Control and Recovery in Database Systems*, Addison-Wesley, Reading, MA, 1987.

37. C. Papadimitriou, *The Theory of Database Concurrency Control*, Computer Science Press, New York, 1986.

38. R. Alonso, D. Barbara, and H. Garcia-Molina, Data Caching Issues in an Information Retrieval System, *ACM Transactions on Database Systems*, Vol. 15, No. 3, September 1990, 359–384.

39. A. Sheth and M. Rusinkiewicz, Management of Interdependent Data: Specifying Dependency and Consistency Requirements. In *Proceedings of the Workshop on the Management of Replicated Data*, Houston, Texas, November 1990, pp. 133–136.

40. S. B. Davidson, H. Garcia-Molina, and D. Skeen, Consistency in Partitioned Networks, *ACM Computing Surveys*, Vol. 17, No. 3, September 1985, 341–370.

41. E. Pitoura, Replication Schema to Support Weak Connectivity in Mobile Information Systems. In *Proceedings of the 7th International Conference on Database and Expert Systems Applications (DEXA96)*, LNCS 1134, Springer Verlag, New York, September 1996, pp. 510–520.

42. H. Garcia-Molina and G. Wiederhold, Read-Only Transactions in a Distributed Database. *ACM Transactions on Database Systems*, Vol. 7, No. 2, June 1982, 209–234.

43. C. Pu and A. Leff, Replica control in distributed systems: An asynchronous approach. In *Proceedings of the ACM SIGMOD*, 1991, pp. 377–386.

44. K. Ramamritham and C. Pu, A Formal Characterization of Epsilon Serializability, *IEEE TRansactions on Knowledge and Data Engineering*, Vol. 7, No. 6, 1995, 997–1007.

45. M. H. Wong and D. Agrawal, Tolerating Bounded Inconsistency for Increasing Concurrency in Database Systems. In *Proceedings of the 11th ACM PODS*, 1992, pp. 236–245.

46. N. Krinshnakumar and A. J. Bernstein, Bounded Ingnorance: A Technique for Increasing Concurrency in a Replicated System, *ACM Transactions on Database Systems*, Vol. 19, No. 4, December 1994, 586–625.

47. K.-y. Lam, T.-W. Kuo, W.-H. Tsamg and Gary C. K. Law, Concurrency Control in Mobile Distributed Real-Time Database Systems, *Information Systems*, Vol. 25, No. 4, June 2000, 261–286.

48. R. J. Abbott and H. Garcia-Molina, Scheduling Real-Time Transactions: A Performance Evaluation, *ACM Transactions on Database Systems*, Vol. 17, No. 3, September 1992, 513–560.

49. V. Kumar and M. Hsu, A Superior Two-Phase Locking Algorithm and its Performance, *Information Sciences, An International Journal*, Vol. 54, No. 1–2, 1991, 147–168.

50. P. Bober and M. J. Carey, On Mixing Queries and Transactions via Multiversion Locking, *Technical Report*, Computer Science Department, University of Wisconsin–Madison, November 1991.

51. S. Goel, B. Bhargava, and S. Madria, An Adaptable Constrained Locking Protocol for High Data Contention Environments. In *Proceedings of IEEE for 6th International Conference on Database Systems for Advanced Applications* (DASFAA,99), April 1999, Taiwan, pp. 321–328.

52. K.-y. Lam, G. Li, T.-W. Kuo, A Multi-version Data Model for Executing Real-Time Transactions in a Mobile Environment. In *Proceedings of MobiDE*, 2001, pp. 90–97.

53. A. Chan, S. Fox, W. Lin, A. Nori, and D. Ries, The Implementation of an Integrated Concurrency Control and Recovery Scheme. In *ACM Proceedings of SIGMOD*, ACM Press, New York, 1982, pp. 184–191.

54. W. E. Weihl, Distributed Version Management for Read-Only Actions, *IEEE Transactions Software Engineering*, Vol. 13, No. 1, January 1987, 55–64.

55. D. Agrawal and S. Sengupta, Modular Synchronization in Multiversion Databases: Version Control and Concurrency Control. In *ACM Proceedings of SIGMOD*, New York, May 1989, pp. 408–417.

56. D. Agrawal amd A. El Abbadi, Constrained Shared Locks for Increasing Concurrency in Databases, *Journal of Computer and System Sciences*, Vol. 51, 1995, 53–63.

57. C. Pu, Generalized Transaction Processing with Epsilon-Serializability. In *Proceedings of Fourth International Workshop on High Performance Transaction Systems*, Asilomar, California, September 1991.

58. J. Gray, P. Helland, P. E. O'Neil, and D. Shasha, The Dangers of Replication and a Solution. In *SIGMOD*, 1996.

59. K.-L. Wu, P. S. Yu, C. Pu, Divergence Control for Epsilon-Serializability. In *International Conference on Data Engineering (ICDE)*, 1992, pp. 506–515.

60. D. Barbara, Certification Reports: Supporting Transactions in Wireless Systems. In *Proceedings of the 17th International Conference on Distributed Computing Systems (ICDCS97)*, 1997, pp. 466–473.

61. V. Kumar, A Timeout-Based Mobile Transaction Commitment Protocol. In *2000 ADBIS-DASFAA Symposium on Advances in Databases and Information Systems*, In Cooperation with ACM SIGMOD-Moscow, September 5–8, 2000, Prague, Czech Republic.

62. V. Kumar, N. Prabhu, M. Dunham, and Y. A. Seydim, TCOT—A Timeout-based Mobile Transaction Commitment Protocol, *Special Issue of IEEE Transaction on Computers*, Vol. 51, No. 10, October 2002, 1212–1218.

63. V. Kumar and M. Dunham, Defining Location Data Dependency, Transaction Mobility and Commitment, Technical Report 98-cse-1, Southern Methodist University, Feburary 98.

64. H. Korth, E. Levy, and A. Silberschatz, A Formal Approach to Recovery by Compensating Transactions, *Proceedings of the 16th VLDB Conference*, Brisbane, Australia 1990, pp. 95–106.

CHAPTER 8

MOBILE DATABASE RECOVERY

This chapter deals with recovery in mobile database systems that is more complex compared to conventional database recovery. It first introduces the fundamentals of database recovery and briefly describes conventional recovery protocols and uses them to focus on application recovery. The chapter also identifies those aspects of mobile database systems that affect the recovery process. Similar to other areas such as transaction modeling, concurrency control, and so on, database recovery in mobile database systems is also in the development stage, so the coverage here is limited to the state-of-the-art research with little on commercial products. A number of mobile database recovery schemes have been developed [1–11], and this chapter discusses a few of them.

8.1 INTRODUCTION

A database recovery system recovers a database from transaction or system failures. Such failures can happen due to a variety of reasons. Some typical reasons are addressing error, RAM failure, incorrect data input, operator error, and so on. Any of these events may cause a system failure or a transaction failure. A transaction and a system failure share the same characteristics; however, in a transaction failure, the effect of data corruption is localized to the failed transaction. A system failure, therefore, can be identified as the failure of all transactions in the system.

In a failure of any kind, the database is corrupted (inconsistent) and the job of the recovery system is to restore the database to a consistent state from where transaction

Fundamentals of Pervasive Information Management Systems, Revised Edition. Vijay Kumar.
© 2013 John Wiley & Sons, Inc. Published 2013 by John Wiley & Sons, Inc.

processing can resume. In a concurrent execution environment, a transaction may be active, blocked, rolled back, or in the middle of a commit. If a failure occurs in this situation, then the task of a recovery protocol is to identify the right operation for recovery for each transaction. These operations are (a) *Roll forward* or *Redo* and (b) *Roll back* or *Undo*. Depending upon the execution status of a transaction, one of these operations is selected to deal with the failed transaction. Thus, in a recovery process, some transactions are undone and some transactions are redone. To implement these operations, a *Transaction log* is required, which is generated and maintained by the system. The log contains committed values of data items (Before Image—BFIM) and modified values of data items (After Image—AFIM). The log is a crucial document for recovery; therefore, it is generated and maintained by a protocol called *Write Ahead Logging (WAL)*.

Definition 8.1 *Undo rule: The BFIM of data item x must be saved in the stable log before its AFIM is generated (before overwritten by the new or uncommitted value).*

The undo rule is often called the WAL protocol because it enforces the undo rule where the BFIMs of data items of a transaction are logged in the stable log before their AFIMs are installed in the final (stable) database.

Definition 8.2 *Redo rule: The AFIMs of data items of a transaction must be saved in a stable log before they are written in the final (stable) database.*

When a failure occurs, the system is rebooted. The recovery system takes over and processes log backward to identify transactions that must be redone or undone. At the end of this scan, it applies Redo and Undo operations on transactions that were in the system when it failed. A Redo completes the commit operation for a transaction and an Undo rolls back a transaction to maintain atomicity. The transactions that are Undone can be rescheduled for execution. Thus, the entire database recovery process is completed by applying Redo and Undo operations.

The way transactions are executed affects the recovery process. A transaction may save all its AFIMs in the log only (log is saved on a stable disk) and writes them to the final copy of the database only at the time of commit. If the system fails under this execution mode, then the recovery system will be able to recover the database only using Redo. On the other hand, if the transaction writes its AFIM to the final copy of the database as soon as it is created under WAL, then recovery from a system failure will require Undo and may need Redo as well. The first way of executing transactions is referred to as *deferred update*, and the second way is referred to as *immediate update*. Thus, the combination of the transaction execution method and Redo and Undo operations provides four different recovery protocols: (a) *Undo–Redo*, (b) *Undo–No Redo*, (c) *No Undo–Redo*, and (d) *No Undo–No Redo*. These protocols are defined briefly here and the detail can be found in reference 12.

Undo–Redo. This protocol applies Redo and Undo to recover the database systems. This means that during transaction execution it uses an immediate update to install

AFIMs to the database. Under this execution, it is possible that some transactions may need Redo during database recovery. If the transaction was active when the system failed, then the transaction is Undone and it is Redone if the transaction was ready to commit.

Undo–No Redo. This protocol does not support a Redo operation and recovers the database by applying Undo operations only. This means that the system forces intermediate updates of transactions to the database immediately under WAL protocol.

No Undo–Redo. This protocol does not support Redo. Thus, it makes sure that no AFIMs of a transaction are installed in the database before the transaction completes its execution (not yet committed). Thus, at the time of recovery, transactions are only Redone; and if a transaction cannot be Redone, then it is removed from the system.

No Undo–No Redo. This protocol does not apply Redo and Undo and recovers the database by using the *shadow* copy of data items. Thus, during execution, a transaction creates a show copy of its AFIMs of the data items. The recovery involves just selecting the right copy of the database (the last consistent version of the database or its shadow copy).

Recovery is a time-consuming and resource-intensive operation, and these protocols require plenty of them. It also reduces the system availability because during recovery, the system does not accept any new transactions. To reduce recovery time and, thus, to increase availability, the database system uses a *checkpointing* process [12]. Although checkpointing has its own processing cost, it does manage to significantly reduce recovery time. A checkpointing operation reduces the amount of Redo and Undo to recover the database.

The management of a log is also a time-consuming process. The cost of these necessary operations significantly increases in distributed systems such as mobile database systems. As a result, a straightforward implementation of conventional log management and checkpointing would not work at all in MDS. The important task in managing recovery in MDS, therefore, is to manage logging and checkpointing in a new way. In this book, we mainly focus on efficient log management.

A Mobile Database System is a distributed system based on the client server paradigm but functions differently than conventional centralized or distributed systems. It achieves such diverse functionalities by imposing comparatively more constraints and demands on the infrastructure. To manage system-level functions, MDS may require different transaction management schemes (concurrency control, database and application recovery, query processing, etc.), different logging schemes, different caching schemes, and so on.

In any database management system, distributed or centralized, the database is recovered in a similar manner and the recovery module is an integral part of the database system. Database recovery protocols, therefore, are not tampered with user level applications. A system that executes applications, in addition to database recovery protocol, requires efficient schemes for *Application recovery* [13, 14].

8.1.1 Application Recovery

The application recovery, unlike database recovery, enhances application availability by recovering the execution state of applications. For example, in MDS or in any distributed system, a number of activities related to the transactions' execution, such as transaction arrival at a client or at a server, transaction fragmentation and the distribution of fragments to relevant nodes for execution, dispatch of updates made from the clients to the server, migration of a mobile unit to another cell (handoff), and so on, have to be logged for recovering the last execution state. With the help of the log, the application recovery module recreates the last execution state of application from where normal execution resumes.

Application recovery is relatively more complex than database recovery because of (a) the large numbers of applications required to manage database processing, (b) the presence of multiple application states, and (c) the absence of the notion of the "last consistent state." This gets more complex in MDS because of (a) unique processing demands of mobile units, (b) the existence of random handoffs, (c) the presence of operations in connected, disconnected, and intermittent connected modes, (d) location-dependent processing, and (e) the presence of different types of failure. These failures can be categorized as *Hard failures* and *Soft failures* [5]. Hard failures include loss of mobile unit (stolen, burnt, drowned, dropped, etc.), which cannot be easily repaired. Soft failures include system failure (program failure, addressing errors, dead battery, processing unit switched off, etc.) and are recoverable.

An application can be in any execution state (blocked, executing, slow data reception, and so on). In addition to this, the application may be under execution on stationary units (base station or database server), or on mobile units, or on both. These processing units, especially the mobile unit, may be (a) going through a handoff, (b) disconnected, (c) in a doze mode, or (d) turned off completely. The application may be processing a *mobilaction* or reading some data or committing a fragment, and so on. If a failure occurs during any of these tasks, the recovery system must bring the application execution back to the point of resumption.

In application recovery, unlike data consistency, the question of application consistency does not arise because the application cannot execute correctly in the presence of any error. Thus, the most important task for facilitating application recovery is the management of the log. The database recovery protocols provide a highly efficient and reliable logging scheme. Unfortunately, even with modifications, the conventional logging scheme would impose an unmanageable burden on resource constrained MDS. What is needed is an efficient logging scheme that stores, retrieves, and unifies fragments of the application log for recovery within the constraints of MDS.

8.2 LOG MANAGEMENT IN MOBILE DATABASE SYSTEMS

A log is a sequential file where information necessary for recovery is recorded. Each log *record* represents a unit of information. The position of a record in the log identifies the relative order of the occurrence of the event the record represents. In legacy systems (centralized or distributed), the log resides at fixed locations that survive system crashes. It is retrieved and processed to facilitate system recovery from any kind of failure. This persistence property of a log is achieved through *Write Ahead Logging (WAL)* [15].

This static property of a log ensures that no additional operation (other than only its access) is required to process it for recovery. The situation completely changes in the systems that support terminal and personal mobility by allowing the processing units to move around. As a result, they get connected and disconnected many times during the entire execution life of the transactions they process. The logging becomes complex because the system must follow WAL protocol while logging records at various servers.

An efficient application recovery scheme for MDS requires that the log management must consume minimum system resources and must recreate the execution environment as soon as possible after MU reboots. The mobile units and the servers must build a log of the events that changes the execution states of *mobilaction*. Messages that change the log contents are called *write events* [9]. The exact write events depend on the application type. In general, the mobile unit records events like (a) the arrival of a *mobilaction*, (b) the fragmentation of the *mobilaction*, (c) the assignment of a coordinator to the *mobilaction*, (d) the mobility history of the mobile unit (handoffs, current status of the log, its storage location, etc.), and (e) the dispatch of updates from *mobile units* to the DBSs. The DBSs may record similar events in addition to events relating to the commit of the *mobilaction*. The two most important issues related to log management are (a) where to save the log and (b) when and how to save the log. These are discussed in subsequent sections.

8.2.1 Where to Save the Log?

Schemes that provide recovery in a PCS (personal communication system) save the log at the BS where the mobile unit currently resides [7, 9]. It is important to note that managing a log for PCS failure is relatively easy because it does not support transaction processing. However, the concept can be used to develop efficient logging schemes for MDS.

A log must be saved at a stable media that survives all types of system failure. There are three places that satisfy this requirement: (a) MSC (mobile switching center), (b) base station (BS), or (c) mobile unit (MU). The reliability and availability of mobile units, however, make it a less desirable place to save the log. The stable storage of a mobile unit may not be reliable because of mobility. In addition to this, it has a number of other issues related to survivability that are explained in earlier chapters.

An MSC has the resources to store a log, but from cost and management viewpoints it is not a convenient location. An MSC may control a large number of BSs and in a cellular network there may be more than one MSC. Thus, in the event of a failure, accessing it from the MSC and its subsequent processing for a specific transaction may be time-consuming. Further, an MSC is not directly connected to the database servers that provide necessary log management applications.

A BS satisfies most of the requirements for saving a log. It is directly connected to the DBSs (and also to mobile units) and has sufficient storage capabilities. Therefore, from connectivity and availability aspects, BSs are comparatively better candidates for saving an application log. Under this setup, a mobile unit can save a log at the current BS and the BS then can archive it on the DBSs.

8.2.2 When and How to Save the Log

Transaction execution continuously adds log records to the log file (application log). To save I/O cost, the log is saved to the stable store (log disk) when some event, such as a defined number of records are added to the log or a number of transactions have committed, and so on, happens. In MDS, an appropriate event or criteria to save the log must be defined to coordinate the movement (handoff) of mobile units and transaction execution. This will take care of when to save the log. The issue of how to save the log to stable storage, needs further investigation. Some of the important issues, such as saving incrementally, using a deferred approach, and so on, require further investigation, and the following explanation covers this issue.

Effect of Mobility on Logging. In conventional database systems, the log generation and its manipulation are predefined and fixed. In a mobile environment, this may not always be true because of the frequent movements and disconnections of mobile units. A *mobilaction* may be executed at a combination of the mobile unit where it originated, a base station, and some fixed hosts. Furthermore, if the mobile unit that executes a fragment of *mobilaction* happens to visit more than one cell, then its log may be scattered at more than one base station. This implies that the recovery process may need a mechanism for *log unification* (logical linking of all log portions). The possible logging schemes can be categorized as follows.

Centralized Logging. Under this scheme, a base station is designated as a logging site where all mobile units from all data regions save their logs. Since the logging location is fixed and known in advance, and the entire log is stored at one place, its management (access, deletion, etc.) becomes easier. Under this scheme, each mobile unit generates the log locally and at suitable intervals or when a predefined condition exists, copies its local log to the selected base station. If a fragment or *mobilaction* fails, then the local recovery manager acquires the log from the base station and recovers the *mobilaction*. This scheme works, but it has the following limitations:

- It has a very low reliability. If the logging base station fails, then it will stop the logging and transaction processing and resume these operations when the *BS* recovers. Adding another backup base station will not only increase resource costs but will increase log management costs as well.
- Logging may become a bottleneck. The logging traffic at the logging base station may become unmanageably heavy, causing significant logging delays.

However, for a lightly loaded system with little MU movement, this scheme provides a simple and efficient way of managing the log.

Home Logging. Every mobile unit stores its log at the base station where it registered initially. Although a mobile unit will roam around in the geographical domain freely and continue to access data from any site, all logging will still be at its base station. This scheme has the following limitations:

- Under this scheme, the entire log of *mobilaction* may be scattered over a number of base stations if its fragments are processed by different mobile units with different base stations. To recover the *mobilaction*, all pieces of the log will require linking (logically).
- It may not work for spatial replicas (location dependent data). Consider a location-dependent query that comes to a mobile unit for processing, but whose base station is not the one that stores the location-dependent data. This may happen if a traveler from Kansas City issues a query on his/her mobile unit for Dallas Holiday Inn data. This scheme can cause excessive message traffic.
- Since the logging location is not distributed, it has poor availability and excessive message traffic during the transaction execution.

At a Designated Base Station. Under this scheme, a mobile unit locally composes the log and (at some predefined intervals) saves it at the designated base station. At the time of saving the log, a mobile unit may be in the cell of the designated base station or at a remote base station. In the latter case, the log must travel through a chain of base stations ending up at the designated base station. This will work as long as there is no communication failure anywhere in the chain of base stations.

At All Visited Base Stations. In this scheme, a mobile unit saves the log at the base station of the cell it is currently visiting. The entire application log is stored in multiple base stations, and at the time of recovery, all log portions are unified to create the complete log. It is possible that two or more portions of the entire log may be stored at one base station if the mobile unit revisits the base station. A number of logging schemes were developed under these two approaches, some of which are discussed below.

Lazy Scheme. In the lazy scheme [9], logs are stored at the current base station, and if the mobile unit moves to a new base station, a pointer to the old base station is stored in the new base station. These pointers are used to unify the log distributed over several base stations. This scheme has the advantage that it incurs relatively less network overhead during handoff as no log information needs to be transferred. Unfortunately, this scheme has a large recovery time because it requires unification of log portions.

The log unification can be performed in two ways: (a) distance-based scheme and (b) frequency-based scheme. In a distance-based scheme [7], the log unification is initiated as soon as the mobile unit covers the predefined distance. This distance can be measured in terms of base stations visited or in terms of cell sites visited. In the frequency-based scheme [7], log unification is performed when the number of handoffs suffered by the MU increases above a predefined value. After unifying the log, the distance or handoff counter is reset.

Pessimistic Scheme. In the pessimistic scheme [9], the entire log is transferred at each handoff from the old to the new base station. This scheme, therefore, combines logging and log unification. Consequently, the recovery is fast, but each handoff requires large volumes of data to be transferred.

The existing mobile network framework is not efficient for full-fledged database transactions running at the DBSs and mobile units. In the above schemes, the location change of MU has to be updated by the DBSs, which would be a big disadvantage. To overcome this, a mobile IP was introduced. In reference 16, log recovery, based on the mobile IP architecture, is described where base stations store the actual log and checkpoint information and the base station or the *home agent* (as defined in reference 17) maintains the recovery information as the mobile unit traverses. This scheme has the advantage that log management is easy and that the database servers need not be concerned with the mobile unit's location update. However, it suffers when the mobile unit is far away from home. Consequently, recovery is likely to be slow if the home agent is far from the mobile unit. The other problem with using a mobile IP is triangular routing, where all messages from the database server to the mobile unit have to be routed through the home agent. This invariably impedes application execution. The schemes discussed so far do not consider the case where a mobile unit recovers in a base station different from the one in which it crashed. In such a scenario, the new base station does not have the previous base station information in its VLR (Visitor Location Register), and it has to access the HLR (Home Location Register) to get this information [18], which is necessary to get the recovery log. HLR access may increase the recovery time significantly if it is stored far from the MU. A similar disadvantage can be observed in the mobile IP scheme of reference 16, where the mobile unit needs to contact the home agent each time it needs recovery.

8.3 MOBILE DATABASE RECOVERY SCHEMES

In this section, a number of recovery schemes have been discussed. These schemes take different approaches, however, they build their scheme on the same mobile database platform. The platform contains a set of mobile units and base stations. These units save logs and checkpoint necessary activities to make sure that the necessary information is available for recovering from failure efficiently and economically.

8.3.1 A Three Phase Hybrid Recovery Scheme

A three-phase checkpointing and recovery scheme that combines coordinated and communication-induced checkpointing schemes is discussed in reference 3. All base stations use coordinated checkpointing, and the communication-based checkpointing is used between mobile units and base stations. The following steps briefly describe the workings of the algorithm. Further details can be found in reference 3. The algorithm uses mobile units MU_1, MU_2, MU_3, and MU_4 and base stations BS_1, BS_2, and BS_3 for describing message traffic.

- Initially, a coordinator (base station) BS_1 broadcasts a request message with a checkpoint index to BS_2 and BS_3.
- Each BS sets up a timer T_{lazy}. It uses a lazy coordination scheme to reduce the number of messages that are especially suitable for mobile database systems. In this approach, infrequent snapshots are taken that only occasionally impose high checkpoint overhead of coordinated snapshots on the low-bandwidth network that connects all mobile units. This approach also prevents the global snapshot from getting outdated; as a result, the amount of computation for recovery from failure is minimized.
- Mobile units MU_2 or MU_3, whichever is active, takes a checkpoint before message m_2 or m_3 arrives from BS_2 or BS_3 during T_{lazy}.
- MU_1 or MU_4 takes a checkpoint when T_{lazy} has expired, and it receives a checkpoint request from BS_1 or BS_3.
- BS_2 and BS_3 respond (send a response message) to BS_1.
- BS_1 broadcasts a commit message to all BSs after receiving response messages from other base stations.
- MU_3 migrates from BS_3 to BS_2 and sends a message to wake MU_4 if it is in doze mode.
- MU_2 takes a checkpoint before it disconnects itself from the network. If MU_2 is already in the disconnected mode, then it does not take any checkpoints.
- In case MU_1 fails, it stops executing and sends a recovery message to BS_1.
- BS_1 broadcasts a recovery message to all BSs.
- Each BS sends a recovery message to all its MUs. These MUs roll back to their last consistent state.

8.3.2 Low-Cost Checkpointing and Failure Recovery

A low-cost synchronous snapshot collection scheme is presented in reference 10 that allows minimum interference to the underlying computation. The working of the algorithm is explained with the following example. Figure 8.1 illustrates the flow of messages that manage the snapshot process. The processing nodes are represented as P_0, P_1, P_2, and P_3, and m_1, m_2, m_3, m_4, m_5, and m_6 represent the messages.

- The node P_2 first collects local snapshots at the point X (time point).
- Assume that nodes P_1, P_3, and P_2 are dependent so a snapshot request message is sent to P_1 and P_3 by P_2. Node P_3 sends message m_4 to node P_1 after taking its own snapshot.

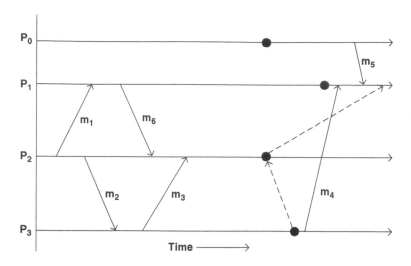

Figure 8.1   An example of snapshot generation.

- Two possibilities arise when message m_4 reaches P_1: (a) P_1 has not processed any message since its last local snapshot or (b) P_1 has already processed a message from any nodes since its last snapshot. In this example, since P_1 has not processed any messages, as a result, it takes its tentative snapshot and records this event before processing message m_4. It then propagates the snapshot.
- Node P_0 takes a local snapshot since it has not received any messages from any nodes and sends a message m_5 to P_1. When m_5 reaches P_1, it finds that m_5 is not a new message to force a snapshot, so P_1 does not take a snapshot.

When node P_i fails, it rolls back to its latest checkpoint and sends rollback requests to a subset of nodes. When a node P_j receives its first rollback message, then (a) it rolls back to its latest checkpoint and (b) it sends a rollback request to a selective set of nodes. Node P_j may receive subsequent rollback messages as a result of P_1's failure, but it ignores all of them. In the case of mobile units, all their rollback requests are routed through their base stations.

8.3.3   A Mobile Agent Based Log Management Scheme

Mobile agents have been successfully used in managing a number of application and system activities. They have also been used to develop a scheme to manage an application log in MDS (mobile database systems). A mobile agent is an autonomous program that can move from machine to machine in a heterogeneous network under its own control. It can suspend its execution at any point, transport itself to a new machine, and resume execution from the point it stopped execution. An agent carries both the code and the application state. Actually, the mobile agent paradigm is an extension of the client/server architecture with code mobility. Some of the advantages of mobile agents as described in reference 19 are as follows:

- **Protocol Encapsulation:** Mobile agents can incorporate their own protocols in their code instead of depending on the legacy code provided by the hosts.
- **Robustness and fault-tolerance:** When failures are detected, host systems can easily dispatch agents to other hosts. This ability makes the agents fault-tolerant.
- **Asynchronous and autonomous execution:** Once the agents are dispatched from a host, they can make decisions independently and autonomously. This is particularly useful for wireless environments where maintaining a connection throughout an executing *mobilaction* may not be economical or necessary. In such cases, the agents can visit the destination, perform any required processing, and bring the final data to the origin, thereby removing the need for a continuous wireless connection. For example, an agent can take a *mobilaction* from a mobile unit, execute it at the most suitable node (could be remote), and bring the result back to the mobile unit.

Agents do have disadvantages, and the one that is likely to affect the logging scheme is its high migration and machine load overhead [20]. This overhead must be minimized for improving the performance. The present scheme uses agent services *only when needed*. It is not possible to develop a scheme that optimizes the performance at all levels and in all different situations. For this reason, some recovery schemes improve their performance by targeting to minimize the communication overhead; some might concentrate on total recovery time, and some may optimize storage space, and so on. Thus, each scheme involves certain tradeoffs. When these issues are taken into consideration, it becomes necessary to build a framework that supports the implementation of the existing schemes and should also be able to support any new scheme. The framework should support the activation/deactivation of a scheme, depending on the particular environment in which it offers best performance. Such a framework should abstract the core base station software, which handles the registration, handoff activities, etc., from handling the recovery procedures, thus allowing for better recovery protocols to be implemented without the need for changing the core software. The framework may also support a rapid deployment of the recovery code without much human intervention.

In an MDS, the coordinator module resides in the base station. It splits a *mobilaction* into fragments, if necessary, and it sends some of them to a set of DBSs. This requirement asks for specific intelligence to be embedded in the base station code. *Mobilaction* initiated by a mobile unit may use different kinds of commit protocols, like 2-phase commit, 3-phase commit, or TCOT (transaction commit on timeout) [21]. The coordinator module needs to support all of these. If such a module at a base station does not support a particular protocol, then there should be an easy way to access such code. An extension to this is, when a new efficient protocol is introduced, all base stations should be able to upgrade to this as easily as possible and with little or no human intervention. From the perspective of mobile unit log recovery, an architecture is required that supports intelligent logging and is able to incorporate any future developments without any difficulty.

Some recovery schemes specify that the logs move along with the mobile unit through a multitude of base stations. The new base stations should be able to handle the logs in the same way as the previous one did, or log inconsistency might result. It is argued that the flexibility and constraints mentioned above could be successfully incorporated on a mobile-agent-based architecture under which the code necessary for recovery and coordination can be embedded in the mobile agents. The coordinator can be modeled as a mobile agent and can be initiated by the mobile unit itself if necessary. During a handoff, if the new base station does not support a specific logging scheme, then the agent in the previous base station that supports this can clone itself, and the new replica can migrate to the current base station without any manual intervention. The same technique can be used in quickly populating the base stations with any new protocols. The mobile agent with the new protocol embedded in it can be introduced in any base station, and it can replicate and migrate to another base station.

8.3.4 Architecture of Agent-Based Logging Scheme

An architecture is presented where mobile agents used to provide a platform for managing logging. The architecture supports the independent logging mechanisms. It is assumed that each base station supports the functionality of mobile agents. The main components of the architecture are as follows:

Bootstrap Agent (BsAg). This agent handles a base station failure. Any agent that wishes to recover, should register with the bootstrap agent. The base station initiates the bootstrap agent. Once loaded, this agent starts all the agents that have registered with it. These agents have the capability to read the log information they have created and act accordingly. The need for such an agent may be obviated if the mobile agent provides an automatic revival of the agents with their state intact.

Base Agent (BaAg). This agent decides which logging scheme to use in the current environment. Such functionality can be decided by its own intelligence or can be given as input. For every mobile unit, it creates an instance of an agent that handles the recovery of *mobilactions* based on the relevant logging scheme.

Home Agent (HoAg). This agent handles *mobilactions* for each mobile unit. It is responsible for maintaining log and recovery information on behalf of the mobile unit. The mobile unit sends log events to this agent, which is responsible for storing them on the stable storage of the base station. The HoAg is a base station interface to the mobile unit for Mobilactions.

Coordinator Agent (CoAg). This agent resides at the base station and acts as the coordinator for all *mobilactions*.

Event Agent (EvAg). In addition to the above framework, the base station provides mobile agents with an interface to the various events taking place—for example, registration of a mobile unit, failure of a mobile unit, handoff of a mobile unit, and so on. This approach abstracts away the core base station functions from application recovery support. When a mobile unit suffers handoff, its HoAg should know about it so that it can perform the required operations. The EvAg is the interface for the base station to the agent framework for dissemination of such information.

Driver Agent (DrAg). The migration of a mobile agent during a handoff involves the movement of its code and the actual data. This might generate considerable overhead [20] even if the actual log transfer is not much.

8.3.5 Interaction Among Agents for Log Management

These agents collaborate with each other to facilitate log management.

Interaction of CoAg and HoAg. An MU sends Mobilaction to its HoAg, which forwards it to the corresponding CoAg. If the CoAg needs to contact the MU, it does so through the MU's corresponding HoAg. When the CoAg sends a write event to the HoAg, it stores it in its local store before sending it to the MU. Similarly, if any event comes to the MU through user input, the MU sends the corresponding log messages to the HoAg.

Action of Agents when Handoff Occurs. The HoAg moves, along with the mobile unit, to the new base station in a handoff. Based on schemes like Lazy and Frequency-based, the agent may or may not take the stored logs along with it to the new base station. When a handoff occurs, a driver agent (DrAg) is sent along with the necessary log information to the new base station instead of the whole HoAg with all its intelligence for log unification. The DrAg has a very light code whose main function is to see whether the code for HoAg is present in the new base station. If so, it requests the resident BaAg in the new base station to create an instance of the HoAg for the mobile unit. If any compatible code is not present, then the DrAg sends a request to the previous base station's BaAg, which clones the necessary HoAg and sends the copy to the new base station. When the mobile unit moves out of a base station, its log information is not deleted automatically, but it is stored unless otherwise notified by the agent of the mobile unit. This facilitates the unification of logs when the logs are distributed over a set of base stations.

8.3.6 Forward Strategy

All schemes reviewed earlier have assumed instant recovery of the mobile unit after a failure, but reference 18 acknowledges the possibility where the mobile unit might crash in one base station and recover in another. A time interval is defined between the mobile unit failing and its subsequent rebooting as expected failure time (EFT). This scheme concentrates on such scenarios where the EFT is not so trivial that the recovery occurs instantaneously. The base station detects the failure of a mobile unit, and agents do not play any part in such detection. For example, if the communication between two mobile units breaks down because of the failure of one of the mobile units, then the corresponding BS will immediately know about this event. Similarly, the base station also knows which mobile unit has executed the power-down registration, which mobile unit has undergone a handoff, and so on.

A base station also continuously pages its mobile units.* If the mobile unit suffers a handoff, then the communication with the last base station is not broken until the connection with the new base station is established (soft handoff). These features of PCS allow MDS to detect mobile unit failure. Thus, while a mobile unit is executing its fragment, its status is continuously monitored by the base station and any change in the mobile unit's situation is immediately captured by the Event Agent (EvAg) interface. Since this detection is system-dependent, the EFT (Expected Failure Time) tends to be an approximate value. The detection can be passed on to the HoAg in many ways. The MDS can provide an interface, which would allow the agents to wait for an event. Another approach would be to provide an agent a readable system variable that would be set on any such event. The agent will periodically poll the variable to check if it is set. Both approaches are possible and easy to implement in languages such as Java in which many agent systems, like IBM's Aglets and General Magic's Odyssey, have been developed [22]. Since a handoff does not occur in the above case, as pointed out in [18], the new base station does not know the location of the old base station. This situation leads to the new base station contacting the Home Location Register (HLR) for the previous base station [6, 7, 10, 18]. This might be a hindrance to fast recovery if the HLR happens to be far from the querying base station. Actually, the Visitor Location Register (VLR) is first queried for the previous base station information, which is stored in the VLR if both base stations happen to fall under the control of the same VLR. If base stations are under different VLRs, then the HLR of the mobile unit has to be queried. Such information is stored in the HLR when a mobile unit first registers with a base station.

In the lazy scheme [18], the base station starts building up the log immediately upon failure of mobile unit. In the schemes presented in reference 7, the mobile unit explicitly issues a recovery call to the base station and the base station begins the log unification. This raises certain questions in the event the mobile unit crashes and recovers in a different base station. If the log is to be unified immediately upon a failure, then it might be necessary for the new base station to wait for the old base station to finish its unification and then present its log. If the failure time is large or the total log size is small, then unification will be over by the time the new base station queries the previous base station. In such a case, recovery can be fast. In the case of a relatively small *EFT (expected failure time)* or a large log size (to be unified), the

---

*The Sprint PCS system pages its mobile units after every 10 to 15 minutes (without generating any overhead), to learn their status. A mobile unit also continuously scans the air by using its antenna to detect the strongest signal.

new base station must wait first for the unification and then for the actual log transfer. This results in increased recovery time and network cost. In such cases, it might be preferable for the log unification to be done in the new base station if the list of base stations where the log is distributed is known. Such a list is transferred in schemes provided in reference 7 and not for those in reference 18. In the approach where the log is unified after a recovery call, the recovery time might not be small enough if the log size to be unified is small. In this case, the unification has to begin after getting the list of base stations involved from the previous base station. Also, if the mobile unit has not migrated to a new base station before recovery, then the log has to be unified, which is likely to increase the recovery time.

Reducing Recovery Time. The scheme of log unification is based on the number of handoffs that occurred since the last log unification or the start of the transaction, whichever is later. The log is unified periodically when the number of handoffs occurred crosses a predefined handoff threshold.

When a handoff occurs, the *trace* information is transferred from the old base station to the new base station. This trace information is an ordered list of elements giving information about the base stations involved in storing the mobile unit's log. Each array element consists of two values: (a) the identify of this base station (BS-ID) and (b) the size of the log stored at BS-IDi (Log-Sizei). When a handoff occurs, then the BS-ID of the new base station and a Log-Size value of zero are added to the end of the trace. The Log-Size value is updated whenever a mobile unit presents a base station with some log information. Optional parameters can also be present in the trace information. Since the trace does not contain the actual log contents and is mostly an array of base stations identities and log sizes, it does not present significant overhead during the handoff. The scheme also assumes the presence of *EFT (expected failure time)* value that can be stored as an environment attribute accessible to HoAg of the mobile unit at the base station. If such support cannot be given by the system, then HoAg can also estimate the *EFT* from the mobile unit's activities. If the agent estimates the *EFT*, then this value is also stored in the trace information. When the system detects mobile unit failure, it informs the agent framework through the *Event Agent* interface. This agent notifies the appropriate HoAg that starts the *EFT* clock. This clock is stopped to get the *Recorded-EFT* value, when the HoAg receives the mobile unit recovery call, which can come from the mobile unit in the same base station or from a different base station in which the mobile unit has recovered. In either case, the agent resides in the base station where the *EFT* clock is started. It estimates the new *EFT* as

$$(\text{K1} \times \textbf{Recorded-EFT}) + (\text{K2} \times \textbf{EFT}), \qquad \text{where } K1 + K2 = 1$$

The new *EFT* is a weighted sum of the previous *EFT* and the *Recorded-EFT*. K1 indicates the reliance on the *Recorded-EFT* while K2 indicates the reliance on the previously calculated *EFT*. The values of K1 and K2 are functions of the environment. In a network where the failure time is relatively stable, K2 is given more weight; and in a network where the failure time varies frequently, K1 can be given more weight.

To improve storage utilization, unnecessary records from the log are deleted. This garbage collection is optional and is done upon log unification. When a mobile unit log is unified at a base station, a garbage-collect message is sent to all the base stations hosting the mobile unit logs as specified in the trace *BS-ID* list. The previous base stations purge these logs on receiving this message. The *BS-ID* and the Log-Size lists are erased from the trace information at the current base station to reflect the unification, and a single entry is created in the trace with the current base station identity and the unified log size.

8.3.7 Forward Log Unification Scheme

Since the trace information contains the size of the log stored at different base stations, the HoAg can estimate the time for log unification based on the network link speed and the total log size. This time is called the *Estimated Log Unification Time (ELUT)*, which can be measured as *Max(BSi-Log-Size/Network link Speed + Propagation Delay)* for all base stations in the trace. The exact characterization of the *ELUT* value depends on other factors such as whether base stations are located in the same VLR area or different areas, queuing delay, and so on. The HoAg should take into consideration as many parameters available from the system as possible to estimate the *ELUT* accurately. Log unification is started if $(\delta * ELUT) \leq EFT$ or else it is deferred until a recovery call is heard from the mobile unit.

The Unification factor "δ" describes what fraction of the log unification will be done by the time the failure time of the mobile unit comes to an end. The default value can be kept as 1, which indicates that the log unification starts only if it can be totally completed by the time the mobile unit is expected to complete its reboot. If the mobile unit reboots in a different base station while the log is being unified in the previous base station, it has to wait for the unification to complete. Variations of this scheme are possible if the HoAg can estimate the effective handoff time. Based on this value, if there is still a long time for the next handoff, then the log unification can start immediately upon a failure, as it is more probable that the failed mobile unit will recover in the base station where it failed rather than in any other base station. In the event the log unification is not performed because $(\delta \times ELUT) \leq EFT$, the HoAg waits for the mobile unit to recover. If the recovery happens in the same base station, the the log unification starts, but if the mobile unit reboots in a different base station, then the HoAg transfers the trace information and the log stored at this base station when requested. In this case, the new base station has to perform the log unification after getting the trace information from the previous base station. This trace contains the newly calculated *EFT* value.

8.3.8 Forward Notification Scheme

This scheme addresses the issue of time spent in getting the previous base station information from the HLR. To minimize this time, a scheme involving forward notifications is proposed. When a mobile unit fails in a particular base station and if the actual failure time (total duration before mobile unit is rebooted) is not too high, then there is a high probability that the mobile unit will recover in the same VLR or in a BS that is in adjacent VLRs. Thus, a VLR and its adjacent VLRs cover a large area and the situation where the mobile unit reboots in a nonadjacent VLR does not occur frequently. If the mobile unit happens to restart in a nonadjacent VLR, then it must have been extremely mobile and most of the recovery schemes are not designed for such unrealistic situations. The other implication is that the mobile unit had been in the failed state for a longer period, and so it is likely that the coordinator could have decided to abort the *mobilaction*. Each VLR also stores each mobile unit's status information (normal, failed, and forwarded).

When a mobile unit fails, its corresponding HoAg informs the VLR about this failure. The VLR first changes the status of the mobile unit in its database from normal to failed. The VLR then issues a message (that the mobile unit has failed) containing its own identity, for example, identity of the VLR that sends this message, the identity of the failed mobile unit, and the identity of the mobile unit that crashed in its adjacent VLRs. The adjacent VLRs store these messages until explicit denotify messages are received. The mobile unit is recorded in these adjacent VLRs with the status as forwarded. The following scenarios may arise when the mobile unit reboots.

Case 1: The mobile unit reboots in the same base station where it crashed. In this scenario, the HoAg informs the VLR that the mobile unit has recovered. The VLR then issues a denotify message to all the adjacent VLRs, indicating that the forward notification information is no longer valid. The status of the mobile unit is changed back to normal from failed.

Case 2: The mobile unit reboots in a different base station but in the same VLR. First, the mobile unit registers with the base station and the registration message is logged on to the corresponding VLR. This VLR identifies the status of the mobile unit as failed, and then it proceeds as in Case 1 and sends denotify messages to the adjacent VLRs. The status of the mobile unit is changed back to normal from failed. The new base station then proceeds to perform log unification from the previous base station.

Case 3: The mobile unit reboots in a different base station and a different VLR. The mobile unit requests registration. The corresponding VLR identifies the mobile unit as a forward notified mobile unit and returns the identity of the previous base station and the identity of the VLR to the HoAg of the mobile unit in the recovered base station. The base station then proceeds to perform log unification from the previous base station. Simultaneously, the new VLR sends a recovered message to the previous VLR regarding the recovered status of the mobile unit and also sends a registration message to the HLR regarding the registration of the mobile unit in the new location. The status of the mobile unit is changed to normal from forwarded in the new VLR. Upon receiving the recovered message, the previous VLR sends a denotify message to all adjacent VLRs except the one in which the mobile unit recovered and removes the registration of the mobile unit from itself as well. In the situation where the mobile unit recovers in a nonadjacent VLR that has not received the forward notifications, the new base station has to get the previous base station information from the HLR and then send the previous VLR a recovered message. Upon receiving this message, the previous VLR acts similarly to the previous VLR of Case 3. The forward notification scheme is unsuitable if the mobile unit suffers failures with a very small *EFT*. In that case, the mobile unit recovers in the same base station where it failed. Hence, the forward notifications and subsequent denotifications generate communication overhead. To alleviate this, we might delay the sending of these notifications immediately on failure of the mobile unit. The HoAg waits for an initial buffer time before it notifies the VLR regarding the failed status of the mobile unit. This time can be estimated by the HoAg in a way similar to the estimation of ELUT without compromising the performance. We can reduce the overhead further if we can reduce the number of recipients of the notifications. If notifications are sent to only those VLRs, the base stations of which are nearer to the base station in which the mobile unit fails, the communication overhead can be reduced.

8.4 SUMMARY

This chapter discussed a number of recovery algorithms for mobile database systems. Some schemes were discussed in more detail than others. These discussions on mobile database recovery clearly indicate that the entire process of checkpointing and logging for recovery are comparatively more complex than conventional database recovery. There are still quite a few research problems that need innovative solutions. Until they are resolved, the mobile database system will continue to remain in the research domain.

EXERCISES

8.1 Do you think that the conventional way of managing the transaction log will work in mobile database systems? Discuss the issues in your own scheme that you develop.

8.2 Explain how TCOT reduces the number of messages under a no failure scenario.

8.3 Log management is a time consuming task. In a shadow approach, a log is not required to recover the database. Do you think that a shadow approach could be better a for mobile database system? Investigate and present your ideas.

8.4 Why does the use of mobile agents provide a good way of handling database recovery in mobile database systems? Explain.

8.5 Investigate the forward notification scheme and discuss possible improvements.

REFERENCES

1. S. Gadiraju, V. Kumar, and M. H. Dunham, Recovery in the Mobile Wireless Environment Using Mobile Agents, *IEEE Transactions on Mobile Computing*, Vol. 3, No. 2, April–June 2004, 180–191.

2. M. M. Gore and R. K. Ghosh, Recovery of Mobile Transactions. In *11th International Workshop on Database and Expert Systems Applications*, September 4–8, 2000, pp. 23–27.

3. C.-M. Lin and C.-R. Dow, Efficient Checkpoint-based Failure Recovery Techniques in Mobile Computing Systems, *Journal of Information Science and Enginering*, Vol. 17, 2001, 549–573.

4. Y. Morita and H. Higaki, Checkpoint-Recovery for Mobile Computing Systems, In *Distributed Computing Systems Workshop, in International Conference*, Tokyo, Japan, April 2001, pp. 479–484.

5. N. Neves and W. Kent Fuchs, Adaptive Recovery for Mobile Environments, *Communications of the ACM*, Vol. 40, No. 1 January 1997, 68–74.

6. T. Park and H. Y. Yeom, An Asynchronous Recovery Scheme Based on Optimistic Message Logging for Mobile Computing Systems. In *20th International Conference on Distributed Computing Systems*, April 2000, pp. 436–443.

7. T. Park, W. Namyoon, and H. Y. Yeom, An Efficient Recovery Scheme for Mobile Computing Environments. In *Eighth International Conference on Parallel and Distributed Systems (ICPADS)*, 2001, pp. 53–60.

8. C. Pedregal and K. Ramamritham, *Recovery Guaranteed in Mobile Systems*, Technical Report 98-12. University of Massachusetts, Amherst,

9. D. K. Pradhan, P. Krishna, and N. H. Vaidya, Recovery in Mobile Environments: Design and Trade-Off Analysis. In *26th International Symposium on Fault-Tolerant Computing (FTCS-26)*, June 1996, pp. 16–25.

10. R. Prakash and M. Singhal, Low-Cost Checkpointing and Failure Recovery in Mobile Computing Systems, *IEEE Transactions on Parallel and Distributed Systems*, Vol. 7, No. 10, October 1996, 1035–1048.

11. D. VanderMeer, A. Datta, K. Datta, K. Ramamritham, and S. B. Navathe, Mobile User Recovery in Context of Internet Transactions, *IEEE Transactions on Mobile Computing*, Vol. 2, No. 2, April–June 2003, 132–146.

12. P. A. Bernstein, V. Hadzilacos, and N. Goodman, Concurrency Control and Recovery in Database Systems, Adison-Wesley, 1987. (Also available at www.research.microsoft.com/pubs/ccontrol)

13. D. B. Lomet, Application Recovery: Advances Toward an Elusive Goal. In *Workshop on High Performance Transaction Systems (HPTS 97)*, Asilomar, CA, September, 1997.

14. D. Lomet and G. Weikum, Efficient Transparent Application Recovery In Client-Server Information Systems. In *Proceedings of ACM SIGMOD Conference*, Seattle, WA. June, 1998.

15. J. Gray and A. Reuter, *Transaction Processing Concepts and Techniques*. Morgan and Kaufmann, San Francisco, 1993.

16. K. Yao, F. Ssu, and W. K. Fuchs, Message Logging in Mobile Computing. In *IEEE Fault-Tolerant Computing Symposium* June 1999, pp. 294–301.

17. C. Perkins, Mobile Networking through Mobile IP, *IEEE Internet Computing*, January 1998, pp. 58–69.

18. P. Krishna, N. H. Vaidya, and D. K. Pradhan, Recovery in Distributed Mobile Environments. In *IEEE Workshop on Advances in Parallel and Distributed Systems*, Princeton, NJ, October 1993, pp. 83–88.

19. D. B. Lange and M. Oshima, Seven Good Reasons for Mobile Agents, *Communication of the ACM*, Vol. 42, No. 3, 1999, 88–89.

20. G. Eleftheriou and A. Galis, Mobile Intelligent Agents for Network Management Systems. In *London Communications Symposium*, London, 2000.

21. V. Kumar, M. H. Dunham, N. Prabhu, and Ayse Y. Seydim, TCOT—A Timeout Based Mobile Transaction Commitment Protocol, *Special Issue of IEEE Transaction on Computers*, Vol. 51, No. 10, October 2002, 1212–1218.

22. J. Kiniry and D. Zimmerman, A Hands-On Look at Java Mobile Agents, *IEEE Internet Computing*, Vol. 1, No. 4, 1997, 21–30.

CHAPTER 9

WIRELESS INFORMATION DISSEMINATION

This chapter introduces the topic of data dissemination (broadcast) through wireless channels. The data dissemination discipline gives the illusion that the space around us is an infinite-sized persistent data storage area from where a user can download desired information. For example, information about airline schedules, weather, stock quotes, and so on, can be downloaded from the broadcast. Initially, the data dissemination system appeared as an information dissemination tool similar to a radio broadcast; but with advances in wireless and satellite communication, it is becoming an information management system as well. This chapter discusses data dissemination technology and development of schemes such as indexing, push and pull, data staging, surrogates, and so on, for incorporating a transactional management facility. The discussion in this chapter is based mostly on research reports because a true data broadcast system (data goes right to the user account without going through the web) has not been developed and deployed for commercial use. It also discusses, in detail, the architecture and workings of a reference data dissemination and processing system called DAYS (DAta in Your Space).

9.1 INTRODUCTION

The discipline of data dissemination through a wireless—channel, that is, data broadcast—has added another dimension in the area of mobile computing. The mobile database systems, discussed in preceding chapters, provided terminal and personal

Fundamentals of Pervasive Information Management Systems, Revised Edition. Vijay Kumar.
© 2013 John Wiley & Sons, Inc. Published 2013 by John Wiley & Sons, Inc.

mobility in information management. The wireless data dissemination took mobile systems one step further and allowed users to tune, access, and process desired information from anywhere in the world.

Accessing data from a wireless channel is a very useful facility because it allows users to get desired data through many computationally enabled devices such as cellular phones, PDAs, or other new devices. Manufacturers continue to develop increasingly more powerful mobile devices while decreasing their size and cost. If it is assumed that there is an abundance of wireless channels, then servers can continue to *push* all data that users would ever need on these channels and users can *pull* whatever they require. This is an ideal scenario. In reality, wireless channels are always less than the number required to satisfy users' demands. Thus, the task of data dissemination technology is to develop ways for satisfying users' data demand with limited wireless resources.

Data Broadcast is predominately user-independent. The users are *passive* in that they can only read what is contained in a broadcast. While this model fits well into some types of data dissemination (such as local traffic information), it is not satisfactory for many different types of applications. Some examples can help to identify its usefulness and limitations.

■ EXAMPLE 9.1

The American Automobile Association (AAA) provides support services for drivers in the United States. One of the major support functions is to provide *Tourbooks* that contain travel information as well as hotel/motel information for areas across the United States. When travelers today plan a vacation to Florida, they can obtain a tourbook on Florida for free. A perfect application of a broadcast would be to broadcast tourbook information.

■ EXAMPLE 9.2

The Kansas City airport has thousands of arriving and departing flights daily. Determining the gate and time for various flights can be challenging for persons traveling to the airport. Current support requires either calls to specific airlines, tuning into predefined stations on local radios, or visiting an airline web site. Instead, the Kansas City airport could provide a broadcast to a local area.

It is possible to obtain this information from the web site of the airline, however, this requires an access to the web, the URL, and the mobile unit must have a browser installed. Under this scheme, the web will serve as the source of data broadcast and changes to the data for the next broadcast can be trigger based.

The traditional view of access to data from a broadcast is shown in Figure 9.1. The mobile client reads data from the wireless broadcast. The *Server* maintains the primary data repository and pushes data (broadcasts data) to users through the base station.

Figure 9.1   Traditional mobile data access from a broadcast.

The architectural model used for data broadcast is shown in Figure 9.2. Clients tune and download desired data from a broadcast.

9.1.1   Data Broadcast Mode

The mode of data transfer is essentially asymmetric, that is, the capacity of the transfer of data from the server to the mobile client (*downstream communication*) is significantly larger than the client or mobile user to the server (*upstream communication*). The effectiveness of a data dissemination system is evaluated by its ability to provide users their required data ubiquitously. There are two basic modes of data dissemination. These modes are motivated mainly by limited power consideration. The lifetime of a battery is expected to increase only by 20% over the next 10 years [1]. A typical AA cell is rated to give 800 mA/hour at 1.2 V (0.96 W/hr). The constant power dissipation in a CD-ROM (for disk spinning itself) is about 1 W and the power dissipation for display is around 2.5 W. The available power source is likely to last for 2.7 hours and to preserve battery power, these activities must be disabled whenever possible. The Hobbit chip from AT&T allows the operation in two modes: (a) *active mode*—the full operational mode where CPU and all other components are in a running state—and (b) *doze mode*—the power conserving mode where the CPU is inactive. The power consumption in the *active mode* is 250 mW, and the power consumption in the *doze mode* is 50 μW. The ratio of power consumption in the active mode to the doze mode is 5000. When the mobile unit (palmtop) is listening to the channel, the CPU must be in the active mode for examining data buckets in the broadcast. The CPU consumes more power than some receivers, especially if it has to be active to examine all incoming buckets. It will, therefore, be beneficial if the CPU can be switched to the doze

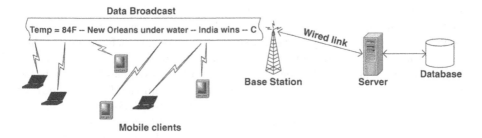

Figure 9.2   Broadcast data access model.

mode whenever it is not being used and switched back to the active mode when the data of interest arrives on the broadcast channel. This facility is called *selective tuning*.

Transmitting and accessing data also consumes power. A number of factors like the terrain, landscape, the height and kind of trees, foliage, season, rain, and so on, play an important role in determining the power required in data dissemination. With distance, the power requirement increases significantly [2]. For large cells, the energy required for transmission could reach tens of watts. For example, a Wavelan card consumes 1.7 W with the receiver powered on and 3.4 W with the transmitter powered on.

The effective bandwidth of wireless networks is only a fraction of the bandwidth that is available in wired networks. The current ATM (asynchronous transfer mode) standards are designed to yield a bandwidth of up to 622 Mbps. This bandwidth is projected to go up to gigabits [3]. The wireless bandwidth varies from 1.2 Kbps for slow paging channels to about 2 Mbps of the wireless LAN.

Data broadcast can be managed with three different modes to satisfy the users needs. These modes are further elaborated upon later in this chapter as *Push* and *Pull* technology.

Broadcast Mode. In this mode, the broadcast server periodically broadcasts the most popular data on some wireless channels from which users can *listen* and, if necessary, download the required data. There is no uplink channel involved in this mode. Simple *filtering* of a broadcast data stream, according to a user specified filter [4], is applied to access the data.

On-Demand Mode. This mode allows a client to request specific data that are not available in the current broadcast or may never appear in the broadcast. The client sends the query for the required data through an uplink channel.

Hybrid Mode. In this mode, broadcast and on-demand modes are combined. The server allows individual data requests from clients through an uplink channel and allows data broadcast through a downlink channel. It also, if necessary, broadcasts on-demand data if its popularity matches the popularity of the broadcast data.

Pull Process. The pull process is user (client)-oriented. A user assumes that the desired information is available in the wireless space and pulls it by tuning the channel. For example, a user keys in a URL on the web browser and pulls the desired information. The server is not concerned with the individual user's access. It is also immaterial whether the user finds the desired data or encounters an error or delay in downloading the data. In day-to-day activities, the pull process is frequently applied in an instance such as: borrowing a book from a library, renting a movie or music cd, buying an airline ticket, and so on. It is clear from these examples that in pull, the user initiates a conditional information flow where the condition is defined by the user with an understanding that the condition is likely to be satisfied. For example, renting a movie with a particular title, purchasing a ticket for a particular destination, and so on. Using an e-mail facility may appear to follow the pull process, but actually it is not so. A recipient of an e-mail does not select the e-mails he receives; rather, they are dropped in the user's space without his knowledge and they just appear on his e-mail directory, some as spam but some quite useful. It is also clear that what a user intends to pull may or may not be present in the pulled information. For example, pulling information from Google with some condition brings quite a lot of trash along with the desired information. An intelligent pull technique, such as semantic web, has yet to be fully developed.

Advantages of Pull. It is user-friendly and provides interactive capabilities to users for accessing the information through a query. The user does not need to search in the wireless information space by tuning several channels.

Disadvantages of Pull. In a wireless data dissemination platform, the pull approach is resource-intensive. A user requires a separate channel to send the request as an SQL query or in some other form to the server for the desired information. The server, after receiving the request, composes the result and must send it to the user on a back channel (downstream) known to the user. Thus, every pull needs two channels for completing the process successfully. If there are a large number of users and they need identical information, then each user will occupy two channels with identical data on all back channels. This is not easily affordable because of the narrow bandwidth available for wireless communication. It appears from these limitations that pull is good for special cases of data retrieval.

Push Process. In the push process, the server broadcast data (pushes data) on one or multiple channels. For example, it can push weather information on one channel, traffic information on another channel, and so on. Clients, depending upon their data requirements, tune into the appropriate channel. In a push system, a client cannot send a specific query to the server, nor can the server broadcast client-specific information.

The push technology was introduced somewhere around April 1996 by an internet company called PointCast, Inc. The company started the push scheme by broadcasting selected news and stock quotes to a client's machine at predefined intervals [5]. The client tuned in and downloaded information at these intervals. This was the beginning of an effective way of reaching a larger number of customers. Developers and researchers found the push scheme quite useful, and since then it was deployed on the internet in many ways such as *webcasting* or *netcasting*. Sometimes it is also called *PointCasting* to honor the company that invented it.

The main objective of push technology was to handle the problem of information overload due to low bandwidth that restricted users to receive multimedia contents. The push scheme provided an effective means to pre-deliver much larger packages of audio, large graphics, or short video clips.

The push technology can be augmented with a number of mechanisms to increase its scope and effectiveness. For example, message indexing can be implemented to speed up a broadcast search, caching can be used to reduce data miss, data staging can be augmented to enhance data availability, personalization of channel contents can help to satisfy specific users, the *smart-pull* approach can assist users to get specific information, and so on. These topics are discussed in detail in subsequent sections.

Push Application. Push technology has been deployed for some time in many real-world activities such as in the financial world to broadcast stock quotes, mutual fund costs, real estate costs and inflation status, news, cable television broadcasts, and so on. Nearly all software manufacturers use push to broadcast application and system updates, and fixes to clients' machines. Many companies use this technology for advertisement. In fact, most of the commercials on broadcast media such as television, radio, and so on, are push-based. Companies are at a great advantage for making use of the push technology that allows them to make instant changes in the broadcast or refresh it entirely based on the users' feedback to increase their effect on consumers. It is not now necessary for them to rely on a human operator to search a site for outdated material. The push technology applies to entertainment and leisure an equally effective basis.

The push technology is specially useful in the intranet market. Companies can push on their intranet corporate information to employees using a predefined schedule. It guarantees identical message delivery, which is highly desirable to all employees.

Accessing Information from Broadcast. Clients can access and download required information in a variety of ways that depend upon how the broadcast was composed and pushed on the channel by the server. In a channel, the push is strictly sequential. Data are dropped in the channel, one at a time. This can be viewed as a string of different categories of data. For example, if the broadcast is composed of weather information, traffic information, and dining place information, then they will appear on the broadcast sequentially in the order they were dropped in the channel. The client will receive the broadcast in the order sent by the server.

At the client's end, the simplest way to access the information is sequentially. In most cases this access is time-consuming. If interested only in dining information, a client has to tune and wait until the dining information appears in the broadcast. In a wireless platform, any waiting (let alone waiting for information) to appear is quite resource-expensive, especially from a bandwidth viewpoint. An ideal scheme is to tune in when the desired information appears (e.g., *selective tuning*) and download the data; that is, the waiting time for information access is zero. It is impossible to implement the ideal scheme, but the access time can be significantly minimized through efficient indexing and carefully composing the broadcast. Such arrangements actually create a notion of *smart-pull* where the client can pull exactly the information he wants with minimum redundancy. Even though push applications are not really push, there is a difference between them. The difference is the automation of the process both for the server and the client. There are a couple of true push technology applications—for example, products like AirMedia Live and Wayfarer (INCISA).

9.1.2 Push Advantages and Disadvantages

Push technology has been a favorite choice of data dissemination because of its several advantages. It has, however, several disadvantages that make it unsuitable, especially for providing transactional management facility [5].

Advantages

- In a large information flow, push technology minimizes the burden of acquiring data. The server can keep the information up to date by broadcasting it on a regular interval, and therefore the user always has the latest information. A user is aware of the broadcast channel carrying the information, along with the exact location of the data in the broadcast. This setup significantly reduces the search time.

- It sends the user the time-critical data for immediate attention.

- It helps organizations (academic, business, or commercial) to identify, focus, and reach those users with precision who are more likely to benefit from their products or services.

- It automatically delivers software upgrades directly to the clients' machines and fixes them faster and, at the same time, reduces or eliminates shipping costs. This facility requires a mechanism to check clients' machines for software and configuration, and then it modifies these configurations.

- It uses incremental updates where only new and changed information has to be sent to the computer that significantly reduces access and download time.

- It helps the server to reserve more processing time for data production by avoiding the handling of numerous client requests individually.

- It shortens response time.

- It easily protects user privacy because push applications run mostly at the client's machine, while the client's profile and the log information about the client's behavior are stored on the client's computer.

- It enables intelligent information filtering based on personalized user profiles describing required information needs.

- It satisfies a large client base using few resources.

Disadvantages. The push technology, although useful in a number of situations, does conserve resources and energy, but it has a number of limitations and disadvantages [5]. Some important ones are given below.

- Push applications are complex and the development costs (time and resources) are generally high compared to creating static pages. Static pages can be viewed by any browser on any operating system, but the push system requires specific tools and applications.

- It requires more powerful hardware and specialized software to provide push service.

- Identifying the location of the desired information in the broadcast and downloading the multimedia contents require a huge amount of disk storage.

- It suffers a number of unresolved bandwidth problems. Problems arise due to the enormous bandwidth that push technologies can require when feeding data to thousands of end users. Caching proxy servers, for example, as well as multicast solutions, will likely solve many of the bandwidth problems of push and allow it to scale. Some providers allow users to choose when the information is downloaded, so users can schedule it for times that they will be away from their computer.

- The push scheme is still not that useful for individual users; however, the emergence of P2P music systems makes it quite popular. Its general usefulness is still confined to organizations who have a good customer base.

- In multiple push schemes, a user can get frequent interruptions. For example, during a song broadcast, some urgent message can appear to notify the user of some serious event. Although users get the information, they may have to live with constant interruptions. Such interruptions cannot be preplanned because they may occur randomly.

- Push system software may suffer with an incompatibility problem. Many vendors (Air Media, Alpha Microsystems, Berkeley Systems, IntraExpress, Marimba, PointCast, etc., to name a few) develop application software with minimum portability and scalability. Competition to dominate the information space in this technology is growing fast, and vendors are unable to develop software compatible to all systems.

- The push technology is not good for the typical knowledge worker who mines information from a variety of sources and then draws conclusions by digesting that information [5].

- Creating and maintaining user profiles is time-consuming. This becomes more expensive with the number of users. One of the main reasons is that users' information needs are constant only to some degree.

- There is no reliable solution to achieve a secured broadcast. Security safeguards are highly needed.

- Standards are currently lacking in this area (competing de facto industry standards are pushed by companies) [5].

Market for Push Technology. Microsoft Corp. and Netscape Communications Corp. are the two leading competitors in push technology. Microsoft is pushing the Extensible Markup Language (XML)-based Channel Definition Format (CDF) for defining push updates. Netscape is using the Meta-Content Format (MCF) that was invented by Apple Computer. For example, Marimba Inc. has begun cooperation with Netscape. Microsoft and Netscape each have created their own push clients for use in conjunction with their latest browsers. The push market can be divided into four basic categories [5]:

- **Application Distributor:** The products of this category, such as Marimba's Castanet, provide automatic delivery of application software to end users.
- **Content Aggregator:** The products of this category—for example, PointCast Business Network—gather and format the contents in a consistent wrapper, and push it to the users' workstations.

- **Platform Provider:** The products of this category—for example, BackWeb—are similar to content aggregators, except they are actually infrastructure to deploy content delivery systems.
- **Real-Time Data Transfer:** The products of this category—for example, TIBCO and Wayfarer (INCISA), and so on—offer the advantage of multicasting. It is expensive to implement, but they guarantee timely delivery of information as quickly as possible.

Push information delivery models can be categorized into at least three main categories [5]:

- **Push Server Model:** It is the most common Push Server Model that provides a client, server, and development tools. A proprietary client is supplied and the applications may use a proprietary protocol. Both users and content providers have control over the content. Some examples of this model are BackWeb and Marimba's Castanet.
- **Web Server Extension Model:** In this model, the push vendor directs feedback and demographic information to an external server, so that information can be retained by the push vendor. No proprietary client is required. These run within the user's installed browser, such as PointCast; or the server delivers content using e-mail, such as ChannelManager and InfoBeat.
- **Client Agent Model:** This model uses a "client agent" to retrieve the information from the web. Each agent is designed to provide different search results and allows to establish an anonymous relationship between the vendor and the subscriber. The user is responsible for deployment and the search-type extensibility.

9.2 BROADCAST DISK

In this section, a novel broadcast scheme called *Broadcast Disk* is discussed. The main idea of this scheme is to efficiently use the available bandwidth to push data to the majority of users. This approach created the notion of multiple disks spinning at different speeds on a single broadcast channel to create an effect of a fine-grained storage hierarchy. The broadcast data on faster disks are pushed (repeated) more frequently than the data on slower disks (channel). Users tune to these disks (channels) and download their desired data [4, 6].

Figure 9.3 illustrates a simple broadcast setup using the broadcast disk approach. The broadcast station has a channel on which it continuously broadcasts (pushes) data items **A, B, C, and D** in that order. The oval represents a broadcast disk (channel) that is accessed (tuned) by a few mobile devices. If the broadcast station has a number of channels with different capacities, then each channel can be used as a different sized disk. This arrangement can be compared with a radio broadcast where different programs are transmitted over different stations (frequencies).

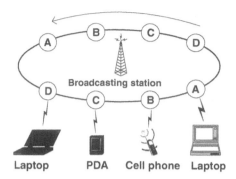

Figure 9.3 A simple broadcast disk setup.

The relative speed of these *disks in the air* (airdisks) significantly affects the broadcast configuration. The speed can be tweaked to satisfy a variety of information needs of its users. In a similar manner, a set of different types of information such as weather, traffic, stock quotes, airline schedule, news flashes, and so on, can be transmitted on different speed channels.

Bandwidth Allocation. The way a set of information is arranged and pushed on to the broadcast channels is called a *schedule*. In an ideal schedule, the *latency time* and *tuning time* are minimal.

Latency Time. Similar to conventional disk access, latency time is (a) the total time for a client request to arrive at the server and (b) the time when the desired data is available in the broadcast channel. This time becomes important especially in interactive applications such as video games that require a fast scan.

Tuning Time. It is the total time required to tune to the channel that is broadcasting the desired data. This time becomes important for fast-changing data such as stock quotes. The client must be able to quickly tune to the right channel to get the data.

Access Time. Another parameter that is called *access time* is the total time to download the desired data from the broadcast channel to the client's local storage. In the push approach, an increase in the length of the broadcast can lead to an unacceptably long access time for the user.

Figure 9.4 illustrates access and tuning time. A client submits a request at T_0 and receives the desired response at time T_7. If the client listens continuously from the time the query was submitted and until the response is received, then the access and tuning times can be expressed as $AT = TT = (T_7 - T_0)$. If, on the other hand, the client intermittently slips into doze mode, that is, tunes selectively (selective tuning), then the actual tuning time will be $TT = (T_7 - T_6) + (T_5 - T_4) + (T_3 - T_2) + (T_1 - T_0)$. In selective tuning, the mobile unit will be in doze mode (DM) for $(T_2 - T_1) + (T_4 - T_3) + (T_6 - T_5)$. If $DM > TT$, then the tuning time saves energy and the saving will be

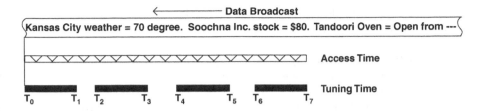

Figure 9.4 Access and Tuning times in a broadcast.

highest only if the client has accurate information about the tuning time for accessing data. The task, therefore, is to find optimal points in the 2D space of access and tuning times. This is quite difficult because there is a trade-off between these two times. The access time depends on the broadcast size, and the tuning time depends on the identification of the exact data location in the broadcast, which is achieved through selective tuning. Unfortunately, selective tuning requires extra information to be appended to the broadcast data, which increases the size of the broadcast. This increase in size affects the access time. An efficient broadcast scheme, therefore, must balance this trade-off.

The broadcast program can be addressed in terms of bandwidth allocation. An efficient bandwidth allocation scheme is directly linked with *data popularity* among the client population. The client information requirement is highly random. Different samples of client populations may have orthogonal data requirements. In some client population, geographical information may be highly important and accessed more frequently while some populations may frequently access stock quotes, and so on. Thus, the relationship among data popularity, client samples, and geographical domain becomes very complex, which makes it very hard, if not impossible, to develop an optimal schedule for all situations. However, with the help of popularity computation, broadcast indexing, and broadcast composition, an efficient schedule can be created.

Figure 9.5 presents three broadcast samples [7]. Schedule (a) is a flat schedule where the data items set, consisting of **D1, D2,** and **D3,** continuously appears in the broadcast. Schedule (b) is a skewed broadcast where data item **D1** appears twice, one after another, followed by **D2** and **D3**. Schedule (c) is a regular broadcast (multidisk) where the inter-arrival time of each page is the same. The difference between schedules (a) and (b) is quite obvious. In (b), data item **D1** is treated as being more frequently

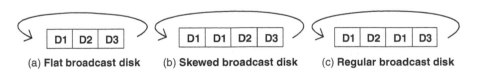

(a) **Flat broadcast disk**   (b) **Skewed broadcast disk**   (c) **Regular broadcast disk**

Figure 9.5 Three broadcast schedule samples.

accessed than the other items on the broadcast. The benefit of a particular broadcast schedule can be understood by its expected access delay.

Access Frequency and Expected Delay. Two cases are considered (a) flat broadcast and (b) skewed and multidisk broadcast.

Flat Broadcast. If there are $D = \{d_1, d_2, \ldots, d_n\}$ data items in the broadcast, then on the average one has to wait for $D/2$ data items to access the desired item d_i. Thus, the expected delay is $= D/2$ broadcast units. In reality, access frequencies of data items vary; and when this value is taken into consideration, the access delay significantly reduces.

Skewed and Multidisk Broadcast. For each $d_i \in D$ the probability p_i that d_i will be accessed is given by

$$\sum_{d_i \in D} p_i = 1 \tag{9.1}$$

The expected delay for a data item d is computed as follows. Since the broadcast time interval $= 1$, the delay in a request for d, with N being the number of transmission intervals, is

$$
\begin{aligned}
Delay_d &= \int_0^1 (t_{max}^{i,d} - t)\, dt \\
&= (t_{max}^{i,d} \times t - \tfrac{t^2}{2}), \qquad t = 0, 1 \\
&= (t_{max}^{i,d} - \tfrac{1}{2}) \\
&= \frac{1}{N}(t_{max}^{i,d} - \tfrac{1}{2}) \\
&= \frac{1}{N}\sum_{i=1}^{N}(t_{max}^{i,d} - \tfrac{1}{2})
\end{aligned}
\tag{9.2}
$$

where

N is the number of transmission intervals (duration of one transmission interval is 1)

t is the arrival time of the request, and

$t_{max}^{i,d}$ is the waiting time when the request arrives at the start of the interval i.

If the transmission of data item d_i has already started, then the client waits for the next broadcast to access d_i.

The expected delay for all data items D with access probability p_i is given by

$$Delay_{total} = \sum_{d_i \in D} p_i\, delay_{d_i} \tag{9.3}$$

Table 9.1   Expected Delay with Access Probabilities [7]

Access Probability			Expected Delay		
D1	D2	D3	Flat	Skewed	Multidisk
0.33	0.33	0.33	1.50	1.75	1.67
0.50	0.25	0.25	1.50	1.63	1.50
0.75	0.125	0.125	1.50	1.44	1.25
0.90	0.05	0.05	1.50	1.33	1.10
1.0	0.0	0.0	1.50	1.25	1.00

Table 9.1 shows the computed expected delays for different access probabilities of data items **D1, D2,** and **D3**.

Mean Access Time. The mean access time can be minimized if each d_i is equally spaced in the broadcast. For any two data items d_1 and d_2 with f_i being the access frequency, we obtain

$$\frac{p_1}{p_2} = \frac{\sqrt{f_1}}{\sqrt{f_2}}$$

$$p \propto \sqrt{f_i}$$

$$p_i = a\sqrt{f_i}$$

$$a = \frac{1}{\sum_{i=1}^{N} \sqrt{f_i}}, \quad \text{since } \sum p_i = 1$$

$$\text{Minimum access time} = \text{Min}\left(\frac{1}{2}\sum_{i=1}^{N}\frac{1}{p_i} \times f_i\right)$$

$$= \frac{1}{2}\sum_{i=1}^{N}\frac{\sum_{i=1}^{N}\sqrt{f_i}}{\sqrt{f_i}} \times f_i$$

$$= \frac{1}{2}\left(\sum_{i=1}^{N}\sqrt{f_i}\right)^2 \tag{9.4}$$

where p is the probability of data access and f is the frequency of data access.

Observations. The data of Table 9.1 demonstrates a number of important points about a broadcast disk scheme. With equal data access probability, the flat schedule has the lowest expected delay followed by the multidisk schedule while the skewed schedule has the highest access delay. In reference 7, this behavior was explained in terms of a fixed bandwidth. In a fixed bandwidth, all data items have equal space in the broadcast. The server composes the broadcast uniformly for pushing it into the channel. If a data item is placed twice (skewed schedule) in the broadcast, then this arrangement will take away some space from other data items. As a result of this, clients are likely to miss tuning and downloading the desired data in the first broadcast and must wait for the subsequent broadcast. On the other hand, in the case of non-equal access probability, the server assigns less "space" to data with low access probability and assigns more to "space" data with high access probability on the broadcast. As a result of this, clients manage to tune and download the desired data from the first broadcast most of the time. Thus, in an extreme case where the access probability of **D1** was 1, the multidisk schedule performed the best because most of the time, clients got the desired data (i.e., **D1**) from the first broadcast.

In real life, the access frequency for data is always nonuniform. Furthermore, this variation in access frequency greatly depends on the geographical location. For example, in a place where the change in weather is quite frequent, such as London, England, users like to query the broadcast system for weather more frequently, compared to residents of California, USA. This real-life scenario indicates that a multidisk schedule may fit better for the data dissemination system.

9.3 BROADCAST INFRASTRUCTURE

The usefulness of the data dissemination system lies in its ability to broadcast a huge amount of data on a number of topics such as weather, stocks, entertainment, traffic, and so on. The future broadcast systems are likely to be used as large data warehouses that store (push) large amounts of data on all topics. It may provide Yellow Page services, encyclopedias, dictionaries, and so on. This will require not only efficient broadcast schedules but also a faster way to reduce the search space of requested data.

So far, data broadcast has been seen as a push-based system, whereas mobile database has been seen as pull-based where users initiate all kinds of transactions. The trend now is to integrate both facilities into one infrastructure. A new generation of data management systems is thus capable of disseminating data for universal access and, at the same time, efficiently process all types of transactions with full database support as we are used to.

The main components of such a system are (a) data access frequency, (b) broadcast schedules, and (c) data access from the broadcast. These components are discussed in detail below.

9.3.1 Data Access Frequency

The aim of the broadcast server is to achieve the highest hit rate for every type of data it pushes. This makes it necessary that the server must first identify the high demand set of data, arrange them in a specific order considering the size of the broadcast channel, and broadcast them. The access frequency identification can be done in many ways— for example, by (a) monitoring the current access pattern by some means, (b) reaching active clients to look at their data access history, (c) studying the market trends and so on. All these approaches essentially identify the access probability.

For achieving the highest data hit rate and highest channel utilization, both static and dynamic approaches can be used. In the static approach, a user notifies the broadcast server of its present and future data pull and the approximate duration for their use. The server will continue to broadcast the static data set for the defined period. In the dynamic approach, the data requirements will be identified using (a) *residence latency (RL)* and *expected departure time (EDT)* [8], (b) *popularity factor (PF)* and *ignore factor (IF)*, (c) user movement, and (d) channel tunability.

RL and EDT. When the server decides to include an item in its broadcast, it also needs to decide the length of time the item will remain in its broadcast set. To identify the residency duration of a data item, an *RL* value is associated with each data set. The *RL* value for a specific data set is the average length of time a mobile user resides in a *cell*, and it can be computed *a priori* based on the advanced knowledge of user movement patterns and cell geography. A data item's *EDT* from a broadcast can be computed by adding the item's entry into the broadcast and the data's *RL*.

PF. The popularity factor of data set D at time T identifies the number of clients in the cell at time T who are interested in D. It can be denoted as PF_D^T or just PF_D. One way to maintain the *PF* of a data item at the server in a cell is to increment it by 1 when a client requests D. The server also records the corresponding time. The popularity of D goes down after its *RL* value and a corresponding decrement of 1 is performed on the value of PF_D at time $(T_D^i + RL)$ where T_D^i denotes the timestamp of the ith increment to PF_D. This reflects the anticipated departure of the client whose request caused the ith increment. In reality, the client population is very large, so the database to support their requests is also very large. Since the increment and decrement are frequently invoked operations, one way to implement them is through an abstract data type—for example, a *PF* queue with these operations.

The *PF* approach implies a priority scheme where the most popular data gets the maximum favor in a broadcast. Starvation is inherent in all priority schemes. One of the side affects of a priority approach is that a client's need for low *PF* data may never be satisfied. This may get worse if the client is highly mobile and suffers frequent handoffs. If it is assured that a client's need for low *PF* data will be satisfied at least once in each cell it visits, then the effect of starvation on the client population can be reduced. A simple approach could be based on the waiting time of a low *PF* data item. Under this scheme, if the waiting time exceeds a predefined limit, then the data item is pushed into the next broadcast. This scheme will work, but individually defining a waiting time for individual data items would be time-consuming and difficult to enforce fairness. A better approach is developed here through the concept of *ignore factor (IF)*. The task of the *IF* is to ensure that less popular but long-neglected data items have a chance to end in the broadcast with a high degree of fairness. The value of the *IF* of a data item can be computed as follows.

Ignore Factor. Suppose that a data item D was last included in the broadcast that ended at time T_0. Data item D was dropped from subsequent broadcast after T_0. At this instance, the *IF* of D (i.e., IF_D) is fixed at 1 [8]. The next request for D arrives at

T_{req}, which means D was "ignored" between T_0 and T_{req}; that is, the IF of D at any time T_i ($T_i > T_{req}$), denoted by $IF_D^{T^i}$, is equal to $NumBroadcast(T_i, T_{req}) + 1$, where $NumBroadcast(T_i, T_{req})$ denotes the number of broadcasts between T_{req} and T_i. If a broadcast period of P_B is considered, then

$$IF_D^{T_i} = \left\lfloor \frac{T_i - T_{req}}{P_B} \right\rfloor + 1 \tag{9.5}$$

Equation (9.5) is valid only for $(T_i - T_{req}) \le RL$. This is because a client requested data item D at time T_{req} and no other request for D came after T_{req}. However, by the definition of RL given above, the client is expected to depart at $T_{dep} = T_{req} + RL$; and if it happens, then there is no point in including D in the broadcast. Thus, after T_{dep}, unless other requests for D arrive, the value of IF_D should be reduced to 1. It can be seen that the following corollary holds for any data item D_i.

$$1 \le IF_{D_i} \le \left\lfloor \frac{RL}{P_B} \right\rfloor + 1$$

A simple way to compute the IF for a data item is explained using Figure 9.6. Points B_1, B_2, B_3, and B_4 denote the start of successive broadcasts. T_{r1}, T_{r2}, T_{r3}, and T_{r4} represent request arrival times for data item D, and T_{dep1} and T_{dep2} show the corresponding times when the client departs from the cells where the requests originated. Suppose that at B_4 all requests (i.e., T_{r1}, T_{r2}, T_{r3}, and T_{r4}) have expired. In general, at all broadcast points where the next broadcast set has to be decided—that is, at successive broadcast points (B_1, B_2, B_3, and B_4)—all requests that arrived prior to the $\left(\lfloor \frac{RL}{P_B} \rfloor \right)$th broadcast and preceding the next immediate broadcast are guaranteed to have expired. This means that IF_D needs to be computed based on the first request that arrived after the $\left(\lfloor \frac{RL}{P_B} \rfloor \right)$th broadcast and preceding the next immediate broadcast. For example, at B_4, IF_D needs to be computed based on T_{r3}. This means that the server requires keeping track of the first request after the broadcast (B_i) and can ignore successive requests until the next broadcast. Thus, the server needs only to maintain a list of $\lfloor \frac{RL}{P_B} \rfloor$. This can be easily done by keeping an ordered list in RAM, along with the request identity and its timestamp. The list will have $\lfloor \frac{RL}{P_B} \rfloor + 1$ elements with identity 1 through $\lfloor \frac{RL}{P_B} \rfloor + 1$, where the timestamp corresponds to the ith element that represents the first request for data item D after the ith previous broadcast. The list is updated at

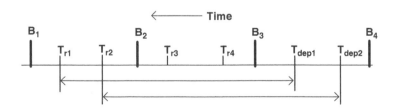

Figure 9.6   Computation of ignore factor for a data item.

each broadcast, so an easy way is to use a circular queue. With this scheme, a data item can be accurately tracked in constant ($\approx \lfloor \frac{RL}{P_B} \rfloor$) time.

The priority of a data item now can computed as follows:

$$Priority = IF^{ASF} \times PF \qquad (9.6)$$

where *ASF* is an *adaptive exponential scaling factor* and its purpose is to increase the inclusion probability of a data item with a low *PF* value. Equation (9.6) explains why the minimum value of *IF* was set to 1 and not 0. It can be seen that when $IF = 0$, the priority value is reduced to 0 and guarantees its exclusion from the next broadcast. The equation also indicates that a data item that has been requested by a large client population has a large *PF* value and relatively low *IF* value as compared to a data item with few requests. With its low *PF* value, it is likely to be omitted from the broadcast that will increase its *IF* in improving its chance to be included in near future broadcasts.

It is possible that an item may be ignored for a long time. In this situation, its *IF* must dominate, which can be achieved through a larger value of *ASF*. *ASF* can be precisely defined using W_{ij}, which denotes the number of broadcasts client i anticipated while waiting for data item j after requesting j. The *average wait count (AWC)* for data item j can be expressed as

$$AWC_j = \frac{\sum_{i \in C_j} W_{ij}}{|C_j|}$$

where C_j denotes the set of clients waiting for data item j.

Suppose the *Maximum Wait Count (MWC)* defines the maximum number of broadcasts a client is prepared to wait for before its request is serviced. In this situation, the values of *AWC* and *MWC* are calculated for computing the priority of a data item. If $AWC > DWC$, then *ASF* is incremented by 1; and if $AWC = DWC$, then *ASF* does not change. *ASF* is initialized to 1 for all data items and is reset to this value each time the item is included in a broadcast.

9.3.2 Data Access Time

Data access time is the total time to download the desired data from the broadcast to the client's local storage. It has two components: (a) the identification of the starting location of the desired data in the broadcast—that is, from where the desired data begins—and (b) the data download from the data location to the local store. The simplest way to reach the data in the broadcast is to continuously listen to the channel after it has been tuned and then start downloading it when the data location is found. Figure 9.7 illustrates a simple broadcast structure that allows a simple sequential search for data without a selective tuning facility.

Each type of data—for example, weather information—constitutes a broadcast segment or data. They are separated by some marker that indicates the starting of a broadcast segment. The mobile unit may tune anywhere in the middle of a broadcast

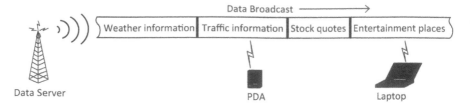

Figure 9.7 Simple broadcast composition.

and must wait for the marker to identify the starting of a segment. In the worst-case scenario, the unit may have to wait the entire broadcast cycle for the desired data.

This scheme is unsatisfactory from every respect of access time and energy costs. Selective tuning is highly desirable, which means that the client tunes only when the desired data are available for download, as explained earlier. Such a reduction in search space is effectively achieved by structuring the broadcast using *indexing*.

9.3.3 Broadcast Indexing

Structuring the data broadcast presents the same set of search problems as conventional data does, and in addition, it has its own set of unique problems. They arise because of the real-time constraints of the broadcast process and its limited bandwidth. The indexing scheme for a data broadcast is time-based. It indicates to the user at what time the desired data will be available from the last tuning to the broadcast channel. For example, if the user tunes at 9:00 a.m., then either the desired data will be available to download or the index will indicate at what time after 9:00 a.m. the data will be available for download. This information will allow the user to go in doze mode or turn off the cell phone and re-tune the channel at the time indicated by the index. Thus, one of the important properties of any index scheme is to indicate precisely the tuning time, which is crucial in saving battery power. The other important requirement is that the indexing structure itself should take much less space in the broadcast to allow the server to push the maximum amount of user data. Thus, indexing shrinks the data search space (i.e., broadcast space), which in turn reduces search time and energy consumption. Figure 9.8 illustrates the position of the index part in the broadcast.

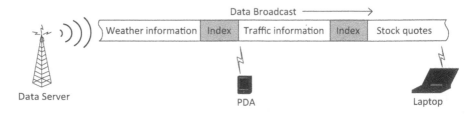

Figure 9.8 Indexed broadcast composition.

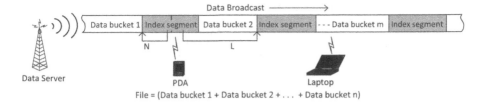

Figure 9.9 Organization of $(1, m)$ indexing scheme.

An indexed broadcast allows selective tuning. The advantage of selective tuning can be maximized by designing powerful indexing schemes. A number of schemes have been developed in the last few years to handle the efficiently varied data access needs of clients. A partial list of the work is given here [6, 9–15]. In this section, some of the earlier and also most of the recent index schemes are discussed in detail.

(1, m) Indexing Structure. A simple indexing scheme called the $(1, m)$ scheme was discussed in references 6 and 14. This scheme and its variants are described here in detail. Under this scheme the index is broadcasted m times during a broadcast of an entire file. This is done by prefixing the entire index in front of $\frac{1}{m}$ fraction of the file. The entire structure is explained in terms of a *data bucket* and *index segment*. The data bucket contains the file and data, and the index segment contains the index. Thus, the index segment precedes a data bucket. To broadcast an entire file, a number of index segments are required. Figure 9.9 illustrates the organization of the $(1, m)$ indexing scheme.

An index segment contains two pointers: N and L. L points to the last data segment in the broadcast, and N points to the data segment to be broadcasted next. To access the desired data block, the user executes the following steps:

- Tunes in to the right broadcast channel. If there is more than one broadcast channel, then some directory is available to identify the correct channel for tuning.
- If this is the data block, then continue tuning for the next index segment. When the next index segment appears, tune to the index segment and get the pointer (N) to the next data segment. In case of multilevel indexing, this search will require continuous tuning until the index for the desired data is found.
- After accessing the desired index, the mobile unit can go into doze mode and resume tuning for the data when it appears in the broadcast. The client can then download all the records of the data item.

The expressions for index tree levels, latency, tuning time, and optimum division of the entire file into data buckets are given below. The complete analysis of this indexing scheme can be found in reference 14.

For a fully balanced index tree, we have

$$k = \left\lceil log_n \left(\frac{Data}{C} \right) \right\rceil$$

$$Index = \sum_{i=0}^{k-1} n^i$$

where k is the number of level in the index tree, n is the size of an index segment in terms of <attribute value, offset> pairs, *Index* is the number of buckets in the index tree, and C is the coarseness of the index attribute.

Latency. $\frac{1}{2} \times \left((m+1) \times Index + \left(\frac{1}{m} + 1 \right) \times Data \right) + C.$

Tuning Time. $1 + k + C$. When a client starts tuning, the first probe gets the pointer to the next index bucket. From here, k probes are needed to follow the pointers in the index block. In addition to C, more probes are required for getting the desired records from the data block.

Optimum m. $m^* = \sqrt{\frac{Data}{Index}}$. The entire file is therefore divided into m^* equal data segments.

Distributed Indexing. The distributed indexing scheme does not introduce a different way of organizing the broadcast, it only restructures and distributes the index segment to optimize the use of broadcast space.

In the $(1, m)$ indexing scheme, the entire index segment is replicated in the broadcast even though the following data segment contains only a part of the file. This observation suggests that only the part of the entire index that covers the following data segment is sufficient and needs to be included. This portion of the entire index is referred to as the *relevant index* and shown in Figure 9.10.

Three different index distribution schemes have been presented here. These algorithms differ in the degree of replication of the index. Figure 9.11 is used to explain the workings of each scheme. This figure shows the layout of a file with 81 data buckets. Each square box at the lowest level represents three data buckets—for example, data bucket 0, data bucket 2, and data bucket 3. The index tree is built on these data buckets. Each index bucket has three pointers—for example, index

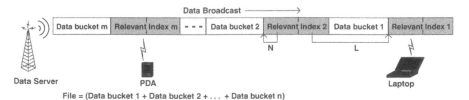

Figure 9.10 The organization of relevant index.

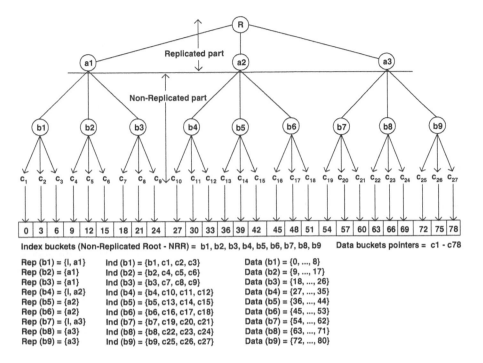

Index buckets (Non-Replicated Root - NRR) = b1, b2, b3, b4, b5, b6, b7, b8, b9   Data buckets pointers = c1 - c78

Rep (b1) = {l, a1}	Ind (b1) = {b1, c1, c2, c3}	Data (b1) = {0, ..., 8}
Rep (b2) = {a1}	Ind (b2) = {b2, c4, c5, c6}	Data (b2) = {9, ..., 17}
Rep (b3) = {a1}	Ind (b3) = {b3, c7, c8, c9}	Data (b3) = {18, ..., 26}
Rep (b4) = {l, a2}	Ind (b4) = {b4, c10, c11, c12}	Data (b4) = {27, ..., 35}
Rep (b5) = {a2}	Ind (b5) = {b5, c13, c14, c15}	Data (b5) = {36, ..., 44}
Rep (b6) = {a2}	Ind (b6) = {b6, c16, c17, c18}	Data (b6) = {45, ..., 53}
Rep (b7) = {l, a3}	Ind (b7) = {b7, c19, c20, c21}	Data (b7) = {54, ..., 62}
Rep (b8) = {a3}	Ind (b8) = {b8, c22, c23, c24}	Data (b8) = {63, ..., 71}
Rep (b9) = {a3}	Ind (b9) = {b9, c25, c26, c27}	Data (b9) = {72, ..., 80}

Figure 9.11 Organization of a file for broadcast.

bucket $b1$ has three pointers. The three pointers of the bucket c are represented just by one pointer pointing to a data bucket—for example, data bucket 0.

- **Nonreplicated Distribution:** There is no index replication. Index segments are disjoints.
- **Entire Path Replication:** The path from the root to an index bucket—say, B—is replicated just before the occurrence of B.
- **Partial Path Replication:** This is also called distributed indexing. If there are two index buckets—say, B and B'—then it is enough to replicate just the path from the least common ancestor of B and B', just before the occurrence of B'. In this arrangement, some additional information is included for navigation to find the correct data segment.

The workings of these three schemes are described in Figures 9.12, 9.13, and 9.14. In these figures, the current broadcast is represented in three levels. The broadcast channel is organized by taking the first level, followed by the second, and then finally by the third level. In order to understand the data access, consider that a client requires a record in data bucket 66. The client makes the initial probe at data bucket 3.

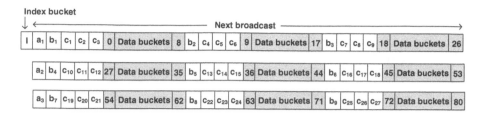

Figure 9.12 Nonreplicated distribution.

Nonreplicated Distribution. Figure 9.12 illustrates the broadcast structure for this scheme. The *bcast-pointer* at bucket 3 directs the client to the beginning of the next broadcast in which the clients probes *a3, b8, c23*, and bucket 66. Since the root of the index is broadcasted only once for each broadcast, the initial probe will result in obtaining the offset to the beginning of the next broadcast. In order to determine the occurrence of the required record, the client has to get to the root of the index. Hence, the probe wait for this scheme will be quite significant and will offset savings in the broadcast wait due to the lack of replication. The offset at data bucket 3 could have directed the client to index bucket *b2*, in which case the client could make the following successive probes: b2, b3, a2, a3, b8, c23, and bucket 66. The client need not have made an extra probe at b3. There are three pointers per index bucket, along with four levels in the index tree, and one extra probe was made. The number of extra probes grows linearly with the increase in the number of pointers in the index bucket, and it also grows linearly with the number of levels in the index tree. This becomes substantial as the number of data buckets and the capacity of the index bracket increase. The tuning time is no longer logarithmic in the number of data buckets.

Entire Path Replication. Figure 9.13 illustrates the index distribution when the entire path from the root of the index tree to each index bucket b_i is replicated. The replication is just before the occurrence of b_i. The offset at data bucket 3 will direct the client to the index bucket *I* that precedes *second_a1*. Then, the client makes the following successive probes: *frst_a3, b8, c23*, and bucket 66. The latency suffers from the replication of index information. In this example, the root was unnecessarily replicated six times, as demonstrated below.

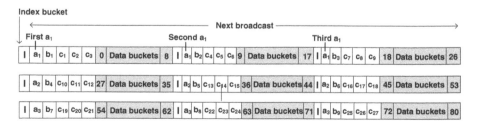

Figure 9.13 Entire path replication.

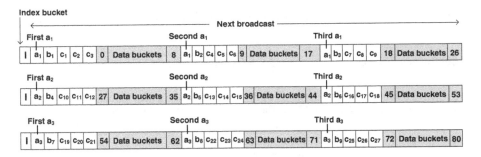

Figure 9.14 Partial path replication—distributed indexing.

Partial Path Replication—Distributed Indexing. Figure 9.14 shows that latency can be further improved by replicating only a part of the entire path. In this arrangement, the root *I* is no longer replicated many times. The offset at data bucket 3 will direct the client to *second_a1*. However, to make up for the lack of root preceding *second_a1*, there is a small index called the *control index* within *second_a1*. If the local index (in *second_a1*) does not have a branch that would lead to the required record, then the control index is used to direct the client to a proper branch in the index tree. The control index in *second_a1* directs the client to i_2. At i_2, the root is available and the client makes the following probes: *frrst_a3*, b8, c23, and bucket 66. In case a record in bucket 11 was being searched for by the client, reading the bucket *second_a1* would provide the client with the required information to successively tune in at $b2$, $c4$, and bucket 11. In this case, having the root just before *second_a1* would have been a waste of space (this is true if the search key was in any data buckets 9 through 26). The additional space that is necessary to store the control index is a small overhead compared to the savings resulting from partial index path replication. Replicated buckets can be modified by removing the entries for records that have been broadcast before the occurrence of that bucket. This will result in some space savings, which, when amortized over all the replicated buckets in the broadcast, will make up for the space taken up by the control index.

Figure 9.15 shows the control index for index buckets that are part of the index tree described in Figure 9.19 and whose layout is shown in Figure 9.14. The first part of each control index element denotes the search key to be compared with during the data access protocol. The second part denotes the pointer to be followed in case the comparison turns out to be positive. For example, if a record in a bucket ≤ 8 is being searched for, then the control index at *second_a1* directs the client to the beginning of the next broadcast. However, if a record in a bucket >26 is being searched for, then the search is directed to i_2. Otherwise, the search in the control index fails, and the rest of the *second_a1* is searched.

Distributed Indexing Algorithm. Given an index tree, this algorithm provides a method to multiplex it together with the corresponding data file on the broadcast

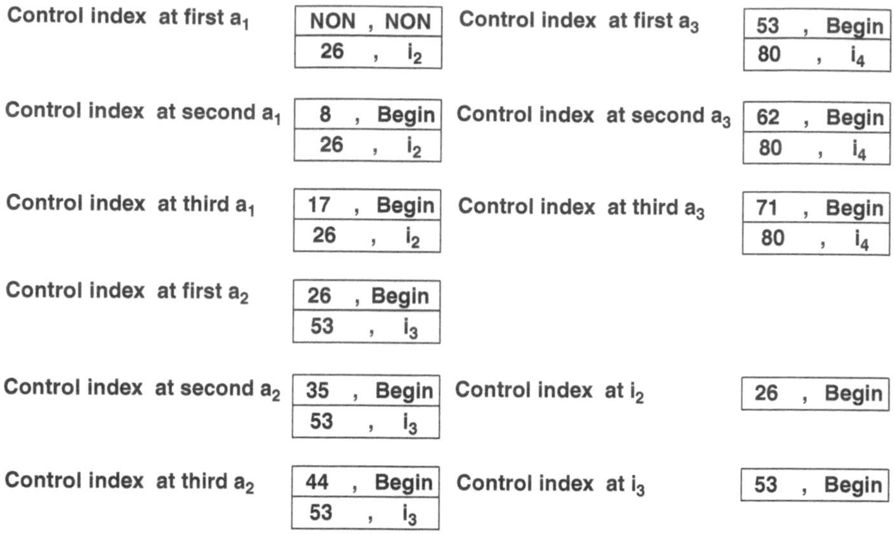

Control index at first a_1

NON	,	NON
26	,	i_2

Control index at first a_3

53	,	Begin
80	,	i_4

Control index at second a_1

8	,	Begin
26	,	i_2

Control index at second a_3

62	,	Begin
80	,	i_4

Control index at third a_1

17	,	Begin
26	,	i_2

Control index at third a_3

71	,	Begin
80	,	i_4

Control index at first a_2

26	,	Begin
53	,	i_3

Control index at second a_2

35	,	Begin
53	,	i_3

Control index at i_2

26	,	Begin

Control index at third a_2

44	,	Begin
53	,	i_3

Control index at i_3

53	,	Begin

Figure 9.15 Control index.

channel. Thus, the distributed indexing method is not a new method of index construction but a method of allocation of a file and its index on the broadcast channel.

The distributed indexing algorithm takes an index tree and multiplexes it with data by subdividing it into two parts:

1. The replicated part
2. The nonreplicated part

The replicated part constitutes the top r levels of the index tree, while the nonreplicated part consists of the bottom $(k - r)$ levels. The index buckets of the $(r + 1)$th level are called *non-replicated roots (NRR)*. The index buckets in NRR are ordered left to right, consistent with their occurrence in the $(r + 1)$th level.

Each index subtree rooted in *NRR* will appear only once in the whole broadcast just in front of the set of data segments it indexes. Hence, each descendant node of the *NRR* index will appear only once in a given version of a broadcast. On the other hand, the number of replications of each node of the index tree that appears above *NRR* is equal to the number of children it has.

Definitions

R = root of the index tree
B = an index bucket belonging to *NRR*
B_I = ith bucket in *NRR*
Path(C, B) = sequence of buckets on the path from index bucket C to B

(excluding B).

$Data(B)$ = set of buckets indexed by B

$Ind(B)$ = part of index tree below B (including B)

$LCA(B_i, B_k)$ = least common ancestor of B_i and B_k in the index tree

Let $NRR=\{B_1, B_2 \ldots B_t\}$ and the first bucket in NRR is $Rep(B_1) = Path((I, B_1), B_1)$. Thus, $Rep(B_i) = Path(LCA(B_{i-1}, B_i), B_i)$ for $i = 2, \ldots t$.

Thus, $Rep(B)$ refers to the *replicated* part of the path from the root of the index tree to index segment B. $Ind(B)$, on the other hand, refers to the non-replicated portion of the index. Figure 9.11 shows the values of Rep, Ind, and $Data$ for each of the index buckets in NRR. Each version of the broadcast is a sequence of triples: $< Rep(B)$, $Ind(B)$, $Data(B) > \forall B \in NRR$ in left to right order.

Let $P_1, P_2 \ldots P_r$ denote the sequence of buckets in $Path(I, B)$. The control index is stored in each of the P_i index buckets.

Let $Last(P_i)$ denote the value of the attribute in the last record that is indexed by bucket P_i.

Let $NEXT_B(i)$ denote the offset to the next occurrence of P_i (which in turn is the index bucket at level i in $Path(I, B)$. Let l be the value of the attribute in the last record broadcast prior to B and let $begin$ be the offset to the beginning of the next broadcast. The control index in P_i that belongs to $Rep(B)$, that is, it precedes $Ind(B)$ and $Data(B)$ has the following i tuples:

$[l, begin]$
$[Last(P_2), NEXT_B(1)]$
$[Last(P_3), NEXT_B(2)]$
$\cdots \quad \cdots$
$[Last(P_i), NEXT_B(i\text{-}1)]$

The control index in bucket P_i is used as follows: Let K be the value of the attribute of the required records. If $K < l$, then the search is directed to the beginning of the next broadcast (i.e., the $begin$ pointer is followed). If the result of the comparison is false, then $(K > Last(P_j))$ is checked for the smallest j to be true. If $j \leq i$, then $NEXT_B(j - 1)$ is followed, else the rest of the index in bucket P_i is searched as in conventional indexing.

The access protocol for a record with attribute value K is as follows:

1. Tune to the current bucket of the broadcast. Get the pointer to the next control index.
2. Tune again to the beginning of the designated bucket with the control index. Determine, on the basis of the value of the attribute value K and the control index, whether to
   - Wait until the beginning of the next broadcast (the first tuple). In this case, tune to the beginning of the next broadcast and proceed as in step 2.

- Tune in again for the appropriate higher level index bucket, that is, follow one of the "NEXT" pointers and proceed as in step 2.
- Probe the designated index bucket and follow a sequence of pointers (the client might go into the doze mode between two successive probes) to determine when the data bucket containing the first record with K as the value of the attribute is going to be broadcast.
- Tune in again when the bucket containing the first record with K as the value of the attribute is broadcast and download all the records with K as the value of the attribute.

Analysis. Let *Index* denote the number of buckets in the index tree. Let *Level[r]* be the number of nodes on the r_{th} level of the index tree and let *Index[r]* be the size of the top r levels of the index tree. Let $\Delta Index_r$ denote the additional index overhead due to the replication of the top r levels of the index tree. Finally, let B denote a nonreplicated root (NRR).

Latency. The latency is a sum of the probe and the broadcast waits. The detailed computation of the following probe waits, the broadcast waits, and $\Delta Index_r$ is described in reference 6.

$$\Delta Index = Level[r+1] - 1$$

$$probe\ wait = \frac{1}{2} \times \left(\frac{Index - Index[r]}{Level[r+1]} + \frac{Data}{Level[r+1]} \right)$$

$$broadcast\ wait = \frac{1}{2} \times (Data + Index + \Delta Index_r) + C$$

$$latency = \frac{1}{2} \times \left(\frac{Index - Index[r]}{Level[r+1]} + \frac{Data}{Level[r+1]} \right) +$$
$$(Data + Index + \Delta Index_r) + C \tag{9.7}$$

Tuning Time. Tuning time primarily depends on the number of levels of the index tree and the coarseness of C of the given attribute. The initial probe of a client is for determining the occurrence of the control index. The second probe is for the first access to the control index. The client is directed to the required higher-level index bucket by the control index. Next, the number of probes by the client is equal to (at most) k, the number of levels in the index tree. The last pointer in the index tree points to the next occurrence of the required data bucket. Finally, the client has to download C buckets of the required records. Thus, the tuning time using distributed indexing is bound by

$$2 + k + C$$

Optimizing the Number of Replicated Levels. Optimizing the number of replicated levels only affects the latency. This optimizing can be accomplished by choosing r in such a way that the following expression is minimal:

$$\Delta_r + \left(\frac{Index - Index[r]}{Level[r + 1]} + \frac{Data}{Level[r + 1]} \right) \qquad (9.8)$$

Given a particular index tree, Eq. (9.8) is evaluated for r ranging from 1 to k (the number of levels in the index tree). The value of r (obtained from Eq. (9.8)) is the optimal number of replicated levels.

Comparison. In general, the distributed indexing algorithm has a much lower latency than the $(1, m)$ indexing scheme. Both $(1, m)$ indexing and distributed indexing have a lower latency than *tune_opt*. Distributed indexing achieves almost the optimal latency (that of *latency_opt*).

The tuning time due to *tune_opt* and $(1, m)$ indexing is almost the same. The tuning time of distributed indexing is also almost equal to that of the optimal (*tune_opt*), the difference is just two buckets. The tuning time of *latency_opt* is very large and is extremely higher than the other three. A detailed comparison between $(1, m)$ indexing and distributed indexing is presented in reference 16.

9.3.4 Nonclustering Index

Usually, at most, one index is clustered. Other indexes are defined over nonclustered attributes. In this section, we discuss index allocation for non-clustered attributes. To this end, we generalize the distributed indexing algorithm developed in the previous section. The proposed generalization is based on the observation that even if a file is not clustered on a particular attribute, it can always be decomposed into smaller fragments that are clustered.

As in the case of a clustered index, first two benchmark define algorithms are defined that are one-dimensional optimal solutions: one that provides optimal latency but has a very poor tuning time and another that provides optimal tuning time but has poor latency.

Noncluster_latency_opt. This algorithm is similar to the *latency_opt* algorithm. The best latency is provided by this algorithm as no index is broadcast with the file. Clients tune into the broadcast channel and listen continuously until all the required records are downloaded.

Noncluster_tune_opt. This algorithm is similar to the *tune_opt* algorithm. The index of the file is broadcast in front of the file. Index entries point to the first occurrence (in the current broadcast) of a record with a given attribute value. Additionally, all records that have the same attribute value are linked by pointers. The client that needs all records with attribute value K will tune in to the broadcast channel at the beginning of the next broadcast to get the index. It then follows the pointers from one index level to another in a successive manner, to the first occurrence of a record with attribute value K. It then downloads all consecutive records with that attribute value. Then it follows the pointer to the next occurrence of records with the same attribute value; this is done until the end of the current broadcast. Assuming that the nonclustering attribute has a coarseness of C (buckets), the tuning time is equal to $(k + C)$, where k is the number of levels in the index tree of the nonclustered attribute. This method has poor latency because the client has to wait until the beginning of the next broadcast even if the required data are broadcast immediately after the initial probe of the client.

Nonclustered Indexing Algorithm. The method of organizing the index for a nonclustering attribute is a generalization of a distributed indexing scheme. The structure of the file is as follows:

- The file is partitioned into a number of segments called *meta segments*. Each meta segment holds a sequence of records with nondecreasing values in the nonclustering attributes. Even though the entire file is not clustered on the index attribute, the meta segments are clustered based on the index attribute. The scattering factor of an attribute is defined as the number of *meta segments* in the file.
- Each meta segment is further divided into a number of data segments. Each data segment $DS(K)$ is a collection of records with the value of the nonclustering attribute equal to K.
- The last element of each data segment $DS(K)$ has an offset to the next occurrence of the data segment $DS(K)$. The last $DS(K)$ of a broadcast has an offset to the first occurrence of the data segment $DS(K)$ in the next broadcast.

There is an index for each meta segment, and it indexes all the values of the nonclustered attributes, rather than being restricted to indexing just the values that occur in the current meta segment. Index entries corresponding to attribute values that are present in the current meta segment will point to the appropriate data segments within the meta segment. For attribute values that do not occur in the current meta segment, the pointer in the Index tree will point to the next occurrence of the data segment for that value. The nonclustered index is organized as in distributed indexing for each meta segment separately.

Each meta segment is partitioned by a set of index segments. Each index segment is a set of index buckets. Let $IS(K)$ denote the index segment immediately following the data segment $DS(K)$ The first element of $IS(K)$ is an offset to the beginning of the next meta segment. Clients looking for records whose attribute value P is less than K use this offset. The remaining elements of $IS(K)$ are built as a directory with offsets to the next data segments $DS(PK < P \leq L)$, where L denotes the largest value of the attribute. The directory here corresponds to $\text{Rep}(B)$ followed by $\text{Ind}(B)$, where B is a bucket belonging to NRR as defined in distributed indexing. As in the case of distributed indexing, even here the index segment contains a control index. However, the first tuple in the control index is a new element. This new element indicates the total number of buckets B in the broadcast. Each data bucket has an offset to the next

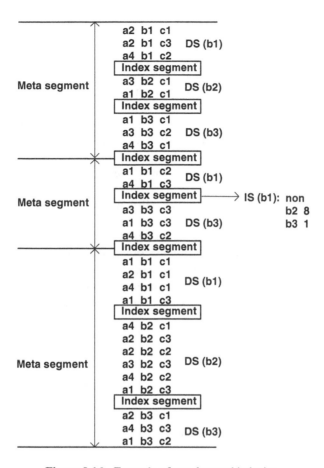

Figure 9.16   Example of nonclustered indexing.

index segment. The access protocol for following the pointers in $IS(K)$ is exactly as in distributed indexing.

■ EXAMPLE 9.3

Figure 9.16 shows a file that has a nonclustering attribute b. It shows various meta segments and data segments. The file is partitioned into data segments for attribute b. The data segments for b are $DS(b1)$, $DS(b2)$, and $DS(b3)$. Figure 9.16 also shows the index segment for $b1$ and $b3$. The index segment in this example appears after every data segment.

Each data bucket contains a pointer to the next occurrence of the index segment for b. Additionally, every data segment of attribute b contains a pointer to the next data segment that contains records with the same value of the attribute. The pointers for attribute value bl is shown in Figure 9.16. Finally, each data segment is followed by an index segment that provides a directory to the nearest occurrence of data segments for other values of b.

Immediately following (the second) $DS(b1)$ is a pointer to the next occurrence of $DS(b1)$. This is followed by the index segment $IS(b1)$. Consider the index segment $IS(b1)$, the first element is *non* because there is no value for the attribute b that is less than bl. The second value indicates that $DS(b2)$ occurs after eight buckets. Note that even though $b2$ does not occur in the current meta segment, there is an entry for it. The third element indicates that $DS(b3)$ occurs in the next bucket. For search keys less than $b3$, the first element (only element) in $IS(b3)$ directs the client to the next bucket.

The access protocol for records with the attribute value K is as follows:

- Probe the current bucket and get the pointer to the next index segment. Go into the doze mode until the next occurrence of the index segment.
- Upon tuning in at the next index segment, get the number of buckets B in the current broadcast. Then follow the pointers to get to the offset for $DS(K)$. The client might go into the *doze mode* between successive probes. Go into the *doze mode* until $DS(K)$.
- Upon tuning in at $DS(K)$, download all the consecutive records of the current data segment and get the offset to the next occurrence of $DS(K)$. Assume that b denotes the number of buckets passed from the point the first index segment was encountered. Repeat until $(b + offset < \#_B)$; then exit.

Analysis. Let C denote the coarseness of the nonclustered attribute. Let M denote the scattering factor—that is, the number of *metasegments* of the attribute. *Data* denotes the total number of data buckets, and *Index* denotes the number of buckets occupied by the index tree.

Latency. Each metasegment has its own index tree that is distributed according to the distributed indexing technique. Let $\Delta Index$ denote the average index overhead per metasegment. The broadcast wait is equal to the size of the whole broadcast, that is

$$M^*(Index + \Delta Index) + Data$$

Note that the broadcast wait is slightly less than that given by the above formula. This is because on the average only half of the last metasegment has to be accessed. This is also true for the noncluster_latency_opt and noncluster_tune_opt algorithms. This small difference is ignored for simplicity. The probe wait is analogous to the probe wait in the case of distributed indexing with respect to a metasegment. Let r denote the average number of optimal replicated levels (within each metasegment) in all the metasegments. Hence, the latency is

$$\frac{1}{2} \times \frac{Index - Index[r]}{Level[r+1]} + \frac{Data}{M \times Level[r+1]} + M \times (Index + \Delta Index) + Data$$

Tuning Time. In the first probe, the client fetches a pointer to the next index segment. After getting to the index segment, a number of probes have to be made to find the required data segment $DS(K)$. The number of probes required for getting to $DS(K)$ is at most $(k + 1)$ (as in distributed indexing), where k is the number of levels in the index tree of the indexed attribute. Once the first data segment $DS(K)$ is encountered, then C probes have to be made to get all the required records. Furthermore, in the worst case, extra M probes may have to be made. This is because the data segments may not occupy an exact multiple number of buckets, in which case the last bucket of a given data segment might contain only a few records belonging to this data segment. Nevertheless, this bucket has to be probed. This factor also needs to be added to the tuning time of non_cluster_tune_opt for a general case. Therefore. the tuning time is bound by $1 + (k + 1) + C + M$, that is, $2 + k + C + M$.

Comparison. The tuning time achieved by nonclustered indexing is always substantially better than the tuning time due to the noncluster_latency_opt. The latency of nonclustered indexing depends on the scattering factor M. Nonclustered indexing achieves a tuning time close to that of the optimum (noncluster_tune_opt algorithm). Nonclustered indexing achieves a latency close to that of the optimum (noncluster_latency_opt algorithm), when the scattering factor is small.

If the latency is very important, then the *noncluster_latency_opt* is used. If the tuning time is important, then either the *non_cluster_tune_opt* or the *nonclustered indexing* is used. *Nonclustered indexing* and *noncluster_tune_opt* have almost the same tuning time; hence, when tuning time is of concern, the decision as to which of the two algorithms to use depends on the latency for the two algorithms.

9.3.5 Multiple Indexes

Since all indexes and data share the same broadcast channel, it is important to specify how indexes and data are going to be multiplexed.

Let each record of the file have n attributes. Assume that the attributes are ordered according to the frequencies of their access. Let the leftmost attribute be the most frequently accessed one, and let the rightmost one be the least frequently requested. Let the sorted attributes be $a_i, a_2, \ldots, a_n$.

Partition the file into metasegments based on each attribute separately. The number of metasegments for the attributes increases with the value of the subscript. Usually only attribute a_1 is clustered and the rest are nonclustered. Let us assume that the indexes are available for the first l attributes. The total index overhead will depend on the subscript of the index attribute–in general, the lesser the subscript of the attribute, the lesser the index overhead.

Let $I = \{a_1, \ldots, a_l\}$ be the indexed attributes. Partition the file separately for each attribute belonging to I. Allocate the file and the index for all the 1 attributes as in nonclustered indexing (except possibly the first attribute that is allocated as in distributed indexing). While allocating the index for a particular attribute, the indexes of the other $(l - 1)$ attributes are treated as part of the file. The index segment of each index attribute has to take into account the additional offset introduced by the presence of the index segment of other attributes. Each data bucket of the file stores a pointer to the next occurrence of the control index for all attributes in I.

If an attribute has a clustering index, then the access protocol for accessing records based on that attribute is similar to that of accessing records in distributed indexing. For nonclustering attributes the access protocol is similar to that of *nonclustered* indexing.

Notice that contrary to disk based files, the latency for accessing records based on some attribute is dependent on the presence or absence of the index for other attributes. Each additional index increases the overall latency while decreasing the tuning time for the indexed attribute.

Consider Figure 9.17, where the records have three attributes: a, b, and c. The file is lexicographically sorted (with a as the most significant attribute, followed by b and then by c). Let a and b be the attributes over which the file is indexed, that is, $I = \{a, b\}$. The file is partitioned into data segments for attributes a and b. The data segments for a are denoted by $DS(a1)$, $DS(a2)$, $DS(a3)$, and $DS(a4)$. The data segments for the attribute are $DS(b1)$, $DS(a2)$, and $DS(a3)$.

A data segment corresponding to the attribute $a(b)$, contains a pointer (following the last record of the data segment) to the next data segment, which contains records with the same value for the attribute $a(b)$. These pointers are shown for attribute value $b2$. Each data segment corresponding to attribute $a(b)$ is followed by an index segment that provides a directory to the nearest occurrences of data segments for other values of $a(b)$. Additionally (not shown in the figure), each data bucket contains a pointer to the next occurrence of the control index for a and the control index for b. In the figure, the index segment for attribute b occurs at every index segment for attribute a. This is not true in general.

Immediately following the (first) data segment $DS(b2)$ is a pointer to the next occurrence of $DS(b2)$. This is followed by the index segment $IS(b2)$. Consider the index segment $IS(b2)$. The first element indicates that if the attribute's value is less than or equal to $b2$ (i.e., $b1$ or $b2$) then the client has to probe the fourth bucket ahead of the current bucket. The second element indicates that if the requested attribute value is $b3$, then the client has to probe the first bucket following the current bucket. The third element indicates that if records with a value of $b4$ (for attribute b) are being searched for, then the client has to tune after 23 buckets. Note that even though b4 does not exist in the current metasegment, there is still an index entry for it.

Analysis. We use the following notations in the analysis:

C_i: the coarseness of attribute a_i (in buckets)
M_i: the scattering factor of the attribute
$Index_i$: the size of the index tree of attribute a_i
k_i: the number of levels in the index tree corresponding to attribute a_i
r_i: the average number of optimum replicated levels in the index tree of attribute a_i
$\Delta Index(i)$: the average index overhead (per meta segment) due to attribute a_i

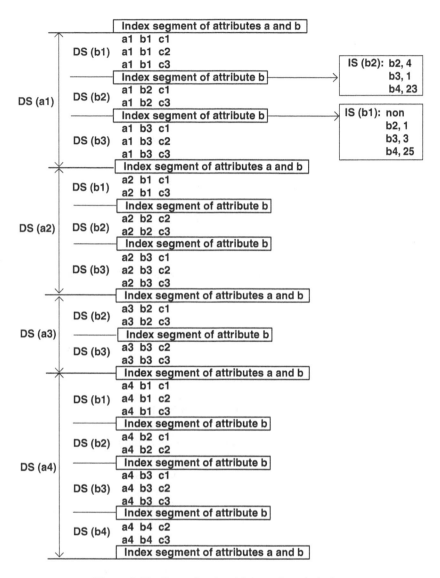

Figure 9.17 Example of multiple attribute indexing.

Latency. Each metasegment of attribute a_i has $(Index_i + \Delta Index(i))$ number of extra buckets due to distributed indexing on the attribute. The total number of extra buckets E_i due to indexing the attribute a_i is

$$E_i = M_i \times (Index_i + \Delta Index(i))$$

The broadcast wait is

$$\sum_{i=1}^{l} E_i + Data$$

For an attribute a_i that is indexed, the probe wait is

$$\frac{1}{2} \times \left(\frac{Index - Index[r_i]}{Level[r_i + 1]} + \frac{Data}{M \times Level[r_i + 1]} \right)$$

Thus the latency for an attribute a_i that is indexed is

$$\frac{1}{2} \times \left(\frac{Index - Index[r_i]}{Level[r_i + 1]} + \frac{Data}{M \times Level[r_i + 1]} \right) + \sum_{i=1}^{l} E_i + Data$$

For an attribute a_i that is not indexed, the probe wait is 0. The broadcast wait and the latency for such an attribute is

$$\sum_{i=1}^{l} E_i + Data$$

Tuning Time. The tuning time for indexed attribute a_i is calculated below. In the first probe, the client fetches a pointer to the next index segment for the attribute a_i. After getting to the index segment, a number of probes have to be made in that index to get to the required data segment $DS(K_i)$. The number of probes required for getting to $DS(K_i)$ is $(k_i + 1)$, where k_i is the number of levels in the index tree for a_i. Once the first data segment $DS(K_i)$ is encountered, then C_i probes have to be made to get all the required records. Furthermore. M_i extra probes may have to be made to get all the required records. This is because the data segments may not occupy an exact multiple number of buckets, in which case the last bucket might contain only a few records belonging to this data segment. The tuning time for the indexed attribute a_i is bound by

$$1(k_i + 1) + C_i + M_i \quad \text{that is,} \quad 2 + k_i + C_i + M_i$$

For a nonindexed attribute a_i the client loses the ability of selective tuning.

In the worst case, the whole length of the metasegment for attribute a_l has to be scanned to get to the next record with the requested value of a_i. This is because the last indexed attribute is a_l. After this, the number of probes required is $(C_i + M_i)$ as described above.

Thus, the tuning time for records on attribute a_i that is not indexed is bound by

$$\frac{Data}{M_i} + C_i + M_i$$

9.3.6 Dynamic Organization

Reorganizing broadcast files is substantially cheaper than reorganizing disk-based files. Indeed, in case of broadcasting, each new broadcast starts from "scratch" because the previous broadcast disappears. The new broadcast can substantially differ from the preceding one, both in terms of data contents as well as index. The reorganization cost is limited to the server's memory reorganization. The reorganization of a broadcast itself simply amounts to a different downloading order by the server. Hence, there is a minimal need for dynamic data organization methods. In fact, dynamic indexing methods such as B-trees are generally inappropriate for broadcasting since, in order to ensure the "locality" of changes, they require a reservation of extra pointer space that would unnecessarily increase the overall broadcast size and consequently the latency.

9.4 EXPONENTIAL INDEX

The basic indexing scheme, as discussed earlier, has overhead related to index management. A scheme called *Exponential Index* [15] used an innovative approach to reduce index management overhead. It is a *parameterized* index that can be tuned to optimize the access latency with the tuning time bounded by a given limit and vice versa.

Figure 9.18 illustrates the structure of the exponential index scheme. Each data block is associated with an index table. An entry of the index table has two fields: *displacement in bucket* and *MaxKey*. The displacement in bucket is a range of buckets where one of the values of this range identifies the number of buckets one has to traverse to reach the desired bucket. For example, if the value of the *displacement in bucket* is 4–7, then more than 4 and less than 7 buckets need to be traversed to reach the desired bucket. An example of a broadcast is given in Figure 9.19.

In this example, stock data for 16 companies is maintained at the server. The data are composed in the broadcast and in ascending order of these companies names. Each company data block is associated with an index table that has four entries. The structure and number of entries in the table are the same for all companies. The index tables for DELL and MSFT are shown in the figure. The entire broadcast has

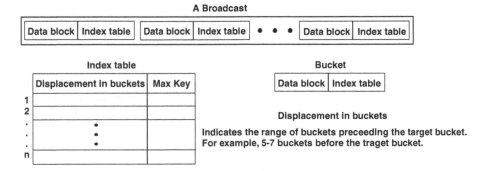

Figure 9.18 Structure of exponential index.

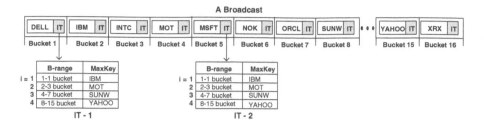

Figure 9.19 A simple exponential index.

been arranged in 16 buckets. The range of buckets (*B-range*) is shown here just for information. In fact, their values can be computed by the position of an entry in the index table. For example, the $i = 3$ (3rd entry of DELL index table) entry is for "SUNW." The range of the buckets for $i = 3$ can be computed as 2^{i-1} to $2^i - 1$, which is (4 to 7). The index table of "MSFT" is a replication of the "DELL" table where some of the entries are different. So in a replication of the index table, the structure does not change but the contents do point to new buckets.

The number of entries in the index table depends upon the size of the broadcast in the buckets. It is important to find a good balance of the size and the number of index tables because their granularity and number significantly affect tuning and latency times. The data access from a broadcast under this scheme can be explained with an example. Suppose a user wants to access stock information for the "NOK" company. The client tunes to the current broadcast and hits "DELL." He downloads the index table *IT-1* and discovers that the position of "NOK" is after "MOT" (that is, after bucket 4) and before "SUNW" (that is, before before bucket 7). This gives us buckets 5 and 6. The client goes into doze mode and wakes up when bucket 5 arrives. He tunes and downloads the index table of bucket 4 (*IT-2*). The first entry of *IT-2* indicates the *B-range* value for "NOK," which is 1–1. This gives us the displacement of 1 bucket from the current position of "MSFT." The client stays active and tunes and downloads the "NOK" bucket.

The total tuning time to get the answer of the query is 3 buckets (i.e., bucket 1 and 5 for initial search and bucket 6 for data download). The worst tuning time for this scheme is $\lfloor log_2(N - 1) + 1 \rfloor$ buckets, where N is the total number of buckets in the entire broadcast. The worst tuning time for this example is ($N = 16$) 5 buckets.

9.4.1 Generalized Exponential Index

In the above example, the *index base*, which is defined as the base for defining the size of the index table, was 2. To generalize the scheme, it can be replaced by any number—that is, $r \geq 1$, where r is the index base. With this index base, the *B-range* can be expressed as

$$\left\lfloor \sum_{j=1}^{i-2} r^j + 1 \right\rfloor = \left\lfloor \frac{r^{i-1} - 1}{r - 1} + 1 \right\rfloor$$

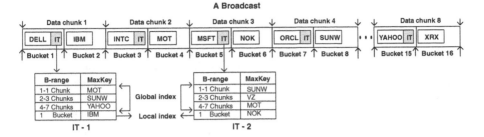

Figure 9.20   A generalized exponential index with r = 2 and I = 2.

to

$$\left\lfloor \sum_{j=1}^{i-2} r^j \right\rfloor = \left\lfloor \frac{r^{i-1} - 1}{r - 1} \right\rfloor$$

The indexing overhead may be reduced by reducing the number of index tables. One way to do this is to group I number of buckets into one bucket (i.e., data chunk). This will reduce the number of index tables and their size (number of entries); as a result, more data items can be accommodated in the same size broadcast. One side effect of this arrangement is that, on the average, $\frac{I-1}{2}$ number of buckets will be searched to find the desired data. A solution to this search problem and for constructing a plain index for all buckets in the group is presented in reference 15. In the plain index an index entry describes the maximum key value for each bucket and the intra-chunk tuning time is either 1 (for the first bucket in the chunk) or two buckets (for the remaining buckets). This is achieved by defining a *global* index for other data chunks and a *local* index for $(I - 1)$ buckets within the local chunk. Figure 9.20 illustrates the layout of a generalized exponential index with $r = 2$ and $I = 2$.

The data search procedure is very similar to the earlier example. Suppose a client wants the stock information of "NOK." He tunes and downloads the index table (IT-1) stored in the "DELL" data block. The desired data information is not in the local index of *IT-1*, so the search is extended to the general index portion where "NOK' falls in the key range specified by the second entry (*2–3 SUNW*). The client goes into doze mode and wakes up when the first bucket of chunk 3 (bucket 5) appears in the broadcast. In the index table of bucket 5, "NOK" falls in the key range specified by the first local index entry and the client accesses the next bucket (bucket 6). The total tuning time is 3 buckets.

The performance of the exponential index can be tuned with r and I parameters. Parameter r controls the number of index entries and I chunk size. Indexing overhead increases with the decreasing value of r, and tuning time is reduced by increasing the value of I. Detailed information about the performance can be found in reference 15.

9.5 LOCATION-BASED INDEXING

Basic indexing schemes discussed so far are unable to handle location-dependent information such as information about Kansas City weather, O'Hare airport congestion, traffic congestion at a segment of I-435, and so on. In order to get location-specific information from the broadcast, the index must contain the necessary pointer to correct the location.

One of the best ways to accomplish this is through the dissemination of highly personalized Location-Based Services (LBS), which allows users to access personalized location-dependent data. For example, a traveler uses his mobile device to search for a vegetarian restaurant in some city. The LBS application would interact with other location technology components or use the mobile user's input to determine the user's location and download the information about the restaurants in proximity to the user by tuning into the wireless channel that is broadcasting *Location-Dependent Data (LDD)*. The following example illustrates the type of indexing required for LDD.

■ EXAMPLE 9.4

Suppose a user issues query "Heaven Coffee on Plaza" to access information about the Plaza branch of Heaven Coffee in Kansas City. In the case of a location-independent setup, the system will list all Heaven Coffee shops in the Kansas City area. It is obvious that such responses will increase access latency and are not desirable. These can be managed efficiently if the server has location-dependent data—that is, a mapping between a Heaven Coffee shop and its physical location.

The tree-based and exponential index schemes discussed earlier are not satisfactory and effective in broadcasting location-dependent data. In addition to providing low latency, they lack properties that are used to address LDD issues. In this section, a new indexing scheme called *location index* is discussed for broadcasting LDD.

9.5.1 Location Index Scheme

The example identifies the need for a mapping function to access location dependent data from the broadcast. This will be especially important for pull-based queries for which the reply could be composed for different parts of the world. The mapping function is necessary to construct the broadcast schedule.

Mapping Function. A *Global Property Set (GPS)* [17], *Information Content (IC) set*, and *Location Hierarchy (LH)* are required to construct a location index. These sets are defined as follows:

Global Property Set (GPS). It is a set of objects or entities that are required to answer a query. For example, traffic, stock quotes, weather, airline, state, country, city, and so on, are the members of GPS. Thus, GPS $= \{e_1, e_2, \ldots, e_n\}$, where e_i's are real-world entities.

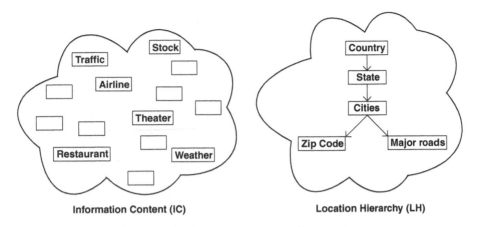

Figure 9.21 Information contents and location hierarchy sets.

Information Content (IC) Set. It is a set of stand-alone entities. Thus, IC = $\{i_1, i_2, \ldots, i_n\}$, where i_i's are real world entities such as traffic, stock quotes, theater, and so on. An IC does not contain any geographical objects such as city, state, and so on, and the relationship $IC \subset GPS$ is always true.

Location Hierarchy (LH). It is a tree of locations. The leaf nodes are the smallest location in the hierarchy. For example: $Country \rightarrow state \rightarrow city$ is a location hierarchy. The relationship $LH \subset GPS$ is always true.

A mapping function is required for correct association between a member of IC and LH. Figure 9.21 illustrates an IC set and LH samples. The mapping scheme must be able to identify and select an IC member and an LH node for (a) correct association, (b) granularity match, and (c) termination condition. For example, $Weather \in IC$ could be associated with a *Country* or a *State* or a *City* or a *Town* of LH. The granularity match between the *Weather* and an LH node depends on the user's requirements. Coarse granularity weather information is associated with a *Country* to get its weather. A finer granularity is associated with a town. If a *Town* is the finest granularity, then it defines the terminal condition for association between IC and LH for weather. This means that a user cannot get weather information about a subdivision in a town. In reality, weather of a subdivision does not make any sense because its area is usually quite small.

A simple heuristic mapping approach scheme based on user requirements is developed here. Let $IC = \{m_1, m_2, \ldots, m_k\}$, where m_i represent its element and let $LH = \{n_1, n_2, \ldots, n_l\}$, where n_i represents LH's member. Define GPS for IC (GPS_{IC}) $\subseteq GPS$ and for LH (GPS_{LH}) $\subseteq GPS$. $GPS_{IC} = \{P_1, P_2, \ldots, P_n\}$, where P_1, P_2, P_3, \ldots, P_n are properties of its members, and $GPS_{LH} = \{Q_1, Q_2, \ldots, Q_m\}$, where $Q_1, Q_2, \ldots, Q_m$ are properties of its members. The properties of a particular member of IC are a subset of GPS_{IC}. It is generally true that the (*property set* ($m_i \in IC$) $\cup$ *property set* ($m_j \in IC$)) $\neq \emptyset$; however, there may be cases where the intersection is null. For example, $stock \in IC$ and $movie \in IC$ ratings do not have any property in common. It is assumed that any two or more members of IC have at least one common geographical property (i.e., location). For example, the stock of a company is related to a country, weather is related to a city or state, and so on. The property subset of $m_i \in IC$ is defined as $PSm_i \forall m_i \in IC$ and $PSm_i = \{P_1, P_2, \ldots, P_r\}$, where $r \le n$. $\forall P_r\{P_r \in PSm_i \rightarrow P_r \in GPS_{IC}\}$, which implies that $\forall i$, $PSm_i \subseteq GPS_{IC}$. The geographical properties of this set are indicative of whether $m_i \in IC$ can be mapped to only a single granularity level (i.e., a single location) or multiple granularity levels (i.e., more than one node in the hierarchy) in LH. The number of granularity and their levels that m_i should map to will depend upon the level at which the service provider wants to provide information about the m_i in question. Similarly, a property subset of LH members is defined as $PSn_j \forall n_j \in LH$, which can be written as $PSn_j = \{Q_1, Q_2, \ldots, Q_s\}$ where $s \le m$. In addition, $\forall Q_s \{Q_s \in PSn_j \rightarrow Q_s \in GPS_{LH}\}$, which implies that $\forall j$, $PSn_j \subseteq GPS_{LH}$.

The process of mapping from IC to LH then identifies for some $m_x \in IC$ one or more $n_y \in LH$ such that $PSm_x \cap PSn_v \ne \emptyset$. This means that when m_x maps to n_y and to all children of n_ym, then m_x can map to multiple granularity levels. If m_x maps only to n_y, then m_x can map to a single granularity level.

In reality, new members can join and old members can leave IC or LH at any time. The deletion of members from the IC space is simple, but addition of members to the IC space is more restrictive. If a new member is to be added to the IC space, then first a property set for the new member has to be defined. Thus, $PSm_{new\_m} = \{P_1, P_2, \ldots, P_t\}$, which is added to the IC only if the condition $\forall P_w$ $\{P_w \in PSp_{new\_m} \rightarrow P_w \in GPS_{IC}\}$ is satisfied. This scheme has an additional benefit of allowing the information service providers to have a control over what kind of information they wish to provide to the users. The following example illustrates the mapping concept.

■ EXAMPLE 9.5

$IC =$	{Traffic, Stock, Restaurant, Weather, Important history dates, Road conditions}
$LH =$	{Country, State, City, Zip-code, Major-roads}
$GPS_{IC} =$	{Surface-mobility, Roads, High, Low, Italian-food, StateName, Temp, CityName, Seat-availability, Zip, Traffic-jams, Stock-price, CountryName, MajorRoadName, Wars, Discoveries, World}
$GPS_{LH} =$	{Country, CountrySize, StateName, CityName, Zip, MajorRoadName}
$PS(IC_{Stock}) =$	{Stock-price, CountryName, High, Low}
$PS(IC_{Traffic}) =$	{Surface-mobility, Roads, High, Low, Traffic-jams, CityName}
$PS(IC_{Important\ dates\ in\ history}) =$	{World, Wars, Discoveries}
$PS(IC_{Road\ conditions}) =$	{Precipitation, StateName, CityName}
$PS(IC_{Restaurant}) =$	{Italian-food, Zip code}
$PS(IC_{Weather}) =$	{StateName, CityName, Precipitation, Temperature}

$$PS(LH_{Country}) = \qquad \{CountryName, CountrySize\}$$
$$PS(LH_{State}) = \qquad \{StateName, State\ size\}$$
$$PS(LH_{City}) = \qquad \{CityName, City\ size\}$$
$$PS(LH_{Zipcode}) = \qquad \{ZipCodeNum\}$$
$$PS(LH_{Major\ roads}) = \qquad \{MajorRoadName\}$$

In this example, only $PS(IC_{Stock}) \cap PS_{Country} \neq \emptyset$. In addition, $PS(IC_{Stock})$ indicates that *Stock* can map to only a single location *Country*. When *Traffic* of *IC* is considered, only $PS(IC_{Traffic}) \cap PS_{city} \neq \emptyset$. As $PS(IC_{Traffic})$ indicates, *Traffic* can map only to *City* and none of its children. Unlike *Stock*, mapping of *Traffic* with *Major Roads*, which is a child of *City*, is meaningful. However, service providers have the right to control the granularity levels at which they want to provide information about a member of *IC* space.

$PS(IC_{Road\ conditions}) \cap PS_{State} \neq \emptyset$ and $PS(IC_{Road\ conditions}) \cap PS_{City} \neq \emptyset$. So Road conditions map to the *State* as well as to the *City*. As $PS(IC_{Road\ conditions})$ indicates, Road conditions can map to multiple granularity levels – to *Zip Code* and *Major Roads*, which are the children of the *State* and *City*. Similarly, *Restaurant* maps only to *Zip code*, and *Weather* maps to the *State*, *City*, and their children *Major Roads* and *Zip Code*.

Push-Based Broadcast Schedule. The following algorithm generates a push-based broadcast schedule. It takes *LH* and *IC* as inputs and generates a series of clustered LDD.

```
Broadcast_Schedule (IC_i, LD)
{
  Bcast = Null;
  for all IC content do
    {
      Check (IC_i);
      LD_i = map (IC_i, LD);
      Bcast = Bcast + LD_i + data_i;
      index = index + IC_i;
    }
}
Map(IC_i,LD) {Comment-Maps the IC_i members with LD}
{
    found = false;
    for all properties in IC_i
      {
      If (property_i == location)
      If(location == Termination-Condition)
      Termination-Condition == property_i;
      }
      While (not found) {Comment-check Termination-Condition in LD}
        {
        For all locations in LD
          If (Termination-Condition == location_i)
```

```
    {
      Termination = Termination-Condition;
      LD_i = Calculate_path (Termination);
      found =true;
      break;
    }
    }
    If (not found)
    {
      Generate (Termination-Condition)
    }
    } End while
} End Map
Generate(Termination-Condition) {Comment- Generate TC, add it to LD}
  {
    for all properties in IC_i
    {
    If (property_i == highest_location)
    (parent_location == property_i);
    }
{Comment-Locate parent_location from GPS to get area code,
zip code, and longitude and latitude. Calculate only Zipcode, Z}
for all Z's in parent_location do
    {
    if (zipcode == Z) then
    New_Location = new [node];
    New_location = Z → child; {add location under Z}
    }
  }
Calculate_path (Termination) in LD
  {
    for all properties in IC_i
    {
    If (property_i == highest_location)
    (parent_location == property_i);
    }
    Path = DFS (parent_location); {Comment - depth first search Return
path.}
    Return
    }
```

Location-Based Index Scheme (LBIS). LBIS is designed to conform to the LDD broadcast. As discussed earlier, the containment property of LDD significantly limits the search of the required data to a particular portion of the broadcast. Thus, the scheme provides bounded tuning time. The scheme contains separate data buckets and index buckets. The index buckets are of two types: (a) Major index and (b) Minor index.

Major Index. It provides information about the types of data broadcasted. For example, if entertainment, weather, traffic, and so on, are broadcasted, then the major index either points to this information and/or their subtypes. The number of main subtypes varies from one type of information to another. This strictly limits the number of accesses to a Major index. The Major index never points to the original data. It points to the sub-indexes called the Minor indexes.

Minor Indexes. These are indexes that point to data. They are also called *Location Pointers* because they point to the data that are associated with a location. Thus, the data search includes accessing a major index and some minor indexes. The number of minor indexes varies, depending on the type of information. LBIS takes into account the hierarchical nature of the LDD, along with the Containment property, and requires our broadcast schedule to be clustered based on data type and location. The structure of the location hierarchy requires the use of different types of indexes at different levels. The structure and positions of the index strictly depend on the location hierarchy as described earlier in the mapping scheme. The scheme is illustrated with the following example.

■ EXAMPLE 9.6

Two information types are used in the broadcast: (a) entertainment and (b) weather. Figure 9.22 illustrates the location tree for entertainment and weather. Ai represents Areas of City and Ri represents roads in certain areas. The leaves of Weather represent four cities. The index structure, along with the broadcast, is given in Figure 9.23. The major index contains Entertainment (E), Entertainment-Movie (EM), Entertainment-Restaurant (ER), and Weather (W). The tuple (S, L) represents the starting position (S) of the data item, and L represents the range of the item in terms of the number of data buckets. The minor index contains the variables A and R and a pointer, Next. Road R represents the first node of area A. The minor index is used to point to actual data buckets present at the lowest levels of the hierarchy. Index information is not incorporated in the data buckets. Index buckets are separate and contain only the control information. The number of major index buckets is $m = N(IC)$,

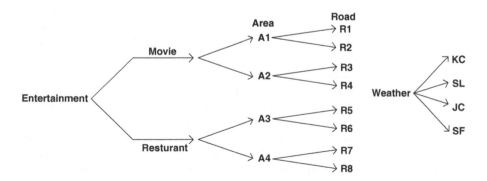

Figure 9.22 Broadcast location tree.

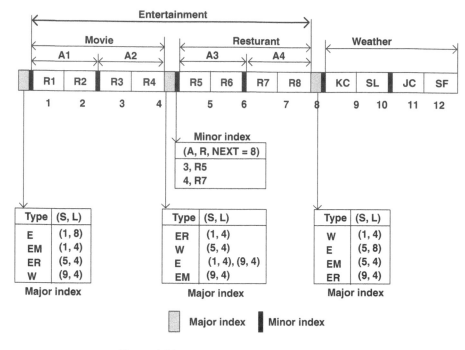

Figure 9.23   Broadcast composition with LBIS.

where $IC = \{ic_1, ic_2, \ldots, ic_n\}$ and ic_i represents information type and N represents the cardinality of IC. In this example, $IC = \{ic_{Movie}, ic_{Weather}, ic_{Restaurant}\}$ and $N(IC) = 3$. Hence, the number of major index buckets is 3.

The mechanism to resolve the query is present in the java-based coordinator in MU. For example, if a query Q is presented as Q (Entertainment, Movie, Road_1), then the resultant search will be for the EM information in the major index, that is, $Q \rightarrow EM$. Information request from a client is processed as follows. Let an MU issue a query (Restaurant information on Road 7, please). This is resolved by the coordinator as $Q \rightarrow ER$. This means that one has to search for the ER unit of the index in the major index. Suppose that the MU tunes the channel at R2. The first index it receives is a minor index after R2. In this index, the value of the Next variable is 4, which means that the next major index is present after bucket 4 and MU may go into doze mode. It becomes active after bucket 4 and receives the major index. It searches for the ER information, which is the first entry in this index. It is now certain that the MU will get the position of the data bucket in the adjoining minor index. The second unit in the minor index depicts the position of the required data R7. It indicates that the data bucket is the first bucket in Area 4. The MU goes into doze mode again and becomes active after bucket 6. It gets the required data in the next bucket.

The information access procedure is presented below:

```
Scan broadcast for the next index bucket,
found = false;
  While not found do
  R: if it is a Major Index bucket then
    Find the Type and Tuple (S, L)
    if S is greater than 1 then
      go in doze mode for S seconds
    end if
    Wake up at the Sth bucket and observe the Minor Index
  end if
  if it is a Minor Index bucket then
    if TypeRequested ≠ Typefound and (A,R)Request ≠ (A,R)found then
    Go in doze mode till NEXT and repeat from R
    end if
    else
      find entry in Minor Index which points to data;
      Compute time of arrival T of data bucket;
      Go into doze mode until time T;
      Wake up at T and access data;
      found = true
    end else
  end if
  end While
```

9.6 ON-DEMAND DATA SCHEDULING

In the push-based system, the server periodically broadcasts a schedule that is computed offline using user access history. This approach is also referred to as *static broadcast* that does not take into account the current data access pattern. The broadcast server composes a broadcast based on the popularity pattern and pushes the entire broadcast on to the wireless channel for users. Its performance is significantly affected when the user access pattern deviates from the one that was used to construct the broadcast schedule. In pull-based systems, which are commonly referred to as on-demand broadcast systems, clients explicitly request data items from the server. The server compiles the requests, and based on the number of pending data item requests, broadcasts the data. In earlier sections, the push-based broadcast was discussed where the broadcast was supported by different kinds of indexing. It is obvious that a push-based approach cannot handle specific requests from a user satisfactorily, and it gets worse if multiple users have orthogonal requests. This situation commonly occurs in transactional requests where a user-initiated transaction through a mobile unit may ask for a number of different data items. An example of this would be a travel planner transaction that makes a reservation for a car, hotel, plane, and so on, and makes the payment through a direct debit. If the mobile unit has to process this transaction, then it will need these data items from the server. A simpler way for the server would be to push these data items on the broadcast channel rather than sending them through a back channel directly to the mobile unit. This scheme may work for a handful of users requesting data items infrequently and would break down if the number of users or requests increases.

A better way to handle such requests is through a data pull using broadcast. This section deals with the pull-based approach for getting the desired data from the broadcast and presents a data scheduling scheme to handle on-demand multi-item requests. Earlier works [7, 18–28] on data scheduling have considered only single-item requests; but in reality, users invariably attempt to download multiple data items to process their requests. For example, database clients often access multiple data items to complete a read transaction. Similarly, web users access HTML documents along with all their embedded objects. In addition to multi-item requests, transactional requests have to handle issues such as consistency, application recovery, and so on.

Some algorithms [18, 22, 26, 27] for a pull-based broadcast system and a push-based broadcast setting are proposed in references 18, 24, and 28. In these approaches, the server delivers data using a periodic broadcast program, which is based on the estimation of the access probability of each data item. Its usefulness is limited to a static environment where access probabilities do not often change. In reference 7, broadcast scheduling algorithms for a hybrid push–pull environment are proposed where the server periodically broadcasts using a broadcast program. A part of the channel bandwidth is reserved for data items that are to be pulled by the client. The client issues a request to the server only after it has waited for a predefined duration for data to become available in a periodic push-based broadcast. Pull-based scheduling algorithms FCFS (First Come First Serve), MRF (Most Request First), MRFL (Most Request First Lowest), and LWF (Longest Wait First) were studied in references 26 and 27. In FCFS, pages are broadcasted in the order they are requested. In MRF, a page with the maximum number of pending requests is broadcasted. MRFL is similar to MRF, but it breaks ties in the favor of the page with the lowest request access probability. In LWF, the waiting time, which is the sum of waiting time for all pending requests for the page is calculated for all the pages. The page with the longest waiting time is broadcasted. It is shown in references 26 and 27 that FCFS performs poorly compared to other algorithms in a broadcast environment when the access pattern is nonuniform. Xuan et al. [22] studied on-demand systems where requests were associated with deadlines. They reported that on-demand broadcasts with an EDF (Earliest Deadline First) policy perform better. Aksoy and Franklin [18], proposed a scheduling algorithm, referred to as $R \times W$, where R stands for the number of pending requests and W stands for the waiting time of the arrival of the first request, which combines FCFS and MRF heuristics. The algorithm computes the product of R and W and selects the data item with the maximum $R \times W$ value for the next broadcasting. Liberatore [21] proposed a scheduling scheme for the push-based system with multi-item requests. The scheme uses the access pattern dependencies of the request as well as the probability of their access and presents a heuristic that exploits the page access dependencies to compute a static offline broadcast schedule.

The schedule presented here considers multi-item and transactional requests that raise new issues.

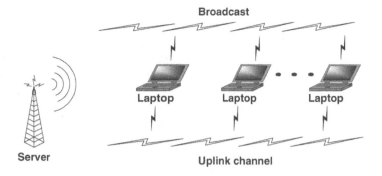

Figure 9.24 On-demand broadcast setup.

Figure 9.24 shows the architecture of a typical on-demand broadcast system. There is a single server that supports a large client population. A client sends queries or update transactions to the server through the uplink channel. The server broadcasts relevant information in response to the queries over the satellite downlink from where the user retrieves the result. Update transactions are executed at the server and the new values are broadcasted if there are requests for them. Similar to previous works on broadcast scheduling, it is assumed that all data items are locally available on the server and they are of equal size and, hence, they have equal service time. The broadcast duration of a data item is referred to as a *broadcast tick*.

One of the limitations of current broadcast scheduling schemes is that they make broadcast decisions at the data item level; that is, they compose a broadcast by considering only the requested set of data items. They do not consider the set of transactions that requested them. The following example illustrates this data access pattern. Table 9.2 lists a number of transactions (t_i) and the corresponding data items (d_i) they need. For example, transactions t_1 needs data items d_1, d_2, and d_7. The *Total* records the total number of transactions that require d_i. For example, data item d_1 is required by transactions t_1, t_3, and t_4. The server broadcasts data items requested by the clients using a scheduling algorithm.

Table 9.2   Transactions and Data Items They Need

t_i/d_i	d_1	d_2	d_3	d_4	d_5	d_6	d_7
t_1	1	1					1
t_2		1	1			1	
t_3	1		1	1			
t_4	1		1		1		
t_5		1		1			
Total	3	3	3	2	1	1	1

A scheduling decision based on the data item level causes consistency problems and also increases data access time. This is illustrated by the following example. The example uses the MRF (Most Request First) scheme because FCFS and $R \times W$ [18] schemes make broadcast decisions at the data item level. Under MRF, data items d_1, d_2, d_3, d_4, d_5, d_6, and d_7 will be scheduled starting from d_1 in one broadcast tick, d_2 will be in the next broadcast tick, and so on.

Consider t_1, which needs d_1, d_2, and d_7. Transaction t_1 gets d_1 and d_2 in the first two broadcast ticks and has to wait for d_7, which arrives in the 7th broadcast tick. This is because the scheduling algorithm makes a decision at the data item level. It has two important consequences: (a) for a single data item the transaction t_1 had to wait until the 7th broadcast tick and (b) in between the 2nd and 7th broadcast ticks, if there are updates to either d_1 or d_2, then transaction t_1 gets stale copies of d_1 and d_2, and the transaction has to be aborted. Another important issue is that the clients have to continuously monitor the broadcast to download their requested data items. There is no provision for broadcasting the data index because: (a) the scheduling decision is made at every broadcast tick, and consequently it cannot predict the data items to be broadcasted in the next broadcast ticks, and (b) the notion of periodicity and the broadcast cycle do not exist.

On-Demand Scheduling with Index. The broadcast scheduling scheme, similar to the push scheme discussed earlier, uses index for tuning. A number of parameters are defined before the scheme is explained.

Response Time. Response time includes (a) transaction wait time, (b) transaction seek time, and (c) transaction span. Figure 9.25 illustrates the relationship among these parameters.

Transaction Seek Time. It is the time between when a request is sent to the server and the first data item of the transaction is broadcasted; that is, $(b - a)$.

Transaction Span. It is the time between when the first and the last data items of the transaction are broadcasted $(b - c)$. The consistency issue is related to the transaction span. As the transaction span increases, the chances of the transaction having an inconsistent view of the data base increases. Hence, the scheduling algorithm aims to reduce the transaction span.

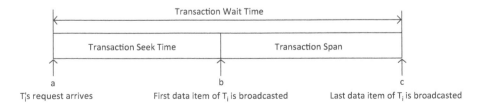

Figure 9.25 Transaction response time.

Transaction Wait Time. It is the time between the data request dispatch and the broadcast of data items. *Transaction wait time = Transaction seek time + Transaction span tuning time.*

Tuning Time. It is the total time the client listens to the broadcast channel.

The following parameters are used to compute the priority of a transactional request called the *temperature* of a transaction.

n = total number of data items in the database D

Database $D = \{d_1, d_2, \ldots, d_n\}$

R_{di} = number of requests for data item d_i

Data items accessed by transaction $t_i = TD_i$, where $TD_i \subseteq D$

num_i = number of data items accessed by transaction, $num_i = |TDi|$

T_{avg} = average transaction size

Temperature of a Transaction: Temp$_i$. It gives the measure of the number of hot data items (frequently accessed data items) that a transaction accesses. *Temp$_i$* is defined as the average number of requests per data item of the transaction. Thus, $Temp_i = \sum R_{di}/num_i$ for all $d_i \in TD_i$. For example, the temperature of transaction t_1 with $TD_1 = \{d_1, d_2, d_7\}$, $R_{d1} = 3$, $R_{d2} = 3$, $R_{d7} = 1$ and $num_i = 3$ is $= (3 + 3 + 1)/3 = 2.33$ (Table 9.2).

In this algorithm, scheduling decisions are taken at periodic intervals that are referred to as *broadcast cycles*. In the push-based system, the content and organization of a broadcast cycle, referred to as schedule, is the same in every cycle and the same schedule is repeatedly broadcast. However, unlike the push-based system, in this scheme the content and organization of each broadcast cycle may vary, depending on the current workload at the server. Thus, the notion of a broadcast cycle is used for introducing periodicity in broadcasts so that indexing can be used as an interval, after which updates at the server can be applied to the database. Each transaction requires a varying number of data items; as a result, it cannot define the exact number of data items in a broadcast cycle as in the case of single item requests. The broadcast cycle is an interval of broadcast ticks whose lengths vary between K to $(K + T_{avg})$ broadcast ticks. In the beginning of the broadcast cycle, the schedule for the current cycle is formed based on the current request volume at the server. The server calculates the temperature for all transactions that were requested by the client population. The transactions are sorted based on their $(Temp_i \times W_i)$ values. First, N transactions are selected from the sorted list so that their total data item requirement does not exceed $(K + T_{avg})$.

The arrangement of data items within the broadcast affects the transaction's span and tuning time. The data items are arranged in a broadcast cycle such that transactions whose data sets T_{Di} overlap are broadcasted together. This helps in reducing the transaction span and tuning time. The data are broadcasted in the order determined along with the index. The index contains the content and order of the data in the broadcast cycle. Update transactions that are received during a broadcast cycle are queued. They are executed at the end of the broadcast cycle and serialized in the order of their arrival. As a result, the state of the database changes only at the end of the broadcast cycle. Data broadcast within a broadcast cycle will always belong to the same database state and hence, are consistent. If the client downloads data from two different broadcast cycles, then it may get an inconsistent view of the database. The client side portion of this algorithm ensures that the client downloads the entire data set T_{Di} of the transaction from a single broadcast cycle by using the index in the broadcast. The algorithm running at the client ensures a consistent view for the client transactions and avoids aborts. The client, after sending the request to the server, monitors the broadcast for the next index and downloads it. If the client does not have its required data in the current broadcast cycle, then it can sleep until the end of the current cycle and tunes for the index in the next cycle.

Server Side Protocol. The term *Request* identifies the set of transactions requested by clients. *Bset* identifies the set of data items selected for broadcasting in the current cycle and *Tlist* identifies the set of transactions that are used to fill the current *Bset*.

1. **Calculating temperature of transactions:** In the beginning of the broadcast, the schedule for the cycle is formed based on the current request volume at the server. The server calculates the temperature of all the transactions in the *Request* set.
2. **Sorting the Request list:** Transactions in the *Request* set are sorted in descending order at the beginning of every broadcast cycle using $(Temp_i \times W_i)$ values, where W_i is the wait time of transaction t_i since its arrival at the server.
3. **Selection for transactions for current broadcast cycle:** Transactions are selected sequentially from the top of the *Request* set until the total data requirement of these transactions exceeds the length K of the broadcast cycle. The contents of set *Tlist* and *Bset* are identified here, and the selected transactions are added to the *Tlist* set and the data items of these transactions are added to the *Bset*.

Procedure

a. Let $Bset = \emptyset$, $Tlist = \emptyset$
b. While $(|\ Bset\ | < K)$
   i. Select next transaction t_i from the sorted *Request* set
     $Tlist = Tlist \cup t_i$
     $Request = Request - t_i$
   ii. $Bset = Bset \cup (TD_i - (Bset \cap TD_i)$
     $|\ Bset\ |$ will be in the range: $K \leq |\ Bset\ | \leq (K + T_{avg})$

---

4. **Arrangement of data items within the broadcast cycle:** The arrangement of data items within the broadcast cycle affects the transaction span and transaction waiting time. Initially the transaction with the highest value of $(Temp_i W_i)$

is selected. Its data items are added to the broadcast set, and then transaction $t_i \in$ *Tlist* is selected so that t_i has a maximum overlap with the broadcast set compared to other transaction $t_j \in$ *Tlist*. $Overlap_i/Rem_i$ is used to measure the overlap of the transaction, where $Overlap_i$ is the overlap of the transaction with the broadcast set and Rem_i is the number of transactions not selected in the broadcast set so far. The transaction t_i with the maximum value of $Overlap_i/Rem_i$ is selected. If there is a tie among the transactions, then transaction t_i with a higher value of $(Temp_i \times W_i)$ is selected. The data items are broadcasted in the same order, as they appear in the broadcast set.

Procedure

a. Broadcast $= \emptyset$

b. Select transaction t_i with the highest $Temp_i \times W_i$ value

c. Add the data items of the selected transaction that are not yet added to the broadcast set and remove the transaction from *Tlist*

    i. Broadcast $=$ Broadcast $\cup (TD_i - ($Broadcast $\cap TD_i))$.

    ii. Tlist $=$ Tlist $- t_i$

    iii. If (Tlist $= \emptyset$), then exit.

d. Calculate for every transaction $t_i \in$ *Tlist*

    i. The overlap of the transaction t_i with the Broadcast set as: $overlap_i =$ *Broadcast* $\cap TD_i$.

    ii. Number of Data items remaining to be broadcasted denoted by rem_i $rem_i = TD_i - overlap_i$.

e. Select transaction t_i with the highest value of $(overlap_i/rem_i)$. If there is a tie in the values $(overlap_i/rem_i)$ among transactions then from these transactions select the transaction that has the highest $Temp_i \times W_i$ value.

f. If $\mid Broadcast \mid \leq K$ then go to step c.

---

5. **Indexing:** Index is a directory of the list of data items that are to be broadcasted in the broadcast cycle. The $(1, m)$ indexing scheme [6] is used to create the index for this algorithm. In this method, the entire index is broadcasted at the beginning of every broadcast cycle and then after every (K/m) broadcast slot, where K is the length of the current broadcast cycle. The major index is at the beginning of every broadcast cycle and the minor index is broadcasted inside the broadcast cycle after every (K/m) broadcast slot. All indexes contain a pointer to the location of the next major index. The minor index contains the list of data items that are not yet broadcasted in the current broadcast cycle. In the push-based system there is no concept of a minor index. All indexes in the push-based system are of the same size and contain a list of the next K element to be broadcasted. In this algorithm, the ith minor index within the

cycle contains the list of $(K - i \times (K/m))$ data items yet to be broadcasted. The major index and all minor indexes that are broadcasted are stored at the server until the end of the current broadcast cycle. The minor indexes are also used for filtering out transactions that were not selected in *Tlist* but were satisfied in the current broadcast cycle.

6. **Broadcast data:** Data are broadcasted in the order determined in the broadcast set in the indexing step above. The major index is broadcasted followed by the data. Thereafter, the minor index is broadcasted after every $(K - i \times (K/m))$ broadcast tick.

7. **Filtering transactions:** At the end of the current broadcast cycle, transactions are removed from the *Request* set that were not selected in *Tlist* during the formation of contents of the current broadcast cycle but still are satisfied completely in the current cycle. Transactions that are filtered out belong to (a) transactions that arrive before the broadcast of the current cycle and (b) transactions that arrive after the broadcast of the current cycle began. A check is made to see if all the data required by the transaction are present in the *Bset* of the cycle to filter the transactions of the first type. If transaction t_i, $TD_i \subseteq Bset$, then t_i is removed from the *Request* set. To filter out transactions that arrived during the current broadcast cycle, the first minor index that was broadcasted after the transaction arrived is used. If the minor index contains all the data required by transaction t_i, then t_i is removed from the *Request* set. If no minor index was broadcasted after the transaction arrived, then the t_i is retained in the *Request* set.

Procedure

$T_{begin} = $ broadcast cycle start time and $T_i = $ transaction t_i arrival time
    For all the transactions that arrived by the end of the current broadcast cycle
      If $(T_i < T_{begin})$, then
        If $(TD_i \cap Bset = TD_i)$ then *Request* $=$ *Request* $- t_i$ Else
          Comment-Transaction arrived after the broadcast cycle began, that is,
          $T_i > T_{begin}$
      i. Select the next minor index (MI) that was broadcasted after time T_i
      ii. If $(TD_i \cap MI = TD_i)$, then *Request* $=$ *Request* $- t_i$

Client Side Protocol. The client sends a request for transaction t_i with data set TD_i to the server: and after sending the request, it tunes the broadcast channel for downloading the index. There are two possible cases: (a) the index could be a major index or (b) it could be a minor index. The client checks if the data required by the transaction are present in the current index; and if they are, then it tunes in the current cycle to download them. If it was the major index, then the client sleeps for the entire current broadcast cycle and tunes in for the next major index in the next broadcast cycle. If the index was a minor index, then it sleeps for the remaining part of the current cycle and tunes in to download the major index from the next broadcast cycle.

Procedure

- **Case 1:** Transaction arrived in the current broadcast cycle.

    a. Tune to download the next minor index.

    b. If $(TD_i \cap Minor\ Index = TD_i)$ then tune and download required data
    Else, tune in for the next major index and sleep

- **Case 2:** Transaction arrived in the previous broadcast cycle and no minor index was broadcasted.
    If $(TD_i \cap Major\ Index = TD_i)$, then tune and download required data
    Else, tune in for the next major index and sleep.

9.7 DATA DISSEMINATION SYSTEM

At present, there is no data dissemination system that supports pull, push, and hybrid schemes. In this section, a hybrid reference data dissemination system called **DAYS (DAta in Your Space)** is introduced. DAYS supports legacy systems (both centralized and distributed), facilitates the use of mobile transactions, allows the execution of location-dependent applications (retrieval and update), and allows users to retrieve and update data from broadcasts.

Figure 9.26 shows the architecture of DAYS. It consists of a *Broadcast scheduler*, *Data server*, and a *Local broadcast space*. The broadcast scheduler schedules push and on-demand data. The data server contains a series of data to be broadcasted that are stored in the pages along with some control information. The control information on each page are of three types: (a) **Broadcast type** (BT), (b) **Page type** (PT), and (c) **Time** (T). BT is a one-bit field with values 0 or 1. $BT = 0$ for popular and is

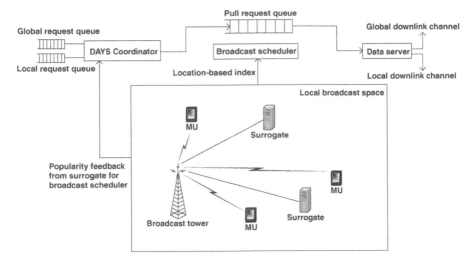

Figure 9.26   DAYS—DAta in Your Space.

intended to be pushed into the broadcast channel, and it is equal to 1 for the remaining pages that are to be pulled. The scheduler decides which page to push, depending on the popularity pattern generated by the DAYS coordinator. *PT* can be described as *PT(x,y)*, where *x* bits denote the page type and *y* bits denote the sequence number of the page type. As the size of the information generated can always increase or decrease, the value of *y* for a particular *x* varies continuously. *T* bits are used to timestamp the pages to identify their old and new versions.

The local broadcast space consists of (a) a broadcast tower for broadcasting data, (b) mobile units, and (c) the data staging machines called the *Surrogates*. Surrogates communicate with mobile units with the help of an 802.11 wireless LANS. They are also connected to the *File Server* that is present in the broadcast tower with a high-speed wired network. The file server periodically caches the broadcast pages. The advantages of a surrogate are numerous. Recent pushed data are cached in the surrogates so that the user may retrieve them if he misses them in a broadcast. This arrangement provides the DAYS coordinator useful information about the access patterns of the user that are used by the coordinator to prepare a popular push broadcast schedule. Some types of requests, such as a specific restaurant, or a hotel, or initiating a financial transaction for buying coffee from a shop, are user-specific. Some of them require update transactions that are not feasible in the push-based broadcast systems due to several reasons. First, the transactions may involve highly personal information such as credit/debit card numbers that cannot be included into the broadcast. It requires a direct exchange of data between the mobile user and the server. Second, it is not realistic to put the response of user-specific requests in the push-based channel because it may involve a significant time lag before the result may reach the user. Also, the user may have to tune the channel continuously for his required data. This is not acceptable for energy constrained mobile units. One solution to this problem is the use of a direct uplink and downlink channel between the mobile user and the data server. Present data rates in wireless channels do not allow these types of services. It is generally accepted that 4G networks will provide more than just wireless voice telecommunications. In fact, the main thrust of 4G technologies is to provide high-speed, high-bandwidth, and packetized data communications. It is expected that in 4G, even voice traffic will be delivered to the handset in packets (as opposed to delivery via dedicated circuit switching).

DAYS has a provision to manage global requests with the use of a separate global downlink channel that delivers to the distant destination through a combination of wireless channels and LEO satellites [29]. In today's world, users demand these types of value added services. With the introduction of 5G technologies, the wireless technologies not only provide voice communication but also possess Internet-like capabilities for doing update transactions.

9.7.1 Data Staging with Surrogates

Staging data in a surrogate allows users to extend their limited caching capacity. This is done by borrowing storage space from the surrogate and by a joint operation of the client proxy of the mobile user, the file server in the base station (broadcast tower),

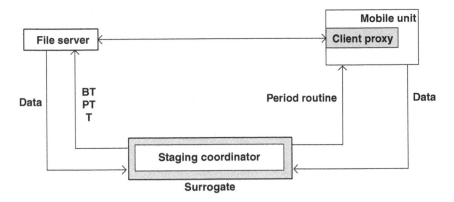

Figure 9.27 Data staging in DAYS.

and the surrogate where data are to be staged. The surrogate is connected to the file server with a high-speed wired network. It is only a single wireless hop away from the mobile unit and is connected by wireless technologies such as 802.11. The client proxy continuously monitors the data access operation of the mobile user. It maintains a log file into which it stores the three control information of each page: BT, PT, and T. The stored control information is for the broadcast and pages that are pulled by the user. Thus, it is able to store the information of the user access pattern without using much cache area. Since it is working internally and does not need to log on to the wireless channel continuously, the power consumption of the mobile unit does not increase. Based on the information stored in the log file, the proxy generates a periodic routine that contains the information about what the mobile user is most likely to access at any time. The routine contains the control information about the pushed data that is requested and the information about particular pulled data that have been frequently accessed by the user. The proxy continuously maintains and upgrades this routine.

Figure 9.27 shows the data staging architecture. It consists of a surrogate that is connected to the mobile user by wireless technologies such as 802.11 and to the file server with a high-speed wired network. The client proxy present in the mobile user has a periodic routine that contains information about the data the user is most likely to access at any point of time. Based on the amount of storage available, the surrogate allows the user to use a certain amount of space for staging data. The user sends the periodic routine to the surrogate. The time of the dispatch of the periodic routine is arbitrary. It may send it periodically or at the time the user requests the data. Since the public data are staged in the machine, we believe that proper handling of data storage in a surrogate can significantly increase the efficiency of data access and thus the overall latency time can be reduced. Figure 9.28 shows accesses of data from the surrogates by a mobile user. The overall aim of data staging is to allow the user to access data at a minimum latency. For this, we calculate a time bound, T_{bound}, for the user to access the data.

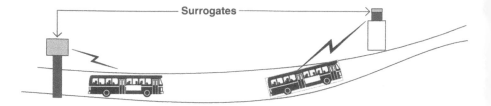

Figure 9.28   Data staging in DAYS.

Let time required for a broadcast $= n$ minutes. Thus, the total number of broadcasts in a day $= 24 \times 60/n$. Let size of the data pages $= M$ Kbytes. The channel bandwidth for broadcast $= B$ Kbps. So, the number of pages broadcast per second $= B/M$ pages. Let the approximate number of pages in a broadcast be N (N may vary, but it is fixed for this calculation). The total time taken for a broadcast is $N/(B/M) = ((N \times M)/B)$. Thus, the average wait for any page in the broadcast equals $((N \times M)/(2 \times B))$. Let the size of an index page be I Kbytes, where $I << M$. There is a time bound for accessing the index that is interleaved in the broadcast so that the user does not have to wait for the entire broadcast to access the index. Let the time bound for getting the index $T_{index} = x$, where $x << (N \times M)/B$ is the total time for each broadcast. Thus, on an average, the user has to wait for $T_{index}/2$ units of time to receive the index. So, the index should be broadcasted after every $(B/M) \times x$ number of pages by the base station. The time required for accessing data from the surrogate are the:

- Round-trip time (RTT) from the user to the surrogate.
- Search time (ST) required by the surrogate to check if data are present.
- File server access time (FSAT) needed by the surrogate to access data from the file server if data are not present in the surrogate.

The response time is $T_{resp} = RTT + ST + FSAT$ time units if data are not present in the surrogate; otherwise it is $T_{resp} = RTT + ST$ time units. Let p be the probability that data are found in the surrogate. The mobile unit contacts the file server with probability $(1 - p)$ when data are not found. The time bound for a user when contacting the surrogate is $T_{bound} = p \times RTT + ST + (1 - p)RTT + ST + FSAT$ or $T_{bound} = RTT + ST + (1 - p) \times FSAT$. The time RTT from the surrogate is about 60–80 msec. Also, the time ST required by the surrogate to search for the data in the surrogate is on the order of milliseconds. Thus, it is $FSAT$ that effectively determines the T_{bound}. The client proxy at any time updates the periodic routine from the log file of the mobile unit. If the user is requesting the data, it first accesses the index from the broadcast and checks the index to see if the required data are there. If the data are not present in the broadcast, it contacts the surrogate. If the data are present in the broadcast, then the proxy checks the T control bit of the data. It matches the T control bit of the data from the index with the T bit present in its periodic routine. If it is the same as in the periodic routine, it means that the data being broadcasted are the last modified data that have been accessed earlier by the user. So the data must be present either in the cache or in the surrogate, and the user accesses the data. If T doesn't match, which means that the data present in the broadcast are the most recent ones, then the client proxy calculates the time for which it will have to wait for accessing the data. This can be done with the help of the t bit of the index. If the time required is less than the T_{bound}, then the proxy waits for the broadcast data. If the time is greater than T_{bound}, then the client proxy doesn't wait for the broadcast and moves on to access the data from the surrogate. It sends the periodic routine or the control information of the data requested to the surrogate. The periodic routine contains control information BT, PT, and T for any requested page. There is a *staging coordinator* (Figure 9.27) that handles the staging of data for the registered clients. The *staging coordinator* first searches the storage area of the surrogate and if found, then it delivers the data to the user if there is a request for it. Otherwise, it gets the periodic routine and sends it to the file server through a high bandwidth network. The file server releases the corresponding data to the staging coordinator. The file server maintains a hit count for each type of page. *Hit count* is the total number of times a data item is accessed or staged in a surrogate. When a page is pulled from the server, or staged to a surrogate, the hit count of that page is incremented. Thus, the hit count of any page gives the file server the information about the number of accesses of that page. When the data for any particular client are accessed from the file server, the *staging coordinator* creates a directory of that type of data using the $PT(x)$ bits of the pages. The $PT(y)$ bit is then used to sequence the data in that directory. When the data are staged, the coordinator informs the client proxy about the arrival of the data. Now if the user wants to access the data, the client proxy picks up the data from the staging machine and makes it available to the user.

9.8 SUMMARY

This chapter discussed the wireless and mobile data dissemination discipline. It started from a brief history of data broadcast and analyzed (in detail) a number of schemes to make necessary data available to people. The discussion began from different modes of data dissemination and two basic approaches, that is, *push* and *pull*. A number of schemes were developed to satisfy the ever-growing data requirements of users. Realizing the potential of data broadcasts in reaching people across the world, researchers began to use the wireless channel space as a persistence storage media. This motivated the development of the broadcast disk followed by a number of air indexing schemes. This chapter discussed (in detail) these developments and a data dissemination system called *DAYS* (*DAta in Your Space*). The *DAYS* system offers location-dependent transactional activity as well as query facilities.

EXERCISES

9.1 Investigate the situations where data broadcast on a wireless channel can play a significant role. Give examples.

9.2 Investigate how data flow through a wireless channel. If a data stream is continuously dispatched on the same channel, then the channel can serve as a stable storage similar to a conventional disk. Thus, the broadcast server could continuously store all its data on a set of channels and eliminate the hard disk altogether. Is this type of storage model acceptable? Explore and explain the issues and problems this model could have.

9.3 Discuss the pull and the push model of data dissemination. Identify some real-world cases where these models are utilized. What type of model (push or pull) would you recommend for data dissemination to reach data consumers? Discuss the advantages and disadvantages of your selection.

9.4 Discuss the concept of broadcast disks. Compare data storage and access costs of using a broadcast disk and a conventional disk for storing the same size of database. Show your computation.

9.5 Explain the purpose of a broadcast index. Suppose you want to broadcast the same information again and again on a single channel. Would this dissemination require an index? Explain.

9.6 Compare the mechanism of centralized, distributed, and nonclustering indexing. Identify the some real-life data dissemination scenario and match them with the most suitable indexing scheme.

9.7 Discuss a wish list of requirements for efficient on-demand scheduling? If you think that the existing indexing schemes do not perform well, then develop your own.

REFERENCES

1. S. Sheng, A. Chandrasekaran, and R. W. Broderson, A Portable Multimedia Terminal for Personal Communication, *IEEE Communications*, December 1992, pp. 64–75.

2. L. William, *Mobile Cellular TeleCommunication Systems*, McGraw-Hill, New York, 1989.

3. C. Partridge, *Gigabit Networking*, Addision-Wesley Professional Computing Series, Reading, MA, 1993.

4. T. Bowen, G. Gopal, G. Herman, T. Hickey, K. Lee, W. Mansfield, J. Reitz, and A. Weinrib, The Datacycle Architecture, *Communications of the ACM*, Vol. 35, No. 12, December 1992, 71–81.

5. T. Käpylä, I. Niemi, and A. Lehtola, Towards an Accessible Web by Applying PUSH Technology. In *ERCIM Workshop on User Interface for All*, Stockholm, October 19–21, 1998, pp. 133–147.

6. T. Imielinski, S. Vishwanath, and B. Badrinath, Energy Efficient Indexing on Air. In *Proceedings, ACM-SIGMOD, International Conference on Management of Data*, Minnesota, May 1994, pp. 25–36.

7. S. Acharya, R. Alonso, M. Franklin, and S. Zdonik, Broadcast Disks: Data Management for Asymmetric Communication Environments. In *Proceedings of ACM SIGMOD Conference*, CA, 1995, pp. 199–210.

8. A. Datta, A. Celik, D. E. VanderMeer, and V. Kumar, Adaptive Broadcast Protocols to Support Efficient and Energy Conserving Retrieval from databases in Mobile Computing

Environments, *ACM Transactions on Database Systems (TODS)*, Vol. 24, No. 1, March 1999, 1–79.

9. D. Acharya and V. Kumar, Indexing Location Dependent Data in Broadcast Environment, *JDIM, Special Issue on Distributed Data Management*, 2005, pp. 114–118.

10. D. Acharya and V. Kumar, Location based Indexing Scheme for DAYS. In *MobiDE05, Sigmod05 Workshop*, Baltimore, MD, 2005, pp. 17–24.

11. M. S. Chen, K. L. Wu, and P. S. Yu, Optimizing Index Allocation for Sequential Data Broadcasting in Wireless Mobile Computing, *IEEE Transaction on Knowledge and Data Engineering (TKDE)*, Vol. 15, No. 1, January/February 2003, pp. 161–173.

12. T. Imielinski, S. Vishwanath, and B. Badrinath, Power Efficient Filtering of Data on Air. *Proceedings 4th International Conference Extending Database Technology (EDBT)*, Cambridge, UK, March 1994, pp. 245–258.

13. N. Shivakumar and S. Venkatasubramanian, Energy-Efficient Indexing for Information Dissemination in Wireless Systems, *ACM/Baltzr Journal of Mobile Network and Applications (MONET)*, Vol. 1, No. 4, December 1996.

14. T. Imielinski, S. Vishwanath, and B. Badrinath, Data on Air: Organization and Access, *IEEE Transactions on Konwledge and Data Engineering*, Vol. 9. No. 3, May/June 1997, 353–372.

15. J. Xu, W. C. Lee, and X. Tang, Exponential Index: A Parameterized Distributed Indexing Scheme for Data on Air. In *Proceedings 2nd ACM/USENIX International Conference on Mobile Systems, Applications, and Services (MobiSys)*, Boston, June 2004, pp. 153–164.

16. S. Viswanathan, Publishing in Wireless and Wireline Environments, Ph.D. dissertation, at Rutgers State University, New Jersey, 1994.

17. N. Garg, V. Kumar, and M. Dunham, Information Mapping and Indexing in DAYS. In *6th International Workshop on Mobility in Databases and Distributed Systems*, in conjunction with the *14th International Conference on Database and Expert Systems Applications*, September 1–5, Prague, Czech Republic, 2003, pp. 951–955.

18. D. Aksoy and M. Franklin, Scheduling for Large-Scale On-Demand Data Broadcasting. In *Proceedings of IEEE Infocom*, CA, 1998, pp. 651–659.

19. M. Franklin and S. Zdonik, Dissemination-Based Information Systems, *IEEE Data Engineering Bulletin*, Vol. 19, No. 3, September 1996, 19–28.

20. S. Acharya and S. Muthukrishnan, Scheduling On-Demand Data Broadcasts: New Metrics and Algorithms. In *Proceedings of 4th Annual ACM/IEEE International Conference on Mobile Computing and Networking*, 1998, pp. 43–54.

21. V. Liberatore, Multicast Scheduling for List Requests. In *Proceedings of IEEE Infocom*, CA, 2002, pp. 1129–1137.

22. P. Xuan, S. Sen, O. Gonzalez, J. Fernandez, and K. Ramamritham, Broadcast On-Demand: Efficiently and Timely Disseminating of Data in Mobile Environment, In *the third IEEE Real-Time Technology and Applications Symposium (RTAS'97)*, 1997, pp. 38–48.

23. K. Stathatos, N. Roussopoulos, and J. S. Baras, Adaptive Data Broadcast in Hybrid Networks, In *Proceedings of the 23rd VLDB Conference*, Athens, Greece, 1997, pp. 326–335.

24. S. Su and L. Tassiulas, Broadcast Scheduling for Information Distribution, In *Sixteenth Annual Joint Conference of the IEEE Computer and Communications Societies. Driving the Information Revolution., Proceedings INFOCOM'97*, 1997, pp. 109–117.

25. M. Karakaya, Evaluation of a Broadcast Scheduling Algorithm, *Lecture Notes in Computer Science*, Vol. 2151, 2001, 182–195.

26. J. W. Wong, Broadcast Delivery, *Proc. IEEE*, Vol. 76, No. 12, December 1988, 1566–1577.

27. H. D. Dykeman, M. H. Ammar, and J. W. Wong, Scheduling Algorithms for Videotex Systems under Broadcast Delivery. In *Proceedings of IEEE International Conference on Communications, ICC '86*, 1986, pp. 1847–1851.

28. N. Vaidya and S. Hameed, Data Broadcast in Asymmetric Wireless Environments. In *First International Workshop on Satellite-based Information Services (WOSBIS)*, 1996.

29. S. Freyth and S. Hartmeier, Introduction to Low Earth Orbit Sattellite, *Communication Network*, 1998.

CHAPTER 10

INTRODUCTION TO SENSOR TECHNOLOGY

This chapter provides a brief history of the concept of sensing that led to the development of the electronic sensors we see today. It then briefly discusses the evolution of a sensor network that forms the backbone of sensor technology. It begins with different types of sensors and explains their workings through a simple block diagram. It then talks about sensor networks that are effectively deployed to collect the type of data they are programmed for. The objective of this chapter is to introduce a type of data called *stream data* that is captured by sensor networks. It discusses the properties of stream data and talks about its management.

The concept of sensing some aspects of an activity seems to go as far back as 1594 when Galileo experimented with a water pump and discovered that 10 meters was the limit to which the water would rise in the suction pump, but was unable to provide any explanation. Then, in around 1644, an Italian physicist, Evangelista Torricelli, experimented with a column of mercury and observed that the column of mercury, when filled in a 1-meter-long tube (closed at one end), settled at about 760 mm from the bottom, leaving an empty space above its level. He could not find any explanation for this drop but used it to sense some force of the earth. A number of scientists (Pascal in 1648, Offo von in 1656, Robert Boyle in 1661, Joseph Gay-Lussac in 1820, and so on) continued to lay the foundation of the sensing process.

It was in 1930 that the sensing process was actually defined the way it is understood today. In 1938, the bonded gauges were developed independently by E. E. Simmons of Caltech and A. C. Ruge of MIT. The development in sensor technology moved further along, and the sensor age started in 1967 when Art R. Zias and John Egan of

Fundamentals of Pervasive Information Management Systems, Revised Edition. Vijay Kumar.
© 2013 John Wiley & Sons, Inc. Published 2013 by John Wiley & Sons, Inc.

Honeywell Research Center in Minneapolis patented their edge-constrained silicon diaphragm. This was followed by the patent of Hans W. Keller for the batch-fabricated silicon sensor in 1969.

Then came the age of sensor networks. In 1978, the Defense Advanced Research Projects Agency (DARPA) organized the Distributed Sensor Nets Workshop (DAR 1978), focusing on sensor network research challenges such as networking technologies, signal processing techniques, and distributed algorithms. DARPA also operated the Distributed Sensor Networks (DSN) program in the early 1980s, which was then followed by the Sensor Information Technology (SensIT) program. In collaboration with the Rockwell Science Center, the University of California at Los Angeles proposed the concept of Wireless Integrated Network Sensors or WINS [1]. One outcome of the WINS project was the Low PowerWireless Integrated Microsensor (LWIM), produced in 1996 [2]. This smart sensing system was based on a CMOS chip, integrating multiple sensors, interface circuits, digital signal processing circuits, a wireless radio, and a microcontroller onto a single chip. The Smart Dust project [3] at the University of California at Berkeley focused on the design of extremely small sensor nodes called motes. The goal of this project was to demonstrate that a complete sensor system can be integrated into tiny devices, possibly the size of a grain of sand or even a dust particle.

The PicoRadio project [4] by the Berkeley Wireless Research Center (BWRC) focused on the development of low-power sensor devices, whose power consumption is so small that they can power themselves from energy sources of the operating environment, such as solar or vibrational energy. The MIT AMPS (micro-Adaptive Multidomain Power-aware Sensors) project also focused on low-power hardware and software components for sensor nodes, including the use of microcontrollers capable of dynamic voltage scaling and techniques to restructure data processing algorithms to reduce power requirements at the software level [5]. While these previous efforts are mostly driven by academic institutions, over the last decade a number of commercial efforts have also appeared (many based on some of the academic efforts described above), including companies such as Crossbow (www.xbow.com), Sensoria (www.sensoria.com), Worldsens (http://worldsens.citi.insa-lyon.fr), Dust Networks (http://www.dustnetworks.com), and Ember Corporation (http://www.ember.com). These companies provide the opportunity to purchase sensor devices ready for deployment in a variety of application scenarios along with various management tools for programming, maintenance, and sensor data visualization.*

10.1 INTRODUCTION TO SENSORS

A *sensor* or a *transducer* is a device that captures external input (physical action, RF or audio–video signals, etc.) and transforms it into an output (physical activity,

---

*This history is adopted from the book Fundamentals of Wireless Sensor Networks by W. Dargie and C. Poellabauer [6] under written permission from John Wiley & Sons.

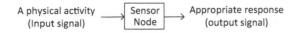

Figure 10.1 A typical sensor node.

light, sound, etc.). In other words, an external command is accepted by a sensor, and it outputs the desired results corresponding to the input command. For example, if a hand is waved (external physical action) in front of a paper towel dispenser, then the unit captures the hand movement and the software interprets this as a request for a piece of paper towel and dispenses the towel. The transformation is done by the embedded program. In the United States and other places, the term used is *sensor*, but in Europe, *transducer* is more commonly used. In this book, the term "sensor" is used. Figure 10.1 illustrates the function of a sensor.

There are many ways to classify sensor types. According to one approach, sensors can be classified as *active* and *passive*. An active sensor pushes some specific type (RF, light, etc.) of signal into the environment and records the interaction between the signal and the environment. Sonar, radar, and metal detectors are a few examples. A passive sensor, on the other hand, pulls existing signals from the environment and interprets the capture. For example, a camera, thermometer, and so on, capture existing signals and record the result. Human eyes, ears, noses, skin types, and so on, are passive sensors that introduce the information about the environment to the human mind.

Table 10.1 lists some common physical entities and types of sensors deployed to capture data representing these entities.

Table 10.1 Physical Entities and Sensor Types

Physical Entities	Sensor Types
Temperature	Thermistors, thermocouples
Pressure	Pressure gauges, barometers, ionization gauges
Optical	Photodiodes, phototransistors, infrared sensors, CCD sensors
Acoustic	Piezoelectric resonators, microphones
Mechanical	Strain gauges, tactile sensors, capacitive diaphragms, piezoresistive cells
Motion, vibration	Accelerometers, gyroscopes, photo sensors
Flow	Anemometers, mass air flow sensors
Position	GPS, ultrasound-based sensors, infrared-based sensors, inclinometers
Electromagnetic	Hall-effect sensors, magnetometers
Chemical	pH sensors, electrochemical sensors, infrared gas sensors
Humidity	Capacitive and resistive sensors, hygrometers, MEMS-based humidity sensors
Radiation	Ionization detectors, Geiger–Mueller counters

Source: Reproduced from W. Dargie and C. Poellabauer, [6] *Fundamentals of Wireless Sensor Networks*, under written permission from John Wiley & Sons.

In recent years, the processing power and the storage capacity of sensors have improved significantly. As a result of these enhancements, sensors have become an essential component of nearly every functional unit (cameras, appliances, watches, garage doors, etc.). A sensor is no longer just an input device, but a programmable, low-cost, low-power, multifunctional *atomic processing unit* that can be networked together to create a truly distributed system. Every node of this network has data processing capabilities (data capture, data validation, and data dispatch) and may function autonomously without going out of sync with other nodes of the network. Each node can be reprogrammed locally or remotely to append necessary capability anytime, and the network topology can be made adaptable to the task it is deployed to complete. Thus, the fully connected information space illustrated in Chapter 2 can only be achieved through all kinds of sensor networks.

A sensor unit (or node) has two main components: (a) *the hardware that captures the external physical action* and (b) *the software* that interprets and transforms the external input (action, RF signal, etc.) to the desired output (action, audio, video, RF signals, etc.) This makes a sensor a multifunctional device that can be programmed to accept any type of input, process the input data and generate the desired result (output). In this book, a sensor node will always mean the following: *Sensor node = {hardware components + software modules}*.

The definition presented here is quite general and in accordance with a device that accepts an input is a sensor. For example, a camera is a sensor, a thermometer is a sensor, the human eye is a sensor, and so on. The discussion in this book refers to a sensing device that can be programmed for a specific task—for example, programmed to sense temperature, humidity, capture audio signals, and so on.

10.1.1   Hardware and Software Components

A generic layout of a sensor node is illustrated in Figure 10.2. It includes memory (Flash or SRAM or both), a software stack, an RF transceiver, a power supply unit, an

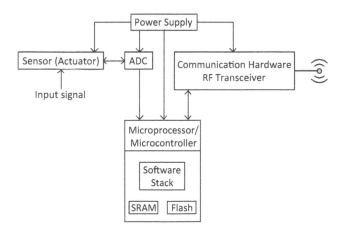

Figure 10.2   Architecture and function of a sensor node.

ADC (analog to digital converter) or a DAC (digital to analog converter) or both, and sensing hardware. The activities of these components can be represented in terms of the following processes:

Amplification. A sensor accepts the input signals. These raw signals are usually quite low in voltage (or current) and cannot be processed for generating corresponding output. For example, an analog signal from a record player, or a signal from a thermostat, and so on, must be amplified before it is processed.

Buffering. A buffer stores data (signal, text, etc.) to be processed at a later time. This becomes necessary for many reasons. If the data capture rate is higher than its processing, then it is buffered to avoid data loss. For example, some DSLRs (Digital SLR) use "Smart" buffering that achieves higher frames per second (fps). Thus, as soon as the shutter is pressed, the input sensor captures and buffers the image's raw data. The buffering helps to achieve a continuous shooting mode (multiple pictures per second). The raw image data are processed and written to another buffer before the image is written to the storage card (flash cards). These steps take place concurrently.

Comparing. A comparator is a chip that compares two input signals (light, temperature, humidity, etc.) and outputs a result, depending upon the circuit logic. Thus, a comparator enables a sensor to compare two numbers and make a decision. For example, if one input is $+6$ V and the second is -3 V, then the sensor output could be $+6$ V. It can also be used to confirm if an input signal exceeds or is below a defined threshold. It does not generate any output if the input signal voltage is less than a defined threshold, and so on.

Data Conversion. It converts an analog signal to its equivalent digital signal and vice versa. For example, if the output of a sensor has to be stored and processed by PCs or displayed on to a TV, or on any other display device, then the analog input must be converted into a digital signal. This conversion is done by an analog-to-digital converter (ADC). In the case when the input is a digital signal, then a digital-to-analog converter (DAC) is required.

The functions of the hardware components of Figure 10.2 can be described as follows:

Energy and Power Unit. The common power sources are alkaline batteries because they provide a high energy density at an inexpensive price. There are some other sources of power such as solar cell, rechargeable batteries, fuel cells, and so on. Although they are better sources of power supply in terms of power delivery, they are not that convenient to use. Rechargeable batteries are not a better option because they have lower energy density, the cost is high, and the need to recharge makes them impractical. For some nodes, neither option is appropriate, that is, they will simply be discarded once their energy source is depleted. Whether the battery can be recharged or not, significantly affects the strategy applied to energy consumption. For nonrechargeable batteries, a sensor node should be able to operate until either its mission time has passed or the battery can be replaced. The length of the mission time depends on the type of application; for example, scientists monitoring glacial movements may need sensors that can operate for several years while a sensor in a battlefield scenario may only be needed for a few hours or days. This defines the common need of using energy efficiently in every deployment and layer of a WSN. For example, the choices made at the physical layer of a sensor node affect the energy consumption of the entire device and the design of higher-level protocols [7].

The medium access control (MAC) layer is responsible for providing sensor nodes with access to the wireless channel. Some MAC strategies for communication networks are contention-based; that is, nodes may attempt to access the medium at any time, potentially leading to collisions among multiple nodes, which must be addressed by the MAC layer to ensure that transmissions will eventually succeed. The downside of these approaches include the energy overhead and delays incurred by the collisions and recovery mechanisms. Also, the sensor nodes may have to listen to the medium at all times to ensure that no transmissions will be missed. Therefore, some MAC protocols for sensor networks are contention-free; that is, access to the medium is strictly regulated, eliminating collisions and allowing sensor nodes to shut down their radios when no communications are expected. The network layer is responsible for finding routes from a sensor node to the base station, and route characteristics such as length (e.g., in terms of number of hops), required transmission power, and available energy on relay nodes that determine the energy overhead of multihop communication. Besides network protocols, the goal of energy efficiency impacts the design of the operating system (e.g., small memory footprint, efficient switching between tasks), middleware, security mechanisms, and even the applications themselves. For example, in-network processing is frequently used to eliminate redundant sensor data or to aggregate multiple sensor readings. This leads to a trade-off between computation (processing the sensor data) and communication (transmitting the original versus the processed data), which can often be exploited to obtain energy savings [8, 9].

Data Processing. The data processing and other activities such as communication are performed by a central processing unit (CPU). The CPU determines the processing power and energy consumption of a sensor node. A sensor may integrate a number of different types of CPUs or manage its processing with a single type. Commercially available CPUs can be identified as microcontrollers, microprocessors, and Field-Programmable Gate Arrays (FPGAs). Each type has its share of advantages and issues. For example, FPGAs consume more power and they are not compatible with some of the high-level programming languages (they do not have a C compiler), but this could change in the future. At present, microcontrollers (MCUs) are commonly used in sensor nodes mainly because of their low power consumption. They have lower clock speeds (a few megahertz), and the memory requirements are determined by the application and the tasks they have to perform. For example, Medusa MK-2 of UCLA and BTnodes of ETHZ use Atmel AVR (a RISC microcontroller), which is a low-cost processor and uses power of about 1500 picoJoules/instruction. Future microcontrollers may have more controlling power and use less energy.

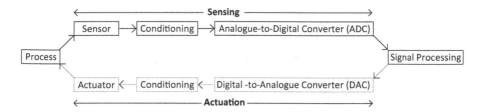

Figure 10.3 Data acquition and actuation. (Reproduced from W. Dargie and C. Poellabauer, [6] *Fundamentals of Wireless Sensor Networks*, under written permission from John Wiley & Sons.)

The software stack stores the software modules (protocols and other system programs) required for data processing. It is a critical component so it must be very small (should be able to fit into an MCPU RAM of about 128KB) and energy-efficient. There are quite a few types of stacks to choose from; however, a chosen stack must be compatible to the MCU.

An example of the steps performed in a sensing (or data acquisition) task is shown in Figure 10.3. The electrical signals that are captured by the sensing device are often not ready for immediate processing, therefore they pass through a signal conditioning where a variety of operations (data cleaning, validation, etc.) are applied to the captured signals to prepare them for further processing. For example, signals often require amplification (or attenuation) to change the signal magnitude to better match the range of the following analog-to-digital conversion. Further, signal conditioning often applies filters to the signal to remove unwanted noise within certain frequency ranges (e.g., high-pass filters can be used to remove 50 or 60 Hz of noise picked up by surrounding power lines). After conditioning, the analog signal is transformed into a digital signal using an analog-to-digital converter (ADC). The signal is now available in a digital form and ready for further processing, storing, or visualization.

The use of actuators is also shown in Figure 10.3. This usage allows WSN to directly control the real-world tasks. For example, an actuator can be a valve controlling the flow of hot water, a motor that opens or closes a door or window, or a pump that controls the amount of fuel injected into an engine. Such a wireless sensor and actuator network (WSAN) takes commands from the processing device (controller) and transforms these commands into input signals for the actuator, which then interacts with a physical process, thereby forming a closed control loop. Further details about this process can be found in reference 6.

10.1.2 Software Component

It is a micro information processing unit that processes the input data captured by the hardware. The type of processing depends on the software components installed in the sensor. This book focuses on the data-centric aspects of a wireless sensor. Since a data-centric task needs a network of wireless sensors, a detailed discussion on a sensor network or *sensornet* is presented.

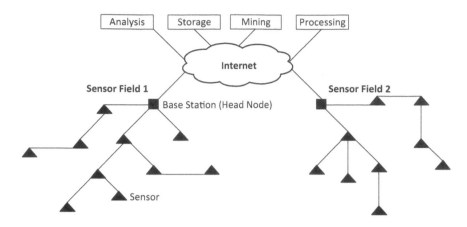

Figure 10.4 Wireless sensor network (WSN) (Reproduced from W. Dargie and C. Poellabauer, [6] *Fundamentals of Wireless Sensor Networks*, under written permission from John Wiley & Sons.)

10.1.3 Wireless Sensor Network

Any data collection application requires a large number of sensor nodes (hundreds or thousands). These sensors are connected together to form a network that is usually referred to as a wireless sensor network (WSN). A WSN is an application-specific network of sensors that may contain many different types of sensor nodes. The structure of WSNs is common; that is, a defined set of different types of sensors are networked together to complete a selected task. For example, a WSN to monitor the health of a bridge may contain a set of sensors to measure the vibration, temperature, stress, and so on. A WSN, therefore, is a real-time data collection, data communication, and data processing system.

Figure 10.4 illustrates a communication setup with two WSNs, each one monitoring (data collection, validation, processing, etc.) two different geographic regions and connecting them to the internet using their base stations (head nodes). It is important to highlight the difference and similarities of a WSN and an *ad hoc wireless network*. A WSN usually contains a larger number (hundreds) of sensors (nodes), but it depends on the task. An ad hoc network, on the other hand, usually has a far less number of nodes that are relatively more powerful and usually are far less energy-constrained. From an operational viewpoint, sensor nodes of a WSN usually need less manual intervention since they can continue to collect data after the WSN is deployed. Since sensor nodes can join and leave a WSN anytime, the question of trust becomes quite important. An ad hoc network may not have these problems.

WSNs need communication protocol to function. The IEEE 802.11 family of standards was introduced in 1997 for mobile systems. It uses different frequency bands (2.4-GHz by IEEE 802.11b and IEEE 802.11g and 5-GHz by IEEE 802.11a protocol). The high energy consumption of 802.11 made it unsuitable for low-power sensor networks. Typical data rate requirements in WSNs are comparable to the bandwidths provided by dial-up modems, therefore, the data rates provided by IEEE 802.11 are typically much higher than needed. This motivated the development of energy-efficient protocols called the IEEE 802.15.4 protocols.

A number of WSNs having different topologies are usually embedded in large network applications. As a result, these WSNs are also referred to as embedded sensor networks. The concept of *Embedded Sensor Space (ESS)* is defined first to discuss the architecture of embedded WSNs.

Definition 10.1 *An ESS is a set of uniquely programmed sensors. Thus, ESS =* $\{s_1, s_2, \ldots, s_\infty\}$*, where s_i (i = 1, 2, ...,∞) are a set of programmable sensor.*

A well-defined set of sensors of ESS is used to form a WSN to perform a specific task. In this book, a WSN that performs a specific task is referred to as an *embedded sensor network (ESN)*. Thus, an ESN could be deployed to regulate the temperature and humidity of a warehouse. An ESN must provide reliable and accurate information and must have the highest degree of availability. To achieve these capabilities, multiple nodes of the same type are connected to the ESN. For example, to measure the temperature in a room, more than one node is connected to the ESN and the final temperature reading is obtained from the data provided by these replicated nodes. Usually, an ESN sensor node collects, validates, and dispatches the reading to a common sensor that is referred to as a *headnode*.

In a network of devices (sensor, processors, printers, etc.), a node has a specific address (IP address) that uniquely identifies the node and is used to communicate with it. Thus, a node in this type of network can send data directly to a specific node using its IP address. In an ESN, where the data stored is more important than the node itself, naming a node through an IP address is not very efficient. This is one of the reasons that sensors in an ESN broadcast their data and the recipient nodes capture the required data from the broadcast. An ESN, therefore, allows the stored data to be named and can be uniquely accessed. The property of the stored data (location, type, column, etc.) can be used to create a unique name. Since this book mainly deals with data-centric activities, the ESN refers to data-centric networks.

Definition 10.2 *A data-centric sensor network is a data-centric storage (DCS) where each sensor data has a unique name. Thus, ESN = $\{< s_1, n_1 >, < s_2, n_2 >,$ $\ldots, < s_\infty, n_\infty >\}$, where s_i is a sensor node and n_i is the unique name of the data stored at s_i.*

A node of an ESN or a sensornet may itself be a network of sensors (micro-sensornet). A micro-sensornet is a set of a small number of fully connected specialized sensors. The headnode of a micro-sensor net is responsible for coordinating the activities of its sensors in the set. The selection of a headnode depends on a number of factors that depend on the type and functions of the ESN. However, the node that has relatively more storage and processing power and is connected to all other nodes is selected as a headnode.

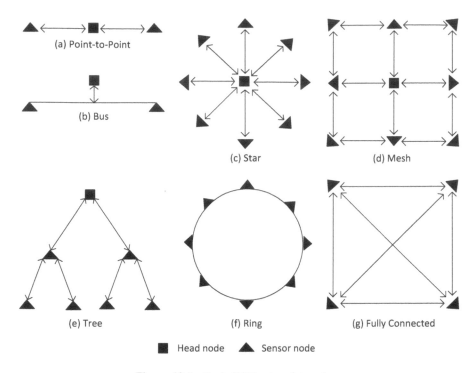

Figure 10.5   Basic ESN network topology.

The unique properties of sensors allow the network to link them in three basic topologies: *point-to-point, star,* and *mesh.* Thus, it is possible to build a globally connected infrastructure where uniquely programmed sensors are embedded at desired places. For example, programmed sensors may be embedded at various points in cars, in the house, in the office, in children's school bags, in parents' briefcases, and so on. On a large scale, ESNs can be deployed at various places (buildings, malls, factories, etc.) of a city for continuous monitoring of events for managing security. Similarly, to protect the water supply, gas pipelines, and so on, programmed sensors can be deployed at strategic locations. Figure 10.5 illustrates basic ESN topologies. A single ESN may include a combination of some of these topologies.

Point-to-Point. This setup represents a direct link between two or more sensor nodes and the presence of a head node may be optional. Figure 10.5a illustrates point-to-point topology. The sensor node broadcasts the message that is captured by the next node in the setup. If this node is not the recipient node, then it broadcasts the message and the next node captures it. Finally, the message is captured by the recipient node.

Bus. In this topology, bus (not the system bus) carries the broadcast message for all nodes. Each node identifies its message through the header packet and downloads it for processing. A node passively listens to the broadcast and does not retransmit any message. Figure 10.5b illustrates this topology.

Star. This topology is a combination of point-to-point setups where the headnode can communicate with all other nodes. Thus, the headnode must have greater processing, message handling, and routing capabilities. Since the headnode is the hub, the topology suffers with a single point of failure problem. However, a single node (other than the headnode) failure does not affect the communication. The star topology is shown in Figure 10.5c.

Mesh. This topology is also referred to as *peer-to-peer*. The inclusion of a headnode is optional. It contains a number of routes, and as a result, a destination node can receive the same broadcast through a number of routes. In a mesh, a node may be directly connected (one hop) to all other nodes. This type of mesh is called a *fully connected mesh*. Some WANs, most notably the Internet, employ mesh routing. Figure 10.5d shows mesh topology. A mesh topology is the most resilient to failure and offers reconfiguration flexibility. Thus, it can be optimized to achieve the lowest latency and to minimize energy consumption. For these reasons, the most practical ESN utilizes some type of mesh topology with peer-to-peer communication links.

Tree. Figure 10.5e illustrates a tree topology. It can be viewed as an integration of a form of star topology deployed using a bus (not to be confused with a computer bus). Each subtree could be managed by a separate headnode, and only the headnode connects directly to the tree bus. An important advantage of a tree topology is that it supports future expandability of the network much better than a bus.

Ring. Figure 10.5f shows an example of a ring topology. In a ring network, there is no headnode and every node has exactly two neighboring nodes. All nodes perform the same function and all messages travel in the same direction (either "clockwise" or "counterclockwise"). The ring topology suffers with a single point of failure, so a failure in any node breaks the loop and can shut down the entire network.

Fully Connected. Figure 10.5g shows an example of a fully connected topology. It is a full mesh ESN where each node is directly connected to all other nodes in the network. The full connectivity reduces communication latency, but creates a serious problem related to the deletion of an existing node or the addition of a new node. When a new node is connected, then it must be linked with all existing nodes and the number of new links increases exponentially with the number of nodes, which in turn makes the routing problem intractable even for high-power computing.

10.2 OPERATING SYSTEMS AND DATABASE SYSTEMS

The brief introduction to sensors and WSN in Section 10.1 highlighted their unique characteristics. The list below summarizes some of the important ones, and it also identifies the need for an operating system that can provide satisfactory service under these constraints. A WSN has the following:

- It has a large number of different types of sensors that are deployed to an event site to capture some specific data. These sensors can be randomly distributed, and self-organizing, and they may move around; thus, their locations cannot be predetermined.
- Any time a sensor may fail, an existing sensor may leave, and a new one can join the WSN. Thus, the number of sensor nodes may not be predetermined.
- A sensor may preprocess the raw data that it captures before broadcasting it to the other sensor nodes of WSN. They only support point-to-point communication. Thus, there is no IP associated with a sensor; as a result, a communication between a sender and a receiver may be completed in multiple hops.
- The network topology may be unknown and may change with time.
- Sensor nodes have limited communication bandwidth (short radio range), limited power, small storage (cache and RAM), low computational capabilities, and computational capacities, and they are vulnerable to failure, malfunction, and so on.

10.2.1 WSN Versus Conventional Networks

A WSN has a number of unique requirements (limitations and management) related to energy consumption [10], communication protocol [11], deployments, and so on. Although WSNs borrow some aspects of conventional architecture such as topology, routing, and so on, they have to work under a number of constraints to provide an acceptable level of performance. For example, sensors are mounted on mobile objects such as cell phones, laptops, and so on, and they are also mounted on moving objects such as vehicles, robots, and so on, that introduce a continuous change in network topology and data capture approaches. Thus, WSNs have to work in a continuously changing environment that requires them to be highly adaptable. A sensor node may fail anytime, and as a result, WSNs need a mechanism to replace failed sensors and recharge energy sources (usually the battery). Table 10.2 lists a number of important differences between conventional networks and WSNs.

10.2.2 Operating System: TinyOS

There are quite a few [12] tiny operating systems for WSN. Some of the relatively most cited and used operating systems are *TinyOS, Contiki, MantisOS, SOS*, and *.NET Micro*. Out of these, this section briefly discusses TinyOS [10] and its recent version. Tables 10.3 and 10.4 summarize the basic capabilities of these tiny systems. A large volume of literature on these systems is available on a number of web sites.

A project called *TinyOS* (a part of the DARPA NEST program) began at UC Berkeley in approximately 1999, and the first TinyOS platform was developed. Since then, it saw significant design and development activities around the world, leading to

Table 10.2   Comparison Between Conventional Networks and WSNs

Conventional Networks	Wireless Sensor Networks (WSN)
General-purpose design; serving many applications	Single-purpose design; serving one specific application
Typical primary design concerns are network performance and latencies; energy is not a primary concern	Energy is the main constraint in the design of all node and network components
Networks are designed and engineered according to plans	Deployment, network structure, and resource use are often ad hoc (without planning)
Devices and networks operate in controlled and mild environments	Sensor networks often operate in environments with harsh conditions
Maintenance and repair are common and networks are typically easy to access	Physical access to sensor nodes is often difficult or even impossible
Component failure is addressed through maintenance and repair	Component failure is expected and addressed in the design of the network
Obtaining global network knowledge is typically feasible and centralized management is possible	Most decisions are made localized without the support of a central manager

Source: Reproduced from W. Dargie and C. Poellabauer, [6] *Fundamentals of Wireless Sensor Networks*, under written permission from John Wiley & sons.

the most recent release of TinyOS 2.1.1 (released in April 2010). A complete history of its evolution can be found in reference 13.

The TinyOS is an open-source system exclusively for WSN. It is designed to support stream data processing with minimal hardware and software requirements in an energy-constrained processing environment. The features of TinyOS can be summarized as follows. It is called TinyOS because its hardware platform is composed of tiny components with the following capabilities: Processor: 4–8 MIPs with 8-bit RISC, Memory 4 KB SRAM for variables and data, and 128 KB Flash for code space. Its peripherals have timers of two 8-bit and two 16-bit, the ADC (analog to digital) uses an 8-channel 10-bit, and the storage capacity is a 512-KB serial flash. It has a single stack, and therefore, all input and output tasks lasting longer than a few hundred microseconds are asynchronous.

It has no kernel and no process management component and does not support virtual memory. As a result, it uses direct hardware manipulation and executes processes serially (one at a time) on an ad hoc basis. It supports only functional calls with no interrupt facility. It is written in a dialect of *C* called nexC, which is optimized for a memory-constrained platform (i.e., WSN). It is also the language for TinyOS applications. The associated libraries and tools (NesC compiler, Atmel AVR binutils toolchains, etc.) are mostly written in C. Since data communication is one of the important activities of WSN, TinyOS provides necessary interfaces and components for communication (routing, sensing, actuation, etc.). To save transmission power, TinyOS uses multihop routing where the route discovery is achieved by a 2-hop broadcast. It uses a simple task scheduling that neither blocks nor preempts

Table 10.3 Comparison of Functional Aspects of Existing Operating Systems

OS	Programming Paradigm	Building Blocks	Scheduling	Memory Allocation	System Calls
TinyOS	Event-based (split-phase operation, active messages)	Components, interfaces, and tasks	FIFO	Static	Not available
SOS	Event-based (active messages)	Modules and messages	FIFO	Dynamic	Not available
Contiki	Predominantly event-based, but it provides optional multithreading support	Services, service interface stubs, and service layer	FIFO, poll handlers with priority scheduling	Dynamic	Runtime libraries
LiteOS	Thread-based (based on thread pool)	Applications are independent entities	Priority-based scheduling with optional round-robin support	Dynamic	A host of system calls available to the user (file, process, environment, debugging, and device commands)

Source: Reproduced from W. Dargie and C. Poellabauer, [6] *Fundamentals of Wireless Sensor Networks*, under written permission from John Wiley & Sons.

Table 10.4 Comparison of Nonfunctional Aspects of Existing Operating Systems

OS	Minimum System Overhead	Separation of Concern	Dynamic Reprogramming	Portability
TinyOS	332 bytes	There is no clean distinction between the OS and the application. At compilation time a particular configuration produces a monolithic, executable code.	Requires external software support	High
SOS	~1163 bytes	Replaceable modules are compiled to produce an executable code. There is no clean distinction between the OS and the application.	Supported	Medium to low
Contiki	~810 bytes	Modules are compiled to produce a reprogrammable and executable code, but there is no separation of concern between the application and the OS.	Supported	Medium
LiteOS	Not available	Applications are separate entities; they are developed independent of the OS.	Supported	Low

Source: Reproduced from W. Dargie and C. Poellabauer, [6] *Fundamentals of Wireless Sensor Networks*, under written permission from John Wiley & Sons.

processes, but does support interrupts. The system is to work with a large number of motes.

The current version of TinyOS is TinyOS 2.0, which has been completely redesigned. A good description of this version can be found in reference 14.

10.2.3   TinyDB

TinyDB [15] is a query processing system that provides a simple SQL-like interface to access the database. In response to a query from a user, TinyDB accesses the database from WSN and displays the result to a PC. One of the objectives of TinyDB is to develop data-driven operations on the WSN. A summary of some of the features of TinyDB is given below.

Metadata. Similar to conventional databases, TinyDB has a catalog that describes data types (attributes, relations, etc.). It also explains the commands available on TinyDB, and provides a TinySchema that is used to create attributes, relations, commands, and so on.

Querying Facilities. TinyDB can process single and multiple high-level queries on the same mote concurrently. It allows data sharing among concurrent queries. The queries are composed in a declarative query language that is a nonprocedure language where a user only describes the required data without specifying how to process it to get the result. Since in a WSN a sensor can appear and disappear anytime, it provides incremental network reconfiguration. This means that when a new sensor node joins the WSN, a copy of the TinyDB can be loaded to the new node, and the connection between the new sensor and the existing ones running TinyDB is configured automatically. Since WSN combines the complexities of distributed and embedded systems and has limited resources and power supply, the software development becomes quite challenging. Further complexity arises with the presence of unreliable, low-bandwidth connections and the requirement of unattended execution of applications. To provide a satisfactory platform for software development, a suite of Java-based tools called the Tiny Application Sensor Kit (TASK) has been developed.

10.2.4   Data Stream

The type of data that a WSN deals with is quite different (type and application), and as a result, its processing needs a new approach. To start with, the monitoring applications of WSN have to continuously capture the stream of data produced by the source. In fact, nearly all real-world events such as gas emission in a mine, traffic flow, audio, video, and so on, continuously generate real-time data that must be captured by the designated sensors and then validated, and any query on them must be answered before the data become stale.

The above example highlighted some of the essential tasks in dealing with sensor data (data capture, validation, formatting, etc.). One of the important tasks from a mobile data management point of view is managing data stream. The next chapter discusses stream data management in more detail.

EXERCISES

10.1 Discuss the difference between passive sensors and active sensors. Give at least one example of each type (refer to Table 10.1).

10.2 WSNs have a limited power source and it is crucial to minimize energy consumption. Investigate and suggest at least three efficient schemes to reduce power consumption without affecting the functionality of WSNs.

10.3 Explain the usefulness of a buffering facility in sensor data processing. Suggest a couple of buffering techniques to improve the performance of a sensor.

10.4 Investigate and identify the set of activities where WSNs are required, along with a set of activities where ad hoc networks are suitable for processing data.

10.5 Investigate and identify the strengths and limitations of various WSN topologies. Explain which one is the most appropriate topology for what activity.

10.6 The TinyDB is a database system for WSNs. Investigate the interaction that takes place (if any) between the TinyDB and the underlying TinyOS in performing a data processing job.

REFERENCES

1. G. J. Pottie, Wireless Integrated Network Sensors (WINS): The Web Gets Physical, National Academy of Engineering: *The Bridge*, Vol. 31, No. 4, 78.
2. K. Burstein, A. Bult, D. Chang, M. Dong, M. Fielding, E. Kruglick, J. Ho, F. Lin, T. H. Lin, W. J. Kaiser, H. Marcy, R. Mukai, P. Nelson, F. L. Newburg, K. S. J. Pister, G. Pottie, H. Sanchez, K. Sohrabi, O. M. Stafsudd, K. B. Tan, G. Yung, S. Xue, and J. Yao, Low Power Systems for Wireless Microsensors. *Proceedings of the International Symposium on Low Power Electronics and Design*, 1996, pp. 17–21.
3. J. M. Kahn, R. H. Katz, and K. S. J. Pister, Mobile Networking for Smart Dust, In *ACM/IEEE International Conference on Mobile Computing and Networking (Mobi-Com'99)*, 1999, pp. 271–278.
4. J. Rabaey, J. Ammer, J. L. da Silva, Jr., and D. Patel, Picoradio: Ad Hoc Wireless Networking of Ubiquitous Low-Energy Sensor/Monitor Nodes, *Proceedings of the IEEE Computer Society Annual Workshop on VLSI*, 2000, pp. 9–12.
5. B. H. Calhoun, D. C. Daly, N. Verma, D. F. Finchelstein, D. D. Wentzloff, A. Wang, S. H. Cho, and A. P. Chandrakasan, Design Considerations for Ultralow Energy Wireless Microsensor Nodes, *IEEE Transactions on Computers* Vol. 54, No. 6, 2005, 727–740.
6. W. Dargie and C. Poellabauer, *Fundamentals of Wireless Sensor Networks Theory and Practice*, John Wiley & Sons, Hoboken, NJ, 2010.
7. E. Shih, S. H. Cho, N. Ickes, R. Min, A. Sinha, A. Wang, and A. Chandrakasan, Physical Layer Driven Protocol and Algorithm Design for Energy-Efficient Wireless Sensor

Networks. In *7th Annual International Conference on Mobile Computing and Networking (MobiCom'01)*, 2001, pp. 272-287.

8. G. J. Pottie and W. J. Kaiser, Wireless Integrated Network Sensors, *Communications of the ACM*, Vol. 43, No. 5, 2000, 51–58.

9. K. Sohrabi, J. Gao, V. Ailawadhi, and G. Pottie, Protocols for Self-Organization of a Wireless Sensor Network, *IEEE Personal Communications Magazine*, Vol. 7, No. 5, Oct. 2000, 16–27.

10. J. Hill, R. Szewczyk, A. Woo, S. Hollar, D. Culler, K. Pister, System Architecture Directions for Networked Sensors. In *9th International Conference on Architectural Support for Programming Languages and Operating Systems (ASPLOS-IX)*, Cambridge, MA, November 12–15, 2000, 93–104.

11. A. Sinha and A. P. Chandrakasan, Energy Aware Software. In *13th International Conference on VLSI Design*, 2000, pp. 50–55.

12. A. K. Dwivedi, M. K. Tiwari, and O. P. Vyas, Operating Systems for Tiny Networked Sensors: A Survey, *International Journal of Recent Trends in Engineering*, Vol. 1, No. 2, May 2009, 152–157.

13. http://en.wikipedia.org/wiki/TinyOS#History.

14. http://www.tinyos.net/tinyos-2.x/doc/html/overview.html.

15. S. R. Madden, M. J. Franklin, J. M. Hellerstein, and W. Hong, TinyDB: An Acquisitional Query Processing System for Sensor Networks. *ACM Transactions on Database Systems (TODS)—Special Issue: SIGMOD/PODS 2003 TODS*, Vol. 30, No. 1, March 2005, 122–173.

CHAPTER 11

SENSOR TECHNOLOGY AND DATA STREAMS MANAGEMENT

This chapter discusses the management of *data stream* or *stream data*. In Chapter 10 the discussion on sensors introduced *data stream* and its characteristics. It was illustrated that a sensor captures data about an event that has the following properties:

- It has temporal (real-time) and may have spatial property. This type of data will become stale (invalid) over some defined time interval; therefore, they must be processed during their validity (deadline) period. This property adds another processing requirement. There is a time lag between monitoring, capturing, and storing the data into the database; as a result, the accuracy of the data may be affected. Furthermore, if a number of nodes in a sensor network are collecting similar or different types of data, then their data capture speed may vary significantly, which will affect the data capture completion time and data accuracy. Consider the example of capturing temperature data continuously in a refrigerator to keep the temperature level constant. This data stream does not have spatial property; on the other hand, flood data collected by sensor networks has both temporal and spatial parameters. If the flood data are collected by multiple sensors for monitoring the rise or fall in the water level, then the result may be approximate if the data collection speed of sensors varies significantly.

Fundamentals of Pervasive Information Management Systems, Revised Edition. Vijay Kumar.
© 2013 John Wiley & Sons, Inc. Published 2013 by John Wiley & Sons, Inc.

- The arrival (capture) order is inherent in the data that show the arrival pattern. For example, traffic data collected by roadside sensors (roadside unit—RSU) has strict arrival order that shows the traffic behavior.

- It is an infinite sequence of continuous arrivals with a predefined structure (hard wired in the sensor). For example, if the sensors of a sensor network are collecting data related to temperature, humidity, pressure, and so on, then each type of data will have a specific format.

Definition 11.1 *A data stream can be formally defined as* $DS = \{< p_1, t_1, l_1 >, < p_2, t_2, l_2 >, \ldots, < p_\infty, t_\infty, l_\infty >\}$, *where* p_i *is a data packet,* t_i *is time of its arrival, and* l_i *is the location (optional) of data.* p_i *is represented in terms of voltage or decibel or in some other unit.*

These properties put data stream into a new category and raise a number of fundamentally new research problems. From a data management viewpoint, they require continuous querying and real-time storing and processing capabilities. Unlike traditional database processing, simply loading the data in the database and processing it there is not feasible. Conventional database management systems are not designed or equipped to deal with continuous query processing. From a data processing viewpoint, conventional database systems emphasize the precise result of a query, while a data stream query is likely to look for approximate answers or statistical inference. The following section deals with a data stream and its management.

11.1 INTRODUCTION

The advent of a large number of inexpensive sensors and the need for processing data 24/7 from data sources, along with the need for real-time and near-real-time processing requirements, have warranted a reexamination of storing, querying, managing, notification (or alerting), and mining of this type of data. Traditional database management systems (DBMSs) were not designed for these application requirements; the use of low-latency disks and a lack of provision for accepting and satisfying quality of service (QoS) requirements makes traditional systems unsuitable for these applications. As a result, customized solutions are developed and currently used.

These data stream management systems (DSMSs) have been proposed to meet the requirements of this new class of applications. In this chapter, we will introduce the general architectural differences between a DBMS and a DSMS. We will briefly indicate the advantages of integrating stream and complex event processing to obtain an end-to-end solution for processing sensor data and data of other similar applications. We will present two different applications that can benefit from the use of stream and event processing techniques: a network management application and processing of multilevel secure data.

A data stream comprises a continuous stream of m tuples τ, consisting of n attribute values $A_i (1 \le i \le n)$ and the represented time interval t_b, t_e.

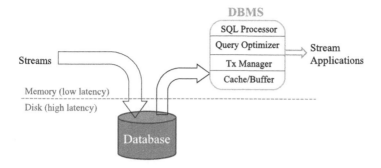

Figure 11.1 Data stream processing using a DBMS.

11.2 DSMS AND DBMS: HIGH-LEVEL ARCHITECTURES

The basic differences between the high-level architectures of a DBMS and a DSMS are summarized in Figures 11.1 and 11.2 (adapted from Stonebraker et al. [1]). Figure 11.1 indicates the use of a traditional DBMS for stream processing. Stream data are first stored in a database (i.e., a secondary storage device), and queries are processed over stored data. This approach incurs two I/Os (input/output) for each data item (actually, at the page level) processed. Because of potential high arrival rates of data items coupled with storage and retrieval latency, processing of data items is likely to lag, resulting in increased response time for query results. In contrast, Figure 11.2 shows an architecture where the incoming streams are processed *directly* by a DSMS. Hence, I/O is not incurred for any data item, thereby decreasing the response time of the query results. This approach, together with enough memory and processing, is more likely to meet the real-time and near-real-time requirements of applications as compared to a DBMS with a low-latency device in the loop. The data may also be stored for archival or other purposes (e.g., processing *ad hoc* queries or queries over past data). However, this archiving is done without affecting the computation and performance

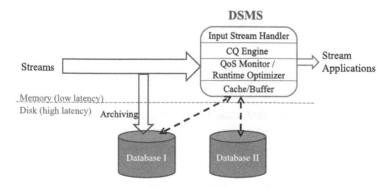

Figure 11.2 Data stream processing using a DSMS.

of DSMS queries (also termed continuous queries). It should be noted that, as part of stream processing, data from a DBMS may need to be accessed (e.g., Radio Frequency IDentification (RFID), and click-stream processing applications, to name a few). This can be done either by efficiently accessing the DBMS or by caching the data required for continuous query processing in memory (or using main memory DBMSs).

Apart from traditional DBMSs, a number of DBMS variants have been researched and developed over the years for specific purposes/applications.

1. Main memory DBMSs [2–7] cache large amounts of data as well as index in the main memory and provide all the functionality of a DBMS.
2. Embedded DBMSs [8–12] are mainly used as a component of larger applications with a small footprint and typically include a subset of DBMS functionality.
3. Real-time transaction processing systems (also termed real-time database systems) [13–51] were developed to schedule transactions (instead of tasks used in real-time processing systems) to satisfy soft, firm, and hard deadlines. The goal was to minimize the penalty (associated with firm deadlines) and maximize the completion of as many firm and hard deadline transactions as possible.

Without going into additional details, there are fundamental differences between each of the above and a DSMS, although some of the goals for the development of the variants were similar. For example, reduction in the footprint and speeding up query processing were the driving forces behind the main-memory and embedded DBMSs. Real-time transaction processing dealt with different aspects of quality of service. For additional details, the reader is referred to reference 52.

11.2.1 DSMS Architecture

There has been considerable research and development of the theory, algorithms, and implementation of DSMS [52–54]. A typical DSMS architecture, based on the STREAM system [55], is shown in Figure 11.3. A continuous query (CQ) can be defined using specification languages [56], or as query plans [54]. The CQs, defined using specification languages, are processed by the input processor to generate a query plan. Each *query plan* is a directed graph of operators (e.g., Select, Join, Aggregate). Each operator is associated with one or more input *queues** and an output queue. One or more *synopses*[†] [56] are associated with each operator (e.g., Join) that needs to maintain the current state of the tuples for future evaluation of the operator. The generated query plans are then instantiated, and query operators are put in the ready state so that they can be executed. Based on a scheduling strategy (e.g., round robin) [52, 57–63], the scheduler picks a query, an operator, or a path, and starts the execution. The run-time optimizer monitors the system for QoS requirements, and it initiates load

---

*Queues are used by in between operators to store unprocessed tuples.

[†] Synopses are temporary storage structures used by the operators (e.g., Join) that need to maintain a state.

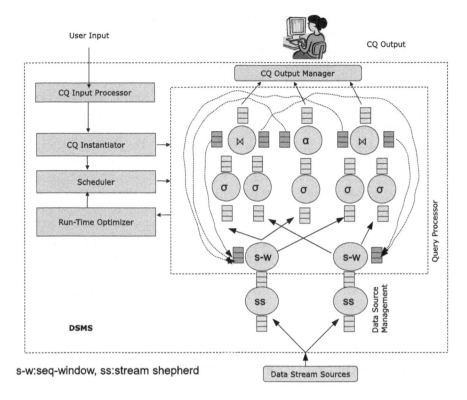

User Input

CQ Output

Figure 11.3 Data stream management system (DSMS) architecture.

shedding [52, 64–68] as and when required. Both scheduling and load shedding (as QoS delivery mechanisms) minimize resource usage (e.g., queue size, tuple latency) and maximize performance and throughput. In addition, other QoS improvement mechanisms such as static and dynamic approximation techniques [69] are used to control the size of the synopses. All the input tuples are first processed by the data source manager that enqueues the tuples to input queues of *all* the leaf operators associated with the stream. In the directed graph of operators, the data tuples are propagated from the leaf operator to the root operator. Each operator produces a stream (can also be a relation) of tuples. After a processed tuple exits the query plan, the output manager sends it to the query creators (or users).

11.3 COMPLEX EVENT PROCESSING (CEP)

Complex event processing, although started as active databases with a need for events, conditions, and rules (or triggers) in the 1980s, has seen a resurgence in the last decade again due to 24/7 monitoring of sensor and other types of data. The foundation for complex (or composite) event processing, in terms of event specification languages, their semantics, event detection algorithms, and integration of event processing with DBMSs as well as stand-alone applications, was formed quite some time ago. The advent of stream processing has brought its synergy with complex event processing and alerts/notifications for a new class of applications to the forefront.

In addition to the research prototypes of active databases, active object-oriented databases, and stand-alone complex event processing systems, a number of commercial stream and complex event processing are available today. A majority of traditional DBMS vendors support complex event processing separately as an engine. Stream processing is also included in a number of them. The middleware approach for complex event processing is also becoming popular. We have proposed a synergistic, integrated architecture (described below) that allows an application to mix and match stream and complex event processing as needed. The following is a partial list of currently available commercial or open source systems related to stream and complex event processing: Aleri [70], Aleri, Apama [71], Apama, AMiT [72, 73], AMiT, Coral8 [74], Coral8, Corona Enterprise Suite [75], Corona Enterprise Suite, Esper [76], Esper (open source), GemFire [77], Gemfire, INETCO [78], INETCO, Oracle CEP [79], Oracle CEP, RuleCore [80, 81], RuleCore, SENACTIVE [82], Senactive, SL RTView [83], SL RTView, StreamBase [84], StreamBase, and West-Global [85], WestGlobal.

11.4 DSMS AND COMPLEX EVENT PROCESSING: ARCHITECTURE

Not only do stream applications need computations (aggregation, merging, join, etc.) on streams, but these computations often generate `computed events` that are domain-specific (e.g., stock price changed by $n\%$ in y units of time, a car slowing down, car stopped, potential fire, a false alarm in a routing network), and several such events may need to be composed or correlated, detected, and monitored for taking appropriate actions. Although each model, namely stream and complex event processing, is useful in its own right, their combined expressiveness and computational benefits far outweigh their individual capabilities.

Our integrated architecture of stream and complex event processing is elaborated in Figure 11.4. Our architecture consists of four stages:

Continuous Query Processing (Stage 1). This stage corresponds to the CQ processing of data streams. Stage 1 represents stream processing that accepts stream data as input, computes CQs, and produces output streams. Output from a CQ can be consumed by an application, and if needed, the output can be designated as events and propagated to the event processing stage.

Event Generation (Stage 2). This stage generates events based on the association of `computed` events with CQs. Stage 2 facilitates seamless coupling of the two systems. This stage allows for stream output to be split to generate different event types from the same CQ.

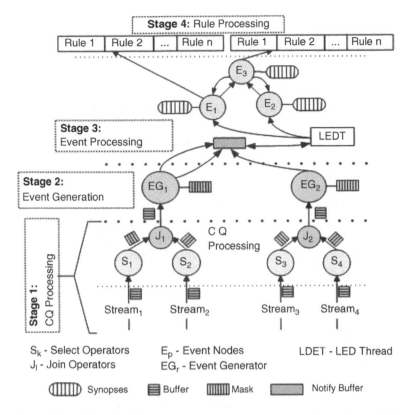

Figure 11.4   EStreams: Four-stage stream and complex event integration model.

Complex Event Processing (Stage 3). This stage represents the complex event processing component, where complex events are detected based on the definition of event expressions. Computed events generated by CQs act as primitive events.

Rule Processing (Stage 4). Rule processing is a component of the CEP system that processes rules that are associated with events. When events are detected, conditions are evaluated, and if they evaluate as true, corresponding actions are performed.

The architecture shown above does not limit the applications to one step of stream processing followed by one step of complex event processing. Incoming streams can be treated directly as events, if necessary, by feeding streams to the event generation operator in stage 2. Also, as the output of all operators (both stream and complex event) is a stream, it can either act as an input to another continuous query (or CQ), act as an application to detect higher-level complex events, or trigger rules associated with that event. In summary, seamless coupling of the two capabilities allows one to process large amounts of raw data in one or more stages of CQ and CEP combinations to derive higher-level abstractions or knowledge. Furthermore, at any point in this process, rules associated with events (primitive or complex) can trigger actions and notifications. Arbitrary composition of stream and complex event processing is readily accommodated by the proposed architecture. Each subsystem can be used to its full potential without additional overhead, and the functionalities can be synergistically combined as needed.

11.5   NETWORK FAULT MANAGEMENT APPLICATION

In this section, we will discuss the network fault management application and illustrate how it can benefit from the above architecture.

Automating network fault management has been an active area of research for a long period because of (a) its complexity and (b) the return on investment it can generate for service providers. However, most fault management systems are currently custom-developed for specific service providers in specific domains. As service providers continuously add new capabilities and sophistication to their systems to meet the demands of a growing user population, these systems have to manage a multilayered network along with its built-in, legacy processing procedures. Our proposed approach is based on leveraging stream and complex event processing techniques to meet the needs of complex, real-word problems.

11.5.1   Network Fault Management Problem

In telecommunication network management, network fault management (NFM) is defined as the set of functions that

a. detect, isolate, and correct malfunctions in a telecommunication network,
b. compensate for environmental changes, and
c. maintain and examine error logs, accept and act on error detection notifications, trace and identify faults, carry out sequence of diagnostic tests, correct faults, report error conditions, and localize and trace faults by examining and manipulating database information.

A typical telecommunication network, illustrated in Figure 11.5, is a multilayered network, in which the bottom layer provides a transport service through SDH/SONET (synchronous digital network/synchronous optical network). Above that, a public

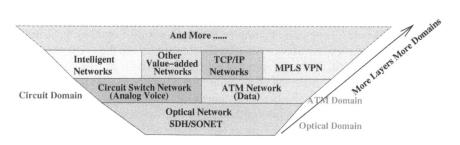

Figure 11.5   A typical telecommunication network.

switched telephone network (PSTN) circuit switch network with a Signaling System 7 (SS7) signaling network is used to provide traditional voice services, and an asynchronous transfer mode (ATM) network is used to provide internet data service. Intelligent networks and other value-added networks can be added above the PSTN switch networks, and the Border Gateway Protocol/Multiprotocol Label Switching (BGP/MPLS) virtual private network (VPN) can be added above the ATM network. The NFM in such a multilayered telecommunication network has been a challenging problem [86–92], addressed by both industry and academia for a long time, because of its high cost and complexity. The recent convergence of data, voice, and cable networks has further compounded the scope of this problem.

Each network element (NE) in this multilayered network periodically (e.g., every 5 minutes) reports the status of each of its components and the status of its environment (e.g., temperature). Some NEs have additional capabilities such as summarizing its status by processing the status message locally in order to reduce the number of messages reported, or to identify trivial messages. Hence, these messages arrive in the form of a message stream, and each NE can be considered as a message stream source. These status and alarm messages from the NE, the Operation System (OS), and the network link are continuously collected in a Network Operations Center (NOC) to be further analyzed by experts to detect and to isolate faults. Once a fault is identified, a sequence of actions needs to be taken locally and remotely. Due to the complexity of the network and different interfaces of multiple-vendor's devices, each layer has one or more independent NFM systems [90, 91]. For example, there is an SDH/SONET fault management system for the transport layer in the network as illustrated in Figure 11.5. There are also individual fault management systems for the circuit switch and Transport Control Protocol/Internet Protocol (TCP/IP) networks. Similarly, each vendor has its own fault management system even when multiple vendors' devices are used. As a result, when a failure occurs at a lower level, it is propagated to all the components at the next level, and hence, a large number of failure messages are reported to independent NFM systems. Moreover, there is a demand for providing an integrated view of the whole network system and to process faults centrally.

Currently, due to the large volume of messages that are continuously reported by each NE and the complex message processing requirements, it is not possible to use traditional DBMSs that support triggers with each independent NFM system. Current NFM systems hard-code (or customize) their data processing logic and specific monitoring rules (queries) in the system. As a result, various filters, pattern languages, and regular expressions are employed to find interesting alarm messages and group these messages into subgroups based on various criteria. These subgroups are finally presented to experts to diagnose root causes or they are routed to an event correlation system to identify causes automatically. Once the causes are identified, a ticket is placed in a ticket system to trace the problem and have it fixed by relevant engineers.

11.5.2   Network Fault Management Issues

Messages from NEs, OSs, and network links are semistructured text messages. First, each type of NE has its own format to report a particular kind of message and can report hundreds (or even thousands) of different kinds of messages. For the same type of NE or OS, different vendors have different message formats. Even for the same type of NE from the same vendor, different versions may have different formats for the same kind of message. In a typical telecommunication network, there are hundreds of different types of NEs and OSs and tens of devices from different vendors. The length of a message ranges from a few bytes to a few thousand bytes.

Second, multilayered telecommunication networks produce a large number of messages. This is not only because each data source (e.g., a message channel of an NE) continuously reports a large number of messages in the form of a data stream, but also because the number of data sources in such a network is quite high. For example, a typical circuit switch produces approximately 250 KB messages per hour, which is about 2000 messages per hour. For a telecommunication network with approximately 400 circuit switches, the switch network can produce 100 MB messages per hour. These messages do not include the messages from the transport network below it, the intelligent network layer above it, data networks, and other OSs.

Finally, the primary role of an NFM system is to detect, isolate, and correct malfunctions in a telecommunication network in a *timely* manner. To detect malfunctions, a fault management system has to continuously monitor incoming messages and find "interesting" alarm messages. Once identified, NFM has to transform the interesting messages into `alarms` by stripping unnecessary fields, adding additional fields, and applying various transformation functions to make the information meaningful and readable by humans. To isolate malfunctions, a fault management system has to continuously process a large set of predefined rules over the alarm streams. These rules are used to trace the root cause of the fault based on correlations, severity, and other properties of various alarms. Rules are usually defined based on the accumulated experience of experts over years. Of course, certain mining tools can also be used to help discover these rules that are beyond the scope of this chapter. Each rule can be considered as a continuous query over the alarm streams. Once a fault is located, sequences of actions must be taken to rectify the faults.

11.5.3 Three-Phase Processing Solution

From the problem description, it is easy to observe that the generation of alarms, their correlation, and notification can be mapped to three distinct phases: processing of continuous queries, processing of event correlations (or compositions), and rules for notification and other purposes. Below, we elaborate on these three phases.

Continuous Query Processing Phase. The first phase in our three-phase model (stage 1 in Figure 11.4) processes continuous queries. It takes the output streams from the message filters (that filter important attributes from the status reports of the NEs) and information extractors (that extract and, if need be, reorganize extracted information) as inputs and generates computed continuous streams to the event detection phase. Note that in this application the computations may not use relational operators but operators that are specific and generic to this domain. In our NFM system, the final results of stream computations are viewed as events (that contain additional information about the event) for detecting faults and isolating faults that use multiple alarm streams and composite events. However, not all current stream processing models support complex event detection and rule processing. Also, in current stream processing systems, it is difficult to detect changes to one or more attributes on the same stream and to suppress the number of output alarms of the same type.

To overcome some of the shortcomings, we have enhanced the stream processing to support additional operators and in other ways to facilitate integration with event and rule processing. Although these enhancements are derived from the NFM application, their formulation has been generalized to make them relevant to any stream-based application (refer to reference 52 for details).

Complex Event Processing Phase. Briefly, primitive or simple events are specific to a domain and are predefined. Primitive events are assumed to be detected by the underlying system along with the time of occurrence. On the other hand, composite events are composed of more than one primitive or composite event using event operators (Snoop event operators are described in references 93 and 94). Some of the event operators proposed in the literature include: and (occurrence of two events in *any* order), sequence (occurrence of two events in *a particular* order), not (nonoccurrence of an event within a well-defined interval or delimited by two events), or (occurrence of one of the two events), aperiodic (aperiodic occurrence of an event in an interval delimited by two events), periodic (periodic occurrence of a temporal event in an interval delimited by two events), frequency or cardinality (number of times an event occurs), and plus (event occurrence based on another event plus a temporal offset). Note that a complex (also referred to as a composite) event can be used as one of the events in the above operators to facilitate construction of larger event expressions to deal with real-world situations.

The NFM application uses a computed event that is the result of an arbitrary computation that can be expressed as a continuous query (part of stream processing in the first phase). In most sensor data applications, the events of interest are computed by processing raw data in various ways. Computed events play the role of primitive or simple events and are composed using event operators. For example, an alarm is the result of a computation or a continuous query in our proposed model. An event processing engine accepts streams of different types of events and performs event correlation by using the above-mentioned and other event operators. Note that the computation algorithm or the semantics of composite event operators do not change because of the computed event. In the three-phase model, computed events, defined on the output of continuous queries, act as primitive events of a complex event processing systems and computed events can be further composed using event operators as needed.

In our integrated architecture, both stream and complex event processing use the data flow paradigm, making the integration seamless with respect to how data flow is handled.

Rule Processing Phase. Although limited human interventions are irreplaceable to correct some malfunctions identified by the alarms, nevertheless, the role of rule processing is critical to automatically triggering a sequence of actions for specific alarm types. Some malfunctions can be corrected without human interaction. Some actions can be performed automatically but require confirmation from an expert, while others require human intervention. For example, when a critical alarm is detected, an audio broadcast (in addition to sending an alarm to a group of experts) may be necessary to get the attention of corresponding experts and administrators in order to respond to it as soon as possible. One alarm can trigger multiple sequences of actions, and different alarms can trigger the same sequence of actions.

In order to improve modularity, multiple rules (condition–action pairs) can be associated with an event in a complex event processing system. Whenever an event is raised (i.e., output as an alarm from continuous queries), it is propagated as necessary to detect complex events, and corresponding conditions are checked to trigger actions (if the conditions evaluate as being true). Components of Event–Condition–Action rules (ECA) are shown below

`Event`	occurrence of a primitive or complex event
`Condition`	condition to be checked
`Action`	action sequence

Thus, whenever an alarm is detected (as an event), associated rules are triggered to evaluate the conditions based on the alarm attributes or temporal properties and associated actions are executed. In addition to the E, C, and A components, a rule may include a coupling mode [21, 23, 95], a consumption mode [93, 96], and priority. In network fault management applications, most of the rules need to be triggered immediately as the problem needs to be brought to the attention of various experts. Priority is used to sequence the notifications. The rule format is shown below

```
Rule rule_name
     (event_name, condition_function, action_function
     [[,coupling_mode] [,priority] [,consumption_mode]])
```

Rules can be assigned priorities. In general, ECA rule processing goes through the following stages: (i) event detection, which is done by a complex event processing system using the alarm events generated by continuous queries, (ii) condition evaluation and scheduling of actions, and (iii) execution of actions.

To summarize, alarm detection from the first stage using continuous queries feeds into the event detection process. Different types and amounts of events are grouped and composed in the third stage using a complex event detection engine. Once an end event is detected, corresponding conditions are evaluated and actions are scheduled. In the final stage, all the scheduled actions are executed. Note that conditions and actions are arbitrary computations and can include triggering other events or starting other continuous queries as well.

11.5.4 Summary

We have briefly described an integrated network fault management solution for a multilayered network monitoring problem. We discussed how stream and complex event processing techniques can be adapted to build a flexible system for a complex, real-world application.

Our solution is in contrast to various solutions for network fault management that have been proposed/discussed in the literature. Proposed approaches [87–89] discuss domain-specific distributed architectures for network management. However, most of the telecommunication service providers employ a central fault management system because of the need for various types of experts and their effective collaboration to fix malfunctions. Medhi et al. [92] propose an architecture for a multilayered network through various interfaces to exchange information between several domain managers and a single interdomain manager; however, like other network fault management systems, it falls short on the aspect of flexibility. Babu et al. [97] propose an architecture for managing data traffic over the internet that is somewhat different from network fault management. The architecture proposed in this chapter takes a totally different approach by leveraging the advantages of stream and complex event processing to modularize the system, reduce its complexity, and improve its ease of use.

11.6 PROCESSING MULTILEVEL SECURE SENSOR STREAMS

In this section, we will discuss the second application, processing multilevel secure stream data using a DSMS. We will discuss how we have extended the DSMS to support multilevel stream data processing. We will also bring out additional issues that need to be addressed.

Oftentimes, the DSMS applications involve data streams belonging to different sensitivity levels (henceforth referred to as security levels), and in such cases it is important to protect the confidentiality and integrity of sensitive data. Consequently, a data stream management system is needed that can collect, process, and disseminate data belonging to different security levels in a manner that ensures that no sensitive information is passed directly or indirectly to a lesser security level. Our proposed approach aims to provide such a system.

Consider a not-so-futuristic application of a DSMS: the battlefield of the future. The battlefield is strewn with "smart dust" that can collect and send data to the command control center that hosts a DSMS. Some of these are wireless magnetic sensors that can detect a passing vehicle's magnetic signature and relay the vehicle's speed and direction. Others are weather sensors that can relay extremely localized weather information. The human soldiers don uniforms made of computing fabric that is implanted with sensors that are capable of monitoring the vitals and precise location of the soldier. Sensors can transmit information pertaining to the health of soldiers, their location, local weather, and location of enemy troops, not all of which are equally sensitive, to the hosted DSMS. The DSMS executes continuous queries (CQs) for various purposes. For example, it may execute the following CQ: *"Alert commanders in ground station when a soldier's pulse rate is low, and he has not moved from the current location for the last n minutes and there are enemy troops nearby."* The DSMS executes such a query that processes live streaming data at various security levels obtained from different sensors, and the execution of such queries continues until there are no more streaming data or when the user explicitly stops it. Traditional DSMSs were not designed for handling these types of queries that involve sensitive data.

Researchers have worked on secure query processing in the context of DSMSs. They focus mainly on providing access control [98, 99] to streaming data [100–105]. Specifically, they focus on providing some form of role-based access control [106–108] where users are assigned to roles, roles are assigned to permissions, and users acquire permissions by activating the subset of roles assigned to them. Access control is oftentimes not adequate for complex applications that process and generate information from multiple domains [109]. Erroneous omission of an access control check may reveal confidential data. Integration of third-party off-the-shelf software may cause policy checks to be bypassed altogether. Multiple domains may have different notions about the sensitivity level of data. Moreover, the existence of covert and overt channels may cause the leakage of sensitive data. Information flow control is greatly needed for processing data in such applications.

The idea of information flow control originated in the military in the context of multilevel secure (MLS) systems. MLS [98, 110–114] not only prevent unauthorized access but also ensure the absence of such an illegal information flow. Multilevel security is being supported by various operating systems (SELinux, FreeBSD, INTEGRITY-178B), database systems [98, 112–117] (Oracle Label Security, SE-PostgreSQL), and other systems (BlueSpace MLS applications to connect to Google Search, Google Earth, etc.). In addition, information flow control in which individual users can change the privilege of the data so as to enable sharing of their private data has been investigated by researchers [118]. Information flow control at the OS level is also being addressed by various researchers [119–121]. The need for information flow control providing decentralized policies in a multidomain environment is being motivated by researchers [109].

MLS systems with their centrally defined labels have very simple and well-understood information flow policies. *Some of the unique requirements (or characteristics) of information flow models are* (i) how system elements are classified via security levels and categories, (ii) information flow policies for preserving secrecy and integrity properties, (iii) prevention of covert storage and timing channels, (iv) trusted components versus untrusted components, and (v) overhead at each component of the underlying system.

On the other hand, some of the unique characteristics of data stream processing systems are as follows: (i) Data items arrive continuously; (ii) the input characteristics of data streams are usually uncontrollable, highly bursty, and typically unpredictable; (iii) data streams are read-only; (iv) raw data streams are generated by stream sources and derived data streams are generated by query operators; (v) data streams are shared between operators to minimize resource usage; (vi) attributes of data stream items are well structured; and (vii) applications have QoS and accuracy requirements.

Supporting access control in DSMSs is very different from MLS support due to the unique characteristics and requirements of MLS systems. Access control support requires additions/modifications to only certain DSMS components such as the query processor, input, and output, whereas supporting MLS involves complete redesign or modifications to all the DSMS components (query processor, input, output, buffers, scheduler, load shedder, etc.) as each and every component has to be classified and satisfy the requirements.

In the rest of this chapter, we discuss the model and issues that need to be addressed to process multilevel secure sensor data. We plan to provide multilevel security in stream processing by addressing the threat that data in stream processing may be leaked or influenced by users who are not authorized to do so. Our threat model is that processing units may contain unintentional bugs or Trojan horses that cause information leakage. We also want protection from honest but curious users who want to know information that they are not authorized to access. We do not address denial-of-service attacks. We assume that the underlying operating system is trusted.

11.6.1 Subjects and Objects in Multilevel Secure DSMS

In MLS systems, each object is assigned to security levels and each subject is authorized to access objects with appropriate security clearances. In this section, we discuss the assignment of security levels and clearances to objects and subjects, respectively, in a DSMS.

A multilevel secure system is associated with a security structure that is a partial order, $(\mathbf{L}, <)$. $\mathbf{L}$ is a set of security levels, and $<$ is the dominance relation between levels. If $L_1 < L_2$, then L_2 is said to strictly dominate L_1, and L_1 is said to be strictly dominated by L_2. If $L_1 = L_2$, then the two levels are said to be equal. $L_1 < L_2$ or $L_1 = L_2$ is denoted by $L_1 \leq L_2$. If $L_1 \leq L_2$, then L_2 is said to dominate L_1, and L_1 is said to be dominated by L_2. L_1, and L_2 are said to be incomparable if neither $L_1 \leq L_2$ nor $L_2 \leq L_1$. We assume the existence of a level U, which corresponds to the level unclassified or public knowledge. The level U is the greatest lower bound of all the levels in $\mathbf{L}$. Thus, any object classified at level U is accessible to all the subjects of the multilevel secure system.

Each MLS DSMS object $x \in \mathbf{D}$ is associated with exactly one security level that we denote as $L(x)$, where $L(x) \in \mathbf{L}$. (The function L maps entities to security levels.) We assume that the security level of an object remains fixed for the entire lifetime of the object.

The users of the system are cleared to different security levels. We denote the security clearance of user U_i by $L(U_i)$. Consider a military setting consisting of four security levels: Top Secret (TS), Secret (S), Confidential (C), and Unclassified (U). The user Jane Doe has the security clearance of Top Secret. That is, $L(JaneDoe) = TS$. Each user has one or more associated principals. The number of principals associated with the user depends on their security clearance; it equals the number of levels dominated by the user's security clearance. In our example, Jane Doe has four principals: *JaneDoe.TS*, *JaneDoe.S*, *JaneDoe.C*, and *JaneDoe.U*. During each session, the user logs in as one of the principals. All processes that the user initiates in that session inherit the security level of the corresponding principal.

Each continuous query Q_i is associated with exactly one security level. The level of the query remains fixed for the entire execution. The security level of the query is the level of the principal who has submitted the query. For example, if Jane Doe logs in as *JaneDoe.S*, all queries initiated by Jane Doe during that session will have the level Secret (S). A query consists of one or more operators OP_i. We require a query Q_i to obey the simple security property and the restricted $\star$-property of the Bell–Lapadula model (BLP) [110].

1. An operator OP_i with $L(OP_i) = C$ can read an object x only if $L(x) \leq C$.
2. An operator OP_i with $L(OP_i) = C$ can write an object x only if $L(x) = C$.

An MLS/DSMS deals with different types of data objects. In a DSMS, we have sensors that capture information. We refer to these sensors as stream sources. One or more sensors can add tuples to a stream. Each sensor or stream source SS_i is associated with a security level $L(SS_i)$. Typically, the location of the sensor can be used to determine its security level. For example, if a sensor SS_i is located in a top-secret location, then its security level $L(SS_i) = TS$. We refer to the data stream generated from the sensors as the source data stream. The source data stream S_i generated from the sensor SS_i inherits the security level of the sensor, that is, $L(S_i) = L(SS_i)$. All the sensors writing to a stream have the same security level as the stream. Each tuple T_{ij} belonging to the source data stream inherits the security level of the stream source, that is, $L(T_{ij}) = L(SS_i)$. All the tuples in the source data stream are at the same level. We assume that each source data stream SS_i is associated with a single security level. This assumption is required to satisfy the restricted $\star$-property of the BLP model. Though we assume that source streams are single level, we consider our stream inside the data stream management system (i.e., once the tuples enter the system) to be multilevel.

Multilevel security can be supported at three *granularities*: attribute, tuple, and stream. Though stream level enforcement may be the easiest, it may not be appropriate for many applications. We have analyzed stream applications from various domains (e.g., battlefield monitoring, linear road benchmark, infrastructure security), and based on our analysis, providing tuple level security would be most beneficial to a large class of applications and sources creating data streams. In this chapter, we will discuss the model and issues for tuple based enforcement.

11.6.2 Multilevel Continuous Query Specification

In this section, we discuss how security levels are associated with tuples and continuous queries in an MLS/DSMS.

The first issue is the classification of tuples and streams in a DSMS. Consider the following data stream.

```
VITALS (soldier id (sid), blood pressure (bp), pulse rate (pr));
```

As discussed in Section 11.6.1, each object (in our case stream, tuple, or attribute) can have exactly one level. Thus, streams and tuples have a security level, and if the stream has a security level, it dominates the security level of its tuples. In this chapter, we delimit our discussion to the tuple-based security level. In order to support tuple-based enforcement, the above stream schema is modified by adding an attribute, termed *level*, representing the security level of the tuple. All the tuples of the stream must have a value for the *level* attribute, and the domain of the attribute is the list of security levels (Unclassified, Confidential, Secret, Top Secret). Only stream sources such as the sensors that create the tuples and certain query operators should be able to modify the *level* attribute. Users and query operators, such as *select* and *project*, should not be allowed to modify the *level* attribute's value. Query operators, such as *join* and *aggregate*, are allowed to modify the value when they create new tuples. When the join operator creates a new tuple, the security level of a newly created tuple is the least upper bound of both the tuples that were processed by the operator for creating that new tuple. For instance, if the join operator joins a *top secret* tuple and a *secret* tuple, the level of the new tuple will be *top secret*. The modified stream schema with the *level* attribute is shown below.

```
VITALS (soldier id (sid), blood pressure (bp), pulse rate (pr),
       level);
```

The next issue is the use of the *level* attribute of a tuple in the Continuous Query Language (or CQL). In which CQL operators can the *level* attribute be used? Also are there any restrictions?

The *level* attribute of a tuple can be used by any of the operators (select, join, project, aggregate, group by, window, etc.). A tuple has exactly one security level. A select operator with AND condition on two or more security levels will always return an empty result. Thus, we allow users to specify OR conditions on the *level* attribute using the set operator IN. On the other hand, a window maintains a set of tuples at any particular instant that is used by blocking operators to compute results. With the existing CQL, the basic windows are tuple-based and time-based sliding windows and are partitioned by the window. In MLS/DSMS, we extend windows to allow users to specify filtering conditions based on the *level* attribute. Similar to the select operator conditions, we allow users to specify conditions on the *level* attribute using the IN operator.

Below, we present a few queries to illustrate how they are specified using MLS/CQL with extensions to the WHERE clause and window.

1. *Compute the average pressure of the last 30 soldiers*:

```
SELECT AVG(bp) FROM vitals [ROWS 30]
```

This query is a regular CQL query using tuple-based windows with no condition based on the *level* attribute.

2. *Compute the average pressure of soldiers using data collected in the last 5 minutes*:

```
SELECT AVG(bp) FROM vitals [RANGE 5 Minutes]
```

This query is a regular CQL query using time-based windows with no condition based on the *level* attribute.

3. *Compute the average pressure of confidential soldiers from the data of the last 30 soldiers:*

```
SELECT AVG(bp) FROM vitals [ROWS 30]
WHERE level IN {"Confidential"}
```

This query includes the *level* attribute in the WHERE clause. The window maintains the last 30 tuples that may or may not contain Confidential tuples. In this chapter, we assume that the WHERE clause is applied after the window selection. If the WHERE clause is applied before, then the window will contain only 30 Confidential tuples. Although applying the WHERE clause before the window will simplify the processing system, it cannot support some specific queries including this query.

4. *Compute the average pressure of Secret and Top Secret soldiers from the last 30 soldiers data:*

```
SELECT AVG(bp) FROM vitals [ROWS 30]
WHERE level IN {"Secret", "Top Secret"}
```

This query will filter all tuples that do not have the security level Secret or Top Secret.

5. *Compute the average pressure of the last 30 Secret or Top Secret soldiers:*

```
SELECT AVG(bp)
FROM vitals [ROWS 30 level IN {"Secret", "Top Secret"}]
```

In this query, the window maintains the last 30 tuples that have either the Secret or Top Security security level.

6. *Compute the average pressure of the last 30 soldiers in each level:*

```
SELECT level, AVG(bp)
FROM vitals [PARTITIONED BY level ROWS 30] GROUP BY level
```

In this query, the *level* attribute is used as part of the window and group by.

7. *Compute the average pressure of the last 30 unclassified soldiers:*

```
SELECT AVG(bp)
FROM vitals [PARTITIONED BY level ROWS 30]
WHERE level IN {"Unclassified"}

SELECT AVG(bp)
FROM vitals [ROWS 30 level IN {"Unclassified"}]
```

As shown, this query can be specified by using either partitioned or tuple-based windows.

11.6.3 Multilevel Continuous Query Processing

In this section, we discuss the issues involved in processing continuous queries. We discuss query rewriting and query sharing in multilevel continuous query processing.

As discussed in Section 11.6.1, continuous queries are assigned the security clearance of the principal who creates the query. The clearance will be used to determine whether a query can access a stream and a particular tuple of a stream. For instance, if the user is a Confidential user, any query created by that user will be attached to the level Confidential. All the queries created by that user will be allowed to access tuples that are dominated by the Confidential. In order to set the security clearance, queries have to be rewritten* by MLS/DSMS. The rewritten query should filter unauthorized tuples from being processed by the query. For nonblocking operator queries, the WHERE clause of SQL is used for filtering. For blocking operator queries, window specification is used for buffering the tuples. Users can also specify a nonblocking operator query with a window. Thus, we have to rewrite all of the above query cases appropriately. The system should be able to identify queries that try to access unauthorized tuples or those that will always produce empty results. In MLS/DSMS, we rewrite the queries using the following rules:

- Nonblocking operator queries without windows and without select conditions involving the *level* attribute can be rewritten by inserting an appropriate WHERE clause condition based on the security clearance.
- Blocking and nonblocking operator queries with windows should be rewritten by inserting a window condition based on the security clearance attribute.
- Queries with conditions based on the *level* attribute in the window or the WHERE clause have to be checked against the security clearance of the user creating it. If the conditions involve unauthorized levels, the query should be rejected.

Consider the following queries issued by a user with security clearance Confidential. We will provide the query description, original query specifications, and the rewritten queries based on the Confidential security level.

1. *Retrieve pressure of soldiers*:

```
SELECT bp FROM vitals
```

The above user query has to be rewritten to include only tuples that are dominated by the level Confidential.

```
SELECT bp FROM vitals
WHERE level IN {"Unclassified", "Confidential"}
```

---

*Note that in some architectures (discussed in the next section), such as replicated, we may not need to rewrite queries, whereas we have to rewrite in the trusted architecture.

2. *Compute the average pressure of the last 30 soldiers*:

```
SELECT AVG(bp) FROM vitals [ROWS 30]
```

The above user query has to be rewritten to include only tuples that are dominated by Confidential level.

```
SELECT AVG(bp) FROM vitals
[ROWS 30 level IN {"Unclassified", "Confidential"}]
```

3. *Compute the average pressure of Confidential soldiers from the last 30 soldiers*:

```
SELECT AVG(bp) FROM vitals [ROWS 30]
WHERE level IN {"Confidential"}
```

The above user query has to be rewritten to include the condition in the window as the window acts as the source relation. The window should not include Secret or Top Secret tuples.

```
SELECT AVG(bp) FROM vitals
[ROWS 30 level IN {"Unclassified", "Confidential"}]
WHERE level IN {"Confidential"}
```

4. *Compute the average pressure of Secret and Top Secret soldiers from the last 30 soldiers*:

```
SELECT AVG(bp) FROM vitals [ROWS 30]
WHERE level IN {"Secret", "Top Secret"}
```

The above user query is rewritten as

```
SELECT AVG(bp) FROM vitals
[ROWS 30  level IN {"Unclassified", "Confidential"}]
WHERE level IN {"Secret", "Top Secret"}.
```

Although this query can be rewritten as shown above, it can also be inferred that this query cannot be issued by a user with a confidential security level. This query can be rejected on that basis. Even if the query is processed with rewriting, there will not be any result from the query. However, scarce computing resources will be consumed for computing an empty answer.

The next issue is the shared processing of queries. Multiquery DSMSs **share** [122, 123] the processing of continuous queries to reduce resource usage and improve quality of service and result accuracy. For instance, if two continuous queries have the same relational algebra operator tree, then the DSMS shares their computation. This is critical as queries are long running, and the resources such as CPU cycles and main memory are limited. This also simplifies scheduling and the need for load shedding. Multilevel queries should be shared whenever possible, to reduce resource consumption. Below, we have summarized the ways in which multilevel queries can be shared: *complete*, *subsumed*, and *partial*.

- **Complete Sharing:** If two queries have the same relational algebra operator tree and have the same levels, then they can be shared. If the two queries have different security levels, then they can be shared only if there is no illegal information flow.
- **Subsumed Sharing:** It is possible to share two queries, if the query plan of one query subsumes the other and they have the same levels. It is also possible to share two queries, if the level of the subsumed query is dominated by the other query. Otherwise, it can create covert channels.
- **Partial Sharing:** If two queries are executing at the same level, then the common relational operator subtree of the queries can be shared. The most complex case is the partial sharing of queries with different security levels. This can lead to covert channels and needs to be analyzed to check whether it is even possible and appropriate.

Note that the exact process of query sharing is dependent on various factors, including operators, window types, and architecture of the MLS/DSMS (discussed in the next section).

11.6.4 Design and Development of an MLS Architecture

In this section, we discuss how to adapt a DSMS architecture to process MLS continuous queries. We focus our attention on the query processor component of the architecture presented in Figure 11.3. The query processor of an MLS/DSMS can have various types of architecture, depending on how logical isolation is achieved across the different security levels. We borrow our ideas in this regard from the various architectures (trusted, kernelized, and replicated) that have been proposed for MLS/DBMS literature [98, 111, 116]. We discuss trusted and replicated hybrid architectures below.

The replicated architecture is based on the replicated model where each level L stores not only the tuples with classification L but also those whose classification is dominated by L. An example replicated query processor is shown in Figure 11.6, although many variants are possible. The query processors are untrusted and replicated at various security levels. Each query processor runs at a security level (L) and is responsible for executing queries submitted by the users who have logged on at the same level. The response to a query may involve data belonging to one or multiple security levels; however, the level of all the tuples returned in the response must be dominated by the query level. The stream shepherd operator must be redefined to ensure that only tuples at the dominated level are passed on to the dominating level. All the other operators are untrusted and are replicated at various levels. The input queues carrying data at dominated levels are replicated at the dominating levels as well. Sequential-Window operators and synopses used for processing blocking operators such as join and aggregation are created as needed for the query processors at that level. When replicated architecture is used, queries can be shared only within that query processor. Queries that run in a query processor are issued by users whose

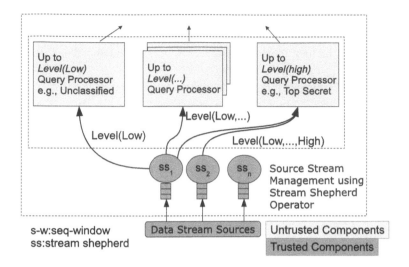

Figure 11.6   Replicated MLS/DSMS architecture.

security clearance is same as the query processor. Thus, when queries are shared, they will not create illegal information flow.

In the trusted architecture, all components shown in Figure 11.3 are made trusted. This allows all components to access tuples at all security levels. Thus, queries specified by users at different levels are run in the same query processor. This architecture allows the sharing of queries across levels. For instance, we may be able to share queries issued by a confidential and a secret user. However, this approach can lead to illegal information flow if sharing is designed incorrectly.

11.6.5   Scheduling and Load-Shedding Strategies for MLS Continuous Queries

In this section, we bring out issues related to scheduling and load shedding that need to be addressed for processing multilevel secure data streams.

A stream processing system handles continuous queries and data and maintains QoS during bursty input periods using scheduling strategies and load shedding techniques [69]. A multiple CQ processing system uses *scheduling strategies* [52, 57–63] to decide the execution order of CQs (operators, operator paths, segments). These strategies are critical to a DSMS as they decide CPU allocation schedules to reduce maximal memory requirement and tuple latency, improve throughput, and avoid starvation. *Load shedding* [52, 64–68], a mechanism that is used to gracefully drop buffered and partially processed tuples during high-input periods, is required to keep a DSMS from violating the QoS constraints specified for the queries. Load shedding techniques are activated by a DSMS when the QoS constraints are violated and the capacity of the system cannot cope with the data rate without severely reducing quality. The main reason for the development of scheduling strategies and load shedding techniques is to keep executing CQs and maintain QoS during bursty input periods. On the other hand, these may also be periods that are critical to security applications. For instance, consider a battlefield application where a lot of data are generated during a crisis. The DSMS should be able to process CQs from soldiers across all levels during the crisis.

The main issue is the execution priority of high-level versus low-level queries. In traditional databases, low-level queries are mostly executed immediately to avoid information leaks. In contrast, in stream processing systems, queries are long running. So, allowing low-level queries to run immediately can make all the high-level queries starve. Based on the nature of stream systems and applications, this can lead to a situation where high-level queries are never executed and all the buffered tuples with high sensitivity are dropped by the load shedder. On the other hand, executing high-level queries immediately may be more important than low-level queries because high-level queries can be monitoring critical and life-threatening situations. But giving priority to high-level queries may lead to covert channels because the high-level user can transfer signals to the lower level by issuing/canceling a large number of high-level queries to manipulate the response time in low-level queries. Thus, we need to design strategies and techniques that should prevent security violation during the normal or a special (bursty input) period and at the same time support execution priorities. In order to support execution priorities and achieve better performance, we need to design new scheduling strategies that interleave scheduling between queries in different levels.

Other issues include the amount of input tuples handled by different processors from the same input stream can be different in a replicated architecture and can affect load shedding. In addition, the following must be kept in mind while developing the scheduling and load shedding strategies. First, users at dominated levels should not be able to infer the activities that are taking place at dominating levels. Second, illegal information flow should not occur through covert channels because of the sharing of CPU time, memory, and operators across security levels. Third, repeatedly not executing queries at dominating levels may cause a starvation and impact the QoS.

11.7 SUMMARY

In this chapter, we have briefly discussed the need for stream data processing and how its goals differ from traditional data management and processing. We have also summarized why both stream and complex event processing are needed for a large class of monitoring applications. We provided two diverse applications where we have shown how traditional, customized solutions can be replaced by general-purpose solutions based on stream and event processing technologies.

A larger question that needs to be addressed is about the choice and development of an effective architecture for situation monitoring applications. How do we progress toward a flexible, composable architecture for analyzing large volumes of data? How do we satisfy real-time (and near-real-time) requirements for applications that need them? These questions certainly need to be answered as we move toward pervasive devices and just-in-time monitoring requirements. The amount of data that will be generated and, hence, needs to be processed is only going to increase dramatically as the technology improves. Application requirements will grow to include distributed data handling, handling of errors, privacy issues, and security as well as collaboration/cooperation among applications. Filtering, fusion, aggregation, and correlation (to name a few) will become preferred mechanisms for dealing with vast amounts of disparate raw data to extract nuggets of meaningful, useful, and actionable knowledge.

EXERCISES

11.1   Formally define sensor data stream and explain how it differs from other types of data stream such as broadcast data, 911 calls, and so on.

11.2   What types of unique requirements are needed to query sensor stream data? Discuss some real-life examples where stream data processing is necessary to manage a situation.

11.3   Investigate and identify the limitations of conventional database systems in processing (querying) sensor stream data.

11.4   The chapter presented a database architecture for processing sensor stream data. Explain the architecture and identify what other features could be added to enhance its capability.

11.5   Discuss the EStreams model and explain the four-stage stream and event integration processing.

11.6   Explain and analyze three-phase processing.

11.7   Identify the security issues in stream data processing and explain the way that the DSMS (Data Stream Management System) handles these issues.

11.8   Identify the issues in multilevel continuous query processing and suggest your scheme for handling some of these issues.

REFERENCES

1. M. Stonebraker, U. Çetintemel, and S. B. Zdonik, The 8 Requirements of Real-Time Stream Processing, *SIGMOD Record*, Vol. 34, No. 4, 2005, 42–47.

2. H. Garcia-Molina and K. Salem, Main Memory Database Systems: An Overview, *IEEE Transactions on Knowledge and Data Engineering*, Vol. 4, No. 6, 1992, 509–516.

3. TimesTen, Oracle TimesTen Homepage, June 2005, http://www.oracle.com/timesten/index.html.

4. J. Baulier, P. Bohannon, S. Gogate, C. Gupta, S. Haldar, S. Joshi, A. Khivesera, S. Seshadri, A. Silberschatz, S. Sudarshan, M. Wilder, and C. Wei, DataBlitz Storage Manager: Main Memory Database Performance for Critical Applications. In *ACM SIGMOD—Industrial Session: Database Storage Management*, June 1999, pp. 519–520.

5. A. Tesanovic, D. Nystram, J. Hansson, and C. Norstram, Embedded Databases for Embedded Real-Time Systems: A Component-Based Approach, Linkoping University, Technical Report, 2002, http://www.mrtc.mdh.se/publications/0366.pdf.

6. P. Boncz, T. Grust, M. Keulen, S. Manegold, J. Rittinger, and J. Teubner, MonetDB/XQuery: a Fast XQuery Processor Powered by a Relational Engine. In *Proceedings of the ACM SIGMOD International Conference on Management of Data*, June 2006, pp. 479–490.

7. Altibase, Altibase Home Page, 2004, http://www.altibase.com/english/.

8. SolidDB, IBM SolidDB Home Page, 2007, http://www.ibm.com/software/data/soliddb/.

9. BerkeleyDB, Berkeley DB and Oracle Embedded Databases, 1996, http://www.oracle.com/database/berkeley-db/index.html.

10. M. A. Olson, K. Bostic, and M. I. Seltzer, Berkeley db. In *USENIX Annual Technical Conference, FREENIX Track*, 1999, pp. 183–191.

11. Empress Embedded Database, Empress Software Inc., 2004, http://www.empress.com/.

12. eXtremeDB, McObject Precision Data Management, eXtremDB home page, 2008, http://www.mcobject.com/.

13. SIAD/SQL6, Trace Mode, Industrial Real-Time DBMS SIAD/SQL 6, 1988, http://www.tracemode.com/products/overview/database/.

14. R. Abbott and H. Garcia-Molina, Scheduling Real-Time Transactions: A Performance Evaluation. In *Proceedings of the Fourteenth International Conference on Very Large Data Bases*, August 1988, pp. 1–12.

15. R. Abbott and H. Garcia-Molina, Scheduling Real-Time Transactions, *SIGMOD RECORD*, Vol. 17, No. 1, 1988, 71–81.

16. S. H. Son (ed.), *Sigmod Record: Special Issue on Real-Time Database Systems*. SIGMOD, Vol. 17, No. 1, 1988.

17. R. Abbott and H. Garcia-Molina, Scheduling Real-time Transactions with Disk Resident Data. In *Proceedings of the Fifteenth International Conference on Very Large Data Bases*, August 1989, pp. 385–396.

18. A. Buchmann, D. McCarthy, and M. Hsu, Time-Critical Database Scheduling: A Framework for Integrating Real-Time Scheduling and Concurrency Control. In *Proceedings of the Fifth International Conference on Data Engineering*, February 1989, pp. 470–480.

19. R. Abbott and H. Garcia-Molina, Scheduling I/O Requests with Deadlines: A Performance Evaluation. In *Proceedings of the Eleventh Real-Time Systems Symposium*, December 1990, pp. 113–124.

20. M. J. Carey, R. Jauhari, and M. Livny, On Transaction Boundaries in Active Databases: A Performance Perspective, *IEEE Transactions on Knowledge and Data Engineering*, Vol. 7, No. 1, March 1991, 78–84.

21. S. Chakravarthy, B. Blaustein, A. Buchmann, M. Carey, U. Dayal, D. Goldhirsch, M. Hsu, R. Jauhari, R. Ladin, M. Livny, D. McCarthy, R. McKee, and A. Rosenthal, HiPAC: A Research Project in Active, Time-Constrained Database Management. Xerox Advanced Information Technology, Cambridge, Technical Report, 1989.

22. S. Chen, J. Stankovic, J. Kurose, and D. Towsley, Performance Evaluation of Two New Disk Scheduling Algorithms for Real-Time Systems, *Journal of Real-Time Systems*, Vol. 3, No. 3, 1991, 307–336.

23. U. Dayal, B. T. Blaustein, A. P. Buchmann, U. S. Chakravarthy, M. Hsu, R. Ledin, D. R. McCarthy, A. Rosenthal, S. K. Sarin, M. J. Carey, M. Livny, and R. Jauhari, The HiPAC Project: Combining Active Databases and Timing Constraints, *SIGMOD Record*, Vol. 17, No. 1, 1988, 51–70.

24. R. Abbott and H. Garcia-Molina, Scheduling Real-Time Transaction: Performance Evaluation, *ACM Transactions on Database Systems*, Vol. 17, No. 3, September 1992, 513–560.

25. D. J. DeWitt, R. H. Katz, F. Olken, L. D. Shapiro, M. R. Stonebraker, and D. Wood, Implementation Techniques for Main Memory Database Systems. In *Proceedings of the ACM SIGMOD International Conference on Management of Data*, June 1984, pp. 1–8.

26. P. Franaszek, J. Robinson, and A. Thomasian, Concurrency Control for High Contention Environments, *ACM Transactions on Database Systems*, Vol. 10, No. 1, March 1992, 304–345.

27. M. H. Graham, Issues in Real-Time Data Management, *Journal of Real-Time Systems*, Vol. 4, No. 3, September 1992, 185–202.

28. J. Gray, B. Good, D. Gawlick, P. Homan, and H. Sammer, One Thousand Transactions per Second. In *Proceedings of the Thirtieth IEEE Computer Society International Conference*, February 1985, pp. 96–101.

29. J. R. Haritsa, M. J. Carey, and M. Livny, On Being Optimistic about Real-Time Constraints. In *Proceedings of the Ninth ACM SIGACT-SIGMOD-SIGART Symposium on Principles of Database Systems*, June 1990, pp. 331–343.

30. J. R. Haritsa, M. J. Carey, and M. Livny, Dynamic Real-Time Optimistic Concurrency Control. In *Proceedings of Eleventh Real-Time System Symposium*, December 1990, pp. 94–103.

31. J. R. Haritsa, M. Livny, and M. J. Carey, Earliest Deadline Scheduling for Real-Time Database Systems. In *Proceedings of Twelfth Real-Time System Symposium*, December 1991, pp. 232–242.

32. J. R. Haritsa, Transaction Scheduling in Firm Real-Time Database Systems, Ph.D. dissertation, University of Wisconsin—Madison, 1991.

33. D. Hong, T. Johnson, and S. Chakravarthy, Real-Time Transaction Scheduling: A Cost Conscious Approach. In *Proceedings, International Conference on Management of Data (SIGMOD)*, 1993, pp. 197–206.

34. D. Hong, Real-Time Transaction Scheduling: Synthesizing Static and Dynamic Factors, Ph.D. dissertation, The University of Florida at Gainesville, December 1995.

35. D. Hong, S. Chakravarthy, and T. Johnson, Locking Based Concurrency Control for Integrated Real-Time Database Systems. In *Proceedings, International Workshop on Real-Time Databases (RTDB)*, 1996, pp. 138–143.

36. S. Chakravarthy, D.-K. Hong, and T. Johnson, Real-Time Transaction Scheduling: A Framework for Synthesizing Static and Dynamic Factors, *Real-Time Systems Journal*, Vol. 14, No. 2, 1998, 135–170.

37. D.-K. Hong, S. Chakravarthy, and T. Johnson, Incorporating Load Factor into the Scheduling of Soft Real-Time Transactions for Main Memory Databases, *Information Systems*, Vol. 25, No. 3, 2000, 309–322.

38. J. Huang, J. A. Stankovic, D. Towsley, and K. Ramamritham, Experimental Evaluation of Real-Time Transaction Processing. In *Proceedings of Tenth Real-Time Systems Symposium*, December 1989, pp. 144–153.

39. J. Huang, J. A. Stankovic, K. Ramamritham, and D. Towsley, Experimental Evaluation of Real-time Optimistic Concurrency Control schemes. In *Proceedings of the Seventeenth International Conference on Very Large Data Bases*, August 1991, pp. 35–46.

40. T. Johnson and D. Shasha, The Performance of Concurrent B-Tree Algorithm, *ACM Transactions on Computer Systems*, Vol. 18, No. 1, March 1993, 51–101.

41. W. Kim and J. Srivastava, Enhancing Real-Time DBMS Performance with Multiversion Data and Priority Based Disk scheduling. In *Proceedings of Twelfth Real-Time Systems Symposium*, December 1991, pp. 222–231.

42. J. Lee and S. H. Son, Using Dynamic Adjustment of Serialization Order for Real-Time Database Systems. In *Proceedings of Fourteenth Real-Time Systems Symposium*, December 1993, pp. 66–75.

43. Y. Lin and S. H. Son, Concurrency Control in Real-time Databases by Dynamic Adjustment of Serialization Order. In *Proceedings of Tenth Real-Time Systems Symposium*, December 1990, pp. 104–112.

44. R. Sivasankaran, B. Purimetla, J. Stankovic, and K. Ramamritham, Network Services Database—A Distributed Active Real-Time Database (DARTDB) Application. In *Proceedings of First IEEE Workshop on Real-Time Applications*, May 1993, pp. 184–187.

45. B. Purimetla, R. Sivasankaran, K. Ramamritham, and J. Stankovic, Real-Time Databases: Issues and Applications. In *Advances in Real-Time Systems*, Prentice-Hall, Englewood Cliffs, NJ, 1995, pp. 487–507.

46. L. Sha, Concurrency Control for Distributed Real-Time Databases, *SIGMOD RECORD*, Vol. 17, No. 1, 1988, 82–98.

47. K. Ramamrithm, Real-Time Databases, *International Journal of Distributed and Parallel Databases*, Vol. 1, No. 2, January 1993, 1–30.

48. J. A. Stankovic and W. Zhao, On Real-Time Transactions, *SIGMOD RECORD*, Vol. 17, No. 1, 1988, 4–18.

49. M. Singhal, Issues and Approaches to Design of Real-Time Database Systems, *SIGMOD RECORD*, Vol. 17, No. 1, January 1988.

50. J. Hansson and M. Berndtsson, Active real-time database systems. In *Active Rules in Database Systems*, Springer, Berlin, 1999, pp. 405–426.

51. A. Buchmann, M. T. Ozsu, M. Hornick, D. Georgakopoulos, and F. Manola, *A Transaction Model for Active Distributed Object Systems*, Morgan Kaufmann, San Francisco, 1992.

52. S. Chakravarthy and Q. Jiang, *Stream Data Processing: A Quality of Service Perspective Modeling, Scheduling, Load Shedding, and Complex Event Processing*, ser. *Advances in Database Systems*, Vol. 36, Springer, Berlin, 2009.

53. B. Babcock, S. Babu, M. Datar, R. Motwani, and J. Widom, Models and Issues in Data Stream Systems. In *Proceedings of the Twenty-first ACM SIGACT-SIGMOD-SIGART Symposium on Principles of Database Systems*, June 2002, pp. 1–16.

54. D. Carney, U. Çetintemel, M. Cherniack, C. Convey, S. Lee, G. Seidman, M. Stonebraker, N. Tatbul, and S. B. Zdonik, Monitoring Streams—A New Class of Data Management Applications. In *Proceedings of the International Conference on Very Large Data Bases*, August 2002, pp. 215–226.

55. A. Arasu, B. Babcock, S. Babu, J. Cieslewicz, M. Datar, K. Ito, R. Motwani, U. Srivastava, and J. Widom, Stream: The Stanford Data Stream Management System, Stanford InfoLab, Technical Report 2004-20, 2004. [Online]. Available: http://ilpubs.stanford.edu:8090/641/

56. A. Arasu, S. Babu, and J. Widom, The CQL continuous query language: semantic Foundations and Query Execution, *VLDB Journal*, Vol. 15, No. 2, 2006, 121–142.

57. B. Babcock, S. Babu, M. Datar, R. Motwani, and D. Thomas, Operator scheduling in data stream systems, *VLDB Journal*, Vol. 13, No. 4, 2004, 333–353.

58. B. Babcock, S. Babu, R. Motwani, and M. Datar, Chain: Operator Scheduling for Memory Minimization in Data Stream Systems. In *Proceedings of the 2003 ACM SIGMOD International Conference on Management of Data*, June 2003, pp. 253–264.

59. Q. Jiang and S. Chakravarthy, Scheduling Strategies for Processing Continuous Queries over Streams. In *21st Annual British National Conference on Databases*, July 2004, pp. 16–30.

60. R. Avnur and J. Hellerstein, Eddies: Continuously Adaptive Query Processing. In *Proceedings of the ACM SIGMOD International Conference on Management of Data*, May 2000, pp. 261–272.

61. D. Carney, U. Çetintemel, A. Rasin, S. Zdonik, M. Cherniack, and M. Stonebraker, Operator Scheduling in a Data Stream Manager. In *Proceedings of the VLDB*, August 2003, pp. 838–849.

62. S. D. Viglas and J. F. Naughton, Rate-Based Query Optimization for Streaming Information Sources. In *Proceedings of the ACM-SIGMOD International Conference on Management of Data*, June 2002, pp. 37–48.

63. S. Chakravarthy and V. Pajjuri, Scheduling Strategies and Their Evaluation in a Data Stream Management System. In *BNCOD*, 2006, pp. 220–231.

64. N. Tatbul, U. Çetintemel, S. B. Zdonik, M. Cherniack, and M. Stonebraker, Load Shedding in a Data Stream Manager. In *Proceedings of the VLDB*, September 2003, pp. 309–320.

65. N. Tatbul and S. B. Zdonik, Window-Aware Load Shedding for Aggregation Queries over Data Streams. In *VLDB*, 2006, pp. 799–810.

66. A. Das, J. Gehrke, and M. Riedewald, Approximate Join Processing over Data Streams. In *Proceedings of the ACM-SIGMOD International Conference on Management of Data*, June 2003, pp. 40–51.

67. B. Babcock, M. Datar, and R. Motwani, Load Shedding for Aggregation Queries over Data Streams. In *Proceedings of the ICDE*, March 2004, pp. 350–361.

68. B. Kendai and S. Chakravarthy, Load Shedding in MavStream: Analysis, Implementation, and Evaluation. In *Proceedings, International British National Conference on Databases (BNCOD)*, 2008, pp. 100–112.

69. R. Motwani, J. Widom, A. Arasu, B. Babcock, S. Babu, M. Datar, G. Manku, C. Olston, J. Rosenstein, and R. Varma, Query Processing, Resource Management, and Approximation. In *Proceedings of the CIDR*, 2003, pp. 245–256.

70. Aleri, Aleri Home Page, 2004, http://www.aleri.com/products/aleri-streaming-platform/.

71. Apama, Progress Software Home Page, 2004, http://www.progress.com/index.ssp.

72. AMiT, IBM, AMiT Home Page, 2004, http://www.haifa.ibm.com/dept/services/stes.html.

73. A. Adi and O. Etzion, AMiT—The Situation Manager, *VLDB Journal*, Vol. 13, No. 2, 2004, 177–203.

74. Coral8, Coral8 Homepage, June 2005, http://www.coral8.com/.

75. Corona Enterprise Suite, Red Rabbit Software Home Page, 2004, http://www.redrabbitsoftware.com/.

76. Esper, Esper Home Page, 2004, http://esper.codehaus.org/.

77. GemFire Real-Time Events, GemFire Real-Time Events Homepage, http://www.gemstone.com/products/gemfire/rte.php, 2008.

78. INETCO, INETCO Homepage, http://www.inetco.com/, 2008.

79. Oracle CEP, http://www.oracle.com/technologies/soa/complex-event-processing.html.

80. RuleCore, RuleCore Homepage, June 2007, http://www.rulecore.com/.

81. M. Seirio and M. Berndtssons, Design and Implementation of a ECA Rule Markup Language. In *Proceedings of the International RuleML Conference*, November 2005, pp. 98–112.

82. SENACTIVE EventAnalyzer, SENACTIVE EventAnalyzer Homepage, http://www.senactive.com/index.php?id=eventanalyzer&L=1, 2008.

83. SL Real-Time Visibility, SL Real-Time Visibility Homepage, http://www.sl.com/solutions/cep.shtml, 2008.

84. StreamBase, http://www.streambase.com.

85. WestGlobal, WestGlobal Vantify Experience Centre Homepage, http://www.westglobal.com/index.php?option=com_content&view=article&id=35&Itemid=62, 2008.

86. J. Baras, H. Lï, and G. Mykoniatis, Integrated, Distributed Fault Management for Communication Networks, University of Maryland, Technical Report CS-TR 98-10, University of Maryland, April 1998.

87. L. H. Bjerring, D. Lewis, and I. Thorarensen, Inter-Domain Service Management of Broadband Virtual Private Networks, *Journal of Network and Systems Management*, Vol. 4, No. 4, 1996, 355–373.

88. R. Diaz-Caldera, J. Serrat-Fernandez, K. Berdekas, and F. Karayannis, An Approach to the Cooperative Management of Multitechnology Networks, *Communications Magazine, IEEE*, Vol. 37, No. 5, 1999, 119–125.

89. M. A. Mountzia and G. D. Rodosek, Using the Concept of Intelligent Agents in Fault Management of Distributed Services, *Journal of Network and Systems Management*, Vol. 7, No. 4, 1999, 425–446.

90. D. Gambhir, M. Post, and I. Frisch, A Framework for Adding Real-Time Distributed Software Fault Detection and Isolation to SNMP-based Systems Management, *Journal of Network and Systems Management*, Vol. 2, No. 3, 1994, 257–282.

91. P. Frohlich and W. Nejdl, Model-Based Alarm Correlation in Cellular Phone Networks. In *Proceeding of the International Symposium on Modeling, Analysis, and Simulation of Computer and Telecommunications Systems (MASCOTS)*, January 1997, pp. 197–204.

92. D. Medhi et al., A Network Management Framework for Multi-Layered Network Survivability: An Overview. In *IEEE/IFIP Conference on Integrated Network Management*, May 2001, pp. 293–296.

93. S. Chakravarthy, V. Krishnaprasad, E. Anwar, and S. Kim, Composite Events for Active Databases: Semantics, Contexts and Detection. In *VLDB*, 1994, pp. 606–617.

94. R. Adaikkalavan and S. Chakravarthy, SnoopIB: Interval-Based Event Specification and Detection for Active Databases, *Transactions of Data Knowledge and Engineering*, Vol. 59, No. 1, 2006, 139–165.

95. U. Dayal, A. P. Buchmann, and S. Chakravarthy, The Hipac Project. In *Active Database Systems: Triggers and Rules For Advanced Database Processing*, Morgan Kaufmann, San Francisco, 1996, pp. 177–206.

96. S. Chakravarthy and D. Mishra, Snoop: An Expressive Event Specification Language for Active Databases, *Transactions of Data Knowledge and Engineering*, Vol. 14, No. 1, 1994, 1–26.

97. S. Babu, L. Subramanian, and J. Widom, A Data Stream Management System for Network Traffic Management. In *Proceedings of the Workshop on Network-Related Data Management (NRDM 2001)*, May 2001, pp. 685–686.

98. S. Castano, M. G. Fugini, G. Martella, and P. Samarati, *Database Security (ACM Press Book)*, Addison-Wesley, Reading, MA, 1994.

99. M. Bishop, *Computer Security: Art and Science*. Addison-Wesley Professional, Reading, MA, 2002.

100. R. Adaikkalavan and T. Perez, Secure Shared Continuous Query Processing. In *Proceedings of the ACM Symposium on Applied Computing (Data Streams Track)*, Taiwan, March 2011.

101. R. V. Nehme, H.-S. Lim, E. Bertino, and E. A. Rundensteiner, StreamShield: A Stream-Centric Approach Towards Security and Privacy in Data Stream Environments. In *Proceedings of the ACM SIGMOD*, 2009, pp. 1027–1030.

102. J. Cao, B. Carminati, E. Ferrari, and K.-L. Tan, Acstream: Enforcing Access Control Over Data Streams. In *Proceedings of the ICDE*, 2009, pp. 1495–1498.

103. R. V. Nehme, E. A. Rundensteiner, and E. Bertino, A Security Punctuation Framework for Enforcing Access Control on Streaming Data. In *Proceedings of the ICDE*, 2008, pp. 406–415.

104. B. Carminati, E. Ferrari, and K. L. Tan, Enforcing Access Control over Data Streams. In *Proceedings of the ACM SACMAT*, 2007, pp. 21–30.

105. W. Lindner and J. Meier, Securing the Borealis Data Stream Engine. In *IDEAS*, 2006, pp. 137–147.

106. D. F. Ferraiolo and D. R. Kuhn, Role-Based Access Control. In *Proceedings of the 15th National Computer Security Conference*, 1992, pp. 554–563.

107. D. F. Ferraiolo, D. R. Kuhn, and R. Chandramouli, *Role-Based Access Control*, Artech House, Boston, 2003.

108. *RBAC Standard, ANSI INCITS 359-2004*, ANSI INCITS 359-2004, InterNational Committee for Information Technology Standards, 2004.

109. M. Migliavacca, I. Papagiannis, D. M. Eyers, B. Shand, J. Bacon, and P. Pietzuch, Distributed Middleware Enforcement of Event Flow Security Policy. In *Proceedings of the ACM/IFIP/USENIX 11th International Conference on Middleware*, ser. Middleware '10. Springer-Verlag, Berlin, 2010, pp. 334–354. [Online]. Available: http://dl.acm.org/citation.cfm?id=2023718.2023741

110. D. Bell and L. LaPadula, Secure Computer Systems: Unified Exposition and Multics Interpretation, The Mitre Corp., Burlington Road, Bedford, MA, USA, Technical Report MTR-2997, March 1976.

111. *Multilevel Data Management Security*, Committee on Multilevel Data Management Security, Air Force Studies Board, Commission on Engineering and Technical Systems, National Research Council, National Academy Press, Washington D.C., March 1983.

112. S. Jajodia and R. Sandhu, Toward a Multilevel Secure Relational Data Model. In *Proceedings, ACM SIGMOD International Conference on Management of Data*, Denver, Colorado, May 1991, pp. 50–59.

113. T. F. Keefe, W. T. Tsai, and M. B. Thuraisingham, A Multilevel Security Model for Object-Oriented System. In *Proceedings, 11th National Computer Security Conference*, October 1988, pp. 1–9.

114. M. Gertz and S. Jajodia, *Handbook of Database Security: Applications and Trends*, Springer, Berlin, 2007.

115. V. Atluri, S. Jajodia, T. F. Keefe, C. McCollum, and R. Mukkamala, Mutilevel Secure Transaction Processing: Status and Prospects. In *Proceedings of the Tenth IFIP WG11.3 Working Conference on Database Security*, July 1996.

116. M. D. Abrams, S. G. Jajodia, and H. J. Podell (eds.), *Information Security: An Integrated Collection of Essays*, 1st ed., IEEE Computer Society Press, Los Alamitos, CA, 1995.

117. I. Ray, Multilevel Secure Rules and Its Impact on the Design of Active Database Systems. In *Proceedings of the BNCOD*, 2003, pp. 226–244.

118. A. C. Myers and B. Liskov, Protecting Privacy Using the Decentralized Label Model, *ACM TOSEM*, Vol. 9, No. 4, 2000, 410–442.

119. P. Efstathopoulos, M. Krohn, S. VanDeBogart, C. Frey, D. Ziegler, E. Kohler, D. Mazières, F. Kaashoek, and R. Morris, Labels and Event Processes in the Asbestos Operating System, *SIGOPS Operation System Reviews*, Vol. 39, October 2005, 17–30.

120. N. Zeldovich, S. Boyd-Wickizer, E. Kohler, and D. Mazières, Making Information Flow Explicit in Histar. In *Proceedings of the 7th USENIX Symposium on Operating Systems Design and Implementation*, Vol. 7, OSDI '06, USENIX Association, Berkeley, CA, 2006, pp. 19–19. [Online]. Available: http://dl.acm.org/citation.cfm?id=1267308.1267327.

121. M. Krohn, A. Yip, M. Brodsky, N. Cliffer, M. F. Kaashoek, E. Kohler, and R. Morris, Information Flow Control for Standard of Abstractions. *SIGOPS Operation Systems Reviews*, Vol. 41, Oct. 2007, 321–334. [Online]. Available: http://doi.acm.org/10.1145/1323293.1294293.

122. M. A. Hammad, M. J. Franklin, W. G. Aref, and A. K. Elmagarmid, Scheduling for Shared Window Joins over Data Streams. In *Proceedings of International Conference on Very Large Data Bases*, September 2003, pp. 297–308.

123. J. Hellerstein, S. Madden, V. Raman, and M. Shah, Continuously Adaptive Continuous Queries over Streams. In *Proceedings of the ACM SIGMOD International Conference on Management of Data*, June 2002, pp. 49–60.

CHAPTER 12

SENSOR NETWORK DEPLOYMENT: CASE STUDIES

Sensors are deployed in nearly every real-world activity to collect data for processing. Some of the typical deployment areas of WSNs are environment monitoring, target tracking, structural health monitoring, precision agriculture, health care, active volcano monitoring, transportation, human activity monitoring, underground mining, and so on. This chapters discusses a few real-life case studies and examples to demonstrate the important role WSNs plays in managing day-to-day activities.

12.1 INTRODUCTION TO DEPLOYMENT

The deployment of a sensor network (WSN) basically can be categorized as (a) space monitoring, (b) real-life activity monitoring, and (c) nature monitoring. Space monitoring includes two categories (a) normal and (b) natural and man-made disasters. The normal category is related to environmental monitoring that includes activities such as habitat, farming, climate control, appliances management, fire alarms, home automation, and so on. The real-life activity monitoring mainly includes outdoor activities such as traffic flow monitoring, medical diagnostics, emergency response, and so on. The nature monitoring includes natural and man-made disasters such as floods, earthquakes, outbreaks of diseases, forest fires, and so on. Among all three categories, the most challenging task is the deployment of WSNs for studying and managing the third category because of its stringent and diverse requirements. Sometimes this

Fundamentals of Pervasive Information Management Systems, Revised Edition. Vijay Kumar.
© 2013 John Wiley & Sons, Inc. Published 2013 by John Wiley & Sons, Inc.

category also includes human-centric activities and overlaps, to some extent, with real-life activity monitoring.

12.1.1 NOW—NOtification by Wireless System

The NOW* system was developed and prototyped at the Computer Science Electrical Engineering Department at UMKC. It is an automatic rapid event notification system that notifies relevant agencies (subscribers of NOW) the occurrence of an event through wireless channels. This type of notification to appropriate emergency medical services (EMS) personnel is essential for sending necessary help to injured patients quickly. Rapid communication is especially crucial during life-threatening events, such as fires, floods, explosions, and traffic accidents, and is especially true for vehicle rollovers. Rollover accidents are among the most likely to leave their victims incapacitated and are particularly hazardous to vehicle occupants, who are often unable to summon help.

An ideal emergency notification system would detect an event and then select and quickly notify (in an automated fashion), the correct set of service providers with necessary information to permit the delivery of the appropriate type of help. This would aid in minimizing the human toll of accidental and traumatic injuries and death.

The need for an automated emergency response system in vehicles is especially important, given the nature of our highly active and mobile society. Drivers or passengers who need assistance following vehicle accidents could be assisted by an event notification system that would automatically locate the site of the incident, especially if the passenger(s) had difficulty or were unable to describe the exact location of the accident. The value of such an automated system is even greater in situations where no occupants are capable of communication. Currently, the emergency notification process available in most vehicles is dependent on capable humans, and it works in the following manner. Following a vehicle accident, the driver, a fellow passenger, or a witness, calls the police via 911, who then notify the EMS or other relevant agencies. This method works but has some limitations. Response time may be prolonged by the levels of complexity inherent in these nonautomated, human-input-requiring emergency response systems. In many cases, for help to reach the victims, notification must transcend more than two levels. In a multilevel human-based communication scheme, each level has its failure probability, reducing the reliability of the response system with each additional level added.

The desire for developing automated emergency notification systems in vehicles is not new [1]. The prototype of NOW was developed with state-of-the-art sensors and mobile communication. It assures users that in the event of a vehicle rollover, necessary information would be seamlessly transmitted to the appropriate emergency service provider immediately, reducing the response time of the EMS providers.

*Dr. Gary Gaddis of St. Luke's Hospital of Kansas City and Dr. Vijay Kumar of the University of Missouri—Kansas City designed and developed the protype.

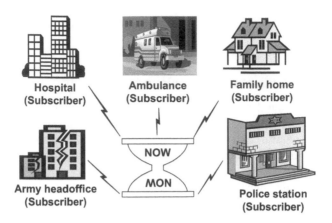

Figure 12.1   NOW concept.

Figure 12.1 illustrates the role of NOW in the notification process. Organizations subscribe to NOW for using notification service.

12.1.2   Architecture of NOW

The general architecture of NOW is illustrated in Figure 12.2. It has three main components: (a) a set of wireless sensors, (b) a wireless server, and (c) a database. The sensors are planted at various strategic locations on the vehicle, with each sensor programmed to continuously collect necessary data about its environment.

The task of the NOW server is to assimilate various portions of the sensor data stream and to monitor the status of the vehicle. If an abnormality is detected, such as excessive shakes, sudden acceleration, or a vehicle hitting a ramp, the server immediately collects and stores the data in the database for later processing. This data

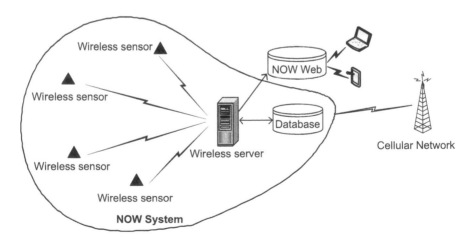

Figure 12.2   A general architecture of NOW.

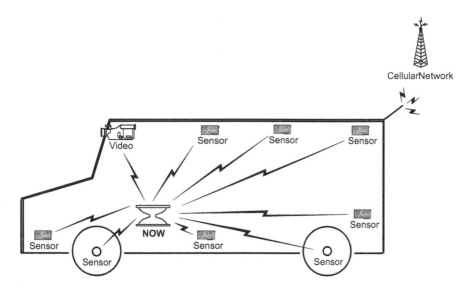

Figure 12.3   A vehicle equipped with NOW.

collection and interpretation are part of the notification process leading to a rollover event. Note that the server does not notify its subscriber about information leading to the rollover; but, if needed, it can be programmed to do so. NOW notifies the necessary service providers only when needed and in order to request help after the occurrence of the rollover event.

The NOW server communicates with its sensors through a WSN. These sensors continuously broadcast the data they collect. The server captures the data stream from these sensors and processes them to identify the state of the vehicle. NOW communicates with the outside world through a cellular network, and the vehicle is connected to a GPS for location identification. Figure 12.3 shows a basic vehicle with the NOW system.

The NOW server is responsible for dispatching the occurrence of an event (rollover, accident, etc.) to the subscribers. When a vehicle rolls over, the NOW system in the vehicle instantly acquires longitude and latitude values and the location of the mishap. A message is composed in a specified format (depends on the subscriber) that is dispatched to the subscriber through the cellular network. At the subscriber's end, depending upon the setup, the message is displayed on a screen or on a mobile device (cell phone, PDAs, etc.)

12.1.3 Landfill Gas Monitoring

The objective of this application is to provide a collaborative and distributed sensing of gas emissions in landfills. Landfilling of solid waste is one of the traditional solutions to waste management and disposal of municipal solid waste (MSW) generated from residential activities. Landfill waste generally consist of approximately 72%

Table 12.1   Typical Constituents Found in MSW Landfill Gas

Component	Percent (Dry Volume Basis) (WSN)
Methane	45–60
Carbon dioxide	40–60
Nitrogen	2–5
Oxygen	0.1–1.0
Sulfides, disulfides, mercaptanes	0–1.0
Ammonia	0.1–1.0
Hydrogen	0–0.2
Carbon monoxide	0–0.2

household waste (MSW), 17.2% commercial waste, and 5.8% construction debris, with the remainder including industrial waste and sludge. The compositions of MSW typically include food waste, yard waste, plastics, papers and boards, textiles, leather, and so on, with a high percentage of organic compositions. These organic components can undergo biological and chemical reactions in the landfill, such as fermentation, biodegradation, and oxidation–reduction. The volume of organic MSW can be reduced due to these reactions, while landfill gases and liquids (leachates) are generated as by-products from both active and closed landfills. The stabilization of the various reactions usually takes two to four years. There are approximately 6000 active landfills in the United States, 93% of which are less than 5.5 million tons in capacity. The percentage of MSW going to landfills is currently 60% and is decreasing due to the development of other waste minimization methods and the rising cost of landfilling [2].

Landfill gas is composed of both principal and trace gases. Main gases include methane (CH_4), carbon dioxide (CO_2), nitrogen, oxygen, sulfide compounds, and ammonia, etc. The relative percentage is listed in Table 12.1. The gases can migrate within the landfill and up to the surface due to physical reactions.

The landfill is a complex system because of its continuous and unpredictable emission activity. In addition to this, it has a number of real-time constraints. These characteristics make its management quite difficult. An effective and efficient scheme for its management must have a reliable and efficient network (static and mobile) infrastructure, an adaptable data management approach and information dissemination platform. Figure 12.4 illustrates the WSN deployment to monitor gas emissions at

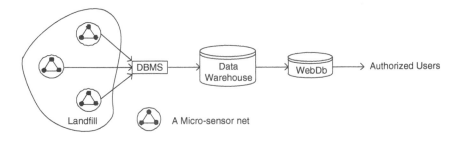

Figure 12.4   Use of ESN to monitor gas emision in a landfill.

various landfills and send the information to the DBMS for further processing and dissemination.

Each micro-sensornet continuously collects and stores data locally. The emission of gases and their volume are not predictable, so these sensors remain continuously active. Sensors will send different types of data with different constraints associated with them. Some data will be temporal in nature with limited validity. In order to handle diverse data types, the raw data are buffered in the database for processing. Thus, sensornets are mainly input devices with limited processing capabilities. This scheme helps to keep sensornets continuously active.

Figure 12.4 identifies the following data management issues that the system manages efficiently:

a. **Stream data capture from specific sensors:** A sensor can send data in any form (pulses, packets, sound, etc.) to the buffer. Since sensors in the network could be location-specific, each sensornet knows its geographical location, which is attached to the raw data packets saved in the buffer.

b. **Validation of captured streams data:** The system uses unique a location for data validation before it is saved. The validation (a) verifies the source of the data (correct sensornet), (b) makes sure that the data are of the right kind for that sensornet, and (b) cleans the captured data.

c. **Storing of formatted data in the database and updating the data warehouse:** After validation and processing, the data are moved from the buffer to the database (relational) that can be queried.

d. **Posting necessary information on the web:** Many organizations (private and governmental) share processed data. This is done by uploading the data on to a web site of a landfill system. The web can be accessed through static and mobile clients.

The sensornets are battery-operated; in order to extend their lifetime, energy efficient schemes are used. To this end, the system minimizes the amount of data being transmitted by the sensors. It uses a hierarchical topology to aggregate data as shown in Figure 12.4.

12.1.4 Active Volcano Monitoring with WSN

There are many natural events such as forest fires, floods, and volcano eruptions that cannot be monitored or studied because it is not possible for humans to reach activity centers to collect the necessary data. In an earthquake, finding victims (alive or dead) buried underneath demolished buildings is not possible by human workers. Sensor networks can be effectively used to accomplish these tasks. A case study presented in reference 3 is briefly described here. Further detail regarding hardware specification and the data collection method can be found in reference 3. The sensor network that was deployed in Volcan Reventador in northern Ecuador.

This case study used seismic-acoustic hybrid sensors that are low-cost and have a simple design. This kind of sensor is usually placed on the ground surface or could be buried in the soil. Once the sensors are deployed (on the surface or buried), they continue to collect data streams for months with little human intervention. They are good for measuring low-frequency acoustic signals (with very low false alarm rates), which are what a volcano emits. They are also not easily affected by normal moisture and weather conditions.

The WSN that was deployed was constructed using (a) 16 wireless sensor nodes with an 8-MHz CPU (TI MSP430) per sensor and (b) a 2.4-GHz IEEE 802.15.4 radio. The radio had data rates up to 80 Kbps. A sensor node captured acoustic and seismic data streams using a microphone. The power to each sensor was supplied by two D-cell batteries that lasted for about one week. One of the nodes was identified as a base station, and data streams from the sensor nodes were relayed to the base station through the radio. The maximum distance between a pair of sensor nodes was 1378 feet. Such large internode separation is necessary to obtain interference-free seismic and infrasonic signals propagation. The base station was responsible for collecting and dispatching the data to a processor (laptop) that was located at about 2.49 miles away.

In a sensor node, data travels from source to destination in multihops because there are no IP addresses that can be assigned to a node. Thus, whenever an event (tremor activity) is detected, a short message was sent by the sensor that reaches the base station through the radio link. The WSN was also equipped with a sensor to transmit data continuously. A continuous data stream is hard to capture because of bandwidth and the energy limitations of WSN. The collected data were shipped to an observatory for further processing. This project collected three weeks of data that represented 230 volcanic events [3]. These data were not only useful to study volcanic activities, they were also very useful for measuring the performance and capability of the WSN. This case study managed to overcome some inherent limitations of a WSN with an innovative design and deployment.

12.1.5 Vehicle Speed Monitoring

Magnetic sensors are used to measure the state (presence, direction, and speed) of a vehicle*. There are three categories of magnetic sensors:

- **Low-field:** It can measure magnetic field strength below 1 μG (micro-Gauss).
- **Medium-field:** It can measure magnetic field strength between 1 μG and 10 G.
- **High-field:** It can measure magnetic field strength above 10 G.

A vehicle can be regarded as a magnetic object because it contains large amounts of steel. Thus, the concentration of magnetic flux (disturbance) changes with the movement of the vehicle, which can be detected from a distance of up to 15 m [5]. Since the degree of change in the magnetic flux is caused by the object, it is possible to identify the type of object, that is, the type and size of a vehicle (car, bus, minibus, truck, etc.) Thus, when a vehicle reaches is to a magnetic sensor, or drives over it, the sensor can detect the vehicle and the variation reveals a detailed magnetic signature.

---

*Adapted from [4] under written permission from John Wiley & Sons.

A prototype was deployed on Vassar Street, Cambridge, Massachusetts. The wireless sensor node consists of two AMR magnetic sensors for detecting vehicular activities and a temperature sensor for monitoring road conditions (snow, ice, or water). The movement and speed of a vehicle is captured by observing the disturbance it creates in the earth's magnetic field. To measure the speed of a vehicle, the node waits until it detects a disturbance and then starts sampling at a frequency of 2 kHz. An AMR magnetic sensor is placed at the front of the node and another at the back. When the signal from the rear sensor crosses the baseline, the node begins to count the number of samples until the signal from the forward sensor crosses the baseline and then computes the speed of the passing vehicle.

Sampling at this rate enables the node to detect vehicles that travel at a higher speed (as fast as 200 mph), with a minimum separation distance of 3 m. The 90 Mica2 sensor nodes were deployed at MacDill Air Force Base in Tampa, Florida, to detect the movement of vehicles, soldiers, and people [6]. Seventy-eight of the nodes were magnetic sensor nodes that were deployed in a 60×25 square foot area. Additionally, 12 radar sensor nodes were overlaid on the network. The magnetic sensor nodes were distributed uniformly. These nodes form a self-organizing network that connects itself to a remote computer via a base station and a long-haul radio repeater. The Mica2 nodes were based on a 4-MHz Atmel processor with 4 kbytes of RAM, 128 kbytes of flash program, and 512 kbytes of EEPROM memory (used for data logging). The TinyOS operating system runs on the nodes. Magnetic fields were sensed by using an in-built magnetometer while the TWR-ISM-002 radar motion sensor was used to detect movement of objects.

12.1.6 Pipeline Monitoring

WSNs are extensively deployed to monitor the movement of gas, water, and oil through pipelines. The vast area they cover makes the task extremely challenging and risky. Sensors are deployed to continuously monitor leakage, deformation, corrosion, wear, material flaws, or damage. Different types of pipelines have different indications of any damage. A leakage of fluid in pipelines is identified by a hot spot, and gas pipelines generate a cold spot. The flow velocity of the material (gas and fluid) also provides useful information.

The PipeNet prototype is a prototype that was developed jointly by Imperial College, London, Intel Research, and MIT. PipeNet monitors water pipelines and measures hydraulic and water quality and the water level in sewer systems. PipeNet is deployed in three different settings to measure pressure data every 5 minutes for 5 seconds, and the pH data are collected for 10 seconds at a rate of 100 Hz. The wireless communication among sensors is established through a Bluetooth transceiver. The pressure sensor is a modified version of the OEM piezoresistive silicon sensor that has a startup time of less than 20 ms and a fast dynamic response. It consumes less than 10 mW. The pH sensor is a glass electrode with an Ag/AgCl reference cell.

The second setting deploys a pressure sensor to measure the fluid pressure in an 8-inch cast iron pipe. Similar to the first setting, the data are collected every 5 minutes for a period of 5 seconds at a sampling rate of 300 Hz.

The final setting deploys a couple of pressure transducers and an ultrasonic sensor to monitor the water level of a combined sewer outflow. The pressure transducers are low-power devices and consume less than 10 mW, whereas the ultrasonic sensor consumes 550 mW. The pressure sensors are employed for periodic monitoring and the ultrasonic sensor only verifies the pressure sensors' readings. In this setting, data collection was carried out at a rate of 100 Hz at 5-minute intervals for a period of 10 seconds. The network supported remote configuration to increase the sampling rate up to 600 Hz.

12.2   THE GATOR TECH SMART HOUSE

A smart house offers a highly comfortable living environment for all age groups. It uses the state-of-the-art electronic devices to create a comfort zone for the inhabitants. The Gator Tech Smart House (GTSH) was developed by the Mobile and Pervasive Computing Laboratory at the University of Florida. It is an assistive environment that extends the typical pervasive computing space into a full-sized, feature-rich home that provides technology and architecture to substantially benefit both elderly or disabled residents and their caregivers.

Figure 12.5 illustrates the structure of the GTSH in terms of "hot spots" that are currently active or under development in the GTSH. The project features numerous existing (E), ongoing (O), or future (F) "hot spots" located throughout the premises.

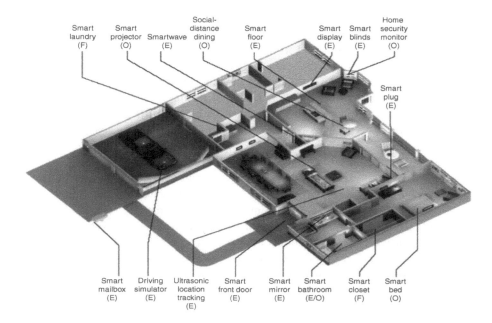

Figure 12.5   Gator Tech Smart House architecture.

The front door area of the GTSH illustrates the use of several devices and services that together comprise the Entry Assistant. A radio-frequency identification (RFID) system built into the wall of the entrance way recognizes residents as they approach the house by means of passive RFID tags attached to their key rings. An electronic deadbolt and an automatic door opener work together to allow the residents access to the house and to secure the premises when the door is closed. The doorbell of the house connects to the smart space that allows the GTSH to easily adapt the notification system to the needs of its residents. The doorbell also triggers the Door View service that is a small video camera built into the peephole of the door. The video is automatically transmitted to the monitor that is located nearest the resident in the house. Access to the house can be granted with a voice command (an audio or text message) using the speakers or LCD display built into the entrance way. The electronic deadbolt has a normal key interface outside and knob inside.

The location of residents in the house can trigger or halt certain applications, affect various notification systems in the environment, and can be used to ascertain data about the health of the residents in terms of daily activity or detecting falls.

The Smart Floor [7] provides a primary location tracking system. Figure 12.6 illustrates the structure of the flooring system. It consists of a residential-grade raised platform with a force sensor installed underneath it that requires no attention from the residents and implements constant, but inoffensive, monitoring throughout the day and night. Applications that make use of the Smart Floor service include the house's notification system. Alerts can be sent to the video or audio device that is located nearest the resident through the house's notification system. The entertainment system makes use of location information by following the resident throughout the house, turning off the television in one room and turning it on in another. The Activity Monitor is able to record a resident's typical amount of movement in a day. If a significant decrease in activity is detected, the house is able to automatically notify the caregivers in case of elderly inhabitants.

Figure 12.6 Tile of the Smart Floor.

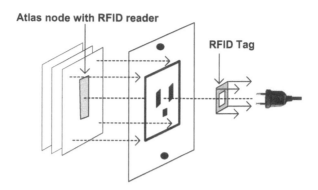

Figure 12.7   Smart Plug deployed behind an electrical socket.

The SmartWave [8], which is a collection of devices and services, provides necessary instructions (remove film, stir ingredients, etc.) for meal preparation. A standard microwave oven was modified to allow computer control of the cooking process. An RFID reader in the cabinet below the microwave allows appropriately tagged frozen meals to be placed in front of the device and recognized by the smart house. The SmartWave sets power levels and cooking times automatically. Once the meal is ready, a notification is sent to the resident anywhere the house.

The Smart Plugs [9] were deployed for remote monitoring and intervention. They include an RFID reader behind each electrical wall socket in the house (Figure 12.7). Each electrical device was given an RFID tag that indicates what the device is and the commands it could issue. This system allows the GTSH to detect devices as they enter or leave the space. A graphical model of the house is updated, providing remote caregivers with an accurate view of the capabilities of the house. For example, if the caregiver notices that temperatures are climbing, they can click on fans so that they turn on.

The detection of passive objects such as furniture, and so on, is performed with PerVision [10]. It uses cameras and a RFID to recognize and extract information about passive objects in the environment. All passive objects were labeled with an RFID tag that identifies some of their characteristics (shape, volume, bounding box, color hues, etc.). RFID readers deployed at the doors detect objects as they enter or leave the space. The PerVision system uses a series of cameras throughout the house to run image recognition techniques to determine the location of these objects throughout the house. The computer vision techniques are assisted by information from the RFID tags and from the Smart Floor.

The PerVision system is assisted by SensoBot [11] (Figure 12.8, a Roomba-based sensor platform that is able to physically map a space and detect the RFID-tagged objects). It provides a camera-less object detection method and generates a floor map of the space that feeds into other aspects of the Self-Sensing Spaces project, such as the 3D model for remote caregivers.

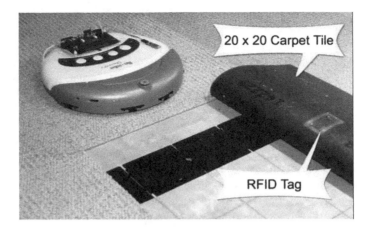

Figure 12.8 SensoBot recognizing an object in the carpet.

The residents control the comfort and convenience settings of the house (temperature or adjustment of the window blinds) with a Smart Phone. The resident can see the view from the front door's peephole camera, open the door, or lock the house at night. By connecting with the health care applications in the house, the residents can either order prescription refills or buy groceries online, with automatic feedback about any dietary restrictions. The Smart Phone is also an integral part of the GTSH's medicine reminder service. The phone includes a barcode scanner that the residents use to scan the bottles or cases of medicine.

12.3 SUMMARY

Sensor technology is the core of smart platforms. Today, all construction (houses, bridges, commercial buildings, etc.) uses some smart platform to provide facilities and the comfort level that are expected at these places. Every day, researchers identify innovative deployment of sensor technology to solve problems of all areas. It appears that the state of the art technology is continuously offering us new tools and challenging us to use them intelligently to shape the future.

REFERENCES

1. D. D. Hrovat, H. Tseng, E. Fodor, and M. Glenn, Rollover Stability Control for an Automotive Vehicle Having an Active Suspension, US Patent No. 608839, June 25, 2003.
2. T. Davis Wayne (ed.), *Air Pollution Engineering Manual, Air and Waste Management Association*, 2nd ed., John Wiley & Sons, New York, 2000.
3. G. Werner-Allen, K. Lorincz, M. Welsh, O. Marcillo, J. Jhonson, M. Ruiz, and J. Lees, Deploying a Wireless Sensor Network on an Active Volcano, *IEEE Internet Computing*, March–April 2006, pp. 18–25.

4. W. Dargie and C. Poellabaur, Fundamentals of Wireless sensor Networks: Theory and Practice, John Wiley & Sons, 2010.

5. Weaver 2003.

6. A. Arora, P. Dutta, S. Bapat, V. Kulathumani, H. Zhang, V. Naik, V. Mittal, H. Cao, M. Demirbas, M. Gouda, Y. Choi, T. Herman, S. Kulkarni, U. Arumugam, M. Nesterenko, A. Vora, and M. Miyashita, A Line in the Sand: A Wireless Sensor Network for Target Detection, Classification, and Tracking, *Computer Networks*, Vol. 46, No. 5, 2004, 605–634.

7. Y. Kaddourah, J. King, and A. Helal, Cost-Precision Tradeoffs in Unencumbered Floor-Based Indoor Location Tracking. In *Proceedings of the third International Conference On Smart Homes and Health Telematic (ICOST)*, Sherbrooke, Québec, Canada, July 2005.

8. J. Russo, A. Sukojo, S. Helal, R. Davenport, and W. Mann, SmartWave Intelligent Meal Preparation System to Help Older People Live Independently. In *Proceedings of the Second International Conference on Smart Homes and Health Telematic (ICOST2004)*, September 2004, Singapore.

9. H. El-Zabadani, A. Helal, B. Abudlrazak, and E. Jansen, Self-Sensing Spaces: Smart Plugs for Smart Environments. In *Proceedings of the Third International Conference On Smart Homes and Health Telematic (ICOST)*, Sherbrooke, Quebec, Canada, July 2005.

10. H. El-Zabadani, A. Helal and M. Schmaltz, PerVision: An Integrated Pervasive Computing/Computer Vision Approach to Tracking Objects in a Self-Sensing Space. In *Proceedings of the 4th International Conference on Smart Homes and Health Telematic (ICOST)*, Belfast, Northern Islands, June 2006.

11. H. El-Zabadani, A. Helal and H. Yang, A Mobile Sensor Platform Approach to Sensing and Mapping Pervasive Spaces and their Contents. In *Proceedings of the International Conference on New Technologies of Distributed Systems*, Morocco, Marrakesh, June 4–8, 2007.

GLOSSARY

A Carrier	Most areas of the United States have two cellular carriers, each of which operates on a different frequency band. One is designated the "A" carrier and the other is designated the "B" carrier. In some markets, there may be only one carrier which may be "A" or "B".
A/B Switching	Most cellular phones have the ability to switch to the "A" or the "B" frequency bands. This feature is useful when roaming outside your home coverage area.
Access Fee	A monthly charge for the ability to connect to a wireless network. This fee is assessed monthly whether the phone is actually used or not.
Activation	Configuration of a wireless phone so that it is ready to be used to transmit and receive calls on the wireless network.
Airtime	Total time that a wireless phone is connected and in use for talking. This includes use for calls both received and placed.
AMPS	Advanced Mobile Phone Service-An analog cellular phone service standard used in the US and other countries.

Fundamentals of Pervasive Information Management Systems, Revised Edition. Vijay Kumar.
© 2013 John Wiley & Sons, Inc. Published 2013 by John Wiley & Sons, Inc.

APC	Adaptive Power Control–A feature of some wireless handsets that helps reduce power consumption to increase battery charge life.
B Carrier	Most areas of the US have two cellular carriers, each of which operates on a different frequency band. One is designated the "A" carrier and the other is designated the "B" carrier. In some markets there may be only one carrier which may be "A" or "B".
Bandwidth	Describes the transmission capacity of a medium in terms of a range of frequencies. A greater bandwidth indicates the ability to transmit a greater amount of data over a given period of time.
Bluetooth	A short range wireless protocol meant to allow mobile devices to share information and applications without the worry of cables or interface incompatibilities. The name refers to a Viking King who unified Denmark. Operates at 2.4 Ghz, see bluetooth.com.
Broadband	Describes a communications medium capable of transmitting a relatively large amount of data over a given period of time; a communications channel of high bandwidth.
BTA	Basic Trading Area. A geographic region defined by a group of counties that surround a city, that is the area's basic trading center. The boundaries of each BTA were formulated by Rand McNally & Co. and are used by the FCC to determine service areas for PCS wireless licenses. The entire US and some of its territories are divided into 493 non-overlapping BTAs.
Cell	The area surrounding a cell site. The area in which calls are handled by a particular cell site.
Cell Site	The transmission and reception equipment, including the base station antenna that connects a cellular phone to the network.
Cellular	The type of wireless communication that is most familiar to mobile phones users. Called 'cellular' because the system uses many base stations to divide a service area into multiple 'cells'. Cellular calls are transferred from base station to base station as a user travels from cell to cell.
CO	(Central Office)–A connection point between the wireless phone system at the MTSO and the landline phone system at the PSTN.

Clone	(Cloning)–A wireless phone that has been programmed to mimic another wireless phone. Often used to defraud a wireless carrier by placing illegal calls without any intention of payment.
Coverage Area	The geographic area served by a wireless system; same as Service Area.
Cross-talk	A signal leak from one channel to another-often the cause of noise and distortion.
dB	Decibel–A unit of measure used to express relative difference in power or intensity of sound.
ESMR	Enhanced Specialized Mobile Radio–Using frequency bands originally allocated for two-way dispatch services, companies such as Nextel and Southern LINC have built digital mobile phone services similar to cellular and PCS systems.
ESN	Electronic Serial Number
FCC	Federal Communications Commission–A US government agency responsible for regulating communications industries.
Follow-Me	Roaming-The ability of a wireless system to forward incoming calls to a handset that is roaming outside its home service area without any pre-notification to the wireless carrier.
GSM	Global System for Mobile–A digital communication technology used by some carriers to provide PCS service. Other technologies used are CDMA and TDMA.
GPRS	General Packet Radio Service)–An emerging technology standard for high speed data transmission over GSM networks.
Handoff	The transfer of a wireless call in progress from one transmission site to another site without disconnection.
Handshake	Signals between a wireless phone and a wireless system to accomplish call setup.
Home Coverage Area	A designated area within which cellular calls are local and do not incur roaming or long distance charges.
HomeRF	A digital wireless communications protocol designed for the transport of voice and multimedia content between consumer electronic devices (including PCs) in a residential setting. Operates at 2.4 Ghz; see homerf.org.

LMDS	Local Multipoint Distribution System–A fixed, broadband wireless system used for voice and interactive data. Generally used as a lower cost alternative to landline connections for businesses and others requiring high bandwidth connections to public networks.
MMDS	Multipoint Multichannel Distribution Service-Often referred to as 'wireless cable' as it is a wireless system used to distribute cable television and other broadband signals to multiple users by way of a single transmitter.
MSA	Metropolitan Service Area–An area defined by the US government for use in grouping census data and other statistics. MSAs include a city of at least 50,000 people or an urbanized area of at least 100,000 people and the counties that include these areas. Not all areas of the US are in an MSA. The FCC used these area definitions to license cellular telephone service carriers. There are 306 regions of the US designated as MSAs.
MTA	Major Trading Area–An area consisting of two or more Basic Trading Areas as defined by Rand McNally & Co. These large areas are used by the FCC to determine service areas for some PCS wireless licenses. The US is divided into 51 MTAs.
MTSO	Mobile Telephone Switching Office–An office housing switches and computers to which all cell sites in an area are connected for the purpose of eventual connection to the PSTN. The MTSO handles the connection, tracking, status and billing of all wireless call activity in an assigned area.
NAM	Number Assignment Module–A component of a wireless phone that holds the telephone number and ESN of the phone in its electronic memory.
Paging	A feature of a wireless device that allows reception of a signal or alphanumeric message.
PCS	Personal Communication Services–Used to describe a newer class of wireless communications services recently authorized by the FCC. PCS systems use a different radio frequency (the 1.9 GHz band) than cellular phones and generally use all digital technology for transmission and reception.
PSTN	Public Switched Telephone Network–A formal name for the world-wide telephone network.

RF Fingerprinting	An electronic process that identifies each individual wireless handset by examining its unique radio transmission characteristics. Fingerprinting is used to reduce fraud since the illegal phone cannot duplicate the legal phone's radio-frequency fingerprint.
RF	Radio Frequency–A radio signal.
RFI	Radio Frequency Interference–An undesired radio signal that interferes with a radio communications signal causing extraneous noise and/or signal dropouts.
RF Noise	Undesired radio signals that alter a radio communications signal causing extraneous sounds during transmission and/or reception.
Roaming	Using your wireless phone in an area outside its home coverage area. There is usually an additional charge for roaming.
Roaming Agreement	An agreement among wireless carriers allowing users to use their phone on systems other their own home systems. Roaming Fee charged for roaming.
RSA	Rural Service Area–Areas not included in MSAs are divided into RSAs. Generally, these are the rural areas of the US. The FCC used RSAs to license cellular carriers in areas not included in MSAs. There are 428 RSAs in the US.
Service Area	The geographic area served by a wireless system; same as Coverage Area.
Service plan	A contract between a wireless carrier and a wireless subscriber that details the terms of the wireless service including rates for activation, access and per minute usage.
Signal-to-noise ratio	A measure of the power of a signal versus noise. A lower ratio means there is more noise relative to the signal.
SMS	Short Messaging System–A feature of PCS phones (primarily GSM) that allows users to receive and sometimes transmit short text messages using their wireless phone.
Spectrum	The entire range of electromagnetic frequencies
Spread Spectrum	A communications technology where a signal is transmitted over a broad range of frequencies and then re-assembled when received.
Standby Time	The time a phone is on but not actively transmitting or receiving a call.

WAP

Wireless Application Protocol–A global protocol used in many newer wireless devices that allows the user to view and interact with data services. Generally used as a means to view Internet web pages using the limited transmission capacity and small display screens of portable wireless devices.

Wi-Fi

A wireless data networking protocol generally used to connect PCs and laptops to a network. Also known as 802.11b and WLAN (Wireless LAN), it is the most common means of wireless networking and operates at 2.4 GHz.

Wireless Carrier

A company that provides wireless telecommunications services.

WLL

Wireless Local Loop–A wireless system meant to bypass a local landline telephone system. A home or business phone system is connected to the public network by a wireless carrier instead of by the traditional local phone company.

INDEX

d-consistent, 163
(Before Image—BFIM), 220

A
absorption, $\bar{A}$ 20
AC, 33
acceptability function, 89
ACID, 135
ACIDL, 157
active mode, 3, 45, 130
adaptive exponential scaling factor, 255
adjacent channel, 28
Adjacent Channel Interference, 27
Aleri, 322
AMiT, 322
AMPS (Advanced Mobile Phone Service), 17
analog, 28
Apama, 322
Application recovery, 221
Atomic Commitment Protocol (ACP), 200
atomic processing unit, 302

B
band, 12
bandwidth, 12
base station (BS), 15
base stations (BSs), 2
basic timestamping, 100
basic timestamping scheme, 101
blind writes, 101
blocking, 94
broadband, 29
Broadband PCS, 29
broadcast channel, 257
Broadcast Disk, 247
broadcast scheduling scheme, 286
BS, 32
BSC (base station controller), 39
BTS (base transceiver station), 32
buffer, 303

C
cascadeless, 80
cascading, 96
cautious waiting, 105

Fundamentals of Pervasive Information Management Systems, Revised Edition. Vijay Kumar.
© 2013 John Wiley & Sons, Inc. Published 2013 by John Wiley & Sons, Inc.